Pioneers, Engineers, and Scoundrels

The Dawn of the Automobile in America

Other SAE titles of interest:

Pioneers of the U.S. Automobile Industry
By Michael J. Kollins
*(Order No. R-251.SET for complete four-volume set,
or order individual volumes as listed below)*

Volume 1: The Big Three
(Order No. R-251/1)

Volume 2: The Small Independents
(Order No. R-251/2)

Volume 3: The Financial Wizards
(Order No. R-251/3)

Volume 4: The Design Innovators
(Order No. R-251/4)

For more information or to order a book, contact SAE at
400 Commonwealth Drive, Warrendale, PA 15096-0001;
phone (724) 776-4970; fax (724) 776-0790;
e-mail CustomerService@sae.org;
website http://store.sae.org.

Pioneers, Engineers, and Scoundrels

The Dawn of the Automobile in America

Beverly Rae Kimes

Leading Our World In Motion

Warrendale, Pa.

For permission and licensing requests, contact:

SAE Permissions
400 Commonwealth Drive
Warrendale, PA 15096-0001 USA
E-mail: permissions@sae.org
Tel: 724-772-4028
Fax: 724-772-4

Library of Congress Cataloging-in-Publication Data

Kimes, Beverly Rae
   Pioneers, engineers, and scoundrels : the dawn of the automobile in America / Beverly Rae Kimes.
      p. cm.
   ISBN 0-7680-1431-X
      1. Automobiles—United States—History. 2. Automobile industry and trade—United States—History. I. Title.

TL23.K55 2005
629.222'0973—dc22   2004056643

SAE
400 Commonwealth Drive
Warrendale, PA 15096-0001 USA
E-mail: CustomerService@sae.org
Tel: 877-606-7323 (inside USA and Canada)
           724-776-4970 (outside USA)
Fax: 724-776-1615

Copyright © 2005 Beverly Rae Kimes
ISBN 0-7680-1431-X
SAE Order No. R-358
Printed in the United States of America.

For my sister Sharon,
whose loving generosity
gave me back my life

Contents

Acknowledgments

IN A WAY, I began writing this book in the autumn of 1963, shortly after *Automobile Quarterly* (*AQ*) publisher L. Scott Bailey took a chance on a fresh college grad who loved history but knew nothing about cars. My first assignment was an article about the curved dash Oldsmobile, and I was hooked. What could be more exciting than automobile history? I told myself that one day I would know enough about it to tell everybody else how exciting it was.

Most of the books in *AQ*'s library at the time had been written in England. Of American authors, the first two volumes of Allan Nevins and Frank Ernest Hill's Ford trilogy were on the shelves, and John B. Rae's *American Automobile Manufacturers* had just been released. We had Floyd Clymer's scrapbooks, bless him, and the popular histories published by Fawcett, Trend, Arco, and True. Ralph Stein had recently given us his *Treasury of the Automobile*, and the incomparable Ken Purdy was awakening an entire generation to the joys of the automobile in *Kings of the Road*. *AQ*'s library consisted of three half sections of shelves built above storage cabinets, and I daresay Scott had every book published on the subject. My library today consists of seven sections of floor-to-ceiling bookcases, and I can't claim to have all the books in the field. The growth of automobile history in forty-odd years has been nothing short of astonishing. I regard myself lucky to have been part of it.

Because this book reflects four decades of automobile research, my acknowledgments must begin with the National Automotive History Collection (NAHC) of the Detroit Public Library. During the years Jim Bradley and George Risley shepherded the collection, I was known as the "lady with the dimes," which I fed relentlessly into an ill-performing copy machine to commit to print as much automobile history as possible. The collection grew as phenomenally as its subject. Today, NAHC is mecca. It is the *sine qua non* of automobile lore in America. Since 1994, Mark Patrick has been curator and is a good friend. When asked, he turned my request for photos for this book into a mission of high adventure, enlisting Terez Franklin and John Bean to join him in combing NAHC's vast files for images reflecting the automobile's birth and adolescence that had rarely or never been published. A formidable task. Formidable thanks.

Revisiting forty years of research has made me aware of the extent to which hobby clubs and museums have contributed to the cause of automobile history. The enthusiasts who vigorously pursue data and documentation have been enormously helpful to those of us who write about automobiles. Poring through my files also brought back fond memories of those who have left us in recent years, particularly Austin Clark (whose Long Island archive was my home away from home) and Ralph Dunwoodie (in whose collection I lived for an extended period). And I found many notes taken during or after visits in Detroit with John Conde, Jeff Godshall, Dave Lewis, and Jim Wren; in Philadelphia with Mary Cattie and Lou Helverson; and in Indiana with many friends at the Auburn Cord Duesenberg Museum. To the museum's Jon Bill goes specific gratitude for help with photos.

To thank everyone who has played a part in helping me realize this book would be impossible. Everyone to whom I expressed gratitude in the lengthy acknowledgments to the *Standard Catalog of American Cars 1805–1942* is extended appreciation again. Other colleagues who have helped, some probably without knowing it, include Leroy Cole, Sue Davis, Kit Foster, Joe Freeman, Ferdy Hediger, Leslie Kendall, David Kolzow, Carl Larson, Dean Lehrke, Skip Marketti, Taylor Vinson, Mike Worthington-Williams, and Bob Zimmerman. Reference notes at the end of the book indicate my gratitude to many others.

Among the reasons for the great strides automobile history has enjoyed since the 1960s has been teamwork, most especially through the Society of Automotive Historians (SAH). Collegiality is the SAH hallmark. We are there to assist each other, which makes moving to the next plateau of our overall knowledge a much shorter trip. When several readers of the manuscript suggested I write an epilogue and I decided upon the industry's Golden Jubilee in 1946 as the focus, one phone call to Jim Wren, who had witnessed the event, sent him to his files to share his notes with me.

Specific research for this book was conducted in areas in which I had not yet delved deeply and entailed countless sessions at the New York Public Library, both the Main Library on Fifth Avenue and 42nd Street and the Science, Business, and Industry Library on 34th Street and Madison. I appreciate the kindness and efficiency I encountered on each visit.

To my old friend, Karl Ludvigsen, and my comparatively new one, Jonathan Stein, thank you for the title and subtitle to this book, respectively. I was the editor for Karl's first story for *AQ* in 1965, Jonathan was my editor three decades later during his tenure there, and both are better at writing book titles than I am.

Three long-time friends read the manuscript for me when I finished it. Profuse thanks to Fred Roe for putting me right where I went wrong, and to Joe Malaney and Matt Sonfield for spotting grammar lapses and typos that had eluded me. Thank you, too, to Kim Strickler, who typed the manuscript, and to her husband Eric, who proofread it for her. Finally, to my husband Jim Cox, for writing chapter titles (again, not my forte) and for his unequivocal support and sainted patience, my boundless gratitude.

This has been a wonderful time.

Beverly Rae Kimes
New York, NY
May 15, 2004

Prologue

GAS LAMPS LIT streetlights, and the only vehicles on Main Street were driven by horses. Big cities hummed to the sound of clomping hooves and moved at equine pace. On a small town's street, cows walked to pasture by day and returned to the barn at night. In rural areas, most people were born, raised, and died within a twenty-five-mile radius of the family farm.

Within a decade, this early twentieth-century scene was being dramatically redrawn. In a "curiosity to necessity" story in 1913, *The New York Times* declared, "the coming of the automobile has literally changed the face of the earth." Given that assessment, it is interesting that the invention was so long in arriving. Its roots dated back to the American Revolution, but for more than a century, inventors faced ridicule and contempt in their struggle to make the vehicle a reality. Then, in a comparative nanosecond, it was here, producing both autophile and autophobe, as well as thousands of would-be entrepreneurs who believed they had a better idea or were anxious to cash in. The transition of America from horse-drawn to horse-less society boasts an epic cast of characters—from stalwart heroes to dastardly scoundrels, from social grandees to street toughs, from wise men to wise guys.

The automobile was the most important invention of the last century. The basic facts of its emergence are known, but the reader has never been taken behind the scenes and introduced to the rollicking saga of what happened, how it happened, and who made it happen. That is what this book has attempted to do.

CHAPTER 1

---■---

Oliver Evans, Where It Began

"IF YOU WILL, amongst the jockeys, make up a purse of $3,000, I will make a steam carriage that will outrun the swiftest horse you can produce..."

Oliver Evans was fighting mad. He had a good idea, and nobody was buying it. Since steam was revolutionizing industry, why could it not also revolutionize travel? It was 1805. Already Evans had spent more than three decades trying to convince somebody—anybody—that a horseless carriage would work.

The desire to transport oneself from place to place without need of human or animal propulsion is as old as recorded time. The twenty tricycles Vulcan built in a single day moved by divine will, Homer's *Iliad* tells us, which did not advance the practical cause much. Nor was significant progress made for centuries thereafter. In the thirteenth century, Roger Bacon prophesied the self-propelled vehicle; in the fifteenth, Leonardo da Vinci sketched one; and in the seventeenth, Isaac

Newton talked about the subject further. Carriages propelled by sails or clockwork proved of dubious merit. In 1771, Nicolas Joseph Cugnot invented a three-wheeled steam tractor he hoped to sell to the French military for towing artillery. That it ran at all was remarkable given contemporary technology, but after being tested at 3 miles per hour, the vehicle was abandoned in a dusty corner of the Paris Arsenal. One year later, in the British colonies across the Atlantic, a teenager named Oliver Evans began thinking about horseless transport, too.

Like 90 percent of the population in New Castle County (Delaware), the Evans family made its living by farming, which bored Oliver to tears. At age fourteen, he begged his father to be apprenticed to a local wheelwright, which provided him access to technical books that he devoured, often by light of wood shavings he burned when his frugal master wouldn't give him a candle. Vehicle propulsion fascinated Evans. Around Christmas in 1772, he learned that a neighboring blacksmith's son had stopped up the vent of a gun barrel, poured in water, rammed down some tight wadding, put the breach into the smithy's fire, and was surprised by a wet explosion. "It immediately occurred to me that there was a power capable of propelling any waggon," he wrote, "provided that I could apply it."

Hitting the books again, Evans came upon a description of Newcomen's atmospheric steam engine, which, so far as he knew, was state of the art. The Newcomen was too bulky and inefficient for his purposes, so Evans set to adapting it. Recuperation from a scythe injury provided him the many hours he needed to build a small wooden model of a self-propelled land carriage. Alternately amused and annoyed, his father had a few words with the blacksmith, who in turn flatly turned Evans down when the lad asked him to build a full-size version.

Unlike many seminal events in history, the onset of the Industrial Revolution cannot be precisely dated. As worthy a year as any other might be 1775, when Scottish instrument-maker James Watt formed a partnership with English engineer Matthew Boulton to produce the low-pressure steam engine that was Watt's monumental improvement on the Newcomen concept. A curious George III stopped by the partners' Soho works one day to ask what was going on. "Power, Your Majesty," Boulton answered, "I possess what all the world desires." What the king replied is not known. He may have been preoccupied by other matters, not the least of them the treason being perpetrated in his colonies.

Oliver Evans' 1778 enlistment in the Continental army is a matter of record; his subsequent service is not. Perhaps he regarded politics as something of an intrusion. Evans was certainly a patriot, but most of the truths he held to be self-evident focused on technology. The previous year, he had invented a machine to process wool. Now he was just another soldier. Fortunately, the revolutionaries had the war won by the fall of 1781.

Managing a country store in Tuckahoe, Maryland, made Evans enough money to marry Sarah Tomlinson, a Delaware farmer's daughter, in 1783. At the same time, he invented the automated grist mill and set out to demonstrate how it worked. Millwrights looked upon Evans' invention warily. A brother was dispatched through the Mid-Atlantic states to offer gratis use of the Evans machines to the first miller in each county who was willing to try them. Few were interested.

If Evans was dismayed at the lackluster reception his milling inventions received, he was devastated by the squadron of deaf ears upon which his automotive ideas fell. Legal protection in mind, he petitioned the Pennsylvania legislature in 1786 for exclusive rights to the automated grist mill as well as his steam carriage. Evans' application was granted by half. "My representations concerning steam waggons made them think me insane," he wrote. Likewise received was a similar petition to the Delaware legislature in 1787. That same year, Evans approached the Maryland legislature, however, and found an advocate.

Among the committee members appointed to hear his case was Jesse Hollingsworth, a Baltimore merchant who had recently been named to oversee the $11,000 budgeted for the building of three roads into the city. Hollingsworth's argument on Evans' behalf was pragmatic; so far as he knew, nobody else in the world had thought of a steam-propelled vehicle, so what harm could be done in granting the inventor an exclusive right to build one? A skeptical committeeman asked Evans how his self-propelled vehicle would get out of the way of horse-drawn wagons? Evans replied that, were the committeeman behind the reins and discourteous enough not to let him pass, he would run over him. The committee room erupted in laughter. On May 21, 1787, the Maryland legislature granted Evans exclusive rights for fourteen years to make and use steam wagons in that state.

Already Evans had designed a high-pressure steam engine for his vehicle. Thomas Masters, a retired sea captain acquaintance, thought it was a natural for transatlantic as well as land travel and volunteered to search out potential investors on his next trip to England. The venture abroad was a complete bust. James Watt declared high-pressure steam a dangerous threat to the public good and adaptation for vehicular use wholly unrealistic.

Back home, Oliver Evans pursued other avenues. A shot in the dark was his suggestion that state governments purchase his invention and sell licenses "to discharge the national debt contracted during the revolutionary war." Evans did think he could convince the Ellicott brothers to invest. Their adaptation of the automated grist mill (on his first-gratis basis) had reduced costs by fifty cents a barrel and made theirs the most successful mill in Maryland. Jonathan Ellicott listened politely to the inventor's proposal for "propelling waggons on good turnpike roads" and politely declined.

In 1790, the establishment of the U.S. Patent Office required all states to relinquish their patents to its jurisdiction. Evans immediately sought protection for his flour manufacturing machines, hoping federal recognition would reduce the number of millwrights liberally borrowing his invention now that its value had become widely known. It didn't. Hiring agents to ferret out the infringers would prove nearly as costly as the royalties recovered. Because of the new Patent Office's confusion in trying to sort through claims "on the supposed discovery of new applications for steam for useful purposes," Evans did not seek a steam patent until 1792. He intentionally omitted steamboat references in his own state applications to avoid involvement in the ongoing fracas between John Fitch and James Rumsey regarding the comparative originality of their inventions.

With no takers at all thus far on his steam engine propositions, and thinking proximity to a center of action might change his luck, Evans moved to Philadelphia. The city abounded in superlatives. It was the biggest, the most modern, the most dynamic—"*the* metropolis of the United States," according to French visitor Brissot de Warville in 1791. There, in 1792, Evans launched himself into business as a "constructor of mills" and began to write a book. *The Young Mill-wright and Miller's Guide* required three years to complete and exhausted his capital. During this period, Sarah Evans made tow cloth, which she sold locally to help feed their growing family. With the book at the printer's—the first edition of 2,000 copies was sold by subscription at $2.00 each—Evans returned to his steam engine work, dispatching drawings and specs to England with the hope that a joint patent might result. Again, no luck. His courier, Joseph Stacey Sampson, inconveniently died in London, leaving forever unresolved the extent to which Richard Trevithick might have profited from Evans' engineering principles had he been introduced to them. The English engineer was in London during Sampson's visit and subsequently suffered the wrath of Britain's ranking steam authority, too. James Watt said Trevithick "deserved hanging" for bringing the high-pressure steam engine into use in England.

In Philadelphia, Oliver Evans endured the brickbats of architect Benjamin Henry Latrobe, whose design for the first waterworks in the United States, which used the low-pressure Watt-type steam engine, was accepted by the City Council in 1799. Because Latrobe had just moved to Philadelphia, Evans was galled that his high-pressure steam principles, for which he had been trying to find an audience since 1792, had been brusquely ignored. Then Latrobe added insult to injury. In a report to the Philosophical Society of Pennsylvania in 1803, he railed against inventors "seized with the steam mania," labeled any notion that steam could power a boat or carriage as absurd, and took on Evans specifically in language so scathing that the American Philosophical Society chose to delete some of his remarks when the report was published. Because vehicular use was impossible with a low-pressure engine, professional jealousy may have motivated the attack. Later that year, Latrobe accepted President Jefferson's appointment as surveyor of public buildings, and Oliver Evans could breathe a little easier now that his most vituperative critic was otherwise occupied.

———

As the nineteenth century dawned, Evans decided to go it alone with his steam wagon project. His stated reason was the fear that he might "suddenly be carried off by the yellow fever" before discharging his "debt of honor to the state of Maryland." But honor had its limits. Evans' pocketbook did, in any case. By now, he and Sarah had seven children. The total cost to build his steam engine was $3,700—$1,000 of that the value Evans put on his own time, the remainder materials and wages for the workers he hired at sixty-four to ninety cents a day. Midway through the project, reality set in. Because the grand total of his income for the past decade had come from his grist mill inventions and no one to date had suggested more than a prayer of a chance for a self-propelled vehicle, Evans decided to put his steam engine to profitable use in milling. Consequently, he dismissed his workmen, set to reworking his engine, and put aside the "steam waggon for a time for more leisure."

Later in 1801, Evans' high-pressure steam engine cut through one hundred feet of marble in twelve hours in a public demonstration. Among those who stopped to watch was the legislative committee chairman who had listened with bemusement when Evans addressed the group fifteen years earlier. To the congratulations the man now proffered, Evans cried in exasperation that "this steam engine goes on the principles which I have intended to propel my steam carriages!"

By early 1802, water was coursing through underground pipes in Philadelphia, but the cost of the Latrobe system had exceeded the architect's estimate by a staggering $93,000. Now truly fired up, Evans redoubled his efforts, convinced that his high-pressure, comparatively inexpensive steam engine might now find a more congenial reception. By early 1803, he began advertising his units for sale. By early 1804, his latest version "to propel boats and land carriages" received a U.S. patent. In September, he wrote Elliston Perot, president of the Lancaster Turnpike Company, whose sixty-two-mile privately owned toll road into Philadelphia was America's first proper highway and, Evans thought, the perfect venue to turn his obsession into a moneymaker at last. Computing comparative costs for transporting merchandise and produce, he argued that his steam vehicle would require one day less and net more than $30 a day more than a horse-drawn wagon. Admittedly, he did weight the case in his favor, including whips, troughs, and feed bags among horse-drawn vehicle costs, while neglecting to include even a monkey wrench on the steam wagon's expense list. Possibly Evans had hidden these costs in his overall estimate, thinking that to delineate tools necessary for repair might scare off the Lancaster company directors. They were scared off anyway.

Together with the Lancaster Turnpike proposal, Evans had submitted a prospectus for his own company to build land carriages. Modest capitalization of $3,450 was asked—enough to get a steam wagon built to demonstrate the efficacy of his idea. The Lancaster rejection, while disheartening, did not dissuade him. Already he had another idea. The yellow fever that routinely raged through Philadelphia during this era—nearly 5,000 died in 1794 alone—had been traced to the filth that collected around the wharves along Water Street. Cleaning the harbor by hand-operated scoop and windlass had proven woefully inadequate. In late 1804, Evans proposed to do the job by steam dredge, and the Philadelphia Board of Health accepted. Equally as important as the money involved, the city contract would allow Evans to prove the point he had been making since 1786. He would drive the dredge to the harbor.

By the following summer, the "Orukter Amphibolos" or "Amphibious Digger," as Evans styled his machine—not getting the Greek translation quite right—was ready for the trip. At his Market Street shop, the weighty dredge had collapsed the first set of axles and wheels put under it. But his workmen—now as excited as Evans—donated their time to make a new and stronger undercarriage for the machine.

During the second week of July in 1805, the first vehicle in the United States to move under its own power slowly made its way to Centre Square. Evans' teenage niece, Eliza Tomlinson (soon to marry William Foster and become the mother of songwriter Stephen), watched the inventor walk with pride beside his machine.

With the approval of the Board of Health, demonstrations followed for several days. Evans advertised the Orukter's performance in *Relf's Philadelphia Gazette*, suggesting an admission charge of twenty-five cents "from those who can conveniently spare the money"—half of which he would retain for further experimentation, the other half to be divided among his workers. Driving the Orukter was sweet revenge. As the ponderous Watt-type engines rumbled in the waterworks at Centre Square, Evans' small high-pressure engine moved the dredge "with a gentle motion" (the inventor's somewhat hyperbolic phrase) for all to see. What a sight it was. Among the spectators, one voluble critic contended, rather belligerently, that the vehicle's speed (about 3 or 4 miles per hour) was too slow for turnpike travel. Oliver Evans retorted with the challenge that opened this chapter. His Orukter was simply a harbor dredge dressed as a land carriage. Three thousand dollars was all he needed to build a proper steam vehicle that he was confident could outrun the best horse power in the city.

No one rose to the challenge. After several days of chuffing around the waterworks, Evans and the Orukter headed for the upper end of Market Street and the Schuykill River. There, at low tide, the machine was positioned down a sloping bank, and a simple paddle wheel was fixed over the stern. As the tide rose, America's first self-propelled vehicle slid off its undercarriage and steamed down the river to fulfill its intended purpose.

———

The Orukter was the best thing that happened to Oliver Evans in 1805. Its performance had proven that his steam engine could not only power a land vehicle but also propel it up the maximum grade (four degrees) allowed by law on turnpike roads. Otherwise, 1805 was dismal. Despite a personal letter to President Jefferson and pleas before a Congressional committee, Evans' mill manufacturing patents had not been renewed. This cost him dearly—or, as he said, "I was left in poverty at the age of fifty, with a large family of children and an amiable wife to support."

His only recourse was to rush to print with *The Young Steam Engineer's Guide*, which he had begun just the preceding year. His millwright's book, now in its second edition, was the standard work in its field. Evans had hoped this manual would enjoy the same success. All he had time for now was an introduction to his high-pressure principles and a miscellaneous hodge-podge of mechanical data. Evans alluded to the premature publication of the book acidly in a new title of *Abortion of the Young Steam Engineer's Guide*.

In 1808, Congress reversed itself, continuing the Evans' milling patent rights for another twenty-two years and authorizing payment due from the expiration of his first patent to the date of re-grant. Some mill owners—Thomas Jefferson among them—paid immediately. But more often, Evans had to resort to expensive litigation. Every plus, it seemed, had a minus. He established the Mars Iron Works in Philadelphia, and his steam engines were finally being bought (ten by 1812, fifty by 1816) for uses as varied as steamboats and the Fairmount Engine Works. But whenever there was a breakdown, he found himself on the other side of a lawsuit.

As America's pioneer in high-pressure steam, Evans had to contend not only with the glitches endemic to any new invention, but considerable calumny because high pressure simply sounded more dangerous than low pressure. When finally the advantages of Evans' principles were realized, his patents were infringed outrageously, and the inventor was back in court again—upbraided as a gross monopolizer of steam, which was now handily categorized as one of nature's wonders and not Evans'. All this was certainly tiresome, although Evans did seem to derive some small pleasure in writing *Patent Right Oppression Exposed; or, Knavery Detected*, in which he lampooned his critics in verse—"The great mechanic called Latrobe/Prig'd out in scientific robe"—and which he published pseudonymously.

At no point, despite the now acknowledged utility of Evans' engine, did anyone come forward to support the inventor's cherished dream of a land carriage. Evans couldn't afford to build one on his own. In 1816, he lost his beloved Sarah. Two years later, when he was sixty-three, he married Hetty Ward, the daughter of a tavern-owning friend from New York. In April 1819, while at Elijah Ward's home in the Bowery, Evans was stricken with a lung inflammation. On April 13, the news was brought to his bedside of the destruction of the Mars Iron Works in Philadelphia. The fire had been set by an apprentice, who offered no reason except "evil genius." All of Evans' plans and patterns were inside—his life's work. It was too much for the already weak inventor. His last act was a trembling signature to a codicil to his will to provide for his young wife. On April 15, Oliver Evans died. Hetty married a lottery agent the following year.

For decades, it appeared that Evans' dream of an automobile had died with him.

CHAPTER 2

■

Steaming from Turnpike to Rail

"I WAS TOO early with my steam projects, and the country was then too poor," Nathan Read lamented, "and I have derived neither honor nor profit from the time and money expended."

Although the most persistent, Oliver Evans had not been alone in envisioning the automobile. Giving up quickly was Nathan Read of Massachusetts. A Harvard graduate and the proprietor of an apothecary in Salem, Read had included a land carriage in his initial petition to Congress following establishment of the U.S. Patent Office in 1790. He did not accept rejection well. When the clerk reading his petition in the House of Representatives came to the section regarding the land carriage, smirks were exchanged throughout the hall. Read promptly returned to Salem, put the small model he had built out of sight, and excluded it from the revised patent petition he submitted eight months later. Reapplication was necessary because of the problems the new Patent Office was having in determining who was first, or original, with what—Oliver Evans, as we have seen, wanting no part of that rat's nest. When it was sorted out in August 1791, the government issued its first patents for steamboats simultaneously to Read, John Fitch, James Rumsey, and John Stevens.

Of that group, both Fitch and Stevens envisioned land carriages, too.

———

Comparatively, Oliver Evans endured soft taps to the life of hard knocks that was John Fitch's. His mother died when he was young, his father didn't much like the frail lad because he couldn't handle work on the Connecticut family farm, he was mistreated by a mate when he ran off to sea and was practically starved by a clockmaker to whom he apprenticed, and he married a woman many years his senior, who made his life miserable. All this had a discouraging effect on his personality. During the Revolution, Fitch served with General Washington at Valley Forge and then sold beer and tobacco to the Continental Army, the profits of which he used to head west and claim land in Kentucky. While there, he was captured by Indians and barely escaped with his life.

In Bucks County, Pennsylvania, in 1785, after a neighbor sped past him in a chaise drawn by a powerful horse, Fitch concluded a steam engine could be adapted to vehicular use. He had never seen such an engine but immediately began the study of steam power, ultimately deciding it might more effectively be applied to a vessel than a carriage. Fitch produced what, most probably, was the first viable steamboat in America. But his genius as an inventor was matched by a fearsome temper and a spectacular talent for driving away associates and prospective investors. Thus, the more congenial and practical Robert Fulton was able to pick up where Fitch's petulance left off and, by popular consensus, enjoy fatherhood of the steamboat ever after.

Fatherhood of the railway locomotive in America is usually accorded John Stevens, who served the state of New Jersey as treasurer during the colonial period and the Continental Army as a colonel during the revolution. As early as 1790, Stevens had pondered the self-propelled vehicle idea, although all of his immediate patents centered on steam engines and their marine application. Only after Fulton steamed on the scene did Stevens return to land use, which remained figuratively virgin territory. By then, Nathan Read had long since decided to forego invention for politics, serving as a Federalist in the House of

Representatives and concluding his career as chief justice for the court of common pleas in Hancock County, Maine.

Poor John Fitch was already dead. Having returned to Kentucky in 1798 to claim his land (unsuccessfully) and to try again to find investors for his steam projects (likewise), he took twelve opium pills instead of the one his doctor had prescribed. Most historians have concluded his death was a suicide.

By contrast, Stevens' life was a bed of roses. Born to wealth, he was also blessed with a wife of great beauty, good humor, and boundless patience. Awakened one morning by her husband's doodling an engine configuration with his fingers on her back, Rachel Cox Stevens suggested that the figure he was drawing was that of a fool but did not otherwise discourage him. Wise lady. Ultimately concluding that a self-propelled vehicle needed help to be effective on land, Stevens built the first steam locomotive to pull a train on a track in America. His failure to stop the construction of the Erie Canal, which he vigorously opposed as less efficient than a railway, was perhaps the only major setback in his life. His final years were spent in comfort, pursuing botany and metaphysics.

———

All this leaves conceptual paternity for the automobile in America squarely with Oliver Evans. Alone among inventors of that era, he doggedly pursued the development of a road carriage, and only he tested his idea by actually producing a vehicle. Granted, calling the Orukter an automobile stretches contemporary definition outrageously, but Evans was constrained to build what he could sell.

Had Evans his druthers and the wider support inventors in Europe generally enjoyed, would the history of the automobile in America have changed significantly? Perhaps not. In France, a couple of years before the Orukter motored to the harbor in Philadelphia, Cugnot's steam tractor—now in the Conservatoire National des Arts et Metiérs— was taken out for testing during the Peace of Amiens, but Napoleon lost interest when war was resumed. Still, both the Frenchman and the American had demonstrated that powered vehicles were possible on the road, a considerable achievement made more so, especially in Evans' case, because it was achieved despite the concerted disinterest of just about everybody.

Moral support was perhaps Evans' most enduring legacy. He provided American inventors the courage to try, although other forces would mitigate against the automobile in this country for far longer than abroad, as we shall see. Indeed, that Evans even envisioned a land carriage betrayed a piquant naiveté, the result no doubt of his location in Philadelphia, the hub of stagecoach enterprises since the colonial period. Quite logically, Evans regarded the Lancaster-Philadelphia Pike, built on concepts pioneered by Scottish inventors Thomas Telford and John Loudon McAdam, as tailor-made for his steam carriage. But that road, at the time, was an epochal exception to the rule. Outside of major metropolitan areas lay "a most howling wilderness," in one contemporary's phrase. Wheeled vehicles of any kind were of minimal use west of the Alleghenies, and in the rural areas to the east, roads that had begun life as Indian footpaths were only marginally better. Twelve days had been required for Washington to travel from Philadelphia to Boston to assume command of the Continental army.

With the Lancaster Pike paving the way, the early years of the republic saw an increase in road building, although it was fitful and sporadic. Chief Justice John Marshall's death in 1835 may have been hastened by his gut-wrenching stagecoach trip from Washington to Richmond earlier that year. Alexis de Tocqueville, who liked much of what he saw in the United States, found the roads "infernal." Most foreign visitors were appalled. To transfer from steamboat to land travel, Baron de Montlezun observed, was to "descend from paradise to hell." Rocking in a contemptible stagecoach over a road with ruts so deep "an army of pygmies might march into them"—that observation from 1833—was one thing. Stagecoach stops were another. Wayside inns served rum brandy and whiskey in copious quantities, perhaps to make travelers forget food that was often unidentifiable. "According to some, it was mutton, to others pork," British visitor Harriet Martineau wrote of one inn meal, "my own idea is that it was dog." Frances Trollop was amazed that Americans put up with the outrages of road travel, as was de Tocqueville.

Real estate was the dilemma. The original thirteen colonies covered a sizable area and, as further states were united into the new nation, America became a very big place. There had to be a better way to get around. Just as engineers harnessing steam as a power turned first to the comparative amiability of water, politicians concluded that canals were a great way to move people and goods, John Stevens' spirited opposition notwithstanding. The canal boom survived until dealt a crushing blow in the Panic of 1837, with the railroads providing the *coup de grâce* soon afterward. "If there is not railroad, canal, or river," a visitor wrote one year, "it is considered impossible to go anywhere." Wrote another only a few years later, "of all my recollections...the most distinct is that of having heard the word railroad occurring once every ten minutes."

History has recognized British inventor Richard Trevithick's high-pressure steam locomotive as the world's first. But well before that, in America and abroad, tracks were used for haulage by groove-wheeled horse wagons in quarries and coal mines. In fact, the Leiper track near Philadelphia had persuaded Oliver Evans to think rails after his Orukter's performance failed to bring any positive response for his road carriage. Ironically, in 1830, five years after the completion of the Erie Canal, the locomotive age began in America when Peter Cooper's Tom Thumb steamed over the B. & O. tracks from Baltimore to Ellicott's Mills, home of the brothers whom Evans had failed to persuade to invest in his steam carriage four decades earlier.

Across the Atlantic, British inventors continued to dominate road-building technology, and Napoleon's military ambition saw to the construction of fine highways on the Continent. But in America, the arrival of the railway had a disastrous effect on the nation's roads. Private turnpikes came to be so little used their income barely paid tollkeeper salaries. The federal government passed the national roads to the states, and maintenance descended to the local level, where the onus of increased taxation led to the adoption of the old English system, whereby repair was seen to by the rural populace "working out" its tax obligation. Soon, most roads in America degenerated into the rough trails they had been originally. There were attempts to halt this retro-gression, the *American Rail-Road Journal* championing "Steam Carriages for Common Roads" and a group in Troy, New York, planning to fix up the wagon road to Schenectady in order to run steam carriages in competition with the Hudson Mohawk Railway. But efforts like these produced only talk followed by inaction.

By 1869, when the locomotives of the Union Pacific and Central Pacific touched cowcatchers at Promontory Point in Utah, the railroad was king in America, exerting a political and economic power unequaled abroad. Soon there were more miles of track in the United States than in all of western Europe. In a land of great distances, the railroad effectively served the migratory nature of the American people and efficiently settled vast areas. But it did not address the American desire for personal mobility, and it created woeful isolation in those areas the tracks did not reach. The railroad's limitations did not go unrecognized, but the paralysis in road building that followed its ascendance made doing anything about it an exercise in futility. For decades, American inventors who attempted an automobile were in essence building a vehicle that had no place to go. The number who tried is surprising.

CHAPTER 3

Frustration, Limitation, Show Business

HIS MASSACHUSETTS farming family regarded Thomas Blanchard as a dullard because of a speech impediment, until at age thirteen he developed a machine to peel apples that could outperform a dozen girls at "paring bees." No one looked askance thereafter as Blanchard went on to patent twenty-five inventions, the most profitable of which was a lathe for turning gunstocks that would be used in armories in both the United States and England. The steamboat he built was the first to navigate Enfield Falls in the Connecticut River and remained in use until the Hartford and New Haven Railroad proved more efficient. Apparently efficient, too, was the steam carriage Blanchard built in 1826 at Bangs' Mill in Springfield and, in his words, "in the middle of one dark night ran up town by way of experiment." Someone was watching, however, because local papers reported the vehicle's ability to run forward and backward, steer properly, and climb hills. But the inventor wasn't very impressed himself, concluding the vehicle was "worthless" and turning his attention to other things. Blanchard was a practical man.

How practical Nicholas and James Johnson were is anyone's guess, but a couple of years after Blanchard, they had their carriage running on the streets of Philadelphia. Reportedly, it was oddly arranged and crudely constructed, with a horizontal single-cylinder engine and a boiler that looked like a big beer bottle. The Johnson brothers tested the vehicle on several occasions until the fateful day when it ran away from them. "Its course could not be changed quick enough," the report read, "and before it could be stopped it had mounted the curbstone, smashed the awning posts, and had made a demonstration against the bulk window of a house at the southwest corner of Brown and Oak Streets." The vehicle was not seen again on the streets of Philadelphia.

The second automobile accident in the United States, most likely, was John Gore's. A builder of stationary steam engines and boilers in Brattleboro, Vermont, Gore completed his vehicle in 1837. A wood-burner like its predecessors, it required two huge vertical boilers that took up 75 percent of the machine's space, leaving room for only a driver and passenger. (By contrast, Blanchard's carriage accommodated eight.) Interestingly, Gore did not endure the official reprisals that would plague many automobile builders for decades, Brattleboro selectmen allowing its use, provided a boy walked ahead, ringing a warning bell. The sound of the bell no doubt was drowned out by the clatter of the machine itself. Although he apparently had no manufacturing ambitions, Gore drove his carriage for more than ten years. His enthusiasm for his invention waned as time passed. On a trip back home from Bernardston, Massachusetts, over particularly rough road, he swerved into a ditch, climbed out, and said that so far as he was concerned, the thing could stay there forever. Later, its engine was removed for a local bakery.

A far briefer life was enjoyed by the vehicle designed by Richard Drury Rice, associate justice of the Supreme Court of Maine. Blueprints made, Rice approached local machinists Frank and George McClench for the actual construction. Rice's boiler looked like a milk can, his carriage was a three-wheeler, and it hit the streets of Hallowell in 1858. In his tall stovepipe hat, Justice Rice was said to cut a dashing figure behind the tiller as the vehicle coursed the neighborhood, a sweating George McClench at the rear, shoveling wood to the ever hungry boiler. Ennui soon set in. Final drive was by chain, and the McClenches were unable to come up with one equal to the two-ton steamer. After several breakages, Rice abandoned the road for the rail and rose to the vice presidency of the Northern Pacific.

More tenacious was John Kenrick Fisher of New York City, who built about a half-dozen steam carriages beginning in 1840. His were not the first in town, however, that honor belonging to William T. James, who built a similar number between 1827 and 1833, and then went to work for the railroad. The steam carriage Fisher built around 1850 was his first requiring only one person to man it, and the 15 miles per hour at which his third vehicle was tested along Broadway in 1853 was an admirable pace. Still, the American Steam Carriage Company he organized for manufacture went nowhere, despite its novel installment plan (periodic five-dollar payments for $100 of stock). When he couldn't find a single buyer for his $2,000 steam carriage, Fisher turned his efforts to fire-fighting apparatus.

———

In 1857, not far from Fisher's shop in lower Manhattan, Richard Dudgeon put the finishing touches to his first steam wagon. Financially secure through his 1851 invention of the portable hydraulic jack now used in locomotive and shipbuilding shops everywhere in the East, Dudgeon was motivated to automotive experimentation less for commercial exploitation than "to end the fearful horse murder and numerous other ills inseparable from their use." He was an ardent animal lover. Reported the *Annual of Scientific Discovery* in 1858, "[The Dudgeon's] speed was about equal with the average speed of horses in stages and it was apparently controlled with much ease, and with more certainty." The inventor was encouraged.

Seeking a wider audience, Dudgeon decided to display the vehicle on his hydraulic apparatus stand at the American Institute's exhibition in the Crystal Palace on 42nd Street. Completed in 1853 as America's largest building and with more gas lights than on all the streets of New York, the Crystal Palace screamed progress and was inspired by the glass and steel edifice of the same name in London. London's Crystal Palace had been home to the first world's fair two years earlier, an event the American Institute wanted to emulate. Pride was the reason. Britain was at its peak as an industrial and technological power; America wanted to prove how inventive it was, too. Moreover, the Crystal Palace needed the business. Unprofitable since it opened, the building's management was now being directed by one Phineas T. Barnum, who knew how to attract attention. Thousands of exhibitors would be on hand with their latest wares—from artwork and "prepared birds" to dental equipment and steam engines. This was the perfect place to promote his steam wagon, Dudgeon thought. At last, New York City's horses would be saved.

But at ten minutes after five o'clock on October 5, 1858, someone in the Crystal Palace yelled "Fire!" Within twelve minutes, the dome fell; within a half hour, most of the building burned to the ground. Arsonists had done their work well. Two thousand visitors were inside when the fire broke out, but, miraculously, not one life was lost. The smoke and flames, visible in many parts of the city, brought hordes of onlookers to watch the destruction of the city's showplace—"such a crowd as has not collected there before since the grand opening," as *The New York Times* wryly commented.

Hurrying as fast as he could because he enjoyed directing the firefighters at such events was Mayor Tiemann, but by the time he arrived, most of the building was gone. The monetary loss of all articles on exhibit was estimated at a half million dollars. Somewhere beneath the rubble and the melted glass was Richard Dudgeon's steam wagon. His only solace was that Daniel Tiemann had missed out on a good time. Dudgeon loathed the man. Despite his vehicle's successful tests, or maybe because of them, Mayor Tiemann, for whom arbitrary exercises of authority were another pleasure, had forbade the inventor's further motoring on city streets. His vehicle had to be towed to the Crystal Palace by the very animals Dudgeon was striving to protect.

"If anyone makes a good, manageable steam carriage at his own cost, and goes everywhere, interfering with no one," Dudgeon asked, why should City Hall "command the steam carriage man never to take it out of his door again?" He determined to build another one when business affairs permitted and New York City had a new mayor. Completed in 1866, Dudgeon's second steamer delighted its inventor. "It will go all day...at fourteen miles an hour, with seventy pounds of steam, the pump on and the fire door open, if desired. One barrel of anthracite coal is required to run at this speed for four hours... It is perfectly manageable in the most crowded streets." Dudgeon used the vehicle to drive his wife and seven children to church on Sunday, and himself to his lower

Manhattan machine shop each day "going fast usually...never really being the cause of a dollar's worth of injury to anybody."

In the 1867 New York City directory, Dudgeon advertised himself as a "maker and patentee of hydraulic jacks, punches, roller tube-expanders, direct-acting steam hammers, and steam carriages for good hard roads." The only one of these products that did not sell was the last named. Still, Dudgeon continued to rail against "the horse-murdering companies" and "the heartless set of politicians" who did not see things his way, and he added an ecological argument that his solution to city travel "does not leave piles of manure in the road." Around 1870, he took up a new cause: the bridge across the East River the Roebling and Kuser families had proposed building, which he thought wholly unnecessary because ferries served the same purpose better and more economically. Dudgeon's vigorous opposition did not halt the building of the Brooklyn Bridge, however, and amusingly, the hydraulic jacks he supplied for its construction made him another small fortune.

Dudgeon drove his second steamer on New York streets for about a decade until officialdom again decided he couldn't. The inventor minced no words in decrying Tammany Hall politics—"If you ever see an honest man nominated who is not an office seeker, vote for him though he be as black, or as Yankee, or as Irish, or as Dutch as the devil"—and Tammany Hall got back at him where seemingly it would hurt most. But by then, Dudgeon was rich enough to have acquired a second home near Locust Valley on Long Island and moved his steam wagon there. Nassau County politicians didn't object to him using it on local roads, which he did until shortly before his death in 1895. The vehicle remains extant in the Smithsonian Institution.

———

Everywhere, inventors were being discouraged. "It seems to us that although it is an ingenious contrivance, it can never supersede horse flesh anywhere," *The Manchester Union* reported of the steamer James S. Batchelder and William H. Writner successfully tested in New Hampshire in 1868. "People who take short journeys for pleasure prefer live stock in harness and long journeys will follow the iron track built expressly for steam carriages of another sort..." During the Civil War and for a decade afterward, local reaction to steam carriages was as dismal as the roads on which they traveled. Inventors returned to more profitable pursuits. In Connecticut, Christopher Miner Spencer commuted to work at Colt's Armory in Hartford in his steam carriage but made his fortune with a repeating rifle that he sold to the Union Army. ("The Yankees loaded on Sunday for the rest of the week," a Confederate officer said.) In Bridgeport, the city fathers okayed the use of the steamer Henry A. House built in 1867 with his brother Joseph, but it was merely a recreational diversion from such moneymaking inventions as an automatic button-holer, a paper-plate maker, a device for blocking felt hats, a fur-picking machine, a parafinned paper cup, and various automatic apparatus for the Shredded Wheat Company of Niagara Falls. With the dawn of the automotive age at the turn of the century, both Spencer and House would return to the automotive vehicle field, Spencer producing steam cars for sale in Connecticut, and House-designed automobiles and trucks being built under license in England.

———

Just who was the first inventor to sell one of his machines is moot. Elijah Ware of Bayonne, New Jersey, is a likely candidate. The steamer he sold in 1866 to a Roman Catholic priest on Prince Edward Island was certainly the first export sale of a U.S. automobile. In New Hampshire, Enos Merrill Clough's 1869 steamer, which he called "Fairie Queen" after the Edmund Spenser epic poem, was traded to A.S. Gordon, a jeweler in Laconia, for a magnificent gold watch and chain. Unfortunately, soon after taking possession, the new owner drove the vehicle into a wall. The first repossession of an automobile in America likely happened in 1867 in Newburyport, Massachusetts, when the client who had ordered a steamer from Francis Curtis (purchase price was $1,000) reneged on the installment payments.

Most commercially minded steam carriage inventors didn't bother trying to sell their vehicles, however. A more certain profit could be made in show business. County fairs offered up to $100 for demonstrations; Oliver Burdette, James Sharp, and Robert Webb of New Athens, Ohio, made a pretty penny with their 1870 creation—"I had my first glimpse of that wonderful steam wagon at the Cadiz Fair," reported an onlooker," "...Mr. Webb standing erect at the helm, on his face a look of pride, his long white beard floating down over his vest, was emblematic of Father Time or Noah steering the ark." Five years earlier, in Massachusetts, the performance of John C. Gardner's steamer at an agricultural fair impressed the *Hingham Journal*: "It runs upon the common road, goes up hill and down, and moves at a two-forty gait without the least apparent difficulty. All that is required is to keep its insides well filled with suitable rations, and it will give full evidence of its capacities and power of speed."

But of all the vehicles of this pioneering era, the most often seen were those of Sylvester Hayward Roper of Roxbury, Massachusetts. Roper, a partner awhile with Spencer in the rifle business, built ten steamers beginning in 1860. His vehicles were the best in the country. Most were four-wheeled, some of them purchased by other steam car builders—such as Joseph Battin of Newark, New Jersey, who was having boiler problems—or would-be builders such as Charles D.P. Gibson of Jersey City, who wanted to study at the tiller of the master before trying his own hand.

The four-wheeler sold to W.W. Austen of Lowell in 1863 made the Roper steamer famous far and wide, although not Roper himself. Professor Austen or Austenius, as W.W. sometimes styled himself, claimed the vehicle as his creation. And he was surely creative in promoting it. "The greatest wonder of the world," his handbills read, "steams noiselessly and unwarily on the public highways, occasionally stopping for a bucket of water, or handful of faggots only."

Actually, this Roper steamed most often on a track, Austen finding that sell-outs were virtually guaranteed whenever he competed against a horse in a match race (the same idea Oliver Evans had more than a half-century earlier). The first appearance of the Roper at a fair sometimes brought a human challenge as well, which Austen naturally was happy to oblige. At Poughkeepsie, New York, the result of a mile race contested by four wheels, four hooves, and two feet was reported as follows: steam buggy, 2:20 minutes; horse, 2:37.5; Rensley on foot, 5:20. "Money flowed in fast, but what at first seemed a pleasure now became work," Austen reminisced.

The downside, apparently, was appearances at such places as Anderson, Indiana, where some locals warned Austen of the havoc they would wreak upon his vehicle—and his person—if the horse didn't win the race. Mulling the alternatives, Austen cut an opening in the fairground fence the night before the event and capped his race victory by escaping to the local police station before the enraged horse lovers could lay a hand on him. "At last I got tired of my now laborious duties," Austen signed, "and feeling that I could retire I did so." Back home in Lowell, Professor Austen put the steam carriage in a shed and got out of show business.

CHAPTER 4

Internal Combustion Arrives

A GREAT SHOW was planned in Philadelphia in 1876. America's wrenching Civil War was history, and most of the scars of the Panic of '73 had healed. The steamboat, the telegraph, the reaper, the cotton gin, and the sewing machine: all these inventions Americans had given the world. The nation was in the mood to celebrate its one-hundredth birthday and to brag. Invitations were sent to all corners of the earth; thirty-eight foreign nations accepted. On May 10, President Grant ceremonially opened the Centennial Exposition in Fairmount Park, just a short distance from the site of the signing of the Declaration of Independence. Only the strains of the march composed for the occasion by Richard Wagner fell flat. Critics panned the piece, and the composer wasn't much more impressed himself, commenting later that the best thing about the march was the $5,000 he was paid for composing it.

The Philadelphia world's fair was huge. In acreage and exhibition hall size, it exceeded any thus far held in Europe. Dignity had been the organizers' aim. On display outside was a huge hand holding a torch, France agreeing to follow with the rest of Frederic Auguste Barthold's colossal statue, provided America pay for building the base. Soliciting donations for the Statue of Liberty's pedestal was decorous enough, but fair organizers were mortified at the ramshackle amusement booths, saloons, and side shows exhibiting such marvels as "learned pigs" and a "five-legged cow," which sprang up for a full mile alongside the world's fair site—and more mortified yet when these attractions brought in more money than the fair itself.

Still, inside the great halls of the Centennial Exposition were marvels far more wondrous than smart swine or a bovine with an extra leg. Alexander Graham Bell demonstrated his telephone, Brazilian emperor Dom Pedro II reportedly jumping out of his seat and shouting "I hear, I hear!" Philo Remington introduced the typewriter, a recent addition to his family's product line of firearms. Among foreign exhibits, the English self-propelled steam road-roller was popular. But among all exhibits, none attracted more attention than the giant Corliss steam engine. Weighing 680 tons, rising 40 feet above the center of Machinery Hall, and supplying power for all exhibits requiring it, the Corliss majestically announced the supremacy of steam. *Atlantic Monthly* editor William Dean Howells eloquently referred to the engine as "an athlete of steel and iron with not a superfluous ounce of metal on it." It was the "symbol of the age," reported Harvard historian Henry Brooks Adams succinctly.

———

Elsewhere, pumping air for the aquarium and operating a printing press for the *London Graphic* were two examples of an engine that was invented perhaps more often than any other mechanical device in history. The concept of internal combustion was born in the late seventeenth century when Dutch mathematician Christian Huygens tried driving an engine with gunpowder, a risky proposition quickly forgotten once the power of steam was harnessed. In the early nineteenth century, in Switzerland, Isaac de Rivaz tried an internal combustion engine in a wagon bed but, similar to Nathan Read with his steam carriage, quickly gave up to devote himself to politics. In Oxford, New Hampshire, Samuel Morey was more persistent, but his engine, which was patented, vibrated so much that the wagon got away from him as he tried to board it for a test run. Persistent too was Alfred Drake of Philadelphia, one of whose engines perished with Richard Dudgeon's steam wagon in the Crystal Palace fire, and New Yorker Stuart Perry, who patented his internal combustion engine in the 1840s.

The principal problem with most of these early efforts was their use of turpentine or alcohol, fuels so expensive as to render them less practical than even the crudest steam engine.

Sticking with the internal combustion idea with the most commercial success was Jean-Joseph Etienne Lenoir, a Belgian who made ends meet during his experimentation by working as a waiter in Paris. The engine he patented in January 1860 used the illuminating coal gas that William Murdock had invented for his boss, James Watt, after being informed in no uncertain terms to forget about building a steam carriage. Using the gas that now coursed through underground pipes to light most of the world's major cities was a clever idea. It was readily available and cheap. "The age of steam is ended," crowed *Scientific American* upon introduction of the Lenoir, "Watt and Fulton will soon be forgotten." The magazine soon ate those words. Installed in factories throughout Europe, the Lenoir engines gobbled prodigious quantities of gas, required copious amounts of grease and oil, and were four times more thirsty for water than a steam engine.

But Lenoir did point the way, and among those following was Nicholas Otto of Germany, whose clumsy, incredibly noisy but infinitely less thirsty internal combustion engine had been introduced at the Paris Exhibition in 1867. Within a decade, with the help of financial angel Eugen Langen and factory manager Gottlieb Daimler, Otto-designed two-stroke engines were in use in factories all over the Continent. And Otto himself was busy at work developing a four-stroke version that would produce more muscle in less space for sale to small factories and workshops. His new engine was successfully tested in the spring of 1876, around the same time his old Otto & Langen (financing the company had earned Eugen co-billing) engine was on exhibit at the Centennial Exposition in Philadelphia.

The second internal combustion engine in Philadelphia was a Brayton, which was as commercially successful in the United States as the Otto & Langen in Europe. Developed by George B. Brayton, an Englishman living in Boston, it was a two-stroke type as well. There were several examples of both the Brayton and the Otto & Langen on hand, the former pumping for the aquarium, the latter for the English printing press.

On hand in Philadelphia, too, was George B. Selden, who exhibited machines he had patented for shaving and for finishing barrel hoops. Those mundane inventions held little interest for Selden, however. In his own grandiloquent words, he was planning "a revolution in loco-motion upon common roads" which would entitle him to "a place in the industrial history analogous to that of the inventor of the steam engine, the locomotive, the cotton gin and the telegraph." George Selden proposed to invent the automobile.

Unfortunately, the Selden family preferred that he become a lawyer. This was not surprising. George's father, Henry R. Selden, was a distinguished member of the Rochester bar, whose clients included Susan B. Anthony (when she was tried for voting) and who served New York State variously as lieutenant governor and judge in the court of appeals. Samuel L. Selden, an uncle, was a successful law-yer as well. His career virtually preordained, young George dutifully studied the classics at Yale, served in the Sixth New York Cavalry and the Hospital Corps during the Civil War, and attended Sheffield Scientific School for a few months until steered back on proper course by his father. Admitted to the bar in 1871, Selden decided to special-ize in patent law, which satisfied his family and kept him close to the field of invention. He was the first attorney hired by photography pioneer George Eastman. But Selden would become most famous as the patent attorney for himself.

Selden's love of mechanics was genuine, and he was a voracious reader of scientific journals. By the mid-1870s, he had discarded the idea of a steam engine for his land carriage—perhaps because of its limita-tions as he saw them, perhaps also because other people had beaten him to it. The internal combustion engine held center stage for Selden now. He built and rejected one operating on nitrous oxide mixed with kerosene. A carbonic gas engine was also a failure. Checking scien-tific journals again, he thought about ammonia, bisulfide of carbon, picric acid, and oil of mirbane. Then came Philadelphia, and he saw the Brayton.

Selden was not alone in his ardor for this internal combustion engine. *Scientific American,* still smarting from the failure of its prediction regarding the demise of Watt and Fulton, judged the Brayton "a fine piece of workmanship...resembling in all respects, externally, a well-proportioned steam engine." Although commended as "ingenious and creditable," too, the Otto & Langen received a less favorable review for failing to look like what it was not. But George Selden's preference for the Brayton was for reasons other than its aesthetic appeal over the awkward Otto & Langen. The latter's fuel supply was tied to the umbilical cord of a gasworks' pipeline; the Brayton used crude petroleum. Granted, Brayton's 1.4-horsepower engine weighed a colossal 1,160 pounds, but scaled down and adapted, it just might work for a land carriage. Selden didn't have the vaguest idea how, but at the moment, neither did anyone else in the world.

"Blow your damned head off if necessary," he told himself back home in Rochester as work began. Making a living routinely interrupted. "Can't carry on about a dozen patent lawsuits and do much experimenting at the same time," he complained. "If ever I get a road wagon it will be by accident." By December 1877, Selden did have specifications for a three-cylinder internal combustion engine, which he took to a local machine shop. A casting was made, although only one of the cylinders was bored out. The following May, the engine was tested and ran in fits and starts, no more than a few minutes at a time, usually at 25 to 30 revolutions per minute, though occasionally revved up to 50. Selden was ebullient. His engine weighed but 360 pounds and developed 2.0 horsepower, a phenomenal improvement on the Brayton's power-to-weight ratio of a single horsepower per half ton. Selden's engine was small enough to be mounted in a vehicle and theoretically had enough muscle to power it. He did not bother trying to build one, however.

———

That the internal combustion engine could propel a land carriage was not George Selden's idea alone. Even the federal government had taken note of the Brayton—in awe mixed with alarm. Reported the Joint Congressional Committee on the Horseless Carriage of 1875, "This discovery begins a new era in the history of civilization; it may someday prove to be more revolutionary than the invention of the wheel, the use of metals or the steam engine. Never in history has society been confronted with a power so full of potential danger and at the same time so full of promise." The report warned against vehicles "hurtling through our streets and along our roads and poisoning our atmosphere..."

Technology would be a while catching up with theory. Meanwhile, steam continued to hold center stage; it was working well on the railroad, and steam engines were easy to build and adapt to road vehicles. As early as 1860, *Scientific American* had editorially hoped that "some of our men of wealth and fashion, who enjoy the exhilarating luxury of driving lightening-going steeds, will get one of these steam carriages and 'clear the track' at the rate of 20 miles an hour." Despite the magazine's advice that one could have a steam carriage built in any locomotive shop, the rich did not rush to do so. Carriages were being built in such shops, however, like the steamer produced by L.T. Pyott, F.A. Morse, and William Devine at the Baldwin Locomotive Works in Philadelphia, which was inspected by Dom Pedro during his visit to the Centennial Exposition. The Brazilian emperor was more impressed with Bell's telephone. In Pittsburgh that same year, building supply tradesman Isaac Mills, Jr., son of the first burgess of the borough of Braddock, drove the steamer of his design in his business until "it was too much trouble to keep out of the way of other wagons."

That steam cars worked was a reality. How well depended on the designer. But the factors mitigating against them far outweighed their relative worthiness. As a novelty, steamers enjoyed some success. As a product, they were unmarketable. Still, the movement toward the automotive age proceeded inexorably. A giant step forward was taken by the state of Wisconsin in 1875. Unfortunately, it was followed by a big step backward.

———

Maryland's no-harm-could-be-done endorsement of Oliver Evans' efforts had been followed with encouragement from the states of Louisiana (1842) and Illinois (c. 1855) to develop a substitute for horses for agricultural work. The federal government chipped in from funds allocated for roads, schools, and churches to help Major Joseph Brown build as many as six Prairie Motors to transport goods in Minnesota in the early 1860s. What made the Wisconsin offer different was its legislated $10,000 price for a vehicle that would be "a cheap and practical substitute for the use of horses and other animals" on both the highway and the farm. There was an impetus and a reason for this.

The impetus was John W. Carhart, a medical doctor and Methodist minister who had built a steam boat to use on the lakes near his New York home in Saratoga Springs, and who, taken ill soon after moving to Racine, Wisconsin, amused himself during convalescence by designing a steam carriage. His brother, H.S. Carhart, a professor of physics at the University of Michigan, worked up the necessary blueprints, and a wealthy Racine resident, George Slauson, was intrigued enough to convert one of his barns into a machine shop for the project. Patterns, castings, and some of the heavier milling were farmed out to the local threshing machine company owned by J.I. Case. Carhart called his steamer "the Spark." "There were no traffic ordinances then to complicate driving," he reminisced, "and, in fact, after one toot of the whistle, we had the street entirely to ourselves." On one of its drives, an expensive trotting horse owned by J.I. Case was scared into breaking its leg, however, and the Racine town council promptly ordered the vehicle off the streets.

But word of Dr. Carhart's steamer had spread far and wide in Wisconsin. Most impressed was George M. Marshall, a state legislator who was a steam enthusiast and enjoyed championing causes. He badgered his colleagues in the legislature into offering the prize. Actually, it made sense. Although not ideally suited by location, Wisconsin's transformation into America's dairy land had already begun. Its network of railways was fine, but alternative ways to get goods to market would serve the state well. The outbreak of distemper, which had sent most of the state's equines to sick bay for several weeks in 1873, suggested that horse power was not reliable.

Initial requirements for the contest enacted in Chapter 137 of the Laws of 1875 called for the machine to be in use for five years, "perform a journey" of at least 200 continuous miles at a 5-miles-per-hour average, be capable of reversing and getting out of the way of horse-drawn vehicles, and ascend and descend a grade of at least 200 feet to the mile. Dr. Carhart, ailing and aging, elected not to participate, but it seemed every other man in Wisconsin who had ever held a wrench felt equal to the task. The legislature had set forth requirements but no rules—and no logistics for monitoring the comparative performance of entrants. Order was brought in a subsequent legislative session with an amendment requiring notice of "progress" to the secretary of state, and the year following, the five-year-use stipulation was replaced by a fixed date for the 200-mile trial to be held along a fixed route by all contestants ready to roll by that time. To supervise, Governor William Smith appointed a three-man Board of Steam Wagon Commissioners: the aforementioned George Marshall; the governor's brother, John M. Smith of Green Bay; and Q.C. Olin, a wealthy farmer from Fort Atkinson.

The 201-mile course selected was Green Bay to Madison by way of Appleton, Oshkosh, Waupun, Watertown, Fort Atkinson, and Janesville, the trial to commence within 20 days after June 10, 1878, and to be concluded within 10 days. The new rules discouraged would-be inventors. Because of the length of the contest, the vehicle would necessarily have to pull a wagon or two, carrying water and fuel, not to mention the race monitors who would be riding along to make sure no tricks were played. All this required a steamer nearly as powerful as a locomotive. A very expensive proposition.

Ultimately, only a half-dozen vehicles entered the Great Steam Race of '78. Despite moving up the starting date nearly a month, only two made it to the starting line. Clearly embarrassed at the paucity of contestants, George Marshall allowed that a couple of entries not quite ready could join the race at intervening points along the course, which did not sit well with the two who were there already. The laggards never did arrive.

The race was between beauty and the beast, literally. The former was called the Oshkosh, all spiff and polish, "a handsome affair and neatly made," according to the *Milwaukee Sentinel*. It had been put together by a committee of five: boilermaker M.G. "Mart" Battis, machinist John F. Morse, fire chief A.W. "Ans" Farrand, and Frank Schomer and Alexander Gallinger, who were in business together "cutting fuel" for the wood-burning locomotives of the Chicago & North Western Railroad. Spreading the work and expense among five had allowed for a comely machine.

By contrast, the second vehicle was the one-man show of machinist E.P. Cowles of Wequiock, who named his creation after the larger neighboring town of Green Bay. So strained were his finances in building his first version that he sold it to a North Woods lumberman, figuring the profit realized would be more than sufficient to make an even better steamer for the contest. What he did not figure on was running out of time. Even the *Green Bay Advocate* conceded that Cowles' steamer appeared to be "thrown together, so to speak." Sniffed the *Oshkosh Daily Northwestern*, "the machine is the most clumsily built and contrived concern it would be possible to imagine."

The proof would be in the plodding. Most of the course paralleled the Chicago & North Western right-of-way, but the roads were so ghastly that no proper assessment of the comparative speeds of the contestants could be made en route. A fairgrounds track was arranged midway for a real race. A lumber-hauling contest would precede it. And because "farm" as well as "highway" had been in the language of the original legislative act, a plowing demonstration was included, too, at the farm of commissioner Olin.

Naming the vehicles by the towns of their origin had been deliberate. Parochial rivalry was fierce. "Talk about your excitement!" Alex Gallinger remembered. "Barnum's circus was no greater attraction." Thousands of people were on hand for the start in Green Bay, and thousands of dollars were bet on the outcome. Most of the wagering was on the Oshkosh. Lest appearances deceive, railroad men with whom Gallinger and Schomer did business confided *sotto voce* that if the Oshkosh crew needed anything along the way to flag a passing train. The Board of Steam Wagon Commissioners' decision to tag along behind the contestants had been a good idea.

At 11:00 a.m. on Tuesday, July 17, the race was on. The Oshkosh vaulted into the lead, reaching Depere by 1:25 p.m. and Appleton a full hour and 45 minutes ahead of the legislated 5-miles-per-hour average. There the Oshkosh crew put up for the night. Appleton was left the following morning at 9:05 a.m., Menasha was reached 80 minutes later, a fine dinner was provided at the Russell House in Neenah around noon, and the Oshkosh arrived in the city for which it was named at 3:00 p.m. Crowds had cheered the vehicle on all along the course, women throwing roses, men throwing cigars. Sometimes wagons were hitched behind the "fuel tender" to join in the ride. Alex Gallinger remembered at least five or six people, including race monitors, back there all the time. But the Oshkosh never faltered.

Meanwhile, E.P. Cowles' Green Bay was proving a sublime metaphor for what haste makes. Soon after the start, its steering gear broke, and the steamer motored straight into a culvert. Dragging it out took hours; more hours were consumed in repair. Back on the road, something else broke in the middle of nowhere. The commissioner riding with Cowles insisted that the vehicle be loaded on a flatbed of the North Western and railroaded to Oshkosh. Cowles was furious, preferring to "work day and night" to fix his machine and "make the whole journey according to stipulation." The Oshkosh crew was upset, too, because announcement was made that the race would be resumed only after the

Green Bay was ready to run again and the rules stipulated a maximum of 10 days for the entire trip to Madison, fairgrounds speed contest, lumber hauling, and all. To move things along, John Morse offered his machine shop, in which the Oshkosh had been built, for Cowles to repair the Green Bay.

Working feverishly, Cowles was ready to roll by Saturday morning. The hauling match was first, which both machines performed admirably. At the fairgrounds speed trial, the Green Bay stormed into the lead, Cowles pouring it on until he was nearly a quarter mile ahead of the Oshkosh. Then one of his makeshift repairs unrepaired itself, and the Green Bay stopped. The Oshkosh sailed past and came under the wire at 4:41 for the mile. Of the hometown machine, the *Green Bay Advocate* reported the next day, "her running and hauling powers are ample, but...her construction is so faulty that she breaks down often, and is constantly delayed for repairs. These difficulties are unfortunate, but by no means fatal." Alas, soon they were. Finally, something broke that Cowles couldn't bang back together, and he gave up about 20 miles from the finish line in Madison.

The rest of the contest was a triumphal procession for the Oshkosh, with several dozen spectators towed behind at one point. Cigars and beer were handed all around as the race winner steamed to the finish line. "We wound up the trip all sound and the boys all well," a reporter riding the Oshkosh commented. "No runaways or broken bridges are left behind to tell the tale." The winner's official running time from Green Bay to Madison was 33 hours and 27 minutes, comfortably within the legislated maximum of 40 hours, and included the refueling stops that the Steam Wagon commissioners had informed the Oshkosh crew only at the starting line would not be considered "free time."

But that was child's play compared to the surprise the commissioners had in store for the Oshkosh owners now. Having won the contest and fully performed all feats (including plowing commissioner Olin's field), they confidently awaited receipt of their $10,000 prize. It did not arrive. Instead, under pressure from the Wisconsin legislature, the Board of Steam Wagon Commissioners concluded that the Oshkosh did not meet "the language and the sprit of the law." At about $1,000 to build and two to six dollars a day to operate, it was not "a cheap and practical substitute" for horses. "Foul!" cried the Oshkosh crew.

The matter was endlessly debated in the Wisconsin legislature and the editorial columns of newspapers in the state. Neither of the contestants had produced an "invention," it was suggested at one point, because neither of the vehicles was the first to be powered by steam on land. "The steam wagons are a fraud and the taxpayers who saw them are mad," sniffed the *Milwaukee Sentinel.* Asked widely now was why the reward had been offered in the first place. And questioned was whether only two vehicles represented a competition.

In the midst of this glorious melee were vocal partisans from the two towns for whom the steam carriages had been named. Allowing that the Oshkosh commended itself "to the superficial eye for its neatness and even elegance," the *Green Bay Advocate* argued that, in principle, the Cowles steamer was superior because it had proven faster in the speed run until it broke down, and it broke down only because of the haste in which it had been constructed; the first Green Bay was still performing to immense satisfaction for that lumberman up in the North Woods. The Board of Steam Wagon Commissioners had suggested compensatory awards to the builders of both machines. The *Oshkosh Daily Northwestern* took immediate umbrage, calling the idea "a queer mixture of acknowledgments toward the Oshkosh machine and sop thrown to the Green Bay machine, the latter evidently to please one of the commissioners from that direction." That was the governor's brother, of course. Quoting George Marshall's comment that the Oshkosh was "the prettiest piece of machinery he ever saw and worked to perfection," the *Northwestern* pointedly noted the matter of good faith on the part of the state: "Its honor is pledged, and whether its offer was wise or not, it is too late to discuss."

Discussion continued anyway for several months longer. Messrs. Schomer, Ferrand, Gallinger, Battis, and Morse threatened to sue the state. Ultimately, the Wisconsin legislature hammered out a compromise, recorded in Chapter 193 of the Laws of 1879. The sum of $5,000 would be provided to the builders of the Oshkosh in "full payment" for the "disbursements and expenses incurred in the construction of a steam wagon on highways... But this act shall not be construed as an admission that said wagon was a satisfactory compliance with the requirements of said acts." At the same time, "said acts" of 1875 and thereafter were repealed. Not mentioned in Chapter 193 of the Laws of 1879 was the ultimatum delivered in a smoke-filled room to the builders of the

Oshkosh that they give $1,000 of their $5,000 award to E.P. Cowles for his Green Bay steamer expenses. "It galled us like thunder," Alex Gallinger said, "but we had to do it."

All of the participants in the Great Steam Race of '78 elected to sit out the rest of the borning automotive age.

CHAPTER 5

∎

Taking a Back Seat
to Little Egypt

ON MAY 8, 1879, in Rochester, New York, George B. Selden applied for a patent for a road vehicle combining his Brayton-type internal combustion engine with the other necessities for locomotion. The elements he described were already known, as Selden was well aware, but their combination was new and therefore patentable. Bearing witness to his application were his draftsman W.M. Rebasz, Jr. and client George Eastman. Selden tried to secure financial backing to build his vehicle but met with the same reception Oliver Evans had nearly three-quarters of a century earlier, and he didn't pursue that course long. What he did pursue was a waiting game in the issuance of his patent.

As a patent lawyer, Selden was a master at the game. U.S. Patent Office law fixed a two-year period for completing applications but allowed that term to be renewed indefinitely. So Selden routinely made revisions, forcing the Patent Office to reconsider the legitimacy of his application each time. After each new claim was either refused or conceded, Selden had another two years to complete his patent. The Patent Office might reply to him in a month or less, but Selden would use the full time allowed to write back and with another change, which started the whole process again. Clearly, he recognized the emergence of the automobile and was determined to be a factor when it arrived.

———

As George Selden shuffled his patent papers, others labored to put together an automobile that would work on the road. The steamer George Alexander Long built circa 1880 in Northfield, Massachusetts, survives in the Smithsonian. He did not attempt a second car. In Lansing, Michigan, Ransom Eli Olds was more persistent. He put his first steamer on the road at three in the morning during the summer of 1887. "I realized I had a colt on my hands," he said, "and did not care to have any spectators." But spectators he had. "An outburst of ripping, roaring noise caused people to leap from their beds and rush to the windows," read one report, "...Civil War rifles and sabers were snatched from walls or attics." The milk-wagon horse bolted, and most of the morning's deliveries spilled onto the street. Admitting that more than one "push to be remembered" was needed to get the vehicle safely back home, Olds was embarrassed that rudely awakened neighbors bore witness. His father was both mortified and worried. "Ranse thinks he can put an engine in a buggy and make the contraption carry him over the roads," Pliny Olds sighed. "If he doesn't get killed at his fool undertaking, I will be satisfied."

Although the vehicle was not a success, Olds developed its steam engine into a worthy product for manufacture that would increase the family machine shop business fourfold and double the workforce to twenty-four. Ransom was much happier with his second steamer, completed in 1892 and the recipient of a laudatory article in *Scientific American,* a journal in which the Olds steam engine was advertised. "It never kicks or bites, never tires out on long runs," its inventor said proudly of the new vehicle, "and during hot weather [the driver] can ride fast enough to make a breeze without sweating the horse." A further advantage was economy because care was not required in the stable, and the vehicle ate only when it was on the road. What Ransom did not admit to *Scientific American* was that he dreaded the sight of a hill. On steep grades, his wife Metta followed behind with a large block of wood should the engine stall. Proper brakes were a factor Ransom hadn't figured out yet. To fund his further experimentation, Olds sold the vehicle to a British patent medicine firm for use in its branch office in Bombay. The ship taking it there is believed to have sunk en route.

How many steam cars were built during this pioneering period will never be known. Dozens of others have been documented; probably hundreds more ran out of steam before their reality was committed to print. By now, too, the internal combustion engine was being looked upon with increasing interest. In 1881, in West Chester, Pennsylvania, Curtis H. Warrington built a three-wheeler powered by common illuminating gas that was carried in a weighted bellows under the passenger seat. "The two-horse engine, with carriage complete, will cost $650," he told the *West Chester Daily Local* before ill health squelched his manufacturing plans. "This is no more than the cost of a good pair of horses, and will travel faster and more steady in the hottest weather, at a cost of only 10 to 12 cents per hour." What Warrington did not mention was that after two hours of running, the driver had best be close to an available gas main or he would not be going anywhere.

The umbilical cord had been the reason Selden favored the crude petroleum-burning Brayton over the Otto & Langen at the Philadelphia Centennial Exposition. Also aware of the Otto's limitations was the manager of the Deutz factory producing the engine in Germany; Gottlieb Daimler realized fuel was the significant key that would make smaller and lighter internal combustion units capable of the same performance as stationary gas engines. Since 1858, when Colonel Edwin L. Drake drilled for oil in Pennsylvania at a place called Titusville, petroleum had been distilled into three distinct products: heavy oil (as used in the Brayton), medium-weight kerosene (which by now had replaced candles and whale oil for all home lighting not supplied by fixtures tied into the local gas works), and petroleum spirit or gasoline (the lightest, the most volatile, and thus far regarded as nearly useless). Daimler decided to use this waste product for the engine he developed after leaving Deutz to experiment on his own in Cannstatt. Sixty miles away in Mannheim, around the same time, engine builder Carl Benz, who had used coal gas previously, was likewise convinced after the explosion of a bowl of benzene a neighboring *hausfrau* had bought to clean gloves. The three-wheeler Benz patented in January 1886 and the four-wheeler Daimler tested later that year were the first gasoline automobiles that truly worked.*

---

* Previous efforts, such as Warrington's, had used city gas for fuel. Among them were Lenoir's vehicle in Paris in 1863, Siegfried Marcus' handcart in Vienna in 1870, and Edouard Delamare-Debouteville's three-wheeler in Montgrimont, France in 1883. These never proceeded beyond the experimental or novelty stage. "After

But being first mattered little then. Neither Daimler nor Benz had come up with a product that would sell. Steam car inventors on both sides of the Atlantic could have told them that. This bothered Daimler not at all; he preferred continued experimentation and was obsessed with the universality of his engine, which he thought could be adapted to vehicles for the road, rails, water, and even the air. Benz's obsession was strictly for the automobile, and he labored mightily for a half-decade, trying to sell his invention in Germany before latching onto Emile Roger, an enterprising Frenchman who sold about two dozen Benz three-wheelers in Paris by the end of 1892 and Benz's new four-wheelers thereafter.

Meanwhile, in America, gasoline car builders were faring dismally. In Ohio City in 1891, John William Lambert—proprietor of a grain elevator, lumber yard, and hardware store—attached a $550 price tag to his three-wheeler, printed a sales brochure, and found no takers. Many others built gasoline cars for their own use or for a single specific client.

Gas and gasoline engines became a fine business, however. And in the years since the Centennial Exposition, a number of manufacturers had risen to challenge the popular Brayton and the Otto, which by now was being manufactured in the United States. Just as with steam, the first commercially successful transport use for these units was on water. George Brayton adapted his motors to launches. In 1887 in Grand Rapids, Michigan, Clark Sintz successfully put his marine engine on the market. In Lansing, P.F. Olds & Son added the gasoline engine that Ransom Olds developed to the company product line.

Another source of power was recommending itself as well. The electric motor was not new. Thomas Davenport, Moses G. Farmer, and Professor Charles G. Page were among those experimenting in the United States before mid-century. But it was not until 1887 when Frank S. Sprague, a former colleague of Thomas Edison's, inaugurated America's first successful electric street railway in Richmond, Virginia,

---

the novelty wore off," as Victor Emerson said of the gas car he built in Cincinnati, Ohio, in 1885, he used it to practical advantage as a grain elevator in his barn. Prior to Daimler and Benz, Delamare-Debouteville did attempt a four-wheeler using liquid fuel, but its chassis was shaken to pieces during a preliminary test. The Frenchman never built another car but did proceed, successfully, into stationary gasoline engine manufacture.

that its practical value was realized. Almost immediately, horse car lines in major cities throughout America began to be electrified. The reason was partly environmental; sanitation experts had estimated the average horse deposited twenty-two pounds of manure and untold gallons of urine on city streets each day.

———

If electric power could work on the rail, it followed that it could work on the road, too. Among those thinking so was Andrew Lawrence Riker, who, at the age of sixteen, attached an electric motor he designed to a Columbia tricycle that he drove across the cellar of the family home in New York City in 1884. For the rest of his life, he called that drive the greatest thrill he ever experienced. William Morrison's electric car hit the streets of Des Moines, Iowa, around 1890. Its subsequent public debut in the Seni Om Sed (Des Moines spelled backwards) parade was picked up by the Associated Press, which resulted in the local post office being deluged with letters to Morrison from all over the world, the majority from fellow inventors of land vehicles who wanted to compare or commiserate.

Probably among them was one from Charles W. Holtzer, who operated the first telephone exchange outside of Boston (fourteen subscribers and one toll line to the big city), and who built an electric car in collaboration with George E. Cabot for local paper baron Fiske Warren. Another letter might have arrived from John D. Perry Lewis of Missouri, whose 1893 electric amazed St. Louis residents—so a local paper said—because "there was no trolley or overhead wire, and how the power was derived was not apparent to the average spectator."

———

Curiosity notwithstanding, thus far the automobile idea seemed to be the answer to a question few were inclined to ask, which was obviously among the problems impeding its progress. Significant, too, was the isolation in which inventors were working—on both sides of the Atlantic. Although Daimler and Benz lived only sixty miles apart in Germany, neither was initially aware of the existence of the other. In America, geography limited interaction even more. Unless an inventor chose to write about his work, and unless a scientific magazine editor took a fancy to it, the likelihood was that the vehicle was not known much beyond the town in which it had been built.

A catalyst was needed. Upcoming in Chicago in 1893 was an extravaganza that just might be it.

———

"Other fairs have shown civilization spreading from field to field like a prairie-fire," *Century Magazine* commented that February. "This fair will flame with the human energy that handed the torch of civilization across an ocean." The city of Chicago had outbid New York, St. Louis, and Washington, D.C. for the privilege of sponsoring the World's Columbian Exposition to commemorate the four-hundredth anniversary of the discovery of the New World. Initially, there were misgivings among "sober-minded people," as *Harper's Weekly* put it, in locating "the World's Fair at a place so distant from the seaboard," but these were quickly dispelled. The Windy City was pulsating with energy and pride. Newly rebuilt from the disastrous fire of 1871, Chicago created a virtual new city for the Columbian Exposition spreading over 150 buildings and 633 acres in Jackson Park. This was nearly four times the area and twice the number of square feet under roof as the Paris Exposition of 1889. A cue had been taken from the Paris event, however, for which Alexandre Gustave Eiffel had been commissioned to build a tower as the centerpiece. The centerpiece ordered for Chicago was a gigantic wheel designed by Illinois engineer George W.G. Ferris to carry visitors 250 feet in the air for a bird's-eye view of the wondrous "White City" buildings that *Scribner's* flamboyantly likened to ancient Greece.

And, a lesson having been learned well from the Centennial Exposition in Philadelphia, "show biz" was big business in Chicago. Although the Midway Plaisance, with its phantasmagoria of villages representing nations around the globe, was officially meant to educate, it was evident that more visitors preferred to be entertained—as demonstrated by the attendance records for the Egyptian exhibit where scantily clad "specimens of oriental beauty" introduced America to belly dancing. Many were scandalized.

But everyone was awed by the enormity of Chicago's fair. From May 1 when, amid a spirited rendition of the "Hallelujah Chorus," President Grover Cleveland pressed the key to give life to the 2000-horsepower Allis steam engine (the largest in the world) that provided power to exhibits as well as the many fountains dotting the grounds, Jackson Park was a kaleidoscope of light and a cacophony of sound that italicized America's growth as an industrial power. Rock drills, band saws, printing presses, and machines of all kinds bellowed in the great halls. Edison's incandescent bulbs burned everywhere. Impressive foreign exhibits there were—so large was the ordnance display sent over by Krupp of Germany that a separate building was necessary to contain it—but America's pride was foremost. The nation had more miles of telegraph wires, more telephones, and more electric lights than any other country in the world. Nowhere else was more timber and steel manufactured; more crude oil refined; more iron, coal, and precious metals mined; or more meat packed, for that matter. But nowhere at the World's Columbian Exposition was America's progress better revealed than in the Transportation Building, where more than fifty of her steam locomotives—highlighted by the New York Central's No. 999, which had recently traveled between Batavia and Buffalo at 112.5 miles per hour—were on display.

But what of automobiles? Fair managers had encouraged inventors to attend, assigning Class 518 in the Transportation Building to "steam and electric carriages, and all vehicles for carrying passengers on common roads operated by other than horse-power." But given the voluminous pre-fair hoopla nationwide that forecast just how gigantic the fair would be, builders of automobiles eschewed participation. Being ignored—or worse, laughed at—on so grand a scale did not appeal. A trio of Chicago electric car proponents—Clyde J. Coleman, Fred Dagenhardt, and E.E. Keller—had hoped to persuade fair management into a lucrative contract to provide motorized transport for visitors but had to settle for a display of one of their pilot models in the Electrical Building. On hand there as well was William Morrison's electric, which the inventor had sold the preceding year to Harold Sturges of Chicago, whose firm had supplied the batteries. Sturges displayed the vehicle in his American Battery Company exhibit and took it out for runs around the fairgrounds, although without the attention the vehicle had commanded the previous year during test drives, which, the *Western Electrician* commented, had been "too much, even for the wide-awake Chicagoan" and required police to hold back the crowds. In the meantime, Sturges had brazenly chosen to rename Morrison's car after himself.

The only steamer at the fair belonged to Achille Philion, a circus performer who had built it to call attention to himself and his act, and who seems to have sneaked onto the Midway Plaisance without an invitation. The only gasoline car was Gottlieb Daimler's. Alone in the Transportation Building it sat, dwarfed by giant locomotives and overwhelmed by exhibits of countless wagon and carriage builders—dominated by the Studebaker brothers of South Bend, Indiana—and the forty-three bicycle exhibitors, the most prominent among them the Pope Manufacturing Company of Hartford, Connecticut.

The presence in Chicago of Daimler's automobile—as well as Gottlieb Daimler himself—was the result of the alliance Daimler had formed several years earlier with William Steinway, whose principal business was the manufacture of pianos in New York City. German born, Steinway had been introduced to Daimler during a trip to his homeland, and Daimler in turn introduced Steinway to his engine with rides in a Daimler-powered car, a boat, and a trolley. Of these, Steinway saw promise for the engine's profitable utilization in boats and trolleys in the United States, but no foreseeable hope for the commercial advantage of his automobile. Steinway's pessimism was not unfounded. Nowhere in the voluminous reportage on the World's Columbian Exposition was Daimler's vehicle—nor the two electrics, for that matter—provided more than a cursory glance. "In each world's fair there has been some exhibit which has played a great part in human affairs," *Scientific American* commented in August 1893. "At the English Exhibition it was the sewing machine; at the Philadelphia Exhibition it was the telephone." In Chicago, the reporter reckoned it would be the elevated railway, the first section of which had already begun its "loop" in the Windy City.

So pervasive was the image and reality of the railroad in America that anything less than its continued dominance seemed unthinkable. On rails, one could ride faster, more smoothly, and less expensively than by any other method of land travel. So strictly also-ran was travel by road that no need had existed to build highways. Outside major cities, fewer than 200 miles were hard surfaced. And few seemed to mind. In Paris, an automobilist could motor from the Champs-Elysées into the countryside, and increasingly, gasoline, steam, and electric cars were being purchased there. But in rural America, where two-thirds of the nation's population lived, the livery stable, the blacksmith shop, and the watering trough were reminders that everyday life in the New World was still reined to a horse.

CHAPTER 6

Pedaling Toward
the Automobile

"WE THOUGHT THE railroad was good enough," Hiram Percy Maxim said, "[until] the bicycle created a new demand which it was beyond the ability of the railroad to supply."

Supplying the bicycle most vigorously was Colonel Albert Augustus Pope, a large man who reveled in wine, women, and song—and who was good at seizing opportunity. Born into a prominent New England family fallen on hard times, young Albert began making his living at age ten. For three years, after school and during summers, he worked on a farm, amassing enough money to buy produce and set himself up in business as a greengrocer. With the outbreak of the Civil War, Pope enlisted in the Union Army and rose rapidly through its ranks. His skill in organizing a provisional regiment of artillery from a convalescent camp to help defend the nation's capital was widely noted. Pope served with Burnside in Tennessee, with Grant at Vicksburg, and under Sherman in Jackson—and turned twenty-two as the war ended. For a while, he marketed ornaments for ladies' slippers and shoe manufacturing supplies and tried Massachusetts politics, serving as a member of the Newton City Council.

At Philadelphia's Centennial Exposition, Pope saw his first high-wheeled velocipede and was enthralled. His return to Newton was delayed while he learned as much as he could about this strange and wonderful device. Pope launched his new career gingerly by importing English velocipedes. After securing the U.S. rights to the French Lallement patents, he began marketing his own under the brand name of Columbia. Their manufacture was seen to by the Weed Sewing Machine Company of Hartford, Connecticut, a firm the Colonel bought out as his business prospered. For good reason, velocipedes were nicknamed "bone-shakers." To increase speed, their front wheels reached diameters of up to 64 inches. They were not for the timid nor the maladroit. Eager purchaser Mark Twain (*nee* Samuel Clemens), who lived a few blocks from Pope's factory, flew over the handlebars and landed on his instructor his first time out.

The mid-1880s invention of the safety bicycle, with its equally sized front and rear wheels, made cycling possible for everyone. The Colonel was in a perfect position to capitalize. His Pope Manufacturing Company became the largest employer in New England. The safety bicycle took the country by storm. Said the *American Machinist,* "this simple machine has for the first time really put the human race on wheels." With a bicycle, a rider was master of his destination once he learned the basics, the lessons often included in the purchase price. Bicycle racing became an immensely popular sport, and women took to the new hobby as eagerly as men. Susan B. Anthony saw the bicycle as the ultimate invention for the emancipation of women, allowing them to discard corsets and bustles for "common sense dressing." The Boston Women's Rescue League dissented, soberly reporting that "thirty percent of the unfortunates who have come within the field of this organization's work have at one time or another been bicycle riders, and therefore wheeling has a demoralizing influence on women."

Factories sprouted everywhere. Colonel Pope did not take kindly to the competition and demanded tribute for manufacture of parts for which he held patent or rights. He was most successful with Lallement infringement, collecting handsomely from the larger producers. Compliance among small-town builders was sporadic, but he was relentless in pursuing them, their number including the Wright brothers' shop in

Dayton, Ohio. Seldom was Pope defeated until, in Chicago, Thomas Jeffery and R. Philip Gormully challenged him in court and, in essence, made America safe for bicycle manufacture. The Chicago partners called their bicycle the Rambler. Fellow Chicagoan Ignatius Schwinn named his after himself.

In Massachusetts, the Duryea brothers began producing the Sylph. In Ohio, erstwhile racer Alexander Winton—who had mourned the passing of the velocipede, lamenting "that was real sport, the safety took the fun out of it"—quit his machinist's job and began the Winton Bicycle Company. By 1896, America boasted 274 bicycle factories, 700 firms making bicycle sundries, and 50,000 retail and repair shops. Bicycling was big business. Despite the competition, the Connecticut colonel remained, figuratively, the cycling pope.

For the bicycle owner, there was a downside. Cyclists venturing from city streets into the countryside came upon the harsh reality that their freedom was limited by more than the power of their legs. The League of American Wheelmen became a propaganda agency for good roads and, with Colonel Pope to champion the cause, a vociferous one. Members besieged city officials, state legislators, and Washington. And they took their case to the public in countless newspaper and magazine articles. Nowhere was the system of highway maintenance by the rural voting population working out its tax obligation more scornfully examined than by N.S. Shaler in the October 1889 issue of *Scribner's Magazine*:

> Arriving on the ground long after the usual time of beginning work, the road-makers proceed to discuss the general question of road-making and other matters of public concern, until slow-acting conscience convinces them that they should be about their task. They then with much deliberation take the mud out of the road-side ditches, if indeed the way is ditched at all, and plaster the same on the centre of the road. A plough is brought into requisition, which destroys the best part of the road... An hour or two is consumed at noon-day by lunch and a further discussion of public and private affairs. A little work is done in the afternoon, and at the end of the day the road-making is abandoned until the next year.

Soon, in many states, convict labor came to be regarded as more efficient. The National League for Good Roads was founded in 1892. In 1893, Congress appropriated $10,000 for a Bureau of Road Inquiry to be established within the Department of Agriculture to determine how bad the situation was and what might be done.

In addition to beginning to literally pave the way for the automobile, the bicycle provided an object lesson in how an automobile might be built. In Ireland in 1888, Belfast veterinarian John Boyd Dunlop developed a pneumatic tire for use on his son's bike. From bicycle manufacturers came steel tube framing, chain drive, ball and roller bearings, and differential gearing. Granted, many of these particulars had been figured out by earlier automobile builders on their own, but the impetus of the two-wheeler encouraged more to try—both bicycle makers (such as J. Elmer Woods and Andrew J. Philbrick in Massachusetts, who built a three-wheeled steamer in 1887) and bicycle purchasers (such as the aforementioned Percy Maxim, son of the inventor of the Maxim gun, who had begun his experimentation into internal combustion with empty shells and small quantities of gasoline, motorizing a secondhand Columbia in 1893).

Equally interested was Charles E. Duryea who, during earlier travels in New Jersey on behalf of his bicycle business, had seen Senator Smith's steamer and chatted with Lucius D. Copeland in Camden, whose efforts included a steam motorcycle (made from a Columbia and a Star) and a steam tricycle. Copeland had promoted his efforts vigorously until, concluding that "nobody would pay more than $500 for a motor vehicle," he left the East Coast for California and retirement. Duryea concluded that Copeland had the right idea but the wrong approach. His car would have four wheels and a gasoline engine. In Springfield, Massachusetts, Charles roughly sketched his ideas and began development with brother J. Frank. But before the vehicle was completed, he left for Peoria, Illinois, to relocate his bicycle business there. Frank, at age twenty-four, eight years Charles' junior, remained in Massachusetts with the car project.

In mid-September 1893, testing of the first Duryea revealed problems that Frank set to solving, taking a break to attend the world's fair in Chicago one month later where Charles was exhibiting his bicycle wares. The World's Columbian Exposition, the elder Duryea would later say, encouraged automotive inventors "who had been discouraged by ridicule and pity [to take] a fresh hitch at their trousers." Most of the Duryea hitching for the next year, however, was done by Frank, with Charles kibitzing via letters from Peoria.

In early January 1894, the first Duryea was driven six miles without untoward incident. In April, Frank began work on an improved second model, to feature two cylinders rather than one and such improvements as a geared transmission and pneumatic tires. That November, Charles returned to Massachusetts to sell his house. The new car was first driven in December, with road tests following into the new year. By February 1895, the brothers were confident enough to take their wives for a ride. By March, when Charles had returned to Peoria, the car was being driven daily. In June, Frank wrote to his brother that "an order received this a.m. says book me for two carriages to be delivered at earliest possible date." That brought Charles back to Massachusetts in July to search for financing. He spent three days in Hartford, Connecticut, with the Pope people and several unrewarding hours with the Colonel himself. Pope was interested in the Duryea, but the negotiations broke down on the matter of money. Duryea wanted a royalty of fifty dollars per unit; Pope offered less than five. All Duryea had that was new was an engine, the Colonel exhorted. The rest of the machine was little more than a steel frame connecting two bicycles, which he knew how to build better anyway. Besides, the Duryea was too far ahead of its time. Nobody he knew wanted an automobile.

A discouraged Charles returned to Peoria. Frank soldiered on in Massachusetts. For the Duryeas, as for the other automobile builders and dreamers in America, there remained the need for a catalyst—an event that would call attention to their achievement.

———

Herman H. Kohlsaat provided it. As a World's Columbian Exposition official, he was aware of the few automobiles exhibited there. As a voracious reader, particularly of European publications, he knew about the burgeoning popularity of automobiles abroad. On a trip to Paris, he had seen many of them. "That the horseless carriage has 'arrived' is beyond question," he wrote, "but its availability to American roads is looked upon with skepticism... The horseless carriage will confer an incalculable benefit upon mankind if it shall hasten their construction."

He proposed to help by sponsoring a contest for automobiles. His motivation was more than altruism. It was also circulation. Kohlsaat was publisher of the *Chicago Times-Herald*.

The idea for an automobile race had been suggested to Kohlsaat by his science reporter, Frederick U. ("Grizzly") Adams. Whether he had been aware of the Great Steam Race of '78 (which the state of Wisconsin had been trying very hard to forget) is not known, but Adams' immediate inspiration was the 1894 run from Paris to Rouen sponsored by *Le Petit Journa*, which inaugurated the fabulous city-to-city races held on the Continent well into the turn of the century. The Chicago Times-Herald would be more than a speed event, however. It would also test utility—as had the unlamented Wisconsin contest, although not with hauling and plowing demonstrations. Instead, a testing contraption was built by the Chicago City Railway Company, and the Studebaker brothers graciously emptied part of one of their city warehouses to store it. On this machine, competing automobiles—which, the rules stated, had to have three or more running wheels and "derive all their motive power from within themselves"—would be tested to determine load carrying, grade climbing, fuel consumption, and efficiency. Only those proving safe, and superior to a horse and wagon, would be certified for the competition run. Initially, that run was planned for Milwaukee to Chicago, but so treacherous were the roads in Wisconsin that a more agreeable ninety-two-mile round-trip course between Chicago and Waukegan was chosen, the start/finish line near the Midway Plaisance in Jackson Park. A maximum time limit of thirteen hours was agreed upon, including all necessary repairs en route, which had to be executed by the automobile's occupants, although the umpire riding along to keep time and enforce the rules could assist if he were so inclined. Prizes overall would total $5,000, to be allocated both for race performance and specific noteworthy elements of design.

Logistics taken care of, Adams began promotion with a vengeance. Competing newspapers in Chicago gave the upcoming event the silent treatment, but it didn't matter. Technical periodicals and major newspapers everywhere else picked up the story. Entries poured in, ultimately nearly one hundred of them. "Astonishing," said *The New York Times*.

Now the problems began. In all the careful planning, one element had been overlooked: timing. The contest was announced in early July, qualifying tests were scheduled for late October, and the race for November 2. That was not very long to build a car, much less make sure it was race prepared. By the time the colors of fall foliage were at their peak, Kohlsaat's face was red. He was besieged by letters from contestants pleading for more time to complete their entries, a number of them also asking for financial contributions—to be repaid, of course, when the prize was won. "If a newspaper publisher thinks it easy to build a motor vehicle in four months," one entrant wrote, "then let him provide the means."

That point was well taken. Earlier builders had learned the hard way how long and costly the period of trial and error could be. Many had not been entirely satisfied with their first efforts but lacked the where-withal to try further. Others had long since consigned their road vehicles to more practical stationary use. Thus, save for those experimenting at the time of the announcement, the Times-Herald entrants would be starting their vehicles from scratch. Ever the optimist, Kohlsaat figured they would be finished on time, despite their complaining, and he did not back down on his contest date.

But he did begin to have other trepidations. As might be expected, when competing Chicago newspapers chose to mention the Times-Herald contest at all, they did so with scorn. To underscore the seriousness of the event, Kohlsaat asked President Cleveland if the War Department might assume overall charge because the vehicles being tested might prove useful to the army. Cleveland agreed, assuring a healthy quantity of be-medaled military types in Chicago in addition to those officials chosen for their vested interest or relative expertise in the vehicle field. Using the only precedent available, some Chicago papers argued that because over-enthusiastic bands of bicycle riders had proven a menace on the road—"scorchers," they were called, the forerunners of the motorcycling Hell's Angels—the danger that speeding motor vehicles would present was too horrible to be imagined. Commissioners of the various parks through which the Times-Herald course was routed were loath to grant permission until Kohlsaat assured them that similar vehicles were in daily use on the Bois de Boulogne in Paris and that the rules formulated guaranteed no danger to life and property.

Officialdom on his side, Kohlsaat awaited late October and the arrival of hordes of cars in Chicago. Only eight showed up. One of them was unfinished (the Columbia Perambulator Company electric entered by the same fellows who had tried to wangle a lucrative contract for world's fair transportation three years earlier), and one was a motorized tandem bicycle that was immediately disqualified. That left six. They were a varied lot.

Among the neater rigs was the Duryea. Charles and Frank were there for a purpose: to promote a company for the manufacture of gasoline automobiles. Following the Pope visit, the brothers had managed to convince Springfield businessmen to put up $23,000 for the organization of the Duryea Motor Wagon Company. That wasn't a lot of capital and was pared down further after repaying obligations to male nurse Edwin F. Markham and stockbroker Henry W. Clapp, who had advanced money for the building of the first and second Duryeas, respectively, but it was a start. In Jackson Park, the Duryeas passed out hundreds of small four-page leaflets, announcing the availability of their car. They didn't know yet how much they would have to charge to make a reasonable profit, indicating only "price $1,000–$2,000" to test reaction.

Reading the leaflet with interest were Times-Herald competitors Henry G. Morris, a mechanical engineer, and Pedro G. Salom, an electrician, who had traveled from Philadelphia with two electric cars they called Electrobats. Manufacture was on their minds, too. From downstate in Decatur, Oscar B. Mueller arrived with the Benz his father Hieronymous had bought for him and which had been modified in the family's plumbing supply factory. Oscar's future plans would depend on his powers of persuasion with his father.

The remaining two vehicles among the half dozen were gasoline victorias that looked like two girl's bicycles with a body and engine slung between them. They were entered by Edward Joel Pennington, the same fellow who had tried to finagle his motorized tandem bicycle into the contest. Had communication been better in 1895, Chicago would already have had Pennington's number. Other communities did. E.J. was a con man of the first rank. The previous summer, he had been in Cortland, New York, where he talked C.B. Hitchcock into manufacturing his motorized vehicles, but the one experimental model he produced couldn't travel a block without overheating. So Pennington left town, and the Hitchcock Manufacturing Company, heretofore a prosperous wagon producer, went into receivership. A few quick and profitable visits to towns as he headed west was followed by real pay dirt in Racine, Wisconsin, where Pennington convinced Thomas Kane, wealthy manufacturer of church and school furniture and stationary engines for dairies, that his patent and Kane's money would result in a world-beater: a vehicle engine capable of operating on virtually any fuel. Pennington was fond of using candle wax in demonstrations and readily agreed to call the vehicles in which the engines were placed Kane-Penningtons. Four had been promised for the Times-Herald, but only two arrived. In truth, the Times-Herald promoters may have been onto Pennington—four years earlier, he had hit the Windy City with an "airship" sideshow—but were glad he was on hand because he swelled the field by a third.

Kohlsaat was devastated by the dismal turnout. Flooding his desk in the past week had been dozens of letters from entrants declaring that with just a little more time, they would be ready to roll. Grizzly Adams, who feared for his job, looked for a way out. Fortunately, the Paris–Bordeaux–Paris race that June had been postponed a few weeks to allow for more participants, and that provided a face-saving precedent for Kohlsaat to move his race up to Thanksgiving Day. Given Chicago's unpredictable weather, a late November date was a gamble but preferable to postponement to spring and enduring an entire winter of editorial abuse from competing Chicago newspapers. To further defuse criticism, Adams proposed that a "consolation" race be held on the originally scheduled November 2 date. Competing in it was clearly not in the entrants' best interests—an accident might put them out of the running for the main event—nor was the $500 consolation prize much of an incentive. Pennington, Morris, and Salom begged off, agreeing only to demonstrate their vehicles in Jackson Park. The Duryeas and Oscar Mueller agreed to race. In retrospect, the brothers were sorry they had.

November 2 dawned clear and cool as crowds gathered at the Midway Plaisance. Thousands more lined the park boulevards of the course, and in Waukegan, the entire town seemed to have turned out for the event. Waukegan would see only one of the two cars. Some miles out of Chicago, the Duryeas came up behind a hay wagon driven by a farmer who, jarred by the toot of the Duryea's whistle, turned his team of horses to the left just as the motor vehicle attempted to pass. In the choice between a collision and a ditch, J. Frank chose the latter and soundly cracked up the Duryea. Neither brother was hurt, but the full damage to the vehicle couldn't be assessed until it was freighted back to Massachusetts and taken apart. The Duryeas' only consolation in the "consolation" race was that the Mueller-Benz average was 10 miles per hour, and the Duryea could easily handle 5 miles per hour more. This boded well for victory in the real race on November 28, provided Frank Duryea could get the car fixed and back to Chicago on time.

But if that was "iffy"—and also presumed a more competitive car than the Mueller-Benz would not show up at the starting line—a bigger "if" was the weather. When the race date was advanced to Thanksgiving, mention was made that, should weather conditions be adverse, the contest could be moved under cover into one of Chicago's large exhibition halls, which brought the expected jeers that, because indoor operation was not the intended purpose of these purportedly wonderful new vehicles, such a test would prove nothing. So Kohlsaat and the Times-Herald contest judges got together and decided on a shorter 52.5-mile run to Evanston and back. The announcement of the new course was made on November 16. Then everybody prayed for good weather. Apparently not hard enough.

Early morning on Monday, November 25, snow began to fall in Chicago. By the time it quit on Tuesday, twelve wet and heavy inches were on the ground, telegraph and telephone wires were down everywhere, and the city was at a virtual standstill. Kohlsaat said the show had to go on. Stalwartly, most of the competitors agreed with him, at least initially. Wednesday's *Times-Herald* published a list of thirty-one prospective starters. But some of those had just wistfully thought they would be ready; others, having finished their cars just under the wire, read the weather report and decided to stay home.

A blustery Thanksgiving Day saw the ranks of competitors diminished to ten. Of those, A.C. Ames and George W. Lewis, both of whose gasoline vehicles had successfully passed the qualifying test, couldn't get their cars started in the cold. Max Hertel, an engineer with the American Biscuit Company, started his car but then broke his steering gear.

Most promising of the newcomers was the Haynes-Apperson, a gasoline car that was the collaborative effort of Elwood P. Haynes and the Apperson brothers of Kokomo, Indiana. Haynes had wanted something other than a horse and buggy to make his rounds as field superintendent for the Indiana Natural Gas and Oil Company. Shopping around at the world's fair in Chicago, he saw the Sintz marine exhibit and placed an order. When the engine arrived, Haynes set it up on saw horses in his wife's kitchen. During the first test, the Sintz shook itself loose and hopped across the room. Because there was a fire on the stove nearby and the engine was spilling gasoline, the kitchen was quickly evacuated. Disaster did not follow, but Mrs. Haynes was not pleased.

Haynes' next stop was the Riverside Machine Works, where all further engine testing was conducted. He brought design sketches for a car that Riverside proprietor Elmer Apperson agreed to build on off-time for forty cents an hour. That labor rate included the services of Apperson's brother Edgar and shop employee Jonathan D. Maxwell, as well as modifications to Haynes' design during construction to make the car work.

Finally, on the Fourth of July 1894, the project was finished. The road test was along Pumpkinvine Pike, just east of Kokomo. So unsure were Haynes and Edgar Apperson of the outcome, the vehicle was towed to the test site by a team of horses. They drove all the way back home. Happy that the car ran, Haynes was less pleased with how it ran; its steering, in his words, was "just the reverse of satisfactory, it was positively dangerous." The partners got back to work.

The second Haynes-Apperson had a stronger Sintz engine and better steering. Postponement of the Times-Herald to a holiday allowed Haynes to travel to Chicago for the race, and Elmer Apperson joined him. They were confident. Alas, on the way to the starting line, at Indiana Avenue and Thirty-Eighth Street, Haynes swerved sharply to avoid a streetcar and smashed a front wheel. The Haynes-Apperson's race was over.

So, only six cars lined up at the starting line on the Midway Plaisance. Among those on hand earlier in November, the Chicago Perambulator Company, having concluded its little electric didn't have a ghost of a chance against the larger cars, did not reappear, and E.J. Pennington was a no-show, too. (By now, he was on his way to England to practice his con artistry there.) Morris and Salom were back with one of their Electrobats. Newly arrived was Harold Sturges with the

Morrison-built electric, which by now had undergone modification in the American Battery Company shops and at least partially deserved its Sturges Electric designation. Possibly Kohlsaat or Adams had prevailed upon their fellow Chicagoan to make the starting lineup more respectable. Under the road conditions, the batteries of the electrics could not possibly stay the course, so it was understood from the outset that these cars would not be running to win the race but simply to demonstrate that even in these god-awful conditions, they could run.

In the race to win were the gasoline automobiles. The Duryea had made it back on time. Oscar Mueller, anxious to repeat his "consolation" race victory of November 2, had been driving his mechanic Charles Reid hard to engineer improvements into the Benz ever since. Two more of the German cars filled out the field. Probably there would have been more Benzes had French dealer Emile Roger been as adept with logistics as he was with promotion. Two years earlier, he had planned to exhibit at the world's fair in Chicago but neglected to make proper application and remained in New York City, wowing local reporters with Benz rides. Gushed Dorothy Dare, "No more cable cars for me. No more elevated roads. No more bicycles and bloomers. For I have ridden in a horseless carriage."

In 1895, arbitrarily assuming that the Times-Herald race was open only to native vehicles, Roger had been leisurely planning his next trip to the New World. Informed that the Benz he had sold to the Mueller company would be competing, he caught the next steamer across the Atlantic. On the starting line in Chicago now was the Benz he had earlier sold to the De La Vergne Refrigerating Company of New York, as well as one of the three Benzes he had brought over on the ship with him, which had been pre-sold to the department stores of Macy's, Gimbel's, and Hilton, Hughes & Company (the predecessor of Wanamaker's). Of the department store sales, Roger had managed to talk Macy's into entering the contest, even convincing bicycle department manager Frank McPherson of the super publicity that would accrue to the store if the car were driven to Chicago. At this point, Roger hadn't been west of the Hudson, and McPherson allowed visions of headlines to take the place of good sense. More than a thousand people had gathered in front of Herald Square at noon on November 15 to wish god speed to McPherson and Macy employee Jeremiah O'Connor. They made it only as far as Schenectady before a snowstorm obliterated the roads and indicated the wisdom of taking the train the rest of the way. Now in snowbound Chicago on November 25, they wondered why they had agreed to participate at all. Emile Roger said everything would be fine.

Even the Times-Herald judges had doubts about that. Because of the conditions, the time limit for the run was waived, although it was agreed that any entrant not making it back to the starting line by midnight would be disqualified because the officials—among them Major General Wesley Merritt, John P. Barrett (city electrician for Chicago), Henry Timken (president of the National Carriage Builders Association), Leland L. Summers (editor of *Electrical Engineering*), and C.F. Kimball (a Chicago carriage maker)—had no intention of sticking around any later than that. The umpires riding with the cars also wondered aloud if some competitors might be the never-say-die sort. So intense was Oscar Mueller that his mechanic had been up all night Thanksgiving eve, pounding and hammering. At the Midway Plaisance and along fashionable Michigan Avenue, the course was lined with thousands of spectators for the start. Few were expected to remain for the finish.

Preliminary ceremonies were held to a minimum because of the cold. The umpire draw put Hiram Maxim with the Electrobat; T.T. Bennett with the Sturges Electric; James F. Bate, Lt. Samuel Rodman, and Charles B. King with the De La Vergne, Macy, and Mueller-Benzes, respectively; and Arthur Wright with the Duryea. Most of the umpires had tinkered with the car-building idea themselves; indeed, King had reluctantly withdrawn his own entry because he couldn't be ready on time. Amusingly, the heaviest of the umpires, Toronto newspaperman Wright, had drawn the lightest car in the race. At 250 pounds, he was a third the weight of the entire Duryea. Frank, lighter than Charles by about 50 pounds, would drive the car. His brother hired a sleigh and team of horses and headed for a midway point to watch.

By 9:00 a.m., most of the cars were racing, save for Mueller's Benz, which was delayed over an hour with a last few hammers and bangs, and the frantic search for sash cord or rope to keep the tires from skidding on the icy surfaces that were sure to be encountered. The start had been cleared of snow, but midway down the Midway, it was apparent to all competitors that this race was insanity. The first to give up was Fred Haas on John Chester De La Vergne's Benz, which had been a last-minute substitution for the company's own car that remained untested. In Washington Park, Haas fought with a snowdrift and lost.

Emile Roger's entreaties notwithstanding, this Benz driver elected not to continue, having been assured beforehand that De La Vergne's reputation was not on the line. By Lincoln Park, both electrics had given up, their batteries and drivers exhausted.

McPherson and O'Connor, aware that Macy's was considering national distribution of the Benz, did not think it politic to quit too easily. Early on, they had slid into the back of an Adams Street horse car, but without discernible damage, and soldiered on. Shortly thereafter, they picked up a passenger, one Everett Ettinger, who hopped off near his home to fetch some Thanksgiving turkey for the hungry Benz drivers. In Evanston, where the grapevine spread word of the approaching racers because telephone/telegraph service had not been restored, the crowd watched as the Macy's Benz slithered into a horse-drawn sled. Still McPherson and O'Connor continued undeterred. Finally, in Douglas Park around 4:00 p.m., something broke, and McPherson and O'Connor, who had only been introduced to the car, indeed any car, merely a few weeks before, couldn't figure out what it was. Ettinger graciously offered to take the streetcar and elevated back to the starting line to find Roger, but the Frenchman was not there. Two hours and another streetcar-and-elevated ride later, Ettinger returned to the shivering Benz drivers and suggested they come home with him. Macy's honor be hanged, McPherson and O'Connor readily accepted.

Now, ten hours from the start, only the Mueller-Benz and the Duryea remained on the course. No one knew quite where. It was rumored that the Duryea's repair to its steering gear near Rush Street had been effected in a blacksmith shop, whose proprietor had to be rousted from bed to open up, which indeed was the case and a rules violation that could have resulted in disqualification. But survival was the paramount rule that day. Snow everywhere, the contestants could not easily follow the prescribed route and wandered off on occasion. Road drifts in some places were two feet deep. When the temperature rose above freezing, and the midday sun shone as the contestants neared Evanston, what had been snow turned into slush. Mueller had help getting pulled out of ruts—another rules violation—a couple of times. Stops had to be made to un-cake tires of coagulated mud. The rough roads beat up the cars unmercifully.

Then, with the setting of the sun, the temperature plunged again, and the cold became unbearable. There were only two people in the

Mueller-Benz now, Oscar and umpire Charles King. Mechanic Charles Reid, overcome by exposure and exhausted from a sleepless night, had been taken by sleigh to the hospital near Riverview Park. "Mr. Mueller seemed to go to pieces quickly after this," King remarked. Shortly thereafter, hungry and numbed by the cold, Mueller fainted in the driver's seat. His absence at the finish would be a rules violation not likely to be overlooked. Somehow, King managed to stop the car, moved Mueller over, and, from Halstead and Fifty-Fifth, finished driving the final hour to Jackson Park, one hand on the tiller, the other arm supporting the semi-conscious Mueller. It was a dramatic finish, but at nearly 9:00 at night, only race officials and reporters were on hand as witnesses. Not quite two hours earlier, Frank Duryea had crossed the finish line to the applause of few but those who had to be there.

The Duryeas retired to the warmth of their hotel to celebrate. "We had power to spare at all places," Frank exulted, "and had no occasion to get out and push." After seeing Oscar Mueller off to the hospital, King hastened to the Del Prado for a late Thanksgiving dinner. He looked a wreck. The flabbergasted hotel clerk said, "You don't belong here, you belong down-the-line," but mention of who he was and what he had just done brought King "the best we have in the house"—and on the house.

The entire front page of the *Times-Herald* was devoted to the race the next day. It was the talk of Chicago. Both the United Press and the Associated Press filed stories at home and abroad. Kohlsaat bragged that the Chicago contest had advanced the automotive art in the United States by no fewer than five years, which would save America untold millions of dollars in royalties to foreign inventors. What Kohlsaat did not know was that a few weeks earlier in Rochester, New York, following the U.S. Patent Office's decree requiring cases of long standing to show cause for delay or face rejection, George Selden had finally moved to have his gasoline car patented.

When the Times-Herald judges met the following week to award prizes, they managed to come up with one for just about everybody. The lion's share of $2,000 went to the Duryea Motor Wagon Company for both the race win and the car's handling in the qualifying tests. The Mueller company received $1,500 for "performance in the road race and economy of operation." On the trip to Evanston and back, the Mueller-Benz consumed six gallons of gasoline, six pails of broken ice, and three pails of snow. Charles King turned down Oscar Mueller's gracious offer of half the cash prize but did accept the gold medal that went with it. Prizes of $500 each went to Harold Sturges of Chicago (local pull seemed to have helped here) and to R.H. Macy & Company of New York (whose Benz did finish the race, Emile Roger fixing the car the next day and driving it back to Jackson Park). A gold medal for best showing in the preliminary tests went to Philadelphia's Morris and Salom for their Electrobat. Even the De La Vergne Refrigerating Machine Company was given $50 for the "counter-balance" on the engine of the Benz that Fred Haas had chosen to drive only a short distance. Of those who hadn't made it to the starting line, prizes of $100 or so for various aspects of design went to George Lewis, the Haynes-Apperson, and Max Hertel, the award for the last named for a device operated from the driver's seat that admirably started the engine, although the engine had trouble starting the car. All of the other gasoline cars in the contest had to be cranked to start.

Reviews of the Times-Herald contest were mixed. The paucity of starters *vis-à-vis* the impressive entry list was harped on by some critics, not really fairly. Even in motor-conscious Paris, the race to Rouen in 1894 had resulted in 21 starters out of 102 entries, and that event was held in midsummer. That no steam cars raced in Chicago was probably because most steam cars were made in New England, their inventors didn't have the money for the trip, and, unlike the Duryeas who had managed to launch an automobile company, had no immediately compelling reason to be there.* Certainly strategic mistakes made by the Times-Herald promoters played a part in the small race field, as most certainly did the weather.

More important than the result was the simple fact that the Times-Herald contest had been held and opened a national dialogue on these potentially important machines. A Philadelphia paper worried, prematurely, that they would "drive down the price of horseflesh." Another reviewer opined that what an automobile had to be was "a mechanism so simple as not to get out of order easily or give trouble to the unskilled

---

* Sylvester Roper, for example, preferred to continue experimentation. His latest vehicle—a steam bicycle—literally scared him to death. While testing at the Charles River track in Boston in 1896, he reached the incredible speed of 60 miles per hour and suffered a fatal heart attack.

operator"—and the automobile was years away from even approaching that. But those critics who declared that the Times-Herald had proven only how unreliable the automobile was—"Old Dobbin Is Still in the Ring" was the headline on the *Chicago Tribune*'s three-inch story about the event—were far off the mark. True, the Times-Herald cars were not appreciably fast; two reporters on a tandem bicycle had to backpedal at times to avoid passing the Mueller-Benz in the consolation race on November 2. But on a snowbound Thanksgiving Day, no bicyclist dared the trip. Grizzly Adams had tried following the Duryea with a two-horse wagon but finally gave up. "No horse on earth could have made those fifty-four miles...," he exclaimed, "there is no doubt that there will be great interest in the manufacture of these horseless carriages now that it has been demonstrated what can be done with them."

But what the Times-Herald provided first was awareness. Previously, American automobile inventors had been "blissfully ignorant," in Hiram Maxim's words, that so many others were working toward the same goal. The Times-Herald brought some of them together in Chicago and many others thereafter, via journals established that year and devoted to a cause that was just beginning to happen. Most important of these was *The Horseless Age*, which E.P. Ingersoll launched from a small office near Wall Street in New York. He took on all critics. To the charge that the automobile would scare horses, he challenged, "Suppose it does. So do locomotives, bicycles, street cars, Fourth of July celebrations, and a dozen other things. Horses must get used to it."

Ingersoll was indomitable. "The appearance of a journal devoted to a branch of industry yet in an embryonic state may strike some as premature...," he admitted. "But those who have taken the pains to search beneath the surface for the great tendencies of the age see what a giant industry is struggling into being there." Ingersoll struggled himself—"often hungry, generally ill-clothed," it was said, "sleeping in his office or in the park"—before his magazine finally began making money. But in his crusade, he had some powerful allies. Even the celebrated Thomas Edison described the horseless vehicle as "the coming wonder."

CHAPTER 7

---■---

Sorting Out and Moving On

THROUGHOUT AMERICA, there arose a mighty clatter in barns, basements, and backyards as news of the Chicago Times-Herald encouraged automobile builders to press on. Among entrants who had not made it to the starting line, William Kappe admitted his gasoline car never left the second floor of the Quincy, Illinois, wagon shop in which he was putting it together; Frank Vanell of Vincennes, Indiana, could afford to spend only $275 on his steamer with predictable results; and retired carriage builder Robert W. Elston of Charlevoix, Michigan, made the mistake of buying a Kane-Pennington engine for his car. Among the more bizarre notions of motive power that doubtlessly didn't work much better were those of A.B. Andrews of Center Point, Iowa, who used a spring motor (it wound itself up going downhill), and partners MacKenzie and McArthur, who tried compressed air in New Haven, Connecticut.

But far more of the Times-Herald entrants successfully completed their cars, most of them for their private use. A few had loftier ambitions. Late in 1895, Aurora (Nebraska) grocer T.R. Gawley advertised for "a capitalist to take hold of my invention." The Hartley Power Supply Company used its own money for three years to market steam, gasoline, or compressed air cars in Chicago, and farm harrow manufacturer M.H. Daley declared the 195-pound gasoline buggy he produced in Charles City, Iowa, the lightest four-wheeled vehicle in the world. None of these efforts survived the turn of the century.

Those who had enjoyed the publicity of participation in the Times-Herald were in a better position to promote their wares but were equally luckless. One month after the contest, A.C. Ames announced his organization of a $100,000 company in Chicago but was never heard from again. In Greenfield, Massachusetts, Max Hertel organized the Oakman Motor Vehicle Company but printed more brochures than he produced cars, a creditors' meeting closing his doors in November 1900. About that same time in Philadelphia, the Lewis Motor Vehicle Company announced a decrease in its capital stock from $10 million to $90,000 "to avoid payment of corporation taxes," the stockholders thereafter deciding to avoid manufacture as well and distributing what assets remained among themselves. George Lewis seems to have enjoyed some success selling his gasoline engine, erstwhile steam-car builder Edwin F. Brown of Chicago among the purchasers. At the request of his friend William Allen White, Brown participated in the Emporia, Kansas, annual fair during which Potawatomi Chief Kack-kack was taken for what was publicized as the first ride of an American Indian in an automobile. Brown sold few cars, however.

Harold Sturges eschewed automobile manufacture, preferring to remain in the storage battery business exclusively. (William Morrison had long since soured on his invention and as late as 1907 would tell a Des Moines reporter that "I wouldn't give ten cents for an automobile for my own use.") Macy's imported the Benz awhile but never contemplated automobile production itself. During the summer of 1896, William Jennings Bryan barnstormed Decatur, Illinois, in the Mueller during his presidential campaign against William McKinley. With the Benz as "training wheels," Hieronymus and Oscar had developed an all-Mueller car, but after the father burned to death when a lighted match ignited the car's gasoline tank, the son had no desire to continue in the automobile business.

Death also foreshortened the automotive life of the De La Vergne Refrigerating Machine Company. By the end of 1895, its own gasoline vehicle now properly tested and in production, De La Vergne announced sales to William Rockefeller, John Jacob Astor, William Waldorf Astor, George Gould, Edwin Gould, and William Havemeyer, as well as beer barons Jacob Rupert of New York and Fred Pabst of Milwaukee. John Chester De La Vergne was a prominent New Yorker and intensely civic minded, spearheading construction of the Third and Willis Avenue bridges and the Grand Concourse in the Bronx, where his factory was located. Of all the Times-Herald entrants, he was best situated and best fixed to profitably champion the horseless carriage cause. But the De La Vergne automobile died when John Chester did, suddenly at age fifty-nine, in May 1896.

By then, matters were moving along well for the Duryeas in Springfield, Massachusetts. The loan of a car to Barnum and Bailey's circus—where it would share exhibition honors with The Wild Man from Borneo and Jo-Jo, The Alligator-Faced Boy—might seem frivolous for so serious a manufacturing venture, but it spread the car's name more widely than the Duryea company's modest treasury would have allowed otherwise. Already manufacture had commenced, with thirteen cars completed by the end of 1896, and the brothers anxious for any opportunity to preach the automotive gospel. When *The Horseless Age* reprised the "deep regret" the *Newark* (New Jersey) *Advertiser* had voiced about "the extinction of so noble an animal as the horse," Frank Duryea shot back that "the horse is a willful, unreliable brute...and not the docile pet of the poet. The mechanical motor is his superior in many respects, and when its superiority has become better known, his inferiority will be more apparent."

Pedro Salom saved his best shot for the vehicle the Duryeas were producing. In Philadelphia, he and partner Henry Morris proclaimed the superiority of the electric. "All the gasoline motors we have seen belch forth from their exhaust pipe a continuous stream of partially unconsumed hydrocarbons in the form of a thick smoke with a highly noxious odor," Salom wrote in 1896 in the *Journal of The Franklin Institute*. "Imagine thousands of such vehicles on the streets, each offering up its column of smell."

Only six cars, all of them gasoline, lined up at the City Hall starting line in New York on Decoration Day in 1896. Inspired by Kohlsaat's contest, John Brisben Walker, publisher of *Cosmopolitan* magazine, staged a race of his own. No-shows proliferated; entries had numbered thirty-four. Four of the cars on hand were Duryeas; Emile Roger entered a Benz. Dr. Carlos D. Booth of Youngstown, Ohio, who became an ardent supporter of the automobile when his wife was killed by a runaway horse, entered the car built for him by the Pierce & Crouch Machine Shop of New Brighton, Pennsylvania.

Again, many entrants had been unable to complete their cars on time. Charles B. King, the Mueller-Benz hero from the Times-Herald, had his car ready but couldn't afford the trip. Earlier, King had written to Walker, asking that the $3,000 total prize money be increased because "this art is at present in a crude state and is mainly in the hands of the inventor who has not as yet been encouraged by capital." Walker was unmoved.

The Cosmopolitan Race was a silk-stocking affair. Judges included Nelson A. Miles, commanding general of the U.S. Army; Chauncey Depew, president of the New York Central; and John Jacob Astor, who listed his affiliation as colonel in the New York National Guard. Despite their considerable clout, permission to race on Manhattan streets was disallowed, so the racers had to drive single file up Broadway to Kingsbridge and proceed all-out from there to the Cosmopolitan Building in Irvington-on-Hudson, then back to Ardsley Country Club for the finish line and lunch, for a total of 16.5 racing miles. Amenities for the officials were fulsome, including a special train to Ardsley arranged by Depew. But the promotion-minded Duryeas complained of the scant provision for competitors to exhibit and demonstrate their cars at the country club.

Save for the Benz, whose driver broke single-file rank on the way to Kingsbridge and was arrested for speeding, all entrants finished the race, which Frank Duryea won. The judges chose to enjoy a lingering lunch and social *tête-a-tête* before announcing that all prize money would go to the Duryea company, which irritated the other two entrants who believed they deserved something for expenses. It had been a good day for the Massachusetts brothers, although part of their winnings had to be used to bail out Henry Wells, the driver of their number four car who collided with a lady bicyclist afterward and spent the night in jail. In *The Horseless Age*, E.P. Ingersoll fumed, "...a wretched fiasco...humiliating, it was worse—it was criminal... The motor carriage business was literally butchered to a Walker holiday."

If the Cosmopolitan Race was *opera bouffe*, the event following in September, sponsored by the Rhode Island State Fair Association of Providence, was pure burlesque. Because Narragansett Park had long seen some of the most exciting horse racing in New England, adding an automobile contest to the festivities promised to boost thrills and attendance. But everything went wrong. Several days of rain saturated the track and postponed the races twice. Entries were slim: Andrew Lawrence Riker with his latest electric, Morris and Salom with their Electrobat, and Frank Duryea. They finished in that order, but only after balky starts and several heats on the soggy track so slow and boring that "Get a horse" immediately entered the American vernacular.

The Duryeas hadn't time to lament their poor Narragansett showing (attributable to the electrics' faster starting speed, the short course, and a sheared tire valve) because their next promotional stop was England. That November, an "emancipation run" from London to Brighton was scheduled to celebrate the demise of the Locomotives on Highways Act, which for decades had limited a horseless carriage's speed (4 miles per hour in the countryside, 2 miles per hour in cities) and required a man with a red flag to precede the vehicle, effectively stifling British automotive development. Awareness that the imminent revocation of the infamous "Red Flag Act" would open the door wide to automobile entrepreneurs had been the reason E.J. Pennington had skipped Thanksgiving in Chicago for a steamer across the Atlantic.

By the time the Duryeas arrived in London, Pennington was in high gear. Although his knowledge of mechanics was slight, E.J. talked authoritatively; although many of his patents were unworkable, they read well. But what sold Pennington to the British were his unbounded enthusiasm, his undeniable charm, and his keen sense of how to overwhelm people. His suite at the Hotel Metropole included a room filled with lady typists under strict orders to begin tapping furiously whenever he entered with a client, and he was aware of the power of Havana cigars, fine brandy, and mellifluous compliments with both potential investors and journalists. Presumably, Pennington started the emancipation run, but that his vehicle made it to Brighton is debatable. Debatable, too, is which car arrived in the resort town first, but the evidence indicates it was the Duryea, which was already famous in England because of its Times-Herald performance.

"Duryea beat everything express," Frank wired home to Springfield. Still, when Harry John Lawson, British bicycle man and promoter extraordinaire, began assembling foreign patents as part of a scheme to monopolize his country's industry, he chose wisely across the channel (acquiring rights to Gottlieb Daimler's inventions in Germany and the pioneering Count de Dion's in France). But, for the New World, he talked to the Duryeas, then bought from Pennington, for a cool £100,000. The ingenious brothers from Massachusetts didn't have a chance against the smooth-talking con man with all the typists at the Hotel Metropole.

———

While most of the automotive activity that made headlines in 1896 happened in the East, progress was being made quietly in the Midwest. In Indiana, Elwood Haynes and the Apperson brothers built a third car, which they exhibited at local fairs alongside its two predecessors, but thought it prudent to keep their day jobs for the time being. Prudent, too, was the course of Ransom Olds in Michigan. His steam cars were strictly an after-hours project, and although each one he built was an improvement over the last, his principal effort remained the family engine-building business. At the Chicago World's Fair, Olds had taken a ride in Gottlieb Daimler's car and was impressed. By 1895, he had completed development of a gasoline engine, convinced of its superiority to steam. Announcement of the Times-Herald tempted him to enter, but gearing up the Olds plant for manufacture of the new engine took precedence.

Olds' first gasoline car was successfully tested on the streets of Lansing during the summer of 1896. "I am thoroughly convinced," he would later write, "that had we placed our vehicle in the Times-Herald contest at Chicago we would have captured first prize easily." Perhaps. Olds did send in an entry to the Narragansett Park race, which he subsequently (and wisely, as it turned out) withdrew, offering as an excuse his objection to the event's rules but probably motivated by the damage to the Olds reputation a possible poor showing would have brought.

Charles King withdrew his Narragansett entry as well, but, as we have seen, money was the principal reason. Sale of patent rights to the railway car brake beam he invented in 1894 had provided him sufficient cash to launch the Charles B. King Company and rent office space at John Lauer's machine shop on St. Antoine Street in Detroit. Lauer manufactured King's patented pneumatic hammer and gave him run of the shop for his other development work. Like Elwood Haynes, King had initially thought the Sintz marine engine viable for vehicle use but, unlike Haynes, ultimately rejected it and began developing his own. Although his failure to complete a car for the Times-Herald had been a big disappointment, King was buoyed by the car's subsequent maiden test on Woodward Avenue at 11:00 p.m. on March 6, 1896. With his young assistant Oliver Barthel at his side, Charles Brady King made history as the first builder of a gasoline car in Detroit.

That achievement wouldn't pay the bills, however, so King concentrated on engine sales, advertising in Ingersoll's *The Horseless Age* and mounting a direct-mail letter campaign to potential purchasers such as steam-car builder Joseph Shaver of Milwaukee. But it was a letter that King received from the Duryeas, whom he had met in Chicago, that seemed most promising. The brothers suggested he might like to produce their engine in Detroit. Lauer's machine shop was certainly adequate, and King regarded the collaboration as beneficial both to himself and the Duryeas. A deal was done, but the Duryea-King project produced only one engine. It was ordered by the carriage-building Emerson & Fisher Company of Cincinnati under contract from the Robinson & Franklin Brothers Circus, which needed an automobile to keep up with Barnum & Bailey. King traveled to Cincinnati to help with the assembly and testing, warning John Robinson that steep hills might be the car's undoing. "Never mind that," Robinson replied, "I will have my biggest elephant behind it..." Robinson also tried to talk King into being the car's driver, noting that his Albino man was "a first class mechanic."

With a tinge of regret, King elected not to join the circus and returned to Detroit to continue experimentation. Convinced now that the single-cylinder Duryea engine had insufficient power, King wrote to fellow experimenter Percy Maxim that his experience indicated "one-lungers" were hard to start, and he was "willing to burn a few dollars for the cause" in further refinement of multi-cylinder engines. His first car had carried a four; now he was refining a two-cylinder unit for marine use because the Great Lakes region afforded a ready market.

Three months after King's Woodward Avenue drive on June 4, 1896, Detroit's second gasoline car was successfully tested. The man who built it was a friend of King's: Henry Ford. As supervisor for the

Edison Illuminating Company of Detroit, Ford had routinely brought repair work to John Lauer's machine shop, generally tarrying awhile to talk engines with King. Engines fascinated him. Repair of an Otto at a Detroit soda bottling plant during the summer of 1891 had convinced him such a motor could be adapted to a road vehicle, but the only person to whom he mentioned this was his wife, Clara. Ford was impressed with the Daimler engine at the Chicago world's fair in 1893, later insisting that his own first engine was completed that year and tested on Christmas Eve in the kitchen sink of the Ford home, with Clara dribbling gasoline into the intake valve as Henry spun the flywheel. Charles King remembered the event as happening in the kitchen sink, but two years later and that he did the dribbling while Clara fretted that the noise being made at three o'clock in the morning was keeping their two-year-old son Edsel awake. Whichever, Ford certainly did not begin building a gasoline vehicle until after the Times-Herald. "I never wanted anything so badly in my life as to go to that race," he told publisher Kohlsaat, "but I could not get anyone to loan me the carfare to Chicago." Instead, he had to content himself with King's firsthand account of what happened there.

When King tested his first car, Ford bicycled behind and then returned to the shed behind his Bagley Avenue home to continue putting together his own. Apparently, an article on the Kane-Pennington motor in the *American Machinist* provided Ford some inspiration for the two-cylinder engine he was building for his vehicle, although thankfully his design deviated considerably. Clara supported her husband's work without reservation and also knew how to keep a secret. "Henry is making something," she would tell neighbors when they asked about the banging in the backyard shed, "and maybe some day I'll tell you." She didn't have to. Only when the car was finally ready did Henry realize that it was bigger than the shed door, a problem he solved with a strongly wielded ax. The willful destruction of his property perturbed the Fords' landlord until he saw the reason for it. Impressed with the car, William Wreford suggested the opening be left as is. In later years, Henry liked to say the result was America's first garage door.

Less pleased with the first Ford car was Henry's father, William. Charles King followed behind on a bicycle when Ford, with Clara beside him and Edsel on her lap, made his first long-distance drive of nine miles out to the family farm in Dearborn. Unable to understand why his son had forsaken the rural life, William Ford made no attempt to hide his displeasure. He refused to sit in the car, much less ride in it. As Henry's sister Margaret remembered, "Father saw no reason why he should risk his life...for a brief thrill." Henry was crestfallen. Finally, close to tears, he turned to King and said, "Come on, Charlie, let's you and me get out of here."

Later that summer, Ford was in New York City for the annual convention of the Association of Edison Illuminating Companies and received encouragement "out of a clear sky," as he remembered, from "the greatest inventive genius in the world." At the convention dinner on August 12, Ford was pointed out to Thomas Edison as the recent builder of a gasoline car. Edison wanted to hear more; Henry was happy to oblige. "Young man, that's the thing, you have it," Edison cried. "The self-contained unit carrying its own fuel with it. Keep at it."

Back home in Detroit, Ford's vehicle brought reactions more similar to his father's or aroused irritating curiosity. "If I left it alone even for a minute some inquisitive person always tried to run it," Henry said. "Finally I had to chain it to a lamp post whenever I left it anywhere." About his motoring experiences, Charlie King would reminisce wistfully, "I was condemned, ordered out of Detroit parks, and subjected to further indignities quite in keeping with progress."

CHAPTER 8

The Electrifying Pope and Whitney

E.P. INGERSOLL thought progress was being made. May 13, 1897 was destined to be a "memorable day in the history of the motor vehicle in America," he said. The Pope Manufacturing Company was entering the automotive field.

Just weeks after the Duryea visit in 1895, the Colonel had decided to pursue the automobile question further. Impetus was the visit to the Pope works of Hiram Percy Maxim, whose M.I.T. engineering degree and vehicle experimentation impressed Pope right-hand man George Day and whose modest salary demand impressed the Colonel. Maxim was taken on to head a new Pope motor vehicle department.

The Pope Manufacturing Company operated on a massive scale. Its mill for fabricating seamless steel tubing was one of the wonders of New England. Its factories employed 5,000. Colonel Pope was a real captain of industry. Once convinced of an idea's potential, he didn't lack follow-through. He hadn't blanched at spending a half-million dollars for a perfect bevel gear nor a million more for a rigid frame for his Columbia gear housing. Most Americans thought he invented the bicycle, and bicyclists knew him as the leading exponent of the good roads movement.

The Colonel was deft at expounding. Earlier automotive efforts, he proclaimed, were "the result of a few months' hasty experimenting [not] as in our case, the outcome of several years of trial and... persevering development." He pooh-poohed as unfortunate that so many motor vehicles had been "seen by the public in circus parades and at races held with some ulterior object of advertising." His vehicle had the nobler purpose of trouble-free service to the purchaser and would be delivered complete with "a few wrenches and other tools necessary to enable your coachman to give the carriage the ordinary attention required by any vehicle." Newspaper and magazine journalists— together with selected V.I.P.s, including General Nelson Miles—were summoned to Connecticut for the Pope motor carriage's public bow to the world. "The Pope Company never bows to anything else," one reporter noted.

Pope's automobile, which would carry his bicycle's Columbia name, was an electric. This was not entirely to Percy Maxim's liking. Prior to joining the Pope organization, his experimentation had been principally with internal combustion engines. "He acted as though he were standing beside a ton of naked dynamite," Maxim said of George Day's reaction to his gasoline car. "...He made me drive around the yard a great many times before he could bring himself to venture in it with me." Maxim admitted that his car "shook and trembled and rattled and clattered, spat oil, fire, smoke and smell," and that to someone accustomed to elegant horse carriages, "it was revolting." The fastidious Pope people made a quick decision. "No one will buy a carriage that has all that greasy machinery in it," George Day cried. "No one will sit over an explosion," pontificated the Colonel.

Principally to placate their talented employee, Percy was allowed to experiment with a gasoline Columbia, but strictly as second fiddle to the pretty and tidy little Columbia Electric. Ten of them were on hand to be driven by guests that May day. Maxim, whose only duty was to mingle, was beside himself with worry. "The knowledge that...my precious darlings were out on the road in the hands of ordinary human beings who might not demonstrate them intelligently nearly wore me down," he said. The cars were not abused, fortunately, and Maxim overcame his anxiety. These were products to be sold, after all. Columbia production in the year-and-a-half following would approximate 500 electrics and a few gasoline carriages.

———

Alone among those thus far captivated by the horseless carriage, Colonel Pope had the facilities to become a major producer right away. But others were joining the Duryea bandwagon in organizing companies specifically for the manufacture of motor vehicles. Prominent among them was Alexander Winton, the Cleveland bicyclist who had earlier mourned the passing of the high-wheeled velocipede.

Winton had grown up along the River Clyde, worked as a machinist in Scottish shipyards, emigrated to America in 1878, and launched the Winton Bicycle Company in 1891. It was immediately prosperous.

Feisty and stubborn, Winton was imbued with supreme confidence. He completed his first gasoline car in 1896 and organized the Winton Motor Carriage Company the following March. His workforce consisted of a tinsmith, a blacksmith, a painter, a trimmer, two woodworkers, seven machinists, and three helpers. Sixty days later, he drove the second, improved model to Elyria and back, proving in his own words "its perfect utility for every purpose to which a horse and wagon can be put." On Memorial Day, the car was driven around Cleveland's famed Glenville Track at a record-breaking 33.64 miles per hour. Equally noteworthy that summer was Winton's drive from Cleveland to New York, a trip undertaken both to prove that his car could travel that distance and to promote sales on the East Coast. Ten days were required to reach New York, Winton described the roads over which he and associate Bert Hatcher bounced with a single word ("outrageous"), and they took the train back home ("we had blisters enough").

Lacking the clout of Colonel Pope, Winton made neither a big splash nor any sales in the East. He was undeterred. Two more test vehicles were built in 1897 as Winton rearranged his bicycle factory for motor vehicle production. Twenty-two Wintons were sold in 1898. Although his 800-mile jaunt to New York had been without breakdown, it was folly to assume that his cars were trouble-free. But he thought so and became enormously exercised whenever anyone suggested otherwise. It was said that in the Winton factory, the mood of the boss could be determined by his derby. If it sat on his head, he was sanguine; if he tossed it in the air, he was elated; if he threw it on the ground and stomped on it, watch out.

One of the first cars Winton sold in 1898 produced a hat-stomping episode. Because its owner lived in Cleveland, a certain diplomacy might have been indicated in dealing with the complaint, but tact was not Winton's long suit. The disgruntled owner finally hitched a team of horses to the car, upon which he placed a placard, reading, "This is the only way you can drive a Winton" and began parading the streets of town. The factory was advised this routine would continue daily until a full refund was given. Winton retaliated with a parade vehicle of his own following the owner's: a factory car towing a farm wagon with a scruffy jackass aboard and a placard reading "This is the only animal unable to drive a Winton." The owner quit his campaign for a refund. The year following, Winton's sales boomed to 100 cars.

In Lansing betimes, although production wasn't booming, Michigan could boast its first company for the manufacture of automobiles. Ransom Olds had taken the plunge. The Olds Motor Vehicle Company was organized on August 21, 1897. Possibly Ransom had waited to make this move until after his father, Pliny, then nearing seventy, retired to California earlier that summer. The success of the Olds engine business was a source of pride to the father. While never discouraging vehicle development, Pliny might not have approved the step his son had to take to get into the automobile business.

The Olds enterprise had always been a family affair, but the family enterprise did not have the money to move into vehicle production. Providing it was Edward W. Sparrow, president of the City National Bank, who interested other local businessmen, principally railroad and mining magnate Samuel Latta Smith. Total capitalization of the new company was $50,000, although only $10,000 was paid in, which Olds believed sufficient to launch manufacture of a vehicle. Now the question was: Which vehicle? The directive from his financial angels specified "one carriage in as nearly perfect a manner as possible." Olds had long since dismissed steam for gasoline, but sales of the latter would total no more than four cars by the end of 1898 as Ransom continued striving for the "nearly perfect," with an excursion into the one major automotive type he had not yet tried. As one of his directors scornfully noted, Olds began "chasing after strange electric gods."

By now, electric proponents Morris and Salom had sold out their company to Isaac L. Rice, originator of the Rice gambit in chess and president of the Electric Storage Battery Company of Philadelphia. The price apparently was handsome. As the nation's leading manufacturer of storage batteries, Rice saw the electric vehicle as a superb customer for his product and thought he might be able to out-Pope the Colonel. His idea was a livery or taxi service, which he inaugurated with a dozen electrics on the streets of New York City. Society columnist Cholly Knickerbocker was immediately summoned. "In search of a new sensation not inconsistent with a proper observance of Lent," the columnist told his *New York Journal* readers, "I went yesterday and rode in a horseless carriage." Knickerbocker was exhilarated by the experience, although not the "wicked glances of the bicycle ladies" on Broadway, nor the jeers, hoots, and "aristocratic elevation of eyebrows" on Fifth Avenue. "Your club chappie likes novelty, but he doesn't want the whole world to watch his indulgence in that direction...," Knickerbocker opined. "I know two or three chappies who have tried the horseless carriage but it has been after dark and along streets where the electric lights were not too bright." He suggested more privacy in the vehicle's coachwork because "as now constructed there is altogether too much publicity about it." Sufficiently encouraged, on September 27, 1897, Rice organized the Electric Vehicle Company and made plans for the production of several hundred electric cabs.

Making plans for the manufacture of steam cars in Massachusetts were Francis E. and Freelan O. Stanley, identical twins who resembled the Smith brothers on the cough drop box and who produced photographic dry plates in Watertown. As early as 1887, after witnessing a demonstration of the Field steam car, they had unsuccessfully tried to build one themselves. Seeing George Whitney's steamer in Boston in 1896 persuaded them to try again, and by the fall of 1898, their car's performance at a meet in Charles River Park convinced them they had a product worthy of sale. Although faster in a two-mile run, the Whitney ran out of steam several feet short of the top of an 80-foot ramp constructed for the "incline contest." Not only did F.E. Stanley breeze to the top, but for a precarious moment, it appeared his car might teeter over it. There was amazement all around, and orders for about 200 of the Stanleys' steamer within weeks. The brothers began procuring parts for an initial batch of 100 cars to be produced in Watertown.

By 1898, in Indiana, county fair appearances of their first three experimental cars had resulted in enough interest for Elwood Haynes and the brothers Apperson to formally establish the Haynes-Apperson Company and acquire a building in Kokomo for manufacture. Among the first decisions made was to advertise the Haynes-Apperson as "America's first gasoline car." This ignored the Duryea, but Haynes didn't see that as a problem.

The Massachusetts brothers had enough problems of their own. Whether the Duryea focus on racing and circus promotion was ill-advised is moot. But, according to Frank, the fundamental reason for their company's decline was "the preference shown by company officials to go after quick money in licensing and patent deals instead of settling down to perfect both the product and a system for quantity sales of cars." This was followed by a vociferous disagreement between the brothers about which of them was responsible for the Duryea's invention. In 1895, Charles had taken out the patent in his name, and he was the only brother pictured in the brochure handed out at the Times-Herald.

Slow to burn, Frank was quick to act once roused. He contacted E.P. Ingersoll, who wrote an article in February 1896, noting that press accounts universally giving credit for the Duryea to Charles overlooked "the very important part performed" by his younger brother. Indeed, *The Horseless Age* suggested that Frank had single-handedly made the car work after Charles moved to Peoria. This peeved Charles. Only a handful of cars was built in Massachusetts in 1897, as angry words were exchanged by the brothers. Within a year, they sold out to their backers, who promptly ran the company into the ground. Frank stayed in the East, and Charles returned to the Midwest.

———

Purloining first gasoline car honors, Elwood Haynes thought, was a safe bet. Even if the Duryeas stopped arguing with each other long enough to take him on, he had another tack ready. The first Duryea was a motorized buggy; his first car had been built from the ground up on a tubular chassis. Automotive sales in Kokomo totaled eight by the end of 1898. "Got twelve hundred and fifty dollars each," Edgar Apperson remembered. "Never tried to sell a car, never advertised. No dealers. If anyone wanted a car he came to the little factory we set up or sent an order by mail. At that, every car was sold before we started on it."

In Michigan in 1898, Henry Ford sold his first experimental car to Charles G. Annesley, a Detroit electrician who had bought Charles King's four-cylinder engine and had visions of becoming a manufacturer himself. Ford hadn't really wanted to sell the car, but the $200 it brought would help pay for the development of a second. His line of credit at the local machine supply store was only $15, and experimentation was straining the family finances. As for Charles King, he took a sabbatical from his experiments to help fight the Spanish–American War as chief machinist on the *U.S.S. Yosemite*.

———

A midsummer issue of *McClure's Magazine* in 1899 declared that in the four months from January to May, "companies with the enormous aggregate capitalization of more than $388,000,000 have been organized in New York, Boston, Chicago and Philadelphia for the sole purpose of manufacturing and operating" motor vehicles. A snowstorm had been responsible for the avalanche.

Watching the storm from his Wall Street office window was William Collins Whitney. Well born, Whitney had married well, too, if tragically. His first wife, Flora Payne, daughter of a Standard Oil magnate, died in 1893; his second, beautiful socialite Edith May Randolph, whom he married in 1896, died in 1899 of injuries sustained the previous year in a horseback-riding accident. But of those matters over which Whitney could exercise control, his grasp was awesome. After contributing to the downfall of the House of Tweed, he virtually controlled Tammany Hall for a while. As Secretary of the Navy during Grover Cleveland's first administration, he effectively overhauled a department desperately in need of it; his efforts largely saw to Cleveland's nomination and reelection in 1892. By then, public office no longer enticed Whitney. He had allied himself with Thomas Fortune Ryan, whom Whitney saw as "the most adroit and suave" man in American finance but whose flexible ethics would earn the public calumny of Robert M. LaFollette and William Jennings Bryan. Early in the 1890s, Whitney and Ryan organized the American Tobacco Company. Late in the 1890s, the Metropolitan Street Railway Company—a Whitney-Ryan collaboration joined by Peter A.B. Widener and Anthony N. Brady—controlled practically every line in New York City. Meanwhile, the partners had come to recognize what a great idea a "holding company" was.

Obviously, Whitney hadn't realized his grand station in life by missing opportunities, and he saw one that winter's day from his window. Below, horse-drawn hansoms had disappeared from the streets, and even his own streetcars were stalled. But on the snow-cleared sidewalks, Isaac Rice's electric cabs remained on the move. Whitney quickly made a move himself.

Earlier, because storage batteries were used in their electric streetcars, he and Ryan had purchased more than a million dollars of stock in Rice's Electric Storage Battery Company. Now they tried to corner the stock in Rice's Electric Vehicle Company. But the electric cabs' snowstorm performance had been noticed by other Wall Street speculators, who plunged in, too. Electric Vehicle shares soared 50 points above the par of 100. Finally, Whitney arranged a private meeting with Rice, who agreed, for what E.P. Ingersoll described as a "snug sum" and retention of the presidential chair, to sell his interest to the Whitney syndicate. It was mid-February. William Collins Whitney had an automobile company and plans for the immediate production of 2,000 vehicles. What he didn't have were the facilities in which to build them. Within days, he asked Colonel Pope to pay a visit.

The meeting resulted in marriage and a honeymoon announcement that 12,000 electric cabs would be built and placed in service in metropolitan areas throughout America. Neither Pope nor Whitney ever thought small. Percy Maxim worried aloud that the Wall Street financier's plan appeared largely a scheme to unload stock on the public. The Colonel said not to worry.

Operating companies were organized with headquarters in cities mentioned in the *McClure's* article; smaller sub-companies were planned for sixteen states from coast to coast. News soon followed from Chicago that Samuel Insull—together with New Yorkers August Belmont and a number of Standard Oil people—had established the Woods Motor Vehicle Company to produce the electric that Clinton E. Woods had been building in small numbers in the Windy City for the two years past and to give the Pope-Whitney people a run for their money. But this venture did not have the same energy. What would derisively be known as the "Lead Cab Trust" (for the lead used in batteries) remained firmly headquartered in New York.

Meanwhile, Colonel Pope had other visions of monopoly, following a conversation later in 1899 with Albert Goodwill Spalding, who suggested that the bicycle end of his thriving sporting goods business might be effectively merged with Pope's bicycle interests. The result was the American Bicycle Company, capitalized at $40 million, which subsequently brought some 45 firms operating 57 plants into its fold. Consolidation made sense to Pope, who saw it, as had the railroad barons, as a way to keep prices high by eliminating the competition. But cycling was an adult sport, and most people who wanted a bicycle now had one. In 1896, there were 3.5 million two-wheelers on the road. The market for bicycles plummeted. By the time President Teddy Roosevelt began concerning himself with monopolies, there was no trust left to bust insofar as the bicycle was concerned. And Colonel Pope had a bunch of idle factories.

All this was in the future, of course, and hardly predictable as Whitney and Pope began laying their grand plans. To assure that production would proceed smoothly, a cycle plant and carriage works in Connecticut were purchased to make bodies and wheels, easing pressure on the Pope motor vehicle department, now renamed Columbia Automobile Company. By August 1899, Pope's George Day had moved from Hartford to New York to oversee the Electric Vehicle and the Electric Storage Battery companies, which Isaac Rice did not like but was paid well enough not to complain about it. Rice probably spent most of his office time now playing chess. Because the patents of Andrew Riker (winner of the Narragansett Park race) were worthy, Whitney and Pope bought out the Riker Motor Vehicle Company of Elizabethport, New Jersey.

E.P. Ingersoll, who had coined "Lead Cab Trust," used the pages of his *The Horseless Age* to lambaste "the rottenest stock speculation that Wall Street has ever seen." Still, he did not see the Pope-Whitney operation as a threat to the burgeoning motor vehicle industry because the possibilities for improvement of the product were so many and the patents relating thereto so limited. But Pope, whose bicycle experience had demonstrated the wisdom of acquiring any potentially exploitable patents, had put Hermann F. Cuntz, his resident expert on the subject, to work searching for prior art in the automotive field.

One gasoline car patent appeared interesting. When Cuntz took it to Pope's resident automotive expert, Percy Maxim snorted in derision. "Utterly impractical and a joke" was his verdict. Cuntz said to forget the drawings and concentrate on the language of George Selden's claim. Maxim still wasn't convinced. But Pope and Whitney were. Rumor had it that five Wall Street speculators also had their eyes on the patent, but Selden was more interested in assigning it to a vehicle manufacturer. Selden may have started the rumor himself. No time was wasted. On November 4, 1899, George Selden and the Pope-Whitney forces came to terms: the exclusive license to the patent for $10,000 up front, a $15-per-vehicle royalty, and a guaranteed annual minimum payment of $5,000.

George Selden still had not built a car.

CHAPTER 9

Growing Pains

HOW MANY CARS had been completed in the Stanley plant in Massachusetts in 1899 when John Brisben Walker paid a visit is not known. But since the race from New York to Westchester County in 1896, the *Cosmopolitan* publisher had been anxious to get into the automobile business. His first trip to Watertown was for the purpose of a trade: advertising space in his magazine for a part interest in the company. The Stanleys weren't interested. They didn't believe in advertising, and they never sold anything except for cash. Moreover, as F.O. Stanley said of his relationship with his twin, "We had difficulty enough in getting along with each other and we did not want to increase our trouble by taking in a third party."

So Walker returned to Watertown with another suggestion: that he buy them out. The Stanleys hedged. Despite some production problems, they were reluctant to sell and finally decided to get rid of Walker by asking for a figure so astronomical he wouldn't accept it. But Walker did. The Stanleys' figure was a quarter of a million dollars; their investment thus far had been twenty thousand.

Leaving a binder with the brothers, Walker returned to New York to search for a financial partner. Even the most speculative of Wall Street speculators were loath to invest in something they had not seen, however. So a few days later, Walker wired the Stanleys to bring one of their cars down. F.O. Stanley drove to Providence, caught the night boat to Manhattan, and for the next week took Walker's millionaire friends for demonstration rides. The most impressed was Amzi Lorenzo Barber. As captain of the American asphalt industry, Barber had a vested interest in the future of road vehicles and agreed to contribute the entire Stanley purchase price for a half-interest in the venture.

Automobile Company of America was the name the new partners chose until, discovering it had been preempted a few months earlier by a New York group for production of a car called the Gasmobile, they switched to Locomobile Company of America. But within weeks of incorporation in June 1899, Walker and Barber quarreled over jobs for their assorted relatives and Walker's arbitrary purchase of land just north of his New York publishing company for a new factory. The partnership was off. Not surprisingly, the separation agreement was in Barber's favor. In addition to the rights to produce the Stanley, he acquired the Watertown factory, the name Locomobile, and most of the steamers the brothers already had under construction. Walker received the rights to produce the Stanley and the undeveloped piece of land in Tarrytown, New York. The former partners would share the consulting services of the Stanleys, a rather bizarre arrangement. Later that summer, Walker organized as the Mobile Company of America and called in Stanford White to design his factory. While it was under construction, Barber enjoyed a splendid head start with the Locomobile. The first Mobile wouldn't arrive until March 1900.

———

By February 1899, the Haynes-Apperson Company was working fifteen hours a day to build two cars a week and had orders enough to keep busy until May. Two delivery versions were among the company sales that year, one for an unnamed Chicago firm that was described in the *Kokomo Dispatch* as "almost as pretty as a woman and much more tractable," and the other for gelatin manufacturer C.B. Knox to advertise his product in Upstate New York. Ashley A. Webber, a physician from Brooklyn, insisted that his Haynes-Apperson be driven to New York to demonstrate its reliability. Haynes and Edgar Apperson personally delivered the car and could thereafter legitimately advertise the "first 1,000 mile run made in America." Ironically, Webber had problems with his Haynes-Apperson, which he concluded were his own fault but no less nettlesome. Writing the factory on the subject, the doctor was wired back to ship the car to Kokomo. With a waiting list of customers, Haynes-Apperson was happy to give a complete refund, which both delighted and surprised the doctor, who declared never having enjoyed "a similar experience with a horse dealer."

In Cleveland, Alexander Winton, who didn't believe in refunds, was claiming he had sold America's first gasoline car, which he hadn't, although unquestionably with the breakup of the Duryeas, he was the gasoline car industry leader. And, more so than his Kokomo rivals, he knew how to attract attention without dipping appreciably into his own pockets to do it. Early in 1899, Winton received the cooperation of the *Cleveland Plain Dealer* and, for a hundred dollars, the freelance services of professional journalist Charles Shanks to accompany him on a trip to New York City that he proposed to make in less than fifty hours using a two-year-old Winton that had already seen thousands of miles. Miffed since 1897 that his first trek to New York had received little press notice, Winton had decided that taking the press along was the best way to guarantee headlines.

Because of rain storms, getting lost in the dark trying to find the road to Buffalo, and an excursion into a ditch that required telegraphing the factory for a new axle, Winton and Shanks didn't arrive in Manhattan until five days after leaving Cleveland, but the actual running time of 47 hours 34 minutes was comfortably under the figure Winton had guaranteed. The Winton trek was "the first real effort at intelligent publicity with which the new industry has been favored," wrote early automobile chronicler J.R. Doolittle. Throughout Shanks had sent dispatches to his own and other newspapers, which generated sales not only for Winton but automobile builders everywhere. As Winton himself put it with characteristic crowing, his previous sales had been largely to engineers or the mechanically inclined "who desired to buy and experiment with an automobile that would really run." Now sales would be made as well to the "public at large."

Not all were impressed. The car Winton sold in July 1898 to a producer of incandescent lamps in Warren, Ohio, was brought back repeatedly to the factory with one problem or another. After a year, Winton became tired of seeing the owner and, worse, hearing his suggestions for improvement. Finally, according to journalist Hugh Dolnar, the Scotsman declared that he would not stultify himself by any departure whatever from his own incontestably superior productions, and if the owner "wanted any of his own cats and dogs worked into a waggon, he had better build it himself." James Ward Packard decided to do just that.

In addition to providing Winton competition in Ohio, Packard persuaded two of Winton's men—George Weiss and Bert Hatcher—to assist him in development. Hatcher, who had accompanied Winton on his 1897 New York trek, had been Winton's shop foreman, and Weiss was one of his major stockholders. The latter took his money out of Winton to invest with Packard, which so enraged his former employer that he banished Weiss' name ever after from the list of the first fifty Winton buyers, despite Weiss having purchased car no. 4.

Shortly thereafter, Winton lost another key employee who was dispatched to California and never returned. The impetus for the trip was a Riverside orange grower who was complaining about his car, but Winton figured Watt Moreland could quickly see to the repairs (which he was convinced were owner caused) and then scout the Pacific Coast for potential Winton outlets. Instead, Moreland happened upon a Riverside planing mill operator who asked him to collaborate on a new automobile to be marketed in California as the Magnolia.*

Departures like these did not represent a mass defection from the Winton camp. Still, the cantankerous Scotsman was obliged to find new people. His chief engineer, Leo Melanowski, suggested a mechanic he had met in Detroit, but Winton didn't think Henry Ford was much of a prospect.

Not that Ford would have been interested. By early 1898, his second experimental car was on the road, with the financial help of Detroit mayor William C. Maybury. Ironically, Maybury's interest was largely occasioned because his father and Henry's had both emigrated to

---

* This was a short-lived venture, as were Watt's subsequent Tourist and Durocar automobiles. He was successful with the Moreland truck, which was produced in Burbank until World War II.

America from the same town in Ireland during the 1830s and had been close friends ever since. William Ford remained adamantly opposed to his son's automotive activity. Maybury was impressed enough with Ford's progress, however, to suggest that friends join him in funding an automobile company. "A group of men of speculative turn of mind," as Henry phrased it, was rounded up.

Among those speculating were wealthy railroad car manufacturers Frank J. Hecker and Senator James McMillan; William H. Murphy, whose fortune had been made in lumber; wholesale hardware dealer Clarence A. Black; and Frank R. Alderman, an insurance salesman. Not much was being risked by these and the other stockholders, the most wealthy of whom invested little more than pocket change. On July 24, 1899, the Detroit Automobile Company was organized with paid-in capital of $15,000. Black was selected president, Alderman secretary, and Murphy treasurer. Ford's title was mechanical superintendent.

Although he put up no money, Henry was given a small quantity of stock and the same $150-a-month salary he had been making with the Edison company. A building on Cass Avenue was leased, and Ford moved in. Nothing happened quickly. Partly this was Henry's fault because he continued experimentation. Partly the problem was inferior parts arriving at the shop, and the inexperience of the few workmen hired to help him. With an appealing innocence, Frank Alderman remarked to a reporter that "You would be surprised at the amount of detail about an automobile." Apparently everyone involved with the Detroit Automobile Company was. And obviously, they were unaware of the money necessary to launch into serious manufacture.

In Lansing, Ransom Olds had learned the hard way. The $10,000 deposited in the treasury of the Olds Motor Vehicle Company was gone, and he was virtually no closer to meaningful production than he had been when he started. Early in 1899, when New York money beckoned, Olds picked out a plant site in Newark, New Jersey but was quickly back home when the deal fell through. His salvation was one of his original investors, Samuel Latta Smith, whose two sons Frederic and Angus had just graduated from college and were fascinated with horseless carriages and in need of gainful employment. But Smith had not made his millions being a bad businessman, and he insisted that any new Olds venture must include the thriving Olds gasoline engine business.

On May 8, 1899, the Olds Motor Works was incorporated with a capital stock of $500,000. Only 3,500 shares (par value ten dollars each) were issued immediately. Smith's cash investment of $200,000 gave him the lion's share; the remainder was distributed among stockholders of the motor vehicle and gasoline engine companies that now composed Olds Motor Works. Ransom Olds' title was vice president and general manager. So anxious was Olds to get into the automobile business, he gave up control of his company to do it. Among the first decisions made by the new corporation was a change of address. A tract of land on Jefferson Avenue near Belle Isle in Detroit was purchased for the new factory. The larger city offered obvious advantages over Lansing. But then, too, the Smiths lived in Detroit. By year's end, Ransom Olds packed up his family and moved. He was still pondering the sort of automobiles he wanted to build, but now, whatever his decision, he had the money to build them.

———

In 1899 in Philadelphia, Mrs. Sarah Terry turned 105. As a birthday present, she asked for just two things: a pension from the government (she was a Daughter of the American Revolution), and a ride in an automobile. The Electric Vehicle Company leaped at the chance to grant half her wish, and the publicity was grand. Taxicab fares had picked up considerably in Philadelphia, as they did subsequently in New York, "club chappies" deciding it was no longer necessary to await the dead of night before entering one. Indeed, some of New York's wealthy residents had an electric cab and a driver constantly on call at the company's home station, a service for which they paid $180 a month.

Although cabs for hire had been the impetus for the founding of the Electric Vehicle Company, cars for sale now became a priority. Production was stepped up in Hartford. A reporter for *McClure's* dropped by the firm's New York headquarters in 1899 and came away mightily impressed by the company's plans for electric charging depots throughout the United States. "It is not hard to imagine what a country touring-station will be like on a sunny summer afternoon some five or ten years hence," he wrote. "Long rows of vehicles will stand backed up comfortably to the charging bars, each with its electric plug filling the battery with power. The owners will be lolling at the tables on the verandahs of the nearby road-house. Men with repair kits will bustle about, tightening up a nut here, oiling this bearing and regulating that gear. From a long rubber tube compressed air will be hissing into pneumatic tires."

Save for Ingersoll's *The Horseless* Age, which continued to lambaste the "Lead Cab Trust," the Electric Vehicle Company enjoyed a fine press for most of 1899. *Scientific American* was enthralled. The company was manufacturing more than half of all the cars produced in the United States, and Hartford, Connecticut, was widely regarded as the automobile capital of the world. Electric Vehicle's resources stood at an imposing $100 million, dividends of 8 percent on both preferred and common stock were declared, and business seemed to be booming.

Matters quickly went awry. Most of the company's money was on paper. The ambitious 8,000-car output was slashed back to the originally planned 2,000, and pink slips were handed to scores of workers in Hartford. Dividends were suspended. Ingersoll filled his pen with vitriol. "They have become grotesque," he wrote of Whitney and friends, "...if they have any saving sense of humor they will retire and leave the field to the mechanics and manufacturers to whom it rightfully belongs." The Electric Vehicle Company promoters knew nothing about automobiles and apparently didn't care to learn. The assumption was that, once the cars arrived from Hartford, the work was ended. Maintenance was ignored; months of use without proper care brought increasing breakdowns. In January 1900, scandal followed revelation of a bit of financial derring-do that saw a $2 million loan secured by Electric Vehicle Company stock made to a dummy director who turned out to be the office boy of Thomas Fortune Ryan, Whitney's closest associate.

That did it for Colonel Pope. He was a manufacturer, not a manipulator, and was sorely embarrassed. That June, he sold out. His Hartford plant as well as the Columbia name became the property of the Whitney syndicate, the Electric Vehicle Company was reorganized as a manufacturing firm, and the numerous operating subsidiaries were allowed to collapse. Perhaps problems with his American Bicycle conglomerate had been partly responsible for Pope's departure from the Whitney group, but chagrin was part of it, too. A $2 million office boy was not the Colonel's style.

With its treasury sorely depleted and its product in disrepute, the Electric Vehicle Company turned to its most important untried asset: the Selden patent. Infringement notices were immediately mailed to producers of gasoline vehicles. Most of them ended up in the wastebasket. But the Whitney syndicate was deadly serious. Less than a month later, in July, lawsuits were filed against the Buffalo Gasolene Motor Company in Upstate New York and in New York City against the Winton Motor Carriage Company and its local sales representatives, Percy Owen and A.W. Chamberlain. Taking aim at the Buffalo firm served warning that the Selden patent was equally applicable to parts makers as it was to automobile manufacturers. The big Whitney group gun was aimed at Winton.

In August, twenty "infringing" manufacturers met at the Iroquois Hotel in Buffalo to plan a counter-assault. Elmer Apperson was elected president of the group. Included on the executive committee were representatives of Buffalo Gasolene Motor and the newly organized Autocar Company of Ardmore, Pennsylvania, as well as Charles Duryea, whose Duryea Power Company, having found the going rough in Peoria, had recently relocated to Reading, Pennsylvania. Scoffed Winton treasurer George H. Brown, "The Selden patent is preposterous...It will not have a leg to stand upon when it gets into the courts." On September 3, the attorney retained by the group formally asked the district court for dismissal of the Winton suit. Everyone involved figured the matter would be quickly over and done with.

CHAPTER 10

The Horseless Carriage Becomes an Automobile

IN 1899, ACCORDING to official estimates, 30 American automobile producers manufactured 2,500 vehicles. Unofficially, *Motor Age* (one of the numerous new magazines that had followed Ingersoll) estimated that experimental automobiles were being built in as many as a thousand more American shops, with manufacture the objective or the invention of patentable features that might profitably be sold to the industry. That October, the National Master Horseshoers' Association worried about the possible effect of the automobile on its business. *Harper's Weekly* suggested that "a good many folks...feel much safer on a machine than behind a quadruped, who has a mind of his own."

At last, that machine had an accepted generic name: automobile. It had been a long time coming. Horseless carriage, which the thing literally was, was unwieldy. Motor vehicle took too long to say. In 1895, the *Chicago Times-Herald*, to further promote its race, had announced another contest with a prize of $500 for the best single word to describe a carriage that did not require a horse. Autobain, petrocar, viamote, motorig, mocle, and mobe were among the entries. ("To mobe or not to mobe, that is the question," one reporter guffawed.) The winning entry, submitted by a New York telephone man, was motocycle. Apparently only the *Chicago Times-Herald* people liked it because, like the magazine of the same name begun in Chicago shortly before Ingersoll's *The Horseless Age*, it was short-lived.

Thereafter, letters were written to the editors of countless newspapers with further suggestions. From Durango, Colorado, came goalone. A physician who abhorred an earlier suggestion of ipsomotor as a bastardization of Latin offered autokinet, "impressing into service the new scientific word 'kinetic' " which could be "easily and musically abridged into 'autokin'." A Detroit man suggested sineque—"since" (without) "equus" (horse), to be pronounced "sineek." Molectros was offered from Brooklyn, and autogo from Yonkers. From Baltimore came the idea of simply adding "ine" to whatever the vehicle was, as in "cabine." One fellow with a droll sense of humor suggested "tommy" because that was his name. But gradually, as the new century approached, automobile—which *The New York Times* described as half-Greek, half-Latin, and all French—came into increasing favor. There was some dissatisfaction that America had to borrow a word instead of coming up with its own. An English professor suggested shortening to "autom" as a way out. During the Cleveland-to-New York trek of '99, in all of his dispatches to newspapers, Charlie Shanks used no other word but automobile to describe the Winton in which he was riding. That sealed the matter. Car, because of its long use with "street" and "railroad," took a while longer to move into the lexicon.

———

Who bought automobiles? Prior to the turn of the century, they were, most conspicuously, the same people who owned private railroad cars, had stables for at least twenty carriages at their estates on Long Island, and summered at their opulent "cottages" in Newport. Society fell in love with the horseless carriage.

In early September 1899, summer residents of Jamestown, Block Island, and other fashionable Rhode Island enclaves joined the entire cottage colony of Newport for an automobile festival. Local florists made a fortune. The cars, mostly Columbia electrics, were smothered with flowers, banners, live doves, and stuffed eagles. Uniformed footmen were everywhere as the car owners set off for a day of amusement, which began with a procession along Bellevue Avenue and Ocean

Drive, the route thronged by more spectators than had enjoyed the recent horse show and yacht races. The parade ended at Belcourt, the estate of Oliver Hazard Perry Belmont, where on the great lawn an "obstacle park" had been laid out, with dummy figures of horse-drawn carriages, policemen, pedestrians, and nursemaids wheeling their infant charges. The game—or "little circus," as the lady of the cottage styled it—was to navigate the course without knocking down any of the figures. Mrs. Belmont, accompanied by J.W. Gerard on a car so laden with blue hydrangeas as to virtually lose them to view, gently cracked a whip of daisies above the figures' heads, which everyone remarked was a clever and symbolic touch.

Less lucky was Mr. Belmont, accompanied by Mrs. Stuyvesant Fish, whose runabout was bedecked with yellow field flowers, an arbor of cat-o'-nine tails overhead, and a floral pole nearly twice the length of the car extending joust-like out front. Belmont knocked down every obstacle. So did Harry Symes Lehr, society's most skilled moocher of the era and Mrs. Stuyvesant Fish's personal court jester, although on this day, he was accompanied by Mrs. John Jacob Astor. The inimitable Harry's performance, however, was not due to a "design flaw" of the flowered vehicle but to the amount of champagne he had imbibed beforehand. Taking the event more seriously was Colonel Astor in a stanhope bedecked with green and white clematis. Wrote an admiring reporter, "He steered with the same cool-headed dash that distinguished him while serving under fire at Santiago." Driving well, too, with Mrs. John R. Drexel as passenger, was Reginald Ronalds, who had distinguished himself as one of Teddy Roosevelt's Rough Riders. When all contestants finished the course, prizes were awarded for the best decorated cars and the most skilled operators. Stuyvesant Leroy took the top driving prize; Mrs. Hermann Oelrichs (*nee* Tessie Fair of the California silver millions) received a silver bonbon dish for her electric floral extravaganza. Dining and dancing at Belcourt followed, and at midnight the automobilists headed home, small lanterns among the wreaths showing the way. Gushed one journalist, it was "like a veritable pageant of fairy chariots."

It cannot be said that enchantment was universal regarding how the very rich had automotive fun. Although floral parades would later become the rage in towns throughout America, Mrs. Belmont's "little circus" gymkhana was not emulated outside the Social Register and drew brickbats in some quarters. "Just now the millionaire is going in for automobiling and, of course, is going to extremes" was the comparatively subdued comment from *The Strand Magazine.*

Meanwhile, the rich did see to it that the automobile was noticed. If the car was a steamer, this involved some difficulty. In 1899, in New York City, the equivalent of a locomotive engineer's license was necessary. Presenting himself at the Steam Boiler's Inspector's Bureau that year was Edward Ringwood Hewitt, whose grandfather was Peter Cooper and whose father would have been mayor of New York longer save for a run-in with Tammany Hall. Young Hewitt had purchased his Locomobile on the same day as Thomas Edison's eldest son. "For two long sessions on two successive days I was examined, both orally and in writing, on the subject of steam and locomotive mechanics," he wrote in his memoirs. "I finally received my license. As I recall, it was No. 25."

Earlier licenses had been granted to Alfred G. Vanderbilt, Harry Payne Whitney (son of William C. and husband of the former Gertrude Vanderbilt), and Amzi Lorenzo Barber of Locomobile, among others. Some who had purchased a steam car but failed to pass the test drove their vehicles anyway; the law quickly became a farce and was rescinded within a year following the court case of Stanley D. Atkinson, who sold Locomobiles at Wanamaker's and who had been apprehended on Fifth Avenue while demonstrating the vehicle's operation to a new owner. Thereafter, three dollars and proving one knew how satisfied the legal requirements for driving a steam car.

Society's ladies preferred electrics, which were infinitely more simple and didn't dirty the glove. After only one demonstration—lever forward to proceed ahead, lever back for reversing, lever up to stop—Mrs. Hermann Oelrichs began making all her afternoon calls in an electric, and Miss Daisy Post likewise. But Mrs. Hamilton Fish had an awful time of it. One day on Fifth Avenue, while motoring at a sedate pace, she struck a pedestrian who got up and was brushing off his hat when she hit him again. In her excitement, the lady couldn't remember which way to move the lever to stop and, after knocking the poor fellow down three times before finally figuring it out, she left the car there and found another way home. Mrs. Stuyvesant Fish learned to drive at Newport, to the great detriment of her lawn. "She didn't mind stone walls, big trees and shrubbery, and finally ran the machine up the wide stone steps of her villa," reported *The Automobile Magazine.* "This experience did not curb her desire to drive an auto, and now there are no more expert than she."

Many of society's more dashing gentlemen, after buying native-built steamers, began importing foreign gasoline cars, principally because America wasn't building any that were fast enough to suit them. At least not on the East Coast. Prominent among them was William K. Vanderbilt, Jr., whose German-built Daimler was the most famous car in Greater New York. There was a reason, in addition to the numerous brushes with the law the millionaire incurred for speeding, which were invariably reported in the press and which Vanderbilt regarded as a badge of honor. Newspaper clippings of his exploits were carefully pressed in a leather-covered album.

But if Willie K. (as he was popularly known, to distinguish him from his father) was a demon at the wheel, he was also possessed of *noblesse oblige*. The record does not indicate that he ever hit a pedestrian, but his Daimler did happen upon a good many animals. "The Long Island farmer has been taught by his parents to 'do' a New Yorker whenever possible," a newspaper reported, "and the Vanderbilt automobile has offered a fine chance. The farmers have discovered that a horse that isn't worth over $6 for glue and fertilizer will bring from $65 to $100 when killed by the Vanderbilt auto." Invariably, Willie K. handed the animal's owner his card and said to send a bill. Thereafter, whenever Vanderbilt approached the Manhattan end of the 34th Street ferry bound for his Long Island home, the news spread like wildfire. Animals were shoved on the road, fights broke out among those shoving as to whose turn it was, and vegetable farmers found it profitable to buy disabled streetcar horses to get in on the act. The newspaper estimate was that it cost Willie K. $47.23 per mile to visit Long Island. Finally, Vanderbilt grew suspicious and publicly announced his intention to hire a claims adjuster. Most of the animals in his path after that wandered there by themselves.

That the automobile was the plaything of the wealthy was the common view during this era, and not wholly accurate, although it would be years before that reputation was worn down. The super rich did a very good job of perpetuating the idea. At the Waldorf-Astoria in June 1899, the Automobile Club of America was founded, partly to counteract the autophobia that was spreading as more cars ventured into the country-side, partly to discourage petty larceny such as that suffered by

Vanderbilt, but mostly to establish motoring as its special and exclusive province. Taking the earlier Automobile Club de France as its model, A.C.A. membership was restricted, its dues were exorbitant, and its club headquarters lavish. And it soon boasted more millionaire members than any other social organization in the world. Interestingly, the American Motor League founded during the Chicago Times-Herald four years earlier by such automotive pioneers as Charles King, Elwood Haynes, and the Duryeas had failed to catch on. Money talked more powerfully than invention. The A.C.A. wielded considerable clout. That November, thousands lined the streets from the Waldorf to watch club members parade in their cars to Grant's Tomb. It was the A.C.A. hope that, like its European counterparts, the club's scope would be national, and that New York City would rule motoring America. That hope was soon dashed.

National press coverage of the run to Riverside Drive encouraged the formation of small local automobile clubs among those who had taken up automobiling in major cities throughout America. The numbers in which cars were being built in this country exceeded society's "Four Hundred" and, unlike Europe, where motoring remained largely an aristocratic pursuit, a certain democratization was already being seen in ownership. Buying a foreign gasoline automobile was an extravagant proposition, to be sure; with freight and the import duty of 45 percent, the total could exceed $15,000. Those were strictly purchases for the Newport set. But an American-built automobile could be had for a bit less than $1,500. Among the first twenty Mobile steamers that William E. Metzger sold in his bicycle store on Jefferson Avenue in Detroit were four to physicians, one to a printer, and one to a plumber. Alexander Winton was selling his gasoline cars to millers, brewers, and dry-goods merchants. The sole requirement to obtain an automobile was sufficient discretionary income. The task of the automobile manufacturer was to persuade more people to indulge themselves. Automobiles were expensive but within the means of thousands who had not yet been enticed to buy one.

———

What was needed was a forum to show off the horseless carriage, a venue more accessible than Mrs. Belmont's lawn, an event less fleeting than a run of cars from here to there. Thus far, automobiles had been exhibited only in circuses, the Electrical Exposition in New York in 1898, and as a drawing card at carriage and bicycle fairs. It was at one of the last named that the promotion manager of the *Chicago Inter-Ocean* decided the drawing card should become the feature attraction. Perhaps a certain chagrin was involved because the *Chicago Times-Herald* could point with pride to its pioneering as increasingly more automobiles were seen on Michigan Avenue. Not wishing to be one-upped again, the rival newspaper announced in July 1900 its sponsorship of the first national exhibition devoted exclusively to the automobile, to be held that September in "God's Great Outdoors" at the Washington Park race track. In addition to viewing the cars, spectators were promised the chance to see them run in a bewildering variety of "general practical utility" contests and all kinds of races, including one with the vehicles being driven backwards and one just for the ladies.

But, as in 1895, Chicago's weather played havoc with *Inter-Ocean*'s extravaganza. For the six days of the event, rain either came down in torrents or threatened to, and spectators stayed away in droves. Manufacturers with cars on hand were reluctant to participate in the contests for fear of a bad showing occasioned by the conditions. Only the mud racing, which was a scheduled event, was wholly successful. And the *Inter-Ocean* had to endure the guffaws of rival Chicago newspapers, save for the *Times-Herald*, which had editorially played that scene itself and was compassionate.

As the rains fell in Chicago, plans were being finalized in New York for an automobile show the following month. Here no chances were taken. The entire event would be held within Madison Square Garden, its perimeter rimmed by an oval track so, as one reporter noted, "a skeptic public might be persuaded that these horseless carriages could go," but there would be no backward races or other amusing novelties. Nor was this event a newspaper promotion. Instead, it was the collaborative effort of the Automobile Club of America and the newly formed National Association of Automobile Manufacturers headed by Samuel T. Davis, Jr., who was Amzi Barber's son-in-law and treasurer of Locomobile. Automobilists and automakers had joined together in a common cause. Rather cleverly, the show organizers persuaded F.P. Dudgeon to send the steam wagon his father had built during the Civil War to lend a touch of history to the proceedings.

The New York Automobile Show opened on November 3 and closed on November 10. Newspaper coverage was lavish, and word of mouth was obviously good because closing day attendance was a record 12,000 visitors. Six thousand or more had visited each day previously, except for election day Tuesday, when attendance fell despite the promise that the returns would be read in the Garden: William McKinley swamped William Jennings Bryan by nearly a million votes to handily win reelection. The verdict on the automobile show was a landslide victory, too. More than 30 manufacturers exhibited, and not one of them dominated, although William C. Whitney's Electric Vehicle Company had tried with a "profuse display" of electrics plus two gasoline cars. From Chicago, the rival Woods Motor Vehicle Company sent a handsome exhibit. Newcomers were the National Automobile & Electric Company of Indianapolis and, from Upstate New York, the Buffalo Electric Carriage Company. Hands-down winner of all contests for electrics (including the gymkhana, which used barrels instead of dummy people figures) was Walter C. Baker, who had just begun manufacturing in Cleveland and who would make a strategic first sale to Thomas Edison.

Among the nine steamers on hand were the McKay and Victor from Massachusetts, the Reading from Pennsylvania, the Keene Steamobile from New Hampshire (designed by Reynold Janney, son of the playwright and novelist Russell Janney), and the Foster from Rochester, New York. Amzi Barber, who by now had decided to move Locomobile production out of the former Stanley plant into a new factory in Bridgeport, Connecticut, had planned well for the show. His old partner had not. In the throes of getting his Tarrytown plant operational, John Brisben Walker had tarried too long in applying for space in the main hall. When told there was none left, the resourceful Walker asked for the roof. There he had a runway constructed up to the water tower, upon which his Mobile steamer's climbing, braking, and reversing virtues could be demonstrated.

In addition to the exhibits of gasoline car manufacturers, a good many European specimens with internal combustion engines were lent for display by their owners. "Society, Auto-Crazed, Will Throng Big Show" headlined *The New York World*. Making a grand entrance on Monday evening was David Wolfe Bishop, with John Jacob Astor as passenger, in the French Panhard that had placed second at the Aquidneck track races in September. Bishop made the ninety-mile trip from Staatsburg-on-the-Hudson in five hours, which, one reporter noted, was a "time that could be beaten by few machines in the Garden." Willie K. Vanderbilt displayed his German Daimler, the winner at Aquidneck.

These sportsmen ignored the mini-powered three-wheeler gasoline efforts of makers such as Harry Knox and Charles Herman Metz of Massachusetts (Springfield and Waltham, respectively) and Charles E. Duryea's gasoline trike, which was exhibited in the restaurant section, thankfully a good distance away from the gasoline runabouts of the Canda Manufacturing Company of New Jersey. Canda had been among the potential licensing deals that went sour for the Duryeas and soured the brothers on each other. Charles didn't seek out Harry Knox for a chat either, because Knox had been encouraged to get into the automobile business by his next-door neighbor, Frank Duryea. "Rigs that Run" was the slogan for the St. Louis Motor Carriage Company exhibit, which society's gentlemen swiftly passed by, and they did not stop by long at the display of Elwood Haynes and the Apperson brothers from Kokomo.

The Winton had enjoyed some sales success among the smart set, but Alexander Winton had little time to generate further business nor even to enjoy the show. His lawyers had bad news. The U.S. Circuit Court for the Southern District of New York refused to sustain the Winton demurrer in the Selden patent case. That the Whitney forces had won round one buzzed through Madison Square Garden as the show was nearing its end. But any apprehension felt by gasoline car manufacturers was tempered by the expectation that Winton would surely take round two—and by the marvelous exhilaration all makers enjoyed showing their cars to an audience of thousands. Particularly delighted were James Ward Packard and his right-hand man, Winton defector George Weiss. William D. Rockefeller stopped by the Packard exhibit, liked the car, and bought two on the spot. Rockefeller's previous automotive purchases, in addition to European cars, had included five Wintons.

Underneath a big sign reading "American Bicycle Company" were a variety of cars—electric, gasoline, and steam—which were being built in various of the conglomerate's plants idled by plummeting bicycle sales. "The automobile will in time be the universal means of transportation," Albert Pope exhorted, "and the future of the American Bicycle Company rests on its adoption and development." The Colonel was right about the American Bicycle Company's future, but that fully 15,000 of his bicycle agents were "fairly howling" for automobiles to meet an "enormous demand" was an exaggeration. It was less a demand for automobiles as no demand for bicycles, and a howl simply for something—anything—to stay in business. American Bicycle Company was arranging for $4.2 million worth of new stock to provide additional working capital to move headlong into the automobile business. Colonel Pope carried his message to all corners of Madison Square Garden.

That the New York Automobile Show was a smashing success was echoed in the press nationwide. Because of the A.C.A. sponsorship, New York society regarded the event as its own and had a fine time. Spectators who were not yet among automobile owners were fascinated. And manufacturers, including a good number selling accessories for the automobile, supported the show rigorously. "More than seventy companies, some from as far west as St. Louis, are represented by exhibits," *The New York Times* had reported midweek. "None of prominence is missing."

Conspicuous by their absence, if only historically, were Ransom Olds and Henry Ford.

———

Henry Ford didn't exhibit at Madison Square Garden because he didn't have anything to sell. As a news release from his Detroit Automobile Company had stated earlier that year, "we have already set one or two dates for the appearance of our motor car vehicle in quantities, and now we have concluded to stop that nonsense." Ford had spent $86,000 and was nowhere near production. A dozen or so vehicles had been built, but Henry was not satisfied with any of them. Even more dissatisfied were some of his investors who, shortly after the Detroit Automobile Company's first birthday, decided not to stick it out for the second. William Murphy and a few others who had not yet lost faith in Ford purchased the company assets, installed Henry in more modest quarters on Cass Avenue, and told him to keep working. They were sure he would come up with something. He did: a race car.

Helping him build it was Oliver Barthel, Charles King's former associate who lost his job when King went off to the Spanish-American War. Ford now prepared to do battle with Winton. It made sense. Not only was Alexander Winton America's number one gasoline car producer (sales would total 700 cars in 1901), he was America's number one race driver, having followed his Cleveland–New York long-distance treks with frequent timed sprints on horse tracks. By now, he was record holder for most distances up to 25 miles. Alexander Winton's reputation was made. Victory over Winton could make Henry's.

The deadline was October 10, 1901. At the Grosse Point dirt track, an ambitious afternoon of racing had been planned by Detroit bicycle and automobile dealer William Metzger, whose committee included former *Cleveland Plain Dealer* reporter Charlie Shanks, now Winton's sales manager. As Ford feverishly worked to finish his car, he was assured of Winton's presence at Grosse Point. Metzger had hoped to entice two other racing luminaries to the event—William K. Vanderbilt, Jr., who had just spent $12,000 for a brand-new Daimler model called the Mercedes, which had taken the Continent by storm during Speed Week on the Riviera, and Henri Fournier, who had piloted the French Mors to victory in the Paris–Bordeaux and Paris–Berlin races. Both cars were now in the United States, but their drivers would elect to confine competition to the East Coast.

Still, enthusiasm ran high for the Grosse Point races. The Detroit Street Railway Company ran special cars out to the horse track, and more than 7,000 spectators attended. Olds Motor Works closed for the afternoon. Because of numerous requests from local attorneys, court also adjourned early that day. In the preliminaries, Olds workers cheered lustily as team drivers Roy Chapin and Jonathan Maxwell placed second and third, respectively, behind a White steamer. In another race, the White was defeated by Edgar Apperson from Kokomo, whose Haynes-Apperson was much faster as well than the entry Charles Duryea had sent from Reading. Then came the main event. Prizes for victory were $1,000 in cash and a cut-glass punch bowl personally selected by Shanks because "it would look well in the bay window of the Winton dining room." Winton's only challenger in the ten-mile free-for-all was the mechanic from Cass Avenue who had never driven in a race.

Riding with Henry Ford was Edward S. "Spider" Huff, one of the few Detroit Automobile Company workers who had remained on the payroll following the firm's move to lesser quarters. Riding with Alexander Winton was Charlie Shanks. The challenger was clearly outclassed. In addition to competition experience, Winton enjoyed a vast power advantage. His racer developed 70 horsepower, Ford's less than 30. But midrace, while leading comfortably, Winton's car began to overheat, a problem Shanks vainly attempted to deal with as Winton kept his foot to the floor. Ford, gaining confidence with each lap, steadily crept up on his rival. "I wish you could have seen him. Also have heard the cheering when he passed Winton," Clara Ford wrote her brother afterward. "The people went wild. One man threw his hat up and when it came down he stamped on it, he was so excited. Another man had to hit his wife on the head to keep her from going off the handle. She stood up in her seat and screamed 'I'd bet Fifty dollars on Ford if I had it.' They were friends of ours."

Ford finished the race almost a mile ahead of Winton and more than four minutes faster than Apperson's winning time in the earlier ten-mile event. But more important than statistics, a hometown boy had won before a hometown crowd. By the following day, Henry Ford's name was as big in Detroit as Winton's ever had been. Ford's backers celebrated by reorganizing as the Henry Ford Company. Now the only problem was the punch bowl. As Clara lamented, "Well, of all things to win... Where will we ever put it?"

———

Ransom Olds' problem had been more complicated. That his product would be called Oldsmobile was the one irrevocable decision he made in 1900 as he vacillated about just what the product would be. Some $80,000 had been spent in automobile development. Upon his return from the Spanish-American War, Charles King had sold his engine business to Olds and joined the company as an engineer in the marine division. Olds Motor Works engine sales were brisk—$186,000 in 1900, an increase of $66,000 over the year previous—which allowed Ransom a cushion in deciding about his automobile. Still, he had to wonder how long the Smiths would tolerate red ink on the automotive side of the ledger. At the *Chicago Inter-Ocean* exhibition, he had displayed an electric. Possibly the fiasco that the show was had been among the reasons he did not display at Madison Square Garden. But he had other things on his mind, too.

Shortly after returning from the Windy City and, after a long sleepless night, Olds called one of his engineers into his office and said, "What we want to build is a small low-down runabout that will have a shop cost around $300 and will sell for $650." A patent application he had prepared in 1896 described a similar gasoline car. Now he directed all his energy toward it. The new model would be the focal point, but it would join a line of electrics. The 35 miles between charges that his electric prototype had demonstrated during testing on Jefferson Avenue compared favorably with the performance of similar cars being produced in the East. Ransom Olds was not prepared at this point to put all of his eggs in one basket. Then fate intervened.

It was a cold day in March 1901 when, returning from a trip to California to see his father, Ransom Olds stepped off the train in Detroit, picked up a newspaper, and discovered that what he was coming home to was no longer there. His factory had burned down. As he walked among the smoldering debris, he rued that "a more inopportune time for such a calamity could not be." Years later, Fred Smith would call the fire "our blessed disaster." They were both right.

Automobiles were a seasonal product in those days. With scant weather protection and no heater, winter motoring was not inviting. Sales picked up with the first inkling of spring, which was just around the corner. And Olds Motor Works was ashes. Only part of the $72,000 property loss was covered by insurance. Of the twenty automobiles inside, only one remained. After turning in the alarm, company timekeeper James J. Brady had dragged, pushed, and shoved the prototype of the little gasoline runabout with its toboggan-like curved dash to safety. Advance announcement had already brought several hundred queries about the car. Now, with time of the essence, wisdom dictated concentrating total company efforts on it. Another decision, reached soon afterward, was to return headquarters to Lansing, where engine production had continued even after the firm's move to Detroit. Assembly operations would be retained in both cities.

Among the other benefits of the Olds fire was the sympathy it generated for the company. With new firms entering the automotive field almost daily, competition for editorial space in automotive journals and newspaper automotive columns was keen. Olds Motor Works, struggling to rebuild under seemingly devastating circumstances, was a real human-interest story. That summer, when the first curved dash Oldsmobile runabouts were put on sale in Chicago, *Motor Age* remarked that the car "attracted more comment and more visitors, in a short time, than any other vehicle that ever came into the city..."

Thus far, Olds Motor Works was a comparative unknown in the East. But Ransom Olds was determined that would not be the case for long. He did not intend to miss the Madison Square Garden show this year.

CHAPTER 11

■

Reaching for the Limelight

BY EARLY FALL, with the Garden rented and plans for the November show well in hand, the Automobile Club of America decided to enjoy itself on a six-day run from New York City to Buffalo, where arrival was scheduled to coincide with the visit of President McKinley to the ongoing Pan-American Exposition. Competition in the stadium as well as a 100-mile road race from Buffalo to Erie were to follow. But as the automobilists relaxed in Rochester after the fifth day, word reached A.C.A. president Albert R. Shattuck that the President had been assassinated. McKinley, whom the Stanleys had taken for a ride in their steamer two years earlier, was taken to the hospital in a Riker electric. The run to Buffalo was immediately canceled.

Prizes were awarded on the performances to Rochester. Overall victory went to David Wolfe Bishop, principally because Willie K. Vanderbilt was a no-show. Incensed that the Newport City Council had disallowed racing on Ocean Drive despite his petition signed by fellow cottagers, Willie K. had, following his domination at Aquidneck

Park where the events had to be held as usual, taken himself and his Mercedes to the Continent. Road racing was allowed there.

Bishop's 15-miles-per-hour average (the maximum allowed) was perfect, but he was not the only winner. First-class certificates were awarded to all cars averaging 12 to 15 miles per hour for the duration. Close behind, at 14.18 miles per hour, was Elmer Apperson on one of his company's cars, another Haynes-Apperson third at 13.78. Four Packards had been entered in the event, with first-class certificates won by each. Likewise splendidly did the quartet of White steamers finish. The White Sewing Machine Company of Cleveland, like Packard, was a newcomer to the automotive field, and a performance such as this was sure to help.

Second- and third-class certificates were awarded for runs of 10 to 12 miles per hour and 8 to 10 miles per hour, respectively. Alexander Winton was furious that his New York agent Percy Owen hadn't managed any better than a second and that Winton owner Alexander Dow (Henry Ford's old boss at the Edison Illuminating Company) received only a third-class certificate. Dow had been in the run solely for enjoyment. That success in competition translated to sales was a given by now, but racing on the East Coast remained dominated by the social set. More irritated than Winton at the outcome of the A.C.A. run were the Gasmobile people from New Jersey. Their product, which had received top gasoline car honors in contests at the 1900 New York Automobile Show, captured two first-class certificates. But more news was generated by Gasmobile owner John Jacob Astor, who hit a bicycle (handing its owner $50 to buy a new one), routinely stopped for such emergencies as one of his passengers losing his hat, and finished the event at a 9.78-miles-per-hour average for a third-place certificate.

———

Roy D. Chapin's drive in the curved dash Oldsmobile later that fall was no joy ride. Son of a prominent Lansing attorney, Chapin had dutifully attended the University of Michigan until a job at Olds Motor Works came through. A fine amateur photographer, the young man was hired at $35 a month to take advertising photos of the Oldsmobile, but his proficiency behind the tiller had quickly earned him a position as test driver. Chapin had lost the Grosse Point race to the White steamer. The event he was now to win was against the roads. Taking a leaf from the Winton book, Ransom Olds (perhaps at the suggestion of

Chapin himself) had concluded that driving the curved dash runabout to New York would make headlines for Oldsmobile before the Madison Square Garden show opened and he had to share news space with all the other cars on exhibit.

On October 29, with a box of spare parts strapped on the back of the car and after a hearty handshake and being wished good luck by his boss, Roy Chapin set out for Manhattan. Seven-and-a-half days later, he arrived. His 14-miles-per-hour running speed would have earned him an A.C.A. first-class certificate the previous month, but his stops had been numerous. At one point, an unseen bump in the road resulted in a bent axle and the spare parts scattered unmercifully in inch-thick mud all around the car. When the roads became even worse, Chapin took to the Erie Canal towpath and endured the verbal abuse of muleskinners, who did not care to share their right-of-way.

The final humiliation was arrival in New York at the Waldorf Astoria. Upstairs, Ransom Olds paced the floor, nervously awaiting news of his car and its driver; downstairs, a bedraggled Chapin was trying to convince a horrified doorman that he belonged there. Finally, he was allowed inside so long as he used the service elevator. "Roy had all the trouble that could possibly be created by one small car," his boss admitted, "but he got there." Olds was disappointed only in the lack of local press interest in the feat, the *Times* ignoring the story altogether, and the *Tribune* giving it short shrift and without mentioning the name of the car. His competitors in Cleveland and Kokomo might have warned Olds that New York wasn't much impressed by cars from the Midwest arriving in town.

Still, the company's own publicity and the display of the mud-spattered car at the show brought more visitors to the Olds stand than otherwise might have been expected. Overhead, a large sign proclaimed that the sporting goods house of Albert Goodwill Spalding had agreed to purchase 100 of the cars for sale in the city. Midway through the show, however, a shamefaced company spokesman took Ransom Olds aside and asked to be released from the contract because Spalding's board of directors—burned once in the bicycle deal with Colonel Pope—didn't think that many Oldsmobiles could be sold in New York during the next year. A perturbed Olds agreed, asking only that the sign remain up until he could figure out something else. Spalding could scarcely refuse that.

Actually, the sporting goods company's cold feet proved to be a boon because the proprietors of a carpet cleaning and rug manufacturing business in Ohio had a better offer. The Owen brothers, Ray M. and Ralph R. (no relation to Winton's Percy Owen), had added manufacture of gasoline vehicles to their floor-covering business prior to the turn of the century but did not pursue this sideline vigorously. By now, they were also selling Oldsmobiles in premises rented in the Cleveland Athletic Club basement, and they recognized the curved dash as a comer. Ray Owen suggested that he take on the New York Olds agency in collaboration with Roy Rainey, a wealthy friend of his. A deal was done and a quota of 500 cars agreed upon.

Then Ransom Olds suggested the announcement should read 1,000 cars so "the public would drop its jaw and take notice." That was fine all around, too. It was also agreed that Ray Owen would move to New York, while brother Ralph would pack up for Lansing to serve as the Olds factory manager. The 1,000-car proclamation—the largest single order for any car in America thus far—was made. Spalding was aghast. But the result in 1902 fell neatly between announcement and quota. Ray Owen's sale of 750 Olds runabouts in Manhattan—one of them to New York Central president Chauncey Depew, who allowed himself to be photographed driving to his office—was a major contributing factor to the curved dash Oldsmobile becoming the most talked-about new car in America.

———

The best-selling automobile in America was the Locomobile steamer, but the talk about it was not good. Amzi Barber thought cars were as uncomplicated and could be made as easily as asphalt. The Locomobile's gallon per mile was terrible water consumption; fixing that with a larger water tank increased fuel consumption. Reliability was a question mark. "I suppose she will settle down some to her conception of duty but just now her record is one of eternal and continuous breakdown," wrote Rudyard Kipling of his Locomobile, "...it is quite true she is noiseless but so is a corpse."

John Brisben Walker's Mobile was a far better car. In 1900, Frank Lambkin drove his all the way from Tarrytown to Chicago "without breakage, interruption or perceptible wear and tear of any kind." Doubtless Lambkin exaggerated. Still, after putting several thousand more miles on the car, he sold it for the full purchase price and bought a new one. By 1903, Virginia Earle was singing "My Mobile Gal" on Broadway in *The Belle of Bohemia*, which nicely advertised Walker's product but did not make up for the head start the Locomobile had enjoyed nor the guilt by association the Mobile suffered. By year's end, Barber's total production in Bridgeport was announced at 5,000 cars, Walker's in Tarrytown at only 600.

In addition to the dozens of other steam car builders in the field, the former partners now faced formidable competition. The Stanley brothers were back with a brand-new steamer that was leagues better than the design they had sold to Barber and Walker. Crying foul, the Locomobile and Mobile makers consulted their attorneys, but the legal hassle was short-lived and the Stanleys were in business in a new plant in Newton, Massachusetts.

Meanwhile, Amzi Barber had made a wise decision: to return to asphalt full time. The Locomobile presidency now belonged to son-in-law Samuel Todd Davis, Jr., who moved to set matters right. The steamer's construction was strengthened, and he contracted with the Overman Wheel Company for the larger boiler and water pump used on the Victor steamer, which Overman had introduced to critical acclaim at the 1900 New York Automobile Show. Overman and Locomobile merged soon afterward, and all of the former's steam-car-building machinery was moved to Bridgeport.

Moving into Overman's Chicopee Falls, Massachusetts plant was Narragansett race winner Andrew Lawrence Riker. A Columbia University law school graduate and the first president of the Society of Automotive Engineers, Riker was now recognized as one of the major talents in the burgeoning industry. Earlier, he had tried to sell a gasoline car design to the Electric Vehicle Company. Now he was hired to develop that car for Locomobile, Davis concluding that the steamer's reputation had become so dismal its long-term commercial success was doubtful. Better the Locomobile should be an all-new product. Riker's work was conducted in the utmost secrecy lest potential purchasers of the steamer be dissuaded from buying a lame duck.

As a further smokescreen, Davis hired George Eli Whitney as his chief engineer in Bridgeport. Grand-nephew of the cotton gin inventor, Whitney had launched a steamer business in Boston in 1896, but because no two cars he built were alike—he was forever experimenting—his profits as a producer were slim, and he began licensing manufacture instead. The McKay steamer, introduced like the Victor at the 1900 Madison Square Garden show, was a Whitney license car. Now, as a Locomobile employee, Whitney was encouraged to sue builders who had presumably adopted some of the Whitney's patented features but neglected to contact the inventor beforehand. In 1902, legal action commenced against the producers of the Grout, Prescott, and Milwaukee steamers, as well as the Stanley brothers.

The action was a bit late with regard to the Wisconsin company, which had declared bankruptcy two months earlier, but the remaining three fought back. In Passaic, New Jersey, the Prescott Automobile Manufacturing Company was gloating about its steamer's fine showing in local reliability contests and was not about to give up easily. In Orange, Massachusetts, the Grout brothers had the formidable resources of their family's New Home Sewing Machine Company to back them. And the Stanley twins never liked being told they couldn't do anything. Still, the lawsuits were nettlesome and took time away from production matters, which had been the Locomobile hope, of course. Once the Riker-designed gasoline Locomobile was on the market and the steamer discontinued, Whitney would be provided new employment designing equipment for the asphalt industry.

––––

In 1902, Ransom Olds sold 2,500 curved dash runabouts, a phenomenal achievement. Granted, at $650, the Oldsmobile was half the price of a Winton or Haynes-Apperson, but in a way, one was buying half as much. Both the Kokomo and Cleveland cars had two cylinders, could be had with accommodations for four, and were substantially built. The Olds runabout was a one-lunger and a two-seater, and hopefully the two people riding in it were of medium size because the lightness of the car and the 4-1/2 horsepower of its engine couldn't manage a lot of weight.

But it was a piquant little car, immediately identifiable by its toboggan-like dash. Most automakers had simply followed carriage practice and retained a straight dash in their runabouts. The curve of the Olds, its makers said, deflected air current downward over the radiator in the footboard, "thereby greatly assisting in the dispersion of the heat." Probably engineering had less to do with the design than the curved dash's individuality, which Olds protected by applying for and receiving a patent.

The Oldsmobile was priced a bit more than a dollar a pound. But it was not the cheapest car in America. That honor belonged to the Waltham Manufacturing Company in Massachusetts and its brand-new Orient Buckboard, which, sharing the curved dash's equation, weighed 400 pounds and carried a price tag of $375. Numerous gasoline, steam, and even a few electric runabouts—basically just carriages made horseless by putting an engine under the seat—were being marketed at or near the Oldsmobile price.

What made the curved dash so successful was its production by a company with an already solid ancillary business in engines, the enthusiastic support of the millionaire Smiths, and a very determined Ransom Olds.

Olds had also chosen wisely in his suppliers. Bearings for his curved dash were purchased from the Hyatt Roller Bearing Company of Newark, New Jersey, and wheels from the Weston-Mott Company in Utica, New York. Virtually everything else Olds needed he found closer to home in Detroit. Coachwork for his curved dash was supplied by the long-time C.R. Wilson Carriage Company and Byron F. "Barney" Everitt's relatively new but thriving body-building establishment. For the runabout's engines, the well-established Leland and Faulconer machine shop was contracted, as was a new but ambitious shop operated by two brothers with flaming red hair who were named Dodge. When Olds stopped by Detroit's largest sheet-metal producer with his radiator, Benjamin Briscoe thought that it was some sort of "antiquated band instrument." For most of these subcontractors, the work for Olds was their first in the automotive field. They would be heard from again.

Likewise, employment at Olds Motor Works became a virtual automotive college for many who went on to illustrious careers on their own or later elsewhere in the automotive industry. "Perhaps we had too many stars," Fred Smith commented wryly. But in 1902, the Olds factory's principal problem was keeping pace with sales, components pouring in one door, curved dash Oldsmobiles out another.

Two Olds employees did graduate from the company that year: Jonathan D. Maxwell (who had helped build the first Haynes-Apperson) and Charles King (who had wearied of his job in the Olds marine division).

First to exit was Maxwell. He had become acquainted with William A. Barbour, who advertised his Detroit Stove Works as the largest in the world and who, upon the recommendation of Detroit dealer William Metzger, was delighted to provide startup money for the organization of the Northern Manufacturing Company. The firm's purpose: to produce a better curved dash Oldsmobile. Plans in place, Maxwell asked Charlie King to join him in partnership. Their new car would be called the Silent Northern.

As for Haynes and the Appersons, their partnership was over. Most probably the principal reason was the Appersons' desire to strike out on their own, but an immediate repercussion was the Duryea-like matter of credit for the 1894 car. Some acrimony followed. It's safe to say that dinner invitations from Haynes to the Appersons, and vice versa, ceased. Both remained in Kokomo, building automobiles under their own names and trying to forget the other existed. For years, the placard accompanying the Pumpkinvine Pike car, which Haynes presented to the Smithsonian Institution in 1907, carried the legend that Elwood had "built" it. Needless to say, both Haynes and Apperson advertising claimed honors for America's first gasoline car.

Neither of the Duryeas vigorously contested the claim at this time. Charles remained struggling to make a profit in Reading; Frank meanwhile had made a fine deal for himself after interesting the J. Stevens Arms & Tool Company of Chicopee Falls, Massachusetts, in a prototype he had built. The armaments manufacturer purchased the nearby Overman factory for production of the new Stevens-Duryea, occupying only the top floor initially while Andrew Riker remained downstairs behind locked doors, designing the gasoline Locomobile. John Lambert, whose first gasoline car had preceded both the Haynes-Apperson and the Duryea, was now a manufacturer, too, although not of a car bearing his name. Instead, it was called the Union because, after years of trying, Lambert had finally found the wherewithal for production, courtesy of the chamber of commerce of Union City, Indiana.

Just about the only gasoline car builder in this saga who had not yet made it into production was Henry Ford.

CHAPTER 12

—■—

Great Minds, Good Maneuvers

"MY COMPANY WILL kick about me following racing," Henry Ford wrote to his brother in January 1902, "but they will get the advertising and I expect to make $ where I can't make ¢s at manufacturing." Ford's company did not see it that way. Unpleasant words were exchanged, and by March, Henry was out of the Henry Ford Company. His settlement was $900, which was viewed by William Murphy and friends as a small price to pay to rid themselves of an investment that wasn't paying off. The name "Henry Ford" would be excised. Ford backers were left with a car company that had no name and had manufactured no cars. Even the drawings for the proposed racer went with the man who had designed it. Crafty Henry engineered the better deal.

His next address was 81 Park Place. And his backer this time wanted to race. "Tom Cooper...has got the racing fever bad," commented Clara Ford. Bicycle champion of America in 1899, Cooper had met Ford at Grosse Pointe when the latter's spectacular racing debut against Winton relegated Cooper's cycling exhibition earlier that same day to only a line or two in the local press. In fact, it had been Cooper who, prior to the Ford/Winton match race, had joined the nervous driver for a couple of test laps to advise him about spots on the track that should be negotiated carefully. Cooper was impressed with Ford; Ford was impressed with Cooper's bank account, which was sufficient to underwrite the building of not one but two race cars, one apiece ostensibly.

Making the move from the old Henry Ford Company with Henry was Spider Huff, who had accompanied Ford in the Winton match race. Oliver Barthel was asked to come aboard, too, in exchange for 10 percent of Ford's future earnings, an offer he declined (and must have regretted to his dying day), choosing instead to remain with Murphy awhile and then accepting financial backing from several Detroit drugstore tycoons for the establishment of the Barthel Motor Company, which produced two cars and was gone by 1904.

Taking Barthel's place was a talented young toolmaker and draftsman whose mother loved Byron: Childe Harold Wills hated his name. He used his initials in business; friends called him Harold. Wills had joined Ford shortly before the upheaval and now remained for the same percentage of future earnings Barthel had turned down. Already Ford and Wills were fast friends. In a heatless office, they had worked together on the race car blueprints until their fingers were so numb they could no longer hold pencils, whereon they donned boxing gloves, punching playfully at each other until their hands were warm again. The amenities in their new surroundings were not much better.

"I must confess I did not feel much enthusiasm when I saw this mechanic's shop which was nothing more than a lean-to...," Roy Chapin remembered years later of his first visit to 81 Park Place. Desperation had taken him there. Following a visit to the C.R. Wilson plant in Detroit on coachwork business, Chapin was headed back to Lansing when the steering on his curved dash Oldsmobile gave out. Chapin's companion knew Ford's shop was less than a mile away, and the car limped there with frequent stops to kick the front wheels back into position. "We went in and found a slender man in blue overalls who came out to see what was wrong with our car," Chapin said. "As soon as he went to work, I saw that he was unquestionably an expert mechanic." Ford quickly fixed the broken spring in the steering, and as the curved dash drove off on its merry way, Chapin's companion waved back and yelled, "Much obliged, Henry." Only then was Chapin aware that his curved dash's savior was the racing hero of Grosse Pointe.

Later that summer, Chapin saw more of Henry Ford in Lansing when the latter visited Olds Motor Works several times to see what was going on.

Ford's visits to Lansing were telling. Unlike Cooper, who was interested in nothing else, Ford looked upon racing as a stepping-stone, an effective way to make money and a reputation to ensure success as a manufacturer once he made up his mind about what he wanted to manufacture. That on two occasions thus far the people providing financial backing had lost faith in him didn't matter at all; Ford had monumental faith in himself. Sharing that faith now, in addition to his always supportive wife, Clara, was Alexander Young Malcomson.

A prosperous coal merchant whose product had long kept Henry and Clara comfortable through the bitter Detroit winters, Malcomson had known Ford since his Edison days when Henry was a wholesale customer for the electrical company. As a motoring enthusiast and Winton owner, Malcomson became interested in the ideas of the Winton vanquisher. What Ford had in mind now was a runabout with twice the cylinders of the curved dash which, given the Oldsmobile's phenomenal success and the name Henry had already made for himself as a race driver, seemed destined to be a winner.

In August 1902, Malcomson and Ford signed their first agreement, whereby the former was to supply the latter with funds for the development of a production prototype, the partnership to be replaced by a corporation once production was imminent. Ford figured $3,500 was enough to fund the prototype stage. While that was a modest outlay, Malcomson insisted that the partnership be silent for the time being. To expand his business, the coal merchant had borrowed extensively from local banks and was worried what involvement in a risky venture like automaking, especially with someone whose track record had been so bad thus far, would do to his credit rating. Thus, a separate account was set up in the name of Malcomson's office manager, James Couzens, who was charged with signing all checks for Ford and keeping tabs on what he was doing.

So the little lean-to on Park Place became both a production studio and a competition shop. The race cars were finished first, one nicknamed the Arrow, the other 999 (after the record-breaking New York Central locomotive that had so impressed Ford at the Chicago world's fair in

1893). They were identical and ugly as sin: four cylinders, 1155 cubic inches, all mechanicals menacingly exposed. Although most powerful gasoline cars had steering wheels by now, Ford chose a tiller for his for safety reasons: if dust momentarily blinded a driver in a race, "he can look at this steering handle...if it is set straight across the machine he is all right..." A single seat was fitted: "One life to a car was enough," Henry said ominously.

Ford tried out 999 in September. The *Detroit Journal* described his appearance afterward: "His collar was yellow, his tie looked as though it had been cooked in lard, his shirt and clothes were splattered and smirched, while his face looked like a machinist's after twenty-four hours at his bench." If driving this beast was a dirty job, it was equally as terrifying. Henry said tackling Niagara Falls in a barrel would have been a mere excursion comparatively. Even Cooper had second thoughts about taking the tiller himself in competition.

The Grosse Point races were fast approaching, so a quick call was made to a man who knew the meaning of the word fear but didn't care: Berna E. "Barney" Oldfield. A champion cyclist and partner of Cooper's (their mutual investments included a coal mine in Colorado), Oldfield had no experience whatsoever in driving a race car. When he saw the two machines Ford had wrought, he likened them to "bedframes on wheels." But the promise of their speed was intoxicating to a man who lived for little else.

On October 25, at Grosse Pointe, Barney stuck a cigar in his mouth and glowered at the opposition. Five cars lined up for the five-lap five-miler. "This chariot may kill me," Barney bellowed, "but they will say afterwards that I was going like hell when she took me over the bank." He knew his only real opposition was Alexander Winton. The Winton conveniently developed mechanical problems and dropped out after the fourth lap; Oldfield romped home the easy victor. A star was born.

Interestingly, before the Grosse Pointe races, Henry Ford's apprehension had become twofold. The racers he had designed still scared the life out of him, but his concern shifted to the effect that their possibly less-than-sizzling performance might have on the Ford production car in development. For this reason, Henry sold his interest in both racers to Tom Cooper, which dismayed Henry's wife not at all. "He thinks too much of low down women to suit me," Clara had said. Ford virtually disavowed the racers until after Oldfield's Grosse Pointe performance with 999. Thereafter, Cooper and Barney teamed up to race both 999 and the Arrow (or "Red Devil," as the second car was sometimes touted) into the next season, with Barney's circling of a mile track in less than a minute the following June a first for a gasoline-powered car. Although both cars were owned by Cooper, Henry lost no opportunity to declare that, whatever their designations, they had been designed by Ford.

———

Meanwhile, matters at the erstwhile Henry Ford Company had taken a dramatic turn. Following Ford's and Barthel's departure, William Murphy and associates had concluded the automobile business was not for them and decided to sell off the building and its equipment. Called in to make an appraisal were Henry Leland and his son Wilfred.

To say that Henry Martyn Leland was patriarchal is rather like suggesting the Empire State Building is tall. Erect in carriage, he wore his sixty years handsomely with a well-trimmed shock of white hair, a meticulously groomed Vandyke beard, cleanly chiseled features, and affectingly kind eyes. Benevolent to his workers, Leland expected them to practice as he preached. He was opposed to drinking and smoking, and he brought his workforce together afternoons to hear him read from the Bible. He regarded work just as religiously. Precision was his doctrine.

During the Civil War, Leland had worked at the United States Armory in Springfield, Massachusetts, and following that for Samuel Colt in Hartford, Connecticut. For the Brown & Sharpe Manufacturing Company of Providence, Rhode Island, he developed a hair clipper that made barbering a more precise art. In 1890, Henry Leland arrived in Detroit. Son Wilfred had been studying medicine at Brown University but was persuaded that his father's calling was equally worthy. Well before the turn of the century, the machine shop of Leland and Faulconer (starting money was wealthy lumberman Robert C. Faulconer's) had established a reputation as the finest in Detroit.

When Olds Motor Works selected two suppliers for engines for its curved dash Oldsmobile, the choice could not have gone to two more dissimilar machine shops. On the one hand was the well-established and respected Leland and Faulconer, headed by the God-fearing, teetotaling Lelands. On the other were the red-haired, round-faced Dodge brothers, who had apprenticed in their father's small Port Huron (Michigan) foundry before moving to Detroit to find work and used the $7,500 royalty profit from a bicycle venture to set themselves up in business as machinists at the turn of the century. When John and Horace Dodge worked, they did it without Scripture reading breaks and often for 16 to 20 hours at a stretch, with maybe a catnap taken on a tool bench. When the Dodge brothers played, they played just as hard. They were big drinkers and consummate brawlers. Every saloon keeper in Detroit knew the Dodges, frequently to their sorrow. At one bar, John, wielding a revolver, persuaded the owner to dance while he smashed glasses against the bar mirror. However damaging their antics, the brothers were invariably sorry afterward and paid for their raucous good times after sobering up. The only similarity the Dodges shared with the Lelands was devotion. John and Horace were as close as brothers as Henry and Wilfred were as father and son.

Dissimilarity extended to the engines they built for Olds Motor Works. The Lelands became aware of the difference at the first automobile show that the energetic William Metzger organized in Detroit in 1901. At the Olds exhibit, Leland and Faulconer and Dodge engines were running side by side, their dials indicating identical speeds. "Father and I stood looking at the dials, and a stranger said, 'Look behind that dial,'" Wilfred remembered. "We saw a cheat brake holding our own engine down to the same speed as the unbraked Dodge-built engine. It amused us."

Some time later, the Lelands became aware that the stranger was Henry Ford, but for the moment, amusement turned to rumination. The robustly built Dodge engine developed 3.0 horsepower; the careful machining of the Leland version had resulted in 3.7. If closer tolerances made for a 23 percent increase, the Lelands reasoned, how much more power might result by redesigning the entire Olds engine for efficiency? The answer was 10.25 horsepower. Elated, the Lelands took their new engine to Fred Smith at Olds Motor Works. Initially, Smith was interested, but after computing the cost of retooling for the stronger chassis components necessary to cope with the increased power, he rejected the Leland engine. The change would delay production, production of 2,500 units for 1902 was not even close to the demand for the curved dash, and Ransom Olds was convinced the power his engine developed was quite satisfactory.

Fortuitously, a short while later, William Murphy needed an appraisal, and Leland was an obvious choice to make it. Although the Lelands vigorously denied it, Oliver Barthel, among others who had worked for the company, insisted that Leland Senior had earlier consulted with Murphy and board directors, the implication being that Henry Leland had helped ease Henry Ford out of his own company. Be that as it may, the assignment this time was specific.

The Lelands arrived at the former Ford plant, parked their curved dash Olds at a hitching post, and looked over the facility and its machinery. The father totted up some figures and then returned to Murphy's office, where associate Lemuel W. Bowen and directors Black (Clarence A.) and White (Albert E.F.) were waiting with Murphy to learn how badly they had been burned investing their money with Henry Ford. In addition to his careful appraisal, however, Leland brought his engine and advised the men that going out of business would be a big mistake. His single-cylinder unit was three times more powerful than the Olds, he said, and he could produce it at less cost than the engine being supplied the Lansing company. Murphy, Bowen, Black, and White were persuaded to try again. Leland and Faulconer would design a car for them and supply the engines. What to call this new venture was quickly decided, too. It would be named for the French explorer who had discovered Detroit two centuries earlier: Le Sieur Antoine de la Mothe Cadillac.

Capitalization of the new Cadillac Automobile Company was $300,000, the men who put in the money distributing executive positions among themselves. Henry Leland was given a seat on the board of directors. The first car was completed on October 17, 1902, and given its maiden test drive by Alanson P. Brush, the 24-year-old Leland and Faulconer engineer most responsible for its design. At $750, the runabout was attractively priced, and for $100 more, a tonneau version to carry two more passengers was available.

The new Cadillac could have sold itself, but among the really smart decisions made by the company was to hire the peripatetic William Metzger as sales manager. Already he had proven himself adept at organizing automobile shows (Detroit), automobile races (Grosse

Pointe), and automobile companies (Northern), and no dealer in the area was more successful in selling cars. He knew the competition—steamers, electrics, the Olds, the Winton—because he had represented them all. At the New York Automobile Show in January 1903, four Cadillacs were on display, and Metzger, accepting deposits of $10, took orders for 2,286 cars before declaring grandly midweek that the Cadillac was "sold out." At the show, Metzger signed up 21 dealers for the new car. "The Cadillac's a cinch," said one. By autumn, the dealership network had risen to nearly 50. Production that year totaled nearly 2,500 cars.

In April 1904, Cadillac wrote to its dealers: "We have had a fire, a bad one, but not as bad as reported, nor bad enough to put us out of business." Work came to a halt for a month and a half; nearly 1,500 deposits had to be returned. The downtime allowed the Cadillac company backers a chance to ponder. Thus far, engine deliveries from Leland and Faulconer had arrived precisely on time, but precision ended at the Cadillac factory door. Bottlenecks in assembly convinced Murphy and Bowen that the superintendents they had hired to produce their car knew little more about the subject than they did. On Christmas Eve, Henry Leland was summoned to the Cadillac office and informed that unless he took over, they would fold the operation. How serious that threat was is not known, but Leland couldn't chance losing the lucrative Cadillac engine contract, so he was stuck with both car and company. The Cadillac and Leland and Faulconer operations were merged into a new Cadillac Motor Car Company, with Henry Leland as general manager at a salary of $750 a month, and son Wilfred assistant treasurer under Murphy with similar take-home pay. Of the 15,000 company shares, the Lelands held under 3,000.

As they arrived to take control with their chief engineer Ernest Sweet, a Cadillac worker muttered, "Well, boys, our troubles are all over now. Here comes the Father, the Son and the Holy Ghost." Wilfred insisted that "it was not long before some of the Cadillac employees asked Father to read the Bible to them at their noon hour as he had been doing at Leland and Faulconer." The year after the fire saw Cadillac production top 4,000 cars.

———

Elsewhere in Detroit, Buick automobile production remained at one. David Dunbar Buick could have given Henry Ford lessons in procrastination and wore out nearly as many financial backers. But there was no deny-ing the man's talent. Prior to the turn of the century, Buick had devel-oped a method of affixing porcelain to cast iron and gave Americans the aesthetic nicety of white bathtubs. But by 1899, his plumbing busi-ness bored him, and he sold out to Standard Sanitary Manufacturing to organize Buick Auto-Vim and Power Company for the production of gasoline engines for farm and marine use. It is indicative of Buick's consummate inability as a businessman that, in 1902, he had to ask an acquaintance for a loan of $650 to finish the automobile he had started.

The acquaintance was Benjamin Briscoe, who had been supplying sheet metal to Buick since his plumbing days and who loved the business of business as much as Buick hated it. In 1901, when the bank holding the Briscoe Manufacturing Company accounts failed and recourse in Detroit proved abysmally slow, Ben had concluded "the place to get money was where money was," and talked J.P. Morgan in New York into investing $100,000. Although he didn't know what an automo-bile radiator was when Ransom Olds first showed him one, Briscoe was happy to launch into its manufacture, which was more challeng-ing than the garbage cans and lawn sprinklers that were his more usual products. Naturally, David Buick's proposal of involvement in an entire car was tantalizing, and Briscoe cheerfully handed over the $650 requested.

Soon Buick had $2,000 of Briscoe's money, and still there was no car. Patent papers had been filed for its valve-in-head engine, which was the work of Walter L. Marr, whose own automobile might have enjoyed commercial success had not the Illinois factory that had been contracted for its manufacture burned down. Factory fires would be routine in the industry for some time. Marr's tenure with Buick was off-again/on-again, and although his French-born colleague Eugene Richard stayed put, he became just as exasperated with Buick's dallying over details.

More exasperated was the man supplying the money. When Buick asked for another loan of $100 in May 1903, shortly after the first experimental car was completed, Briscoe agreed but only on the con-dition that the Buick Manufacturing Company metamorphose into the Buick Motor Company with a capital stock of $100,000 ($99,700 for Briscoe, $300 for Buick). Buick had the option to purchase the Briscoe stock by simply repaying his loans and the ultimatum that had he not done so within four months, Briscoe would take over the operation.

Actually, all Briscoe wanted was out. Earlier, he had asked Jonathan Maxwell to drop by Dave Buick's place to see what was going on. Reporting back, Maxwell carefully avoided saying anything "that could be construed as favorable or unfavorable about the Buick" but at the same time casually dropped the suggestion that maybe the two of them could "hook up" in the automobile business. By now, he wanted his own name on a car.

Compared to Buick, Maxwell's automotive background was impressive. A veteran of both Haynes-Apperson and Olds, Maxwell was at the moment allied—none too happily—with Charlie King in the manufacture of an Olds look-alike called the Silent Northern. The disenchantment was a matter of personalities. Maxwell's and King's didn't mesh. Maxwell had designed the Northern; King insisted that only his extensive revisions made the car run properly. Thus far, only 300 had been produced. Maxwell wanted out of his alliance as much as Briscoe did his. The curious deal the latter had negotiated with Buick was simply to get his money back or, barring that, to get the Buick shop, which Maxwell could use to get their joint venture going.

As it happened, neither the Buick nor the new Maxwell would be built in Buick's hometown of Detroit. Instead, James H. Whiting of the Flint Wagon Works purchased the whole of Buick's operation and moved it to Flint. Although Briscoe had been frustrated by Buick, he genuinely liked the man; Buick's repaying his loans with interest "justified my high opinion of his integrity." Ben worried aloud to his friend that the deal just concluded with Whiting was abjectly not in his favor, but Buick declared all he really wanted was a place to work and enough money with which to work.

Briscoe was thinking leagues bigger. When the substantial capital he asked for to get the Maxwell-Briscoe Motor Company off the ground was not available in Detroit, Ben returned to Wall Street and J.P. Morgan. The Morgan interests sold more than a quarter of a million dollars in bonds for the new company and, anxious to be close to where the money would be spent, insisted on Tarrytown as home for the new Maxwell. By 1904, John Brisben Walker had given up on the Mobile and was anxious to unload the factory. (The year following, he would sell *Cosmopolitan* magazine to William Randolph Hearst and retire to Colorado.) Tarrytown was fine with Ben Briscoe, too. Brother Frank would stay in Detroit to manage the Briscoe sheet-metal business. Jonathan Maxwell remained there only long enough to finish his production prototype in John Lauer's machine shop and then joined Ben. These native Midwesterners were now part of the East Coast automobile manufacturing establishment.

CHAPTER 13

Eastward, Ho!

UNLIKE MICHIGAN, where the focus was on the gasoline car almost exclusively, the East Coast was equally as prolific in electric and steam automobiles. New England particularly teemed with steamer manufacturers, the Stanleys most prominent among them. The Greater New York area had dozens of small electric producers. In Manhattan in 1902, a reporter assigned to the corner of 42nd Street and Fifth Avenue to take an American automobile census counted twenty steamers, twelve electrics, and eight gasoline cars passing by at midday.

But with the introduction of J. Frank Duryea's Stevens-Duryea and the reintroduction of the Locomobile as a gasoline car, among other high-powered and expensive automobiles, wealthy East Coast purchasers began regarding native products sporting internal combustion engines as equally meritorious to the European cars that they had imported at the turn of the century. Most Eastern makers, like the newly trans-planted Maxwell and Briscoe, continued to confine efforts to the pro-duction of one automobile and in one place. But not Albert Pope.

By the time the Maxwell was in production in Tarrytown, Colonel Pope, now sixty, had five factories humming. He never could think in other than multiples. Initially, his foray into automobile manufacture had been haphazard and to find quick lucrative use for idle factories of the America Bicycle Company. Now the Colonel had a plan. The Waverley electric continued in production in Indianapolis, but steam apparently turned him off because the Ohio factory previously producing the Toledo steamer was assigned a gasoline car. Obviously, the Colonel had a change of mind about the marketability of "sitting over an explosion" because his three other new cars had internal combustion engines, too.

Still, it was not the power of these cars that was paramount to Pope so much as their diversity to the pocketbook. His Pope-Tribune (built in Hagerstown, Maryland) was a heftier runabout than the curved dash Olds, sported shaft drive *vis-à-vis* its rival's often troublesome chain, and sold for the same $650. The Pope-Waverley ranged from $850 to $1,050. The Connecticut-built Pope-Hartford rose upwards of $1,000; the cheapest Pope-Toledo was $2,000. Most expensive was the Pope-Robinson produced in Hyde Park, Massachusetts, which was the only non-Pope-created car in his empire. After buying the Robinson Motor Vehicle Company, the Colonel kept John T. Robinson on as president and dispatched nephew Edward W. Pope to Hyde Park to serve as secretary-treasurer and to watch out for his interests.

Unlike his American Bicycle Company which was a bit late, this Pope idea was perhaps a little premature. And based as it was on the salvaged wreckage of the American Bicycle Company debacle, it would not have an easy birth. Further, with the sellout to the Whitney group, Pope had lost the estimable talents of George Day and Hiram Maxim. Most managerial posts in his new empire were held by relatives. The Colonel would have a passel of problems.

———

In Cleveland, Alexander Winton's annual sales were nearing the thousand mark, his car's price tag had climbed to $2,500, his newly completed factory complex was the largest in the nation, and he was finishing a lakefront mansion he would call Roseneath (after a similarly named Scottish town). Winton was just forty-two. He had one really big problem: the Selden patent. By now, he was fighting it alone. After contributing $6,500 to the Cleveland manufacturer's defense fund, the protective association organized in Buffalo had fallen apart. In court, Winton's lawyers cited 126 American, British, and

French patents dating from 1794 to 1881, argued forcefully that Selden's delaying tactics represented fraud, produced voluminous exhibits, took more than 2,000 pages of testimony, and spent a lot of Winton's money. But the Whitney syndicate had not been idle as all this was happening. Lawsuits were instituted against a few backyard builders and financially troubled firms powerless to respond, with the hope that these victories by default would strike the fear of Selden in other more prominent manufacturers.

The strategy worked. During the summer of 1902, Fred Smith visited Cleveland and reported back to Ransom Olds that Alexander Winton "is hot foot (or blows off that way) to wipe the Electric Vehicle Co. off the globe." But by that fall, word reached Cleveland that seven producers of gasoline cars had approached the Electric Vehicle Company regarding a Selden license. Winton's lawyers suggested he settle. Being forced to capitulate did not appeal to him, but neither did waging a losing battle that might also lose him his company. In November 1902, Winton approached the Electric Vehicle Company to talk settlement. The negotiations were in secret.

The year 1903 proved devastating for Winton. In September, the body of his wife, the mother of his six children, was discovered floating in Lake Erie, 75 feet below the cliff at Roseneath. The Wintons had been married 20 years. Whether the death was accident or suicide was discussed endlessly in Cleveland parlors.

———

Alexander Winton's best news that year had arrived earlier and from an unexpected source: Dr. H. Nelson Jackson, whom no one in Cleveland knew. A native of Vermont, Jackson was visiting San Francisco and, while enjoying a convivial evening and automobile talk at that city's University Club, heard someone say that nobody would ever drive an automobile across the continent. Given the prevailing condition of U.S. roads generally, and the utter lack of them in sections where the West remained wild and woolly, the prophesy was not outlandish. Indeed, the ever publicity-conscious Winton and his sales manager, Charlie Shanks, had attempted such a run from San Francisco in 1901, only to abandon it after eleven days. But Dr. Jackson bet the naysayer $50 that he could accomplish the trip in three months. The bet was immediately accepted.

Within days, Jackson had purchased the brand-new Winton of a Wells Fargo agent (for $500 above the purchase price) and secured the traveling companionship of Sewall K. Crocker (a Tacoma chauffeur and mechanic who also was visiting San Francisco at the time). The duo did not travel light. Stuffed into or strapped onto the Winton were waterproof sleeping bags, rubber mackintoshes, leather coats, canvas overalls, tin canteens with cooking utensils, a canvas bag for water, a fireman's ax and shovel, a compass, a telescope, a set of machinist's tools and spare parts, a vise and pair of jack screws, and a block and tackle. Also packed was some rather heavy artillery: a rifle, a shotgun, and two automatic pistols, for protection against outlaws and to secure game for food in sparsely populated areas. Two fishing rods were added for an occasional change of cuisine. Gasoline carried onboard totaled thirty-two gallons in two tanks, room was found somewhere for an extra five gallons of oil, and two spare tires were fitted over the hood. The Winton was not a pretty sight.

On May 23, the pair took off from San Francisco. Aware that on their aborted trip Winton and Shanks had headed straight east, Jackson and Crocker elected for a northern route that would take them into Oregon, then across Idaho, and into Wyoming. Barely had they made it into Oregon, however, than they were stalled for three days, waiting for the new tires to arrive for which they had wired Goodrich in San Francisco. The original rubber on their car was ruined already. For awhile, they had traveled with their wheels wrapped with rope, but that was not a solution to carry them all the way across America. With Idaho came heavy rain and mud. In one day, the block and tackle had to be used seventeen times, and the car made a grand total of six miles. On another occasion, a red-headed woman on a white horse gave them directions that took them more than fifty miles out of their way because she wanted them to pass her house since no one in her family had ever seen a car. In fact, in some of the hinterlands, people had never even heard of an automobile and thought the Winton was a small railroad locomotive that had somehow derailed and was searching madly for its tracks.

The going was relatively fun for awhile. In one small western town, Dr. Jackson brought a mascot aboard: a pit bull terrier he rescued from a dog fight, which he nicknamed Bud. Bud was provided a pair of goggles to protect his eyes from the dust; he took to wearing them as deftly as he did to traveling. In virtually every small Rocky Mountain town, the travelers approached and saloons emptied as ranchers, traders, cowboys, and Indians crowded into the street to witness the extraordinary sight of an automobile. But then, someplace in Wyoming, Jackson and Crocker found themselves completely deserted. No villages, no streams in which to fish, nothing flying overhead for dinner. A good supply of drinking water remained in the water bag, and alkali water could be used for the car. But after thirty-six hours without food, Jackson and Crocker began looking at Bud in a new light. Fortunately for the dog, the men didn't have the heart to make a meal of their mascot and decided they would all starve together if necessary. Just hours later, a shepherd was spotted.

It was in Wyoming, too, that Dr. Jackson learned he had competition in this mad drive of his. Two men in a Packard were already traveling east through Nevada. Two others, in a curved dash Oldsmobile, were about to leave San Francisco. Both cars were headed for New York. Now, in addition to his $50 bet, Jackson thought whimsically, he was involved in a race.

———

To the manufacturers, the treks were very serious. Both the Olds and the Packard trips were factory inspired. Aware by now of Jackson's attempt, the Winton company shipped him whatever parts he needed whenever he needed them. These three transcontinental runs, like all others for years, were started from the Pacific Coast because it was thought best to get through the worst first. West of Denver, the only roads or bridges were those built by the railroad, and the only map was that published by the Union Pacific. That an automobile could survive a trip from coast to coast suggested a spirit of adventure concomitant to the forging of a new frontier and spoke volumes about the worthiness of the vehicle that accomplished the feat. Thus it was that when news traveled across the Rockies about Dr. Jackson and his Winton, the makers of the Olds and Packard set plans in motion to assure that not all the transcontinental news in 1903 would go to the Cleveland manufacturer.

In fact, James Ward Packard had begun considering the trip even before Dr. Jackson's departure from San Francisco, probably as early as 1901 when he learned of the aborted Winton attempt. Because of Alexander Winton's arrogant "If you're so smart, build one yourself" rejoinder when Packard had complained about the Winton he owned, James Ward had to relish the divine revenge that would be his if the automobile he produced could accomplish what Winton's had not. Now the transcontinental trip would be among his last major achievements for the car that bore his name because Packard was no longer in control of his company.

The scenario was typical. James Ward Packard had enjoyed a critical success with his car. The 165 Packards that his Ohio Automobile Company turned out in Warren from 1899 to 1901 represented a modest profit but did not provide him the resources to expand production. So Packard began scouting for financial assistance. His approach to the Cleveland Chamber of Commerce brought a quick rebuff. "We already have the Winton factory," Packard was told, "and besides, we have just induced the largest clothes pin manufacturer in the country to build a local plant." Subsequently, Youngstown rubber millionaire Henry Wick, who had just spent $800 to have a car custom built for himself locally, offered Packard the money he needed, but by now, Detroit money was beckoning, too—a lot of it.

The first Detroit millionaire to become interested in the Packard was Henry B. Joy, whose family's fortune had been made with the railroad. Joy had become fascinated by the automobile when it was still called a horseless carriage. As early as November 1895, he wrote the Duryea Motor Wagon Company in Massachusetts about a purchase, and in Detroit, he talked with both Charlie King and Henry Ford, asking the latter if he could purchase one of his experimental cars. Henry said to "Wait for the next one, it would be a better car."

By the turn of the century, Joy apparently still had not purchased an automobile. On a trip to New York in 1901 with his brother-in-law Truman Newberry, he stopped at the Locomobile agency and asked for a demonstration. While the boiler was heating, the glass pressure gauge broke, showering Joy and Newberry with water and creating an immediate aversion to steamers for both men.

Their next stop along Broadway's "Automobile Row" was Adams and McMurtry, the New York agency for the Ohio Automobile Company. Two Packards sat at the curb outside. As the Detroiters approached, a horse-driven steam fire engine clanged past, and George Adams and Alden McMurtry rushed out of the showroom, cranked the two cars, and set off in pursuit. Joy was sold on the gasoline car from Warren.

Given the choice of "losing either my legs or my Packard," he would say, he wasn't sure which he would rather hold on to. In addition to becoming a Packard owner, Joy became an investor and encouraged his brother-in-law and other millionaire friends in Detroit—including the all-powerful McMillan family—to do likewise.

Soon James Ward Packard had twice as much money as he had been seeking, an extra $125,000 added to the till for the building of a factory in Detroit "when indications and conditions should warrant it." For Joy, that was already *fait accompli*; Warren did not fit into his plans. Architect Albert Kahn was summoned, the Ohio Automobile Company became the Packard Motor Car Company, and, although James Ward Packard told a local reporter that a move out of Warren was neither in the works nor being considered, he knew it had in essence happened already. Controlling interest in his company was in Detroit. The actual move was completed by October 10, 1903, when the last two freight car loads of office furniture left Warren. James Ward Packard remained company president, but it was obvious the title was strictly honorary.

———

Perhaps it was the weight of these impending events, in addition to the desire to one-up Winton, that energized Packard on the transcontinental trek. The Detroit group's indifference helped, too. Truman Newberry thought "the money could be spent more wisely on the back cover of *Collier's*," but there was no attempt from Detroit to call off the trip. "If this is the plan you want and...can make a lot of noise about it," Joy wrote, "go ahead."

The transcontinental trek was well planned in Warren. Earlier, Packard had suggested to Marius C. Krarup, editor of *The Automobile*, that notes kept of each day's run might be submitted with pictures for weekly progress reports to be published in the magazine. Krarup said he would like to make the trip himself, which was even better. Selected to drive the Packard was Tom Fetch, an automobile enthusiast, expert mechanic, and valued employee since Packard electric company days. A car, which would be nicknamed Old Pacific, was selected from factory stock and shipped to Harold W. Larzalere, the company agent on the West Coast.

The Packard's transcontinental gear was similar to the Winton's but with some substitutions and additions: a stout shovel, two six-by-twenty-foot canvas strips and heavy logging chains for mud and sand,

and rather more complete instrumentation including a compass, thermometer, barometer, gradiometer, and an extra cyclometer. A spare axle was packed, as well as a large umbrella for desert motoring—and the requisite .38. Better equipped than the Winton, the Packard would also be better supplied, with gasoline shipped ahead by rail to various prearranged destinations. (At one point, when the Cleveland car ran out of gasoline completely, Sewall Crocker had to walk twenty-nine miles to the next town to buy two gallons.) But if the factory-sponsored Packard trek, which began from San Francisco on June 20, was more organized than the Winton's, Fetch and Krarup would share many of their rivals' zany adventures. They arrived in Carson City, for example, shortly after a murder had been committed, and everybody in town, including the sheriff, left the scene of the crime for a look at the car. In another village, they arrived on a Sunday morning and left the church pastor preaching to rows of empty pews as the entire congregation hastened outside.

Shared, too, were many terrifying moments and frustrating days. Tom Fetch liked to talk afterwards of holding on for dear life all the way down mountains and at the bottom "spitting on the brake band to watch it bounce off." In Colorado, rain made the alkali roads like soap, which rendered steering impossible and resulted in the Packard sliding its way through much of the state, with Fetch behind the wheel, Krarup outside to guide the car. Or vice versa. As the transcontinentalists approached Ohio, James Ward Packard prepared a gala celebration. The Warren factory was closed for the day so his fellow workers could join Tom Fetch in Jefferson, his hometown, for a well-publicized reunion. The reunion that mattered the most to Tom was with his wife, whom he hadn't seen in two months. Warren itself was bypassed to avoid possible rumors that the stop there had been made for repairs, a decision prompted by the Winton trek. With their head start, Jackson and Crocker had already arrived in New York to monumental acclaim, followed by rumors variously alleging that two cars had been used for the trip or that the Winton had crossed the worst sections of the country comfortably ensconced in a railroad car. The Winton company was convinced this talk originated from jealous competitors in the industry and offered a $10,000 reward to anyone who could prove the accusations. An irate Dr. Jackson added $15,000 of his own money. The reward was never collected.

By mid-August, Old Pacific had reached Tarrytown, New York, for another gala celebration. Packard agents Adams and McMurtry, with the help of *The Automobile* and the Automobile Club of America, had arranged for two hundred cars to gather there to follow Old Pacific on its triumphal run into the city. The Packard arrived in Manhattan on the evening of August 21, sixty-one days after leaving San Francisco. That beat the Winton's time across the country by two days.

No speed record was set by the Oldsmobile, which started trekking east from San Francisco on July 1. Principally, this was because the little tiller-steered curved dash runabout had half the number of cylinders and about half the horsepower of its rivals, but drivers L.L. Whitman and Eugene Hammond had many more misadventures as well. And endured much worse weather. In the Midwest, it rained six times in five days; in one twenty-four-hour period, ten inches fell. After laying up for a week, waiting for the rains to subside, the Oldsmobile drivers decided to flounder on, regardless. "The Missouri spread itself with blatant egotism," Whitman wrote afterward; Council Bluffs needed only a few gondolas and the palace of Doges to become a Venice. "We took to a hill whenever we sighted one," he went on, "shook ourselves like water spaniels, baled out the machine and splashed on." A nicer splash was the celebration Ransom Olds arranged for the curved dash runabout's drivers in Michigan. Thirteen days later, the car arrived in New York. Total time for the trip had been seventy-three days, ten more than the Winton and twelve more than the Packard.

The time scarcely mattered. Breaking the transcontinental record would henceforth become a favorite activity among manufacturers. But in 1903, surviving the continent was the big news. For the Winton, the Packard, and the Oldsmobile, the achievement was glorious. And certainly better advertising than the back cover of *Collier's*.

CHAPTER 14

■

Licensing the Industry

IN NEW YORK CITY, George Day was as anxious over the Selden patent as Alexander Winton was in Cleveland. Winton's willingness to negotiate followed his being told seven gasoline-car manufacturers had approached the Electric Vehicle Company, of which Day was president, regarding a Selden license. This was true, but only by half. The approach to the manufacturers had been made quietly by Day himself through his associate Hermann Cuntz, the former Pope man who had first brought the Selden patent to the attention of William Collins Whitney. The Whitney syndicate favored pummeling the industry into submission; Day saw acquiescence as the wiser course. If gasoline car manufacturers could be persuaded that banding together under the Selden patent was in their best interests, a protracted and costly court fight—which Day regarded as counterproductive for both sides—could be avoided. Therefore, his overtures downplayed royalty and emphasized regulation. The Selden would be a protective license awarded the worthies of the industry and denied the wastrels. Day's gasoline-car community concept was favorably received until the subject of royalty was broached. The Whitney syndicate would accept no less than 5 percent on the retail price of each car sold. Every one of the manufacturers balked.

The initiative shifted. In early January 1903, a conference in Detroit was arranged by Fred Smith of Olds and Henry Joy of Packard. Attending were representatives of the Locomobile, Haynes, and Apperson companies, the Autocar Company (Ardmore, Pennsylvania), the Searchmont Automobile Company (Philadelphia), the Knox Automobile Company (Springfield, Massachusetts), the George N. Pierce Company (Buffalo, New York), and the Peerless Manufacturing Company of Cleveland. Secrets in the industry were no better kept then as now. Because Winton lawyers were known to be at the bargaining table with the Electric Vehicle Company, the Winton company was pointedly not invited. Neither Smith nor Joy could know how close the Cleveland company might be to selling out to the Selden patent holders.

The stated purpose for the Detroit get-together was to determine whether to fight or capitulate, although privately the two Detroit men had already agreed they would argue forcefully to negotiate instead, from the strength of a new organization to be known as the Manufacturers' Mutual Association. All present heartily endorsed that idea. The automakers were agreeable to a license but wanted control of the patent. As for the royalty, the Electric Vehicle Company was informed one-half of 1 percent would be happily paid, which the Whitney syndicate regarded as insulting.

Within a month, the Manufacturers' Mutual Association had met again, elected Smith as president and Joy as secretary-treasurer, and extracted $2,500 from each participating member for what Smith called a "fighting fund." Joy let Winton know what was going on. The showdown came in March, in the drawing room of the Whitney mansion on Fifth Avenue.

Of all the New York social grandees, William Collins Whitney was arguably the most grand, indulging, in Lucius Beebe's words, "the sybaritic taste of an authentic Corinthian as no American has ever done since." He was famous for the number of his estates, no fewer than ten. His city residence at the corner of Fifth Avenue and 68th Street was valued at two million turn-of-the-century dollars (the equivalent of more than $42 million today). Designed by Stanford White in Italian Renaissance style, it was regarded as one of the most magnificent city homes in America. Inside, rare tapestries competed with paintings of old masters, and the furnishings were royal in their splendor.

Calling an "informal" meeting in the midst of this palatial and unabashed opulence was, Fred Smith said afterward, "a strategic mistake of the enemy." Perhaps intimidation had not been the plan, but the manufacturers who attended thought so and didn't like it. In addition to Smith, they included Joy, Charles Clifton from Pierce, Samuel Davis from Locomobile, and Elihu H. Cutler, the no-nonsense New Englander from Knox.

Even before the meeting, Day had been informed that if its demands were not met, the Manufacturers' Mutual Association would join forces with Winton for a united opposition front. Riding up Fifth Avenue in an electric cab, the committee appointed Cutler to do all the talking, and Cutler scribbled their requirements on the back of a blue envelope: total royalty of 1-1/4 percent, 3/4 percent for the Electric Vehicle Company, and the remainder for the treasury of the manufacturers' association; the association to determine who would and would not be sued under the patent; likewise, the association to determine who would and would not be licensed. After the committee was ushered into Whitney's plush drawing room and the usual pleasantries were exchanged, Cutler announced the three-point proposal. Whitney lawyer Frederic Betts asked one committee member, then another, then another, to elaborate. They said nothing and turned to Cutler. To every entreaty for discussion, Cutler just read from the back of the blue envelope. It became monotonous after awhile. Whitney knew he was beaten.

On March 3, the Association of Licensed Automobile Manufacturers (A.L.A.M.) was formally established. Smith and Joy continued as president and secretary-treasurer, respectively. Barclay Warburton of Searchmont became vice president, and George Day general manager. An executive committee was appointed. Office space for the A.L.A.M. was secured at 7 East 42nd Street. Now the former belligerents of the Selden patent were its overseers and got together to determine whom to license and whom to sue. The first ten licenses were accorded the members of the Manufacturers' Mutual Association and the Electric Vehicle Company (which was producing a gasoline Columbia in addition to a variety of electrics). Invited to join next was Winton, with the understanding that the Cleveland company's legal expenses (as well as those of the firms that had contributed to the Winton defense fund) would be rebated by the Electric Vehicle Company from its own royalties. Victory was so sweet.

Now began the propaganda campaign. Full-page advertisements in all major city newspapers were directed to "manufacturers, dealers, importers, agents and users of gasoline automobiles," announcing the A.L.A.M. and its power: only licensed manufacturers were authorized to make or sell gasoline automobiles, and anyone else so doing was liable to prosecution for infringement. The immediate effect was a staggering apprehension throughout the rest of the industry. Looking on the bright side, *Motor World* commented, "Happy the man who makes or sells only steamers or electrics or the parts thereof! There is no Selden patent or ghost of other patents to cause him to shudder by day or to see bugaboos by night."

By early summer of 1903, seventeen more manufacturers had been invited into the A.L.A.M. Among them were Colonel Pope and Frank Duryea; the Cadillac and Northern companies in Detroit; H.H. Franklin of Syracuse and E.R. Thomas of Buffalo, New York; U.S. Long Distance and Commercial, both from Jersey City, New Jersey; from Ohio, the makers of the Yale in Toledo and the Elmore in Clyde; Waltham in Massachusetts; and the importing firm of Smith & Mabley in New York City. One invitation had been turned down.

Thomas Jeffery wanted nothing to do with the A.L.A.M. No one abhorred monopolies more than the avuncular maker of the Rambler automobile in Wisconsin. During his bicycle days, Jeffery and his partner Philip Gormully had been among the few to successfully challenge Pope patents in the courts. Following his partner's death, Jeffery had sold out to Pope's American Bicycle Company, partly because he had no inclination to compete against a conglomerate whose objective was the general elimination of competition in the cycle field—and most especially because the "princely sum" offered was sufficient to launch him into the automobile business. His timing couldn't have been better. Within months, the gigantic building in Kenosha that had been home to the Sterling bicycle was offered for sale at a bargain $65,000. There, with his son Charles, Jeffery had set up the best-equipped automobile plant in the industry, and one of the first that would bring manufacture of most of the automobile's component parts under one roof.

The $750 Rambler runabout was an instant success in 1902. "Rare value for the money," *Motor World* reported. Said *Motor Age*, "it may be taken as certain that in the machine...Mr. Jeffery has embodied all that is good." An enthusiastic owner wrote that "it starts immediately, runs like a jackrabbit and stops only at our will." First-year sales of 1,500 Ramblers were exceeded in the gasoline car field only by Ransom Olds' curved dash. The courtship of Jeffery by the A.L.A.M. was ardent but unavailing. Jeffery stood firm and issued a press release stating that his company would protect Rambler purchasers from any action by the Selden patent holders.

Daunted by the idea of challenging a manufacturer in court who had a history of success in such litigation, the A.L.A.M. chose to ignore Jeffery and take on a relative newcomer who would be easier to handle and hopefully quicker to knuckle under. Henry Ford hadn't really given the A.L.A.M. any choice.

———

In November 1902, less than a month after Barney Oldfield's triumph at the Grosse Pointe track with 999, Alexander Malcomson and Henry Ford established the Ford & Malcomson Company Ltd. Of its 15,000 shares, the partners would take 6,900 as payment for everything accomplished up to that time plus an additional 350 shares for a $3,500 cash investment. Remaining to be sold were 7,750 shares, but to whom? A month later, Malcomson arranged for a Mack Avenue wagon shop to be converted into an assembly plant for the forthcoming arrival of all necessary components for production, but from whom?

Parts suppliers were contracted first, and first to come aboard in February 1903 were John and Horace Dodge. To do so, the brothers had to forego renewing their association with Olds, for whom they were now building transmissions, or entering a new one with Charlie King and Northern. Hindsight would vindicate the wisdom of casting their fortunes with Ford, but at the time, they were taking a risk that ostensibly their business could ill afford. All of their money was tied up in the machine shop. Two years earlier, when John's first wife, Ivy, had died, his aunts lent him the money to bury her. The following year, Horace borrowed two dollars for a marriage license, married Anna Thomson on his lunch break, and then went back to work.

The Dodges liked risks, had known Ford for some time, and believed he was a potentially better long-term proposition than Olds or Northern. The deal arranged was a good one for Henry and a reassuring one for the brothers: 650 rolling chassis to be supplied by the Dodges at $250 each, with $10,000 to be provided the brothers in two increments within the next two months for their startup expenses, and another $5,000 due when the first chassis were delivered to Mack Avenue. That agreement signed, Ford and Malcomson sallied forth to sign contracts with body, tire, and wheel suppliers. The completed two-cylinder Ford car was slated to sell for $750 in runabout form, with an extra $100 for a tonneau seating two more passengers. With component costs fixed and assembly costs estimated, Jim Couzens figured the resulting profit margin would be $200 and $150, respectively. That boded well.

Contracts were going out faster than capital was coming in, unfortunately. Henry Ford's performance as an automobile producer thus far was hardly inviting to potential investors. Although doors were not slammed in Malcomson's face, they weren't opened very wide either. For a while, he hoped to link up with the Daisy Air Rifle Company in Plymouth, suggesting that the car be called a Daisy as inducement. Henry wouldn't stand for that, and the deal fell through anyway because the Daisy company charter disallowed outside investments. When the first $5,000 was due to the Dodges on March 15, Couzens didn't have the funds to pay it. The brothers, perhaps ruing their penchant for risk taking, demanded their money, as Couzens was well aware they would the next $5,000 a month later. Clearly, something had to be done.

To the rescue came John S. Gray—uncle to Malcomson, erstwhile candy tycoon, and now head of the German-American Bank—who exchanged the needed $10,000 plus an additional $500 for 105 shares of stock and the Ford company presidency. Gray had little choice. Malcomson had borrowed heavily from the German-American Bank to expand his coal business, and if he were unable to repay that loan, the bank would be in trouble. Helping a relative in crisis may have been part of Gray's motivation, too. Certainly he had no love for the automobile. Until his death in 1906, the Ford Motor Company president would remain convinced that "this business cannot last"—and the only reason he didn't sell his stock was his conscientious unwillingness to unload it on friends.

After receiving their initial $10,000 in cash, the Dodges' further grumblings were quieted by an agreement that brought them the same amount in stock, $7,000 being written off immediately for the expenses accrued in buying material to fulfill the Ford contract, the remaining $3,000 for which they gave a note due in six months, providing them a cushion of time to determine whether the company would succeed or fail. But that was small change. Retooling for Ford production had cost the brothers upwards of $60,000, so the future of the Dodges' machine shop was inextricably linked to Henry's performance.

By June 1903, finally, matters seemed to be falling into place. On June 16, incorporation papers were filed in Lansing for the Ford Motor Company, absorbing Ford & Malcomson and leaving by the wayside the Fordmobile Company, Ltd. Selling the Ford as Olds did with "mobile" tacked on the end had been tried first, an idea Henry hadn't liked much better than calling his car a Daisy. His discomfiture was brief. After a few advertisements touting the Fordmobile, the name was unceremoniously dropped for Model A Ford.

Investors in the Ford Motor Company numbered twelve, Malcomson and Ford sharing 520 of the 1,000 shares of stock, with the remainder divided among the Dodge brothers, Gray, and assorted folks rounded up by Malcomson. Charles J. Woodall was a clerk in Malcomson's coal company, Vernon Fry managed the notions department of a Detroit store and was a cousin, lawyers John Anderson and Horace H. Rackham had the Malcomson Fuel Company as their major client, and Albert Strelow held the lease on the Mack Avenue building in which the Fords would be assembled. Their arms didn't have to be twisted too hard. Coming aboard with personal funds because he actually had faith in Ford's car was Charles H. Bennett, vice president of Daisy Air Rifle. The most enthusiastic was Malcomson alum Jim Couzens, who had told Anderson that he intended to "beg, borrow or steal" all the money he could to invest. That amounted to $2,500, a thousand in cash ($100 of that his sister Rosetta's), and a note for the rest, which both Malcomson and Ford endorsed.

Already Couzens had chosen his favorite between the two majority stockholders. Driving together from the incorporation meeting, Henry turned to him and said, "Jim, what do you think we ought to ask those fellows in the way of salary?" A week later, at the election of officers, Ford's compensation was fixed at $3,000 per year, and Couzens' at $2,500. For the two men, it was us-against-them thereafter. Ford and Couzens were running the business; the rest of "those fellows" were just along for the ride.

Of the $100,000 in Ford stock issued, only $28,000 was paid in cash and not all of it immediately. On June 26, the Ford Motor Company bank balance was $14,500. At the beginning of July, chassis from the

Dodge works began arriving by horse-drawn wagons, to be united with wheels and bodies already delivered. The small crew labored fever- ishly. "We would work our hearts out to get fifteen out a day," one of the dozen Ford workers remembered. But no one worked harder than Ford and Couzens: their schedules from the outset had been twelve hours per day, often a seven-day week—Ford in the shop and Couzens in the office. By the morning of July 11, expenses and parts payments had whittled the Ford checkbook down to $223.65. Not one Ford had been sold. By afternoon, Strelow's $5,000 check covering his stock subscription arrived, however, and four days later, so did an $850 check from a Chicago dentist ordering the first Ford car. By month's end, further orders increased the Ford treasury to $3,831.77, and all out- standing bills were paid.

On July 26, as Ford, Couzens, engineer Harold Wills, and a few other workers loaded the first batch of Fords into freight cars bound for points south and east, someone brought that day's *Detroit News* with its full- page A.L.A.M. advertisement announcing the illegality of what mak- ers like Ford were doing. Both Ford and Couzens were furious.

———

Earlier, Ford had asked Fred Smith about a license, Smith responding "not as the exalted president of the A.L.A.M. but as one man to another" that he did not think a Ford application "at that moment would be con- sidered favorably." The implication was that because Ford had not proceeded into sustained production in two previous attempts, there was no reason for the A.L.A.M. to believe he would succeed any better on the third. John Gray had insisted on another meeting, putting forth the Ford case himself this time. Although he had "a guilty feeling of 'sassing' my elders," Smith didn't budge. Further, he allowed that Ford's operation was nothing more than an "assemblage plant," which had to irritate Henry, especially because that comment neatly side- stepped the fact that no A.L.A.M. licensee had begun by manufactur- ing all of its parts nor were any of them yet wholly self-sufficient.

On July 28, Ford responded to the A.L.A.M. *News* ad with one of his own in the *Free Press*, declaring (like Jeffery) that he would protect Ford owners against prosecution. The ad quoted Ralzemond A. Parker, the most illustrious of Detroit's patent lawyers, regarding the worth- lessness of Selden's 1895 patent, pre-dated Henry Ford's first car three years to 1893, noted his race victory over Winton and Oldfield's track record on 999, and ended with the defiant note, "We have always been winners."

A month and a half later, Gray called stockholders into his office to hear Parker expound further on the Selden patent. The attorney was sure it could be beaten. Although Gray had little faith in the Ford business, the aging tycoon had fond memories of the vigorous battle he waged years earlier in the glucose patent wars and rather liked the idea of having a last hurrah in court. Ford and Couzens were enthusiastic, too. Since production began, they had had just one falling out, in early August when a complaint arrived from Pittsburgh, to be followed by a few others, that the Ford would not climb hills. Henry was all for stopping shipments until the problem was remedied, but Jim Couzens informed him that "you stop shipping and we go bankrupt...discounting the bills of lading is all that stands between us and that right now." Couzens won the argument. Mechanics were dispatched to the field to fix cars already sold, while Ford worked out a solution using the crude ramp to the second floor of the Mack Avenue assembly building as his proving ground. On the matter of Selden, the two men were in solid agreement; they had already told Smith where he and his associates could go with the patent. The Ford Motor Company assault was stepped up in a flurry of full-page ads. Ford even told a Detroit reporter that he would give the A.L.A.M. people $1,000 if they would advertise his business by commencing suit against him.

The A.L.A.M. was mortified. Its national propaganda campaign had been aimed at a bloodless victory, quick compliance through artful intimidation. Privately, many of the Selden licensees shared Ford's opinion of the patent. Now the A.L.A.M.'s back was to the wall. Unless Ford was taken to court, the new association would be laughed out of business. A humiliated Henry Joy threatened to withdraw Packard from the A.L.A.M. unless something was done immediately.

On October 23, Henry Ford was informed that a suit against C.A. Duerr (his New York agent) and the Ford Motor Company had been lodged in the U.S. Circuit Court for the Southern District of New York, that venue chosen, as previously, both because of New York's position in the world of trade and because it was the debarkation point for most foreign automobiles arriving in this country. Within three months, further suits were filed against the O.J. Gude Company (one of the first purchasers of a Ford in New York), the French firm of Panhard et Levasseur (and its New York branch manager), John Wanamaker (who had succeeded Duerr as the Ford New York agency), and Henry and Albert C. Neubauer (Dutch importers of French cars in the city). Subsequently, these five separate actions were consolidated into two cases: Ford and foreign. Henry made sure his was the most talked about.

———

Even before that, Ford was page one news again. Barney Oldfield was the reason. Shortly after Ford's first anti-Selden ad with its "We are always winners" coda, Oldfield had left Cooper to race for Alexander Winton. No soul-searching went into his decision. Barney's only allegiance was to speed and having a good time. "I'd rather be dead than broke," he said often—and, like the Dodge brothers, he required a lot of cash to pay for his carousing. Winton offered a sweet deal: a more powerful car than the Ford, a $2,500 retainer, expenses, and all the prize money he could win. Oldfield's defection proved a godsend for Ford. Malcomson had decreed that a four-cylinder $2,000 model be added to the Ford line, which Henry, who had no desire to enter that high-priced a market, abhorred. Still, with the car a reality, he had to find a way to sell it, as well as prove the continuing truth of his "We are always winners" boast.

The two problems were solved with one race car. Ford resuscitated the old Arrow, whose battered remains had come to rest in Detroit after a race accident earlier that year, and overhauled its four-cylinder engine, which he said was substantially identical to that of the new $2,000 car. Because Oldfield had made the name 999 more famous than Arrow, Henry blithely provided the refurbished car the 999 designation and announced that he planned to take on the world land speed record, which since the turn of the century had been broken a dozen times and always by French cars. Because Michigan roads were not as worthy as those on the Continent, Ford chose January 1904 and frozen Lake St. Clair for his try.

Shortly after New Year's, he bundled up Clara and young Edsel, summoned engineer Wills and mechanic Spider Huff, and set off for Anchor Bay. Snow was scraped and the ice cindered over a four-mile straight-away course. Spider laid himself over the hulk of 999, Henry settled himself into the driver's seat, and they were off. The surface was none too smooth. "At every fissure the car leaped into the air. I never knew how it was coming down," Henry said. "When I wasn't in the air I was skidding." But they stayed the course, Spider substituting his foot whenever Henry's bounced off the throttle. The run ended in a snowbank because of a breakdown in communication. Puffing into a rubber hose leading into the gas tank was one of Spider's duties; one kick from Henry signified "blow harder," and two kicks meant "stop." In his excitement, Spider forgot the code and the more Henry kicked the harder he blew. It didn't matter. The car and its occupants emerged unscathed—and with the straight-away mile accomplished in 36 seconds flat for 100 miles per hour. At a victory dinner that night at the Hotel Chesterfield, the entree was muskrat, which Henry declared delicious, although few others at that table agreed.

The official run was made several days later, with American Automobile Association (A.A.A.) timers on hand. (Begun as an amalgam of local automobile clubs, the A.A.A. was the democratic answer to the elitist Automobile Club of America, although the earlier organization remained powerful enough to ensure that the A.A.A.'s first president was A.C.A. man Winthrop E. Scarritt.) Getting their signals straight this time, Henry and Spider ran the mile in 39.4 seconds for 91.37 miles per hour, which was nearly 7 miles per hour faster than the previous French mark. The A.A.A. debated awhile whether a run on frozen water constituted a "land" speed record, but ultimately certified the speed. European officialdom would not recognize the Ford achievement, but Henry didn't care about that. Convincing America of the merits of his car had been his sole aim. By the end of 1904, Ford production stood at 1,700 cars, and he was preparing to challenge the Rambler and the Cadillac for the number two spot in the industry.

———

In January 1904, as Ford raced on the ice at Lake St. Clair, Ransom Eli Olds walked out the door of Olds Motor Works in Lansing. "It was a hard thing for me when I had been manager since 1885," he wrote, "besides working day and night to develop the business to a wonderful success."

And the business *was* a wonderful success. The 5,500 curved dash runabouts produced in 1904 would be more than the Cadillac and Rambler output combined, and the car was soon to be forever immortalized as Vincent Bryan and Gus Edwards tunefully invited Lucille for a ride "In My Merry Oldsmobile."

However, matters had been anything but merry in the front office of Olds Motor Works for some time. First, Fred Smith decreed the company should focus on production of larger, more luxurious models, which sorely exercised Olds, who was no more amenable than Henry Ford to being told what cars should be built. Second, Olds opposed the entry of his company into the A.L.A.M., which sorely exercised Smith because he had been instrumental in the organization's founding. Third, Smith thought strict adherence to quality control was worthy preventive medicine; Olds' philosophy tended to be produce first and wait for customer complaints later. The two men seemed not to agree on anything. Geography soothed tempers for awhile; Olds had moved back to Lansing, while Smith remained in Detroit. But when the latter man set up an experimental engineering department, whose first project was a spring setup to improve on the version Olds had developed, Ransom hit the ceiling. "I have had all I want of this treatment," he advised Smith, reminding him that overall company management was his province. Well, not exactly. Although the company was called Olds, controlling interest belonged to the Smiths. In a power play, Ransom had no power to play with.

In exchange for leaving quietly, the Smiths promised to assist Olds in disposing of his company stock at a favorable price. An argument followed on this, but Olds did leave a very rich man. And he kept his side of the bargain; "for certain reasons" was the only phrase he used officially to describe his retirement from Olds Motor Works. Privately, the feelings were bitter on both sides. Like Haynes and the Appersons, Olds and the Smiths studiously avoided public mention of the other ever after.

Within seven months, Ransom Olds was back in the automobile business in Lansing. Having learned a lesson well, Olds not only was president and general manager of this new venture but also controlled 52 percent of the stock. To help, he latched onto numerous Olds Motor Works people, which had to irritate the Smiths, although they were helpless to do anything about that but watch. They leaped into action, however, upon learning that the proposed name of this new venture was the R.E. Olds Company. The use of the name Olds, the Smiths mentioned pointedly, was an infringement of the right sold to them in

January. Ransom doubted that but was not anxious to begin his new business under the specter of a possible injunction. He had not sold the Smiths his initials. So, the Reo Motor Car Company was born. Its founder had no intention of joining the A.L.A.M. But then, he had no expectation of being invited either.

CHAPTER 15

Hopping on the Bandwagon

THAT THE ASSOCIATION of Licensed Automobile Manufacturers thought it could control the industry was amusing. By 1904, A.L.A.M. member companies numbered thirty-one. Hundreds more were producing gasoline cars. Not since the gold rush had so many been lured so quickly by the promise of fame and fortune. Not a day passed when someone somewhere did not tread stalwartly into the automobile field.

Experience as an engine builder, machinist, blacksmith, or bicycle or wagon maker, while no guarantee of success, did provide a helpful background from which to start. But seemingly the manufacture of anything was deemed sufficient qualification to give this new field a whirl. Automobiles arrived from the E.T. Burrowes Company, makers of house screens in Portland, Maine; from the United Shirt & Collar Company of Troy, New York; from the incubator-producing Hiawatha Manufacturing Company of Kansas; from Reid Manufacturing of Detroit, makers of showcases and store furnishings; from the Bonebrake hardware company of El Reno, Oklahoma; and from the makers of the Crompton loom in Worcester, Massachusetts, and the

Walterscheid pump in Wichita, Kansas. Automobile companies were also begun by Simon Mayer and Ross Phillips, policemen respectively from Chicago and Los Angeles; Oscar J. Friedman, a florist from the Windy City; William Forest Meserve, a watchmaker from Canobie Lake, New Hampshire; and John F. Klink, a photographer from Dansville, New York.

Not surprisingly, a background on rails persuaded many to try their hand at vehicles for the road, among them John Parsons, a locomotive engineer for the Pennsylvania Railroad from Wilmington, Delaware; O.E. Glugler, superintendent of the Union Pacific shops in Omaha, Nebraska; James E. Belger, baggage master at the Natick railroad station in Massachusetts; and George N. Randall, a trolley-car conductor from Meadville, Pennsylvania. Doctors, who took to motoring earlier and more enthusiastically than those in any other profession, occasionally tried a sideline business in automobiles, with the view that patients were a likely market. The Reverend Hiram Frantz of Cherryville, Pennsylvania, thought he could secure investors aplenty from his congregation. None of these efforts was long-lived, but dubious origin was not the reason. In the manufacturing past of two prestigious A.L.A.M. companies were clothes wringers (Peerless of Cleveland) and birdcages (Pierce of Buffalo).

Public awareness of the automobile via shows and competitions, or simply one showing up in a neighbor's stable, created a demand for the vehicles. Ostensibly, getting into the business was a breeze, the only requirement a little money, a little mechanical ability, and a place to put the car together. The Climax from New Salem, Massachusetts, was initially assembled in a henhouse. The Dixie from Houston, Texas, was built in a church. One day in 1901, Walter W. Schultz, president of the farm-implement-producing Wayne Works of Richmond, Indiana, walked into his tool room and asked engineer Jack St. John to build an automobile because "everyone else is."

The necessary components were readily available: engines from stationary and marine producers, bodies and wheels from carriage makers, other parts from metal- and wood-working shops, and hardware from a hardware store. Also readily available were bicycle dealers, blacksmiths, farm machinery salesmen, and others anxious to sell automobiles. Notice in the trade press of "live agents wanted" usually brought a flood of queries. Parts for an automobile were purchased on thirty to ninety days credit; an automobile was sold to the purchaser or dealer for cash. Requiring advances could take care of a small payroll. "Dealer deposits often paid half the sum necessary to bring out a full year's production," Roy Chapin of Olds commented, "and if the assembling were efficiently directed, drafts against the finished cars could be cashed as rapidly as the bills from parts makers came in." The trick was to master the timing, which, as the Ford Motor Company bank balance in July 1903 indicated, wasn't always easy.

With few exceptions, the entire industry was undercapitalized during these early years. The lure of an operation that could virtually finance itself was irresistible. Because it was possible to get one's feet wet so simply, many makers plunged in and were soon up to their necks in trouble.

The period between grand announcement of a new automobile and the arrival of the sheriff was often painfully short. "We could sell one thousand cars in three months if we could make them," American Populaire boasted in March 1904; eleven months later, its Sanford factory had been turned into a weaving shed by the Maine Alpaca Company. In Fairmount, Indiana, all William Carey left to be divvied up among his creditors was one partially completed automobile.

Purchasers could be as testy as creditors. When the runabout that Nels J. Herby said would do 30 miles per hour managed only 24, the car's owner successfully sued the Oakland, California, builder for fraud. New York socialite James L. Breese graciously waited two months past the promised delivery date for his American De Dion, then had the sheriff visit the Brooklyn factory.*

Even adequate capital, or its semblance, was no key to success. Philo Remington, of the arms and typewriter family, had to declare his automobile venture "financially embarrassed" within two years. Wellington P. Kidder, inventor of the Kidder press and the Wellington and Franklin

---

* Some $150,000 had been invested in this venture to produce a U.S. version of the popular French car. Among the problems apparently were the unforeseen delays necessary to beef up the little voiturettes to withstand the pounding of American roads. De Dion engines had been successfully used by a number of U.S. manufacturers (Pierce and Peerless among them) to enter the industry.

typewriters, quit after making only three cars. Millionaire sportsman Harry Harkness thought better of establishing an automobile company in Flushing, New York, very soon after he got the idea. The "fire balloon" from nearby Coney Island that landed on the roof of the Vehicle Equipment Company provided sugar king William F. Havemeyer the opportunity to suggest that his two sons find something else to do. Ardent automobilists Albert Bostwick and Winthrop Scarritt (A.C.A. and A.A.A. presidents, respectively) were but two of the wealthy backers of the Pan-American Motor Company of Mamaroneck, New York, that took over the Gasmobile in 1902. By 1903, all concerned had concluded they would rather drive than make. Automobiles were not predictable. Even the best of them broke down occasionally, which might be a tolerable nuisance to an enthusiast owner who could turn the matter over to his chauffeur, but became an aggravating problem for the enthusiast turned manufacturer who had to deal with the complaints.

At the turn of the century, there were 76 million people in the United States. About 4,000 were automobile owners. The Census Bureau lumped motor vehicles with "miscellaneous." By 1904, total automobile ownership had risen by perhaps 40,000, a healthy percentage increase but one that did not appreciably change the "miscellaneous" character of the industry. Ford president Gray's dubious regard for the future of the automobile was not a minority opinion. Cars were generally thought of as novelty items, and for many manufacturers, the novelty wore off quickly. "The stockholders of the Star Automobile Company have decided that the automobile business is not the bonanza that they believed it to be..." was the report from Cleveland in 1903. "The company built about twenty cars and nearly all of these have been disposed of at fair prices, so that the company comes out about even."

Even securing the capital to proceed that far eluded many makers. In 1906, Walter F. Flynn tried to persuade fellow townsman Henry Wick to invest in the manufacture of his Falcon, but the Youngstown rubber millionaire, who earlier offered to back James Ward Packard, had experienced so many problems by now with his custom-built $8,000 car that he had sworn off automobiles for the moment. Capital to expand was often just as illusory. Elsewhere in Ohio, the Geneva Automobile & Manufacturing Company built about twenty steamers per year beginning in 1901, but received the same cold shoulder Packard had in trying to secure capital in Cleveland. "Gents—," H.E.

De Loura wrote *Cycle and Automobile Trade Journal* in March 1902 from Rochester, New York, "I am desirous of finding some city that is willing to donate a site and building for me to move my factory into." Apparently, there was a hint of interest from Iowa because for the next year, De Loura reported in from Ottumwa, Ft. Madison, Perry, and Ft. Dodge—and then was heard from no more. October 1901 had found William E. Taft of Boston touring the state of Massachusetts and disposing of enough stock at fifty cents per share to set up shop in a former bicycle plant in Westboro, but it was in the hands of the mortgagee by February 1902.

In St. Louis, Missouri, the automotive venture of Semple and Ashley Scott ran aground when backer Charles Drummond lost interest soon after the purchase of a plant and equipment. In Hudson, Massachusetts, successful machinists Frank Knight and his son George found that the earlier demise of the Marlboro steam car produced by Orrin Walker made it impossible for them to secure financing in the area. "A New York capitalist who undertook to raise $50,000 in the funds failed to connect," John Leach wrote wistfully in 1901 of his Everett, Massachusetts, venture, "and the works have been closed until the necessary capital can be secured." It never was. Frank Merrill's bold plan to raise $300,000 in Springfield, Massachusetts, for his Veerac ("valveless explosion every revolution air cooled") was a quick fizzle in 1905, as earlier had been the plan of the Western Automobile Company of Chicago to talk the citizens of Stevens Point, Wisconsin, out of $200,000 to locate there. Even in Michigan, when the Lansing Business Men's Association lured Olds Motor Works back to that city following its Detroit fire, local enthusiasm was lukewarm at best—despite the solid Olds gas engine business and the prestige of the super-wealthy Smiths. Of the $5,200 necessary to buy land for the factory, the Business Men's Association was able to raise only $1,800 and had to borrow the rest.

Factory fires eliminated many automobile companies, as did the incendiary words exchanged among the people behind automobile companies. Quarreling in the nascent automobile industry reached epidemic proportions. In addition to the Duryeas, Haynes and the Appersons, Ford and Malcomson, King and Maxwell, and Olds and the Smiths, among others thus far mentioned, arguments spelled *finis* for the partnerships responsible for the Binney & Burnham steamer in Boston and the Hammer-Sommer gasoline car in Detroit. That their automobile would be called the Croesus was one of the few matters on which photographer

George W. Curtiss and W.L. Bell, a school furniture salesman, could agree. This Kansas City, Missouri, enterprise came to a tawdry end when Curtiss filed suit, alleging that he was to furnish the brains and skill, and Bell the cash and salesmanship. But Bell had made no attempt to sell any cars at all. In Greeley, Colorado, the Millers, a doctor and machinist related only in name, came to words when the former claimed design credit. "I doubt the doctor's ability to run the auto, to say nothing of the building of it," scoffed the machinist.

T.J. Henderson, the San Francisco machinist responsible for building the Hill Climber, was so irked at the $150 in back pay owed him that he appropriated the car he had just finished for a local customer. The customer objected, Henderson was arrested on a charge of grand larceny, and the Hill Climbing Automobile Manufacturing Company faded into oblivion. Count was lost of the number of managerial shakeups the Duquesne from Jamestown, New York, endured, but after the last one, president LeRoy Pelletier, a former newspaper man who had covered the rush to the Klondike for *The New York Times*, moved to Detroit and got a job as Henry Ford's private secretary.

Keeping one's hand in the business but in another area was common for many early automobile builders. Herschell-Spillman, Inc., producers of merry-go-rounds in North Tonawanda, New York, built a few cars and then decided to focus on producing engines for other manufacturers. While motoring in New York City in the car he built, Joseph W. Jones' wife asked how fast they were going; Jones didn't know and invented a device he called a speedometer. In Bradford, Pennsylvania, George M. Holley gave up cars and took up carburetors.

"All of us were trying to capitalize the boom," Alfred P. Sloan, Jr., wrote in his memoirs, "and having a hard time doing it." An M.I.T. graduate with a degree in electrical engineering, Sloan found the going tough for the Hyatt Roller Bearing Company of Harrison, New Jersey, until he and partner Peter Steenstrup received an inquiry from Elwood Haynes in 1899. Steenstrup went to Kokomo and reported back on the "dirty little factory about as primitive as our place," with most of the work being done on a dirt floor. But the Indiana visit woke them both to the fact that other manufacturers might be interested in something better than greased wagon axles for their cars. Olds Motor Works came through with a big order. "Orders grew and grew, but so did our financial problems," Sloan said. "You would use every dollar you could get to put into bearings to make more dollars to buy more machinery to make more and more bearings. Whether you made axles, engines, wheels, bodies, lamps or hardware, it was the same story."

And the same story, too, for the people who were putting all those parts together. Elwood Haynes might graduate to a cement floor, and Henry Ford quickly outgrew his 250-by-50-foot Mack Avenue assembly building, but for every manufacturer struggling with success, there were a dozen more dealing with failure.

Still, they arrived in torrents. A veritable herd of Buffaloes was planned in Upstate New York, no fewer than fifteen companies organized to build cars of that name. Tonawanda mayor Frank I. Alliger chose a cute variation, but his Bison from Buffalo didn't make it into manufacture. Others, once in, were reluctant to give up easily. Despite two lawsuits for design infringement by Olds Motor Works that plunged his company into receivership, Henry F. Spaulding considered bankruptcy a mere inconvenience and, in August 1903, was testing his latest model on the tow path of the Erie Canal when he drove in and drowned. In six years, Albert F. Clark had three different electric car companies. No fewer than five different automobiles were produced by the indefatigable C.H. Blomstrom: the Queen, the Gyroscope, the Rex, the Frontmobile, and the Blomstrom. Everett S. Cameron used his own name for all the cars he manufactured, but he manufactured them everywhere: Rhode Island, Massachusetts, Connecticut, Michigan, and Ohio. Sometimes, one factory saw a plethora of different cars, viz., the Caps, the Kansas City, the Kansas City Wonder, and the Gleason in the same Missouri plant. Sometimes, the same car had different lives, as the electric from Cleveland that was called the DeMars, the Blakeslee, the Williams, and the Byrider, depending on the financial backer at the time.

If an automobile builder couldn't make it on his own, he was always assured a new job designing for an entrepreneur with more money than car sense. William H. Birdsall created the Regas for Frederick Sager (his name spelled backwards, an affectation of the period that also produced the Odelot in Ohio), as well as the Mora for Sam H. Mora and its smaller companion car, the Omar (anagrams were popular, too), and in New York State, cars for D.D. Dunn (the inventor of Sen-Sen) and a consortium desirous of producing the Buckmobile (a dreadful choice of a car name). Gilbert Loomis enjoyed a distinguished career as an automobile designer for Pope-Tribune, Payne Modern, and Speed-well after failing to find commercial happiness with his Bluebirds. The Loomis vehicle had been worthy enough to attract the attention of Bloomingdale's department store in New York, and Loomis signed a contract for delivery of 500 Bluebirds in two months, an impossible deadline for his small machine shop, and the store called off the whole thing.

Automobile Fore Carriage in New York City, Tractobile in Carlisle, Pennsylvania, and Standard Motor Vehicle Company in Oakland, California, offered motorized attachments to convert a horse-drawn carriage to horseless, but these did not work at all well. More successful, at least technically, were the cars offered in kit form by three entrepreneurs in St. Louis (Andrew Lee Dyke, J.H. Neustadt, and H.F. Borbein), two in Cleveland (the People's Automobile Company and the partnership of Francis O. Brew and William A. Hatcher, Hatcher having quit his engineering job at Packard with the move of the company from Warren to Detroit), and the Crest Manufacturing Company in Massachusetts. But probably fewer of these kits were sold to would-be owners than to unimaginative entrepreneurs who wanted to get into the automobile business with the least amount of fuss.

Instead, most do-it-yourselfers really did do it themselves. A.V.A. McHarg of Edgewater, New Jersey, admitted that his reasoning—"If one horse pulled a wagon satisfactorily, a one-horsepower motor should be able to do as much"—resulted in an automobile with a pace not much faster than a walk. But a better performance was realized by Hiram H. Bardwell of Flint, Michigan, who built his car strictly by the book (specifically, *Horseless Vehicles, Automobiles and Motor Cycles* by Gardner D. Hiscox). Dudley Brown of Stonington, Connecticut, used a steam engine from a thresher, wheels from an old mowing machine, and rough timber for the body of a car that wasn't very pretty but was capable, Brown said, "of rolling off 25 miles an hour." A young man from Berwick, Pennsylvania, who had to travel through life with the formidable name of Willie Westinghouse Edison Myers, was able to build his car after trading marbles for knives, the knives for a nanny goat, the goat for a pony, the pony for a horse, and finally the horse for a gasoline motor. "The machine is now on the streets," *Motor World* reported, "and its speedy careenings are giving all other traffic the shivers."

Practical reasons lay behind the car Lincoln H. Fey built for himself in Northfield, Minnesota (he was allergic to horses), and the Racine, Wisconsin, car built by Charles F. Brietzke (his wife was afraid of them). Robert E. Sheldon built his car in 1905 because that was the only way he would have one in Skagway, Alaska. In Decatur, Illinois, George A. Henderson bought a used steamer that was so awful "I came near becoming involved in litigation with the firm that sold me the outfit but concluded that the same money that would pay for a course of law might possibly pay for a course of study in steam"—so he rebuilt the car he had, sold it, and with the proceeds constructed a worthier one for himself. Many of these home-built automobiles were easily the equal, or better, of cars being manufactured during this era. Charles V. Randall of San Jose, California, declared that his runabout "taken as a whole exceeds my expectations by about forty percent." In Carrington, North Dakota, milkman Clarence Cummings was so proud of his creation that he declared himself ready to take on anybody with a store-bought automobile.

Save for George Henderson's steamer, all of the aforementioned cars, according to the Association of Licensed Automobile Manufacturers, had been built illegally.

———

The A.L.A.M. had no intention of sending process servers into the backyards of gasoline automobile builders throughout the nation, of course, but the arrogance of its all-inclusive posturing couldn't have played well among those often ingenious tinkerers who could afford a car only if they built one themselves. The A.L.A.M. did demand licenses, however, from individual users of foreign gasoline automobiles. Some dutifully paid up right away. The tribute exacted was a trifling, given the wealth of most foreign-car owners. Those who objected on principle were hauled into court and soon recognized the wisdom of paying rather than incurring attorney fees far in excess of the $500 demanded.*

---

* Signing his check promptly was Harry Payne Whitney, for his French-built Léon Bollée. The estate he had inherited after the sudden death of his father in 1904 included a major interest in the Electric Vehicle Company—and its rights to the Selden patent. The stock exchanges had hushed up the news of Williams Collins Whitney's death until the market closed; the New York State legislature adjourned.

The A.L.A.M. heralded these victories as upholding the validity of the Selden patent, which, of course, they did not. But the publicity was helpful as counterpoint to the Ford advertising that had become increasingly strident. "Get a Ford car and enjoy it," agent John Wanamaker ballyhooed. "The Trust has no car to show in competition with it—hence the scare-crow and tom-toms....We'll take care of the tom-toms." It was David versus Goliath. The homespun Midwesterner against the Eastern establishment. The hard-working inventor against the dastardly trust. It was very effective.

The A.L.A.M. was in the unenviable position of wishing to monopolize without appearing to be a monopoly. President Roosevelt had made himself clear on the matter of trusts. At first, so had the A.L.A.M. "It would be impossible for all who have attempted to go into the business to make a success of it," member H.H. Franklin declared. "Those already licensed can more than supply the demand." The A.L.A.M. firms, it was explained, commanded 90 percent of U.S. gasoline-car production. The companies within the A.L.A.M. competed with each other, which was quite enough competition for the association. Ford answered with ads, noting sarcastically that the A.L.A.M. was not a philanthropic institution but "in the business to make money at the expense of five or six times as many competitors...and we are endeavoring to do our level best to reduce [the percentage of the market the A.L.A.M. claimed]."

No doubt the A.L.A.M. underestimated the ferocity with which Ford would fight the Selden patent. Some association members figured Darwinian ruthlessness would take quick care of the mere hopefuls in the gasoline car industry, and the A.L.A.M. could easily take care of the rest. "Well, we are disposed to be fair," Fred Smith had said to Ford stockholder Anderson. "We will take an inventory of their stocks, machinery, equipment, whatever they may have, and give them fair value for it. Then they quit business." That may have been more bombast than promise, because even the A.L.A.M., money powerful as it was, wasn't possessed of enough funds for a sweeping cleanup of the industry.

The litigation was costing a fortune. From the outset of the Ford challenge, it was apparent the case would be protracted. A patent suit always was, partly because proceedings were not held in open court. If the witness lived more than 100 miles from the seat of action, the court went to him. Testimony was taken in law offices, hotels, wherever; without judicial power, the examining officer could do no more than maintain order if the witness wandered far afield. Testimony in the Selden case would fill a steamer trunk. From three to five years was routinely required for taking of depositions and evidence in a patent case.

The Selden litigation looked like it might drag on even longer. It was possibly for this reason that Fred Smith offered to reconsider Henry Ford's worthiness for an A.L.A.M. license in 1904. Ford rejected the offer. The A.L.A.M. had more money than he, but Henry liked the fact that much of its royalty income was earmarked for "a soft pension fund" for A.L.A.M. lawyers. Taking on the association when he did, at the onset of production, had been gutsy, but as sales climbed, Ford had the satisfaction of knowing that what he was paying in attorney fees was offset by what he was not paying in royalties. And he was reaping wonderful good will for his company.

Put on the defensive, the A.L.A.M. tried a benevolent offense. Association manager George Day insisted that the A.L.A.M. had recognized and was attempting to avert the "imminent danger of overproduction." Association member Elihu Cutler warned of the peril of "large quantities of machines that have not been fully tested." Further pronouncements held the A.L.A.M. did not intend to "shut out reputable and established manufacturers," only "unreliable upstarts" in order to "protect the public and be a boon to all purchasers of gasoline automobiles."

Quite correctly, the A.L.A.M. pointed to the flagrant abuses in the nascent industry. Fraud was being perpetrated everywhere.

CHAPTER 16

Cads and Bad Autos

A NEWS ITEM from Wisconsin in 1902 that the Hotel Racine had recouped part of its bill by selling off the expensive clothes Edward Joel Pennington had left behind in a hasty departure indicated that this con man of Chicago Times-Herald renown had worn out his welcome in England and returned home. Subsequently, he jumped hotel bills in Cincinnati and Pittsburgh, and, in the fall of 1903, paid for his lavish entertaining in the best suite in the best hotel in Cleveland with four checks, all of which bounced. Pennington was the man behind the Tractobile, which didn't work, and a 16-horsepower $300-car promoted in Milwaukee that was never built. There were other towns and other swindles. When his movements were unknown, the likelihood was that someone somewhere had caught up with him, and his accommodations for the moment were courtesy of the state. The irony was that many of his later automotive ideas were as worthy as his schemes were not. "But for the weakness of his moral equipment," *The Autocar* wrote when he died in 1911, "he would have been a great man."

The Compound car, one of several produced by John W. Eisenhuth, was apparently an admirable vehicle; less admirable was the number of times its promoter was arrested. Forged promissory notes and angry creditors were all that remained when the Upstate New York promoters of the Ripper Motor Carriage Company (Buffalo) and the Foster Automobile Manufacturing Company (Rochester) left town. W.H. Kitto, who promoted three different cars in three different states, was the smooth-talking Pennington type; he sued 129 delinquent subscribers to one of his stock schemes, contending that if all subscriptions had been paid, he could have opened his factory—and he won. When the creditors appealed, he departed.

A hastier exit was Walter K. Freeman's of the Auto-Acetylene Company of New York City. Wrote Ingersoll in *The Horseless Age* indignantly, "He never had any patents, knew nothing about motors, and when his schemes had ripened, and a considerable sum had been realized from his advertisements in part payment for acetylene carriages, which neither he nor anybody else had ever succeeded in building, he took train for other parts, leaving his pretentious offices and his dupes behind him." Of San Francisco's Sparks Automobile Company, *The Horseless Age* commented wryly, "The picture which adorns the front page of the company's prospectus bears a striking resemblance to the electric phaeton of the Woods Motor Vehicle Company." Similarly, a company's factory in a stock prospectus was frequently a drawing and not a photograph.

There was the expected backlash. In Marlboro, Massachusetts, machinist O.D. Wheeler and his son E.O., a graduate of Worcester Polytechnical Institute, approached a Boston bank in 1902 for the money to gear up for manufacture of their automobile. The bank was favorably impressed by the Wheelers until it discovered that another financial institution in town had recently been bilked by a flim-flam artist. That scenario was replayed many times during the automobile's early years. Given the quick rise and fall of the bicycle craze, banks were generally reluctant to invest in a proposition as dicey as the automobile business anyway. The performance of automobile swindlers served only to harden that resolve.

Swindlers insinuated themselves into going automobile concerns, too, with disastrous results. The company representative who was handed a good deal of cash from the safe to set up the Prescott export business in Europe was never heard from again. Neither, shortly thereafter, was the Prescott, a steamer from Passaic, New Jersey, which had made a fine name for itself in the New York–Boston Reliability Run.

The A.L.A.M. could appoint itself policeman of the industry, in part because the government raised no controlling hand. But then the government wasn't much interested in the automobile either. The U.S. Patent Office's turn-of-the-century declaration that "It is obvious to the least observant of laymen that [the self-propelled vehicle] has come to stay" was not the consensus in Washington. The Library of Congress, the Bureau of Standards, and the Government Printing Office bought a few electrics, as did the Signal Corps, but its communiqué announcing the fact betrayed misgivings: "Each is equipped so that a mule may be hitched to it, should it refuse to run." Similarly, when the President of the United States was given his first ride in an automobile—one of Colonel Pope's in Hartford, Connecticut—an aide commented that "Roosevelt's display of courage was typical of him." A horse-drawn carriage had followed the Rough Rider at a respectable distance, just in case of emergency.

Certainly there was some official awareness of the automobile's potential utility, but from a distance. After attending French maneuvers, Major T. Bentley Mott reported that motor vehicles could be put to military advantage in Europe because of the fine highways and the ever-present possibilities of "war on its soil," neither of those conditions prevailing in the United States. At the turn of the century, John Brisben Walker made a "war car" out of his Mobile steamer, which, its own deficiencies notwithstanding, was greeted with indifference by Elihu Root's Department of War. Only General Nelson Miles, whose advocacy of the automobile dated back to the Chicago Times-Herald, continued to champion the cause. His view that the Spanish-American War had demonstrated the horse as a liability in battle did not dissuade the romantics of the cavalry, however. Nor did the "great stunts" performed with automobiles at various maneuvers, including the Massachusetts State Militia trials in the summer of 1905, during which Miles drove the Surgeon General "3,000 feet into the woods at top speed" in a White steamer to get to a drowning man who was "only saved by prompt arrival."

Initially, the Post Office Department had thought the mail might arrive more promptly by automobile. Collection from street boxes was tried in New York City as early as 1896; an 1899 experiment in Buffalo cut in half the time required to collect mail from forty boxes along a six-mile route. Reports of these and other community experiments were relayed to Washington for deliberation. The conclusion was that, for best mail-delivery performance, automobiles required "asphalt or other smooth pavements," but the vehicles might be built better in the future, which neatly put the solution to the problem of America's deplorable roads on the other foot. The sale of a steamer to the Boston post office, together with the hint of an order for a full fleet, was cause for celebration at the Easton (Pennsylvania) factory of the Eclipse Automobile Company in 1901; the only eclipse that followed was the company's. For years, motorized postal delivery would be tried only experimentally. The government was not about to commit itself to the automobile.

———

If a recalcitrance to bow to the inevitable is suggested by the foregoing, there were mitigating circumstances. A lot of truly awful cars were being placed on the market and tended to give motoring a bad name. "There was no research to it at all," a mechanic of the Burdick Motor Car Company of Eau Claire, Wisconsin recalled, "...just a matter of buying a front end and putting it here, buying a transmission and putting it there, getting a rear axle and putting it there. Sometimes the parts fit and sometime they didn't." An automobile that was custom built by a blacksmith in Helena, Montana, sat on a slant because the carriage wheels used were different sizes and vibrated so badly the owner often slid out; after also sliding under, breaking a few bones, he sued the blacksmith.

———

There was no really definitive answer to what an automobile should be yet and some bizarre notions of what it might be. The Kent's Pacemaker from Boston had one wheel in front and three in the rear (the outside wheels were raised at speed so the car could coast like a bicycle); the Philadelphia-built Autocycle put a single wheel fore and aft with two parallel side wheels; and the Tincher from Chicago sported a compressed air device that braked the car, pumped the tires, and tooted the whistle. L.P. Madsen of Council Bluffs, Iowa, put the engine cooling water in the hollow fenders on his runabout; George T. Glover's Chicago-built four-wheeled steamer mounted a hollow traction wheel midship to be filled with hot water from the engine boiler to melt snow in wintry motoring; and in Utica, New York, D.B. Smith flamboyantly curved the coachwork of his steam runabout and ornamented it with a tiara. None of these cars was on the market long.

Just as short-lived was the four-cylinder touring model of the Mahoning Motor Car Company of Youngstown, Ohio, whose power-to-weight ratio was so dismal that upon approaching any sizable hill, all passengers had to get out and walk. Residents of Elmira, New York, called the two-cylinder air-cooled friction-drive product of the Watrous Automobile Company the "waterless, gearless, powerless, useless Watrous." In Hyattsville, Maryland, Howard O. Carter was convinced he had solved the engine failure problem and ushered in "an epoch of transportation unparalleled in the history of the world" when his Carter Motor Car Corporation introduced the Duplex, sporting two separate four-cylinder engines (each with its own radiator, exhaust, and ignition) that could be operated either together for high performance or singly in case of emergency.

Better mousetraps were attempted awhile in how the automobile should be powered in the first place. Some were genuine, if ill conceived, such as W.G. Caffrey's electric that operated like a trolley car by hooking into overhead electrified wires in Reno, Nevada. Others were scams like the American Liquid Air Company, which demonstrated its car at the first Madison Square Garden show and, in the scathing words of *Motor Age*, drew "into a charmed circle of hashish-laden atmosphere all the smart gentry who have succeeded in getting a little money ahead at the cost of fellow-beings and whose idea it is to get something for nothing." Carbonic acid was the soda-fountain-like approach chosen by the New Power Company of Trenton, New Jersey, and the American Automobile, Motor & Power Company of Brooklyn, New York. Compressed air was the choice of the Pneumatic Carriage Company of New York City; the Cosmopolitan Power Company of Jersey City, New Jersey; and John S. Muir of Norfolk, Connecticut, who offered a hand-compressor as standard equipment so that the owner could easily "fill up" himself. The Chicago Motocycle Company offered the Caloric with a hot-air engine that required the cylinder head to be heated by a torch for starting.

But overwhelmingly, the manufacturers' choice came to be limited to three types: electric, steam, and gasoline. Each was a mixed blessing.

———

The electric was simple in construction, as quiet as a kitten's purr, clean, odorless, and the easiest of the three to operate, the hapless Mrs. Stuyvesant Fish notwithstanding. There was nothing to freeze, burn, or explode in an electric; the car started immediately on demand; there was no waste of material when not running; and a single lever controlled the power while another steered. But the earliest electrics had a top speed of about 12 miles per hour and a range of about 20 miles between charges. And they were approximately twice as expensive both to buy and to run as steamers and gasoline cars.

At the outset of the industry, however, the electric's advantages were attractive enough to lure many entrepreneurs into producing them. "The Shrewdest Dealers are pushing electrics," the Centaur Motor Vehicle Company of Buffalo, New York, advertised in the trade press in 1902, "and will be established when the Boom comes for the pleasure vehicle." From Syracuse, M.E. Walshe & Sons proclaimed that "any person of ordinary common sense will be able to charge [the Walshe] from any place where there is an electric light or arc light." In New York City, the Ajax Motor Vehicle Company tried to counteract the electric's low-performance reputation with a biceps-and-clenched-fist trademark that rendered the famous Arm & Hammer logo a muscular also-ran. In Chicago, the Graham Automobile & Launch Company priced its "Swellest Electric Vehicle Made" at $850, but apparently the car was as lamentable as the company's grammar.

Dealers, who often represented all three vehicle types, gave the electric short shrift. Perhaps it was the vehicle's simplicity that lulled both seller and user into thinking all one had to do with an electric was drive it. "Such a thing as learning how to charge a battery never occurred to the dealer as essential," one electric maker complained. "Put the cat out and the car on charge"—a popular catchphrase of the era—was seen by owners who installed their own charging apparatus as completing the nightly chores. Consequently, batteries were burned up by overcharging or, conversely, were put to work without being sufficiently charged, which was equally ruinous. Cleaning the commutator was often ignored as well, which further lessened the electric's already minimal speed and mileage.

Unlike the steamer or gasoline car, which volubly announced its need for attention, the electric did not noisily indicate something was wrong. Unfortunately, most of the electric noise was made by manufacturers, who saw exaggeration as the best tactic to counter the steamer's and gasoline car's advantages. Saying that his product traveled three times as far between charges as it actually did might make for more initial sales, but repeat business or further sales through recommendations of satisfied owners was nil. And the electric as a genre was not helped either. As M.L. Goss wrote in *Harper's Weekly*, there was "a mushroom growth of unwarranted prejudices against electric cars."

Unwittingly, Thomas Edison created another problem. Since as early as 1889, America's most celebrated inventor, who detested horses as irresponsible, had been predicting that within twenty-five years, "electricity will have superseded horse power in New York." In the mid-1890s, he was impressed awhile with the gasoline car concept because, as he had enthused to Henry Ford, it was a "self-contained unit carrying its own fuel." But by the turn of the century, Edison had concluded the internal combustion engine's defects were unlikely to be swiftly overcome. "The inventors will hang their heads with disgust," he was reported as saying in 1899 of those practicing the gasoline car art. He was going to create an electric car that would put them to shame. "I have solved the automobile problem," Edison announced in 1902. "I can make an automobile that will go so fast a man cannot sit in it. The speed of storage battery machines is unlimited." Moreover, he said such a car could be sold for $350. "Edison Will Make Automobiles the Poor Man's Vehicle" was the headline in the *New York Journal*.

Unfortunately, Edison had not produced such a car yet. But he was valiantly trying. He borrowed a carriage from the Studebaker brothers to begin experimentation and talked Albert Pope into lending him an engineer. The Colonel had quick second thoughts about helping a potential competitor, however, and recalled the fellow to Hartford. Actually, Edison had no intention of being a car manufacturer himself. His aim was to supply storage batteries to the electric vehicle industry.

The heavy lead-acid battery then in use was the electric car's Achilles' heel. The alkaline version Edison developed weighed about a third less, had a quarter more useful capacity, and was faster charging, longer lasting, and promised infinitely better performance in an electric car. But it was also much less durable and cost three and a half times as much to produce. The Edison name assured sales to electric car makers; when extended use revealed the battery's fragility, Edison conscientiously recalled them all and returned to the drawing board. That his "miniature reservoir of electric force" was not the immediate world-beater he had hoped was agonizing for the now aging and nearly stone-deaf inventor.

In Charles Duryea's view, "one of the greatest sales obstacles the gasoline car had to overcome was the general conviction that any day Edison would invent a miraculous auto that would sweep the market." But that same conviction backfired on the electric car, too. Too much was expected too soon.

Electric vehicle performance did improve. As early as 1902, Walter Baker had raced his electric Torpedo Kid a mile in less than a minute on the same Glenville track that had made Alexander Winton famous. The year before that, the installation of six charging stations in New Jersey made it possible for an electric to motor from New York to Philadelphia. In 1906, Frank Babcock of Buffalo, New York, managed that one-hundred-mile trip on only one charge in his new electric car fitted with batteries of his own manufacture. Babcock's easy 30-miles-per-hour touring speed compared favorably with those of the gasoline runabouts, but the cheapest he could sell his Babcock Electric for was $1,400. Walter Baker was selling his electric runabout at the same price in Cleveland.

A comparatively short period of time had seen the electric's range increase from twenty to one hundred miles, and it was believed that in time, production costs of an electric would concomitantly decrease. General magazines of the period, while frankly admitting the electric's shortcomings, were vociferous in their belief that it was the ideal car for doctors making house calls, for salesmen making rounds, and for general urban use. "In cities the electric automobile stands without rival," wrote Cleveland Moffet in *Review of Reviews*. Careful appraisals such as those were lost, however, in the hoopla surrounding Edison's any-day-now revolution in the "world of power."

Perhaps the electric's fall from first place in the industry to third in less than a half decade had something to do with image, too. The smooth riding comfort of an enclosed carriage had made the car an early favorite of society ladies and dandies such as Diamond Jim Brady, who ordered his Baker with curved glass windows so that his jewelry and his lady of the moment would be properly displayed on drives to the theater. But for most men, the electric was anathema. In an era of careful division between the sexes, the masculine sensibility could not equate with a vehicle of charm and good manners. *Real* motoring was a robust activity. Seldom was an electric the only vehicle in a household. It was a second car or, in the case of John Jacob Astor, arrived at some midway point in the acquisition of the thirty-two automobiles that graced his garage shortly after the turn of the century.

———

The steamer did not have a feminine image and had history on its side, which was aggressively played upon by early manufacturers. "Steam is our oldest artificial power," said the Milwaukee Automobile Company. Commented the Lane Motor Vehicle Company of Poughkeepsie, New York, "It propels our great ships, pulls our railway trains, runs our factories." John Brisben Walker had declared his Mobile steamer "represents a power that is absolutely understood, and its reliability known beyond a question," whereas "the operation of a gasoline machine requires the employment of an expert of high intelligence and thorough training..." These were effective selling points.

The steamer was quieter than a gasoline car and faster than an electric. Indeed, Fred Marriott's run of 127.66 miles per hour at Daytona Beach in 1906 in a Stanley was a world land speed record. And the steamer, with its greater elasticity, was a wonderful hill climber, all of the cars so powered making it to the top of Eagle Rock (West Orange, New Jersey) in a 1902 automobile club hill climb; Frank Duryea's Stevens-Duryea was the only gasoline car to manage the same feat that day.

With fewer mechanical parts, the steamer suffered fewer mechanical failures than the gasoline car. And it was easier to locate the source of the trouble when a breakdown did happen. The steamer's engine, lubricated with special cylinder oil fed into it with the steam, required less attention than its gasoline counterpart because it was running at a much slower rate of speed and did not wear out as quickly. Water in horse troughs was readily available, and the kerosene the steamer generally used was easier to purchase for awhile than gasoline.

The steam-powered car's principal disadvantages were the time required to raise steam (as much as forty-five minutes) and the vehicle's incredible thirst. (Steamers ran out of steam almost as rapidly as electrics did electricity.) With design improvements, these vices abated. The flash boiler could raise steam in a few minutes, and leaving the pilot light on allowed instant starts. Automated controls were seen as a real boon. "If everything works perfectly, the water level, the steam pressure and the fire are all looked after automatically," a journalist wrote, "and the operator has only to manage his levers and enjoy the scenery." That was a big "if," although no more so than a gasoline car proceeding from here to there without difficulty. Clogged valves, pump failures, frozen pipes in cold weather, and the occasional annoyance of finding the soft water the steamer preferred were irksome.

Most attractive was the steamer's promise of a vibration-less ride with little more sound than the hiss of a teakettle and without gearshifting, smoky exhausts, or backfiring. The promise of explosion was scarcely appealing, however. A joke popular in electric and gasoline car circles was that the owner of a steamer could never be sure whether he would travel straight ahead or straight up. "This is in reality the greatest argument against the steam machine," a critic concluded. Even President McKinley was overheard to remark that he "expected to be blown to bits at any minute" while riding in the Stanley. Fatalities due to boiler explosions were certainly no more numerous than vehicle-related deaths in gasoline cars. Still, a steamer was generally seen as the more dangerous of the two types.

———

In a way, the gasoline car became the ideal by default. Compared to an electric, it was as noisy as a Chinese firecracker, and its odor was leagues more noxious than a steamer. "The automobile industry will surely burgeon in America," a reporter wrote following the 1900 New York Automobile Show, "but this motor will not be a factor." A correspondent in Paris noted how his nostrils were offended "as these machines sweep past, with that sickening smell of imperfect combustion." The gasoline car's only saving grace at first was its need for only one kind of replenishment and its greater range between replenishing stops. Spark plugs fouled, carburetors lacked finesse, and engines overheated.

Starting a gasoline car could be a real chore. Guffaws of the day included one published in *Collier's* that the four hours and fifteen minutes an Ohio doctor had to crank before his engine turned over was a new U.S. record. Less funny was the blood poisoning that "Punk" Allen of Valley City, North Dakota, suffered after repeatedly bruising his right hand in cranking, as well as the number of arms broken elsewhere. But the gasoline car was improved, dexterity in starting could be learned by new owners, and further practice made some of the car's foibles fixable by home remedy. Moreover, recourse to a local "professional" brought satisfaction to a gasoline car owner more readily;

one's neighborhood machinist might tackle a steamer, but an electric was quite beyond him.

More significantly, manufacturers found that, pound for pound, a gasoline car was the most lucrative proposition. From the beginning of automobile development, finding a light and compact power package had been the goal. Steamers and electrics wasted a lot of weight just hauling their bulk around. The comparative power-to-weight figures were: electric, 840 pounds; steam, 371 pounds; and gasoline, 185 pounds. Because the potential for a gasoline car was more attractive than its rivals, makers who had marketed steamers or electrics, or both, often switched over completely. Rarely did gasoline car makers go the other way. Manufacturing a gasoline car was easier, and could be accomplished more quickly, than laboring at solutions to the electric's or the steamer's technical shortcomings. When Spindletop gushed near Beaumont, Texas, in 1901, lowering the price of petroleum below five cents per barrel and suggesting that gasoline would be forever cheap and plentiful, many more rushed into the gasoline car field.

Personality was a factor, too. Entrepreneurial gasoline car engineers in the Midwest were more committed to both improving their product and finding a wider market for it than were their steamer and electric counterparts in the East. And they were far better in promotion. "Anybody that runs a car and uses gasoline dislikes it," James L. Eck commented, citing its volatility and the danger of fire in the barns where automobiles were generally stored. But Eck, who built steamers as a sideline to his Boss Knitting Machine Works in Reading, Pennsylvania, wasn't heard from often. He didn't compete in races, reliability runs, or any of the events that brought the automobile to national attention. Nor did many makers of steamers or electrics.

Walter Baker was a *rara avis* in racing an electric, and the steamer producers who competed were soon overwhelmed by the hordes of gasoline car manufacturers who chose competition as an effective way to sell the product. In advertising, too, gasoline car makers were far more aggressive. The Stanley brothers, who had as many customers and were making as much money as they desired, didn't believe in advertising at all. Electric manufacturers, satisfied with high per-unit profits, turned to ad campaigns that were as decorous as their cars.

——

Sheer numbers tell the story. Overall in the history of the American automobile, about 300 makers built electrics, and about 500 built steamers. Companies attempting the gasoline car field numbered in the several thousands. The swiftness of the transition was dramatic. Production figures industry-wide for 1900 totaled more than 1,600 steamers, more than 1,500 electrics, and fewer than 1,000 gasoline cars. By 1904, annual steamer and electric production remained at approximately the same level, but well over 10,000 gasoline cars were produced by the top four (Olds, Cadillac, Rambler, and Ford) alone.

And, finally, ready to come on strong was Buick.

CHAPTER 17

High Gear and Turbulence

"THE CAR SIMPLY ran to perfection," Hugh Dolnar wrote in *Cycle and Automobile Trade Journal* of Herbert H. Hills' Buick. "...[It] flew down the hills and flew up the hills, all the same rate, and the engine purred and the wind whistled past and the soft September sun smiled benignly on the fine farms we ran by, and it was all delightful." Hills, a physician at the Oak Grove Sanitarium in Flint, had been seventeenth in line for the new Buick but moved to the top when he agreed to allow his vehicle to be used as a demonstrator. This was a wise decision on the doctor's part because he received delivery a lot quicker than he would have otherwise. Manufacturing the car remained lower on David Dunbar Buick's priority list than experimenting with it. Naturally, this worried James H. Whiting, whose Flint Wagon Works controlled Buick's operation.

Like Ben Briscoe before him, Whiting had quickly realized that business management was not among David Buick's skills. The $37,500 earmarked to move the car into production was exhausted before a wheel had turned, and a further $25,000 had been borrowed from each of three Flint banks. That was a considerable sum. If Buick failed, not only would Flint Wagon Works be brought down with it, but the entire economy of the city of Flint could be affected. Nearing retirement age, Whiting didn't think he was up to coping with the problem. What Buick needed was more working capital and a go-getter who could make the business work.

As Buick production inched toward the thirty-seven cars that would be the total output for 1904, James Whiting and Fred A. Aldrich, secretary of the Durant-Dort Carriage Company of Flint, discussed the situation aboard the train taking them to a carriage convention in Chicago. Aldrich suggested a man the very mention of whose name shed sunshine throughout Flint: the ambitious, energetic, bold, indefatigable, engaging, star-studded, and success-storied William Crapo Durant. He was in New York at the moment, playing the stock market and playing it well, and he wasn't much interested in cars. But if anyone was the answer to Whiting's problem, Aldrich was sure it was his boss.

Durant was the grandson of Henry Howland Crapo, a Michigan lumber magnate and two-term governor of the state, and the son of William Clark Durant, whose excesses were alcohol consumption and stock speculation and who, one day when his son was nine, left home and was never seen again. A reckless spirit of adventure was the chief character trait Durant inherited from his father. He drank little and was shamelessly devoted to his mother for the rest of her long life. His family called him Willie; to friends, he was Billy. He was always in a hurry to do things. A half year shy of high-school graduation, Durant had abruptly quit to make his way in the world. The family lumber business occupied him awhile, but the boy preferred being his own entrepreneur. Billy had a phenomenal ability to sell anything. And almost anyone. He peddled patent medicines and then cigars; he tried insurance and real estate.

One day in the mid-1880s, while traveling around Michigan, he happened upon a road cart with a novel method of suspension and borrowed $2,000 from a Flint bank to buy rights to its manufacture. Within hours of obtaining the loan, he had talked Josiah Dallas Dort, manager of a local hardware store, into partnership. Neither of them knew anything about manufacturing road carts, a problem easily solved by hiring people who did. Dort was a practical administrator; Durant was the consummate idea man. They were an unbeatable combination. By

the turn of the century, the Durant-Dort Carriage Company was producing more than 50,000 vehicles a year, far in excess of its local rivals,
the Flint Wagon Works and W.A. Paterson and Company. And Durant-
Dort had a dozen more carriage plants, either established or acquired,
in Michigan and elsewhere. Billy Durant was a millionaire before he
turned forty. He needed a new challenge.

Like many carriage men, Durant had doubts about the automobile. In
1902, when his daughter Margery excitedly told him, "Pops, I've ridden in a horseless carriage," he scolded her for foolishly risking her
life. That same year, he was taken for a ride by Charles H. Wisner, a
local judge who had built his own automobile and was looking forward to leaving the bench if Durant could be talked into helping him
finance manufacture. Durant was unimpressed, particularly when the
car had to be pushed over curbs. A cousin had a Mobile steamer in
which Durant rode once and thereafter declared himself "mighty pro-
voked" that a relative "would drive around annoying people that way."

Still, Durant liked Whiting and loved his hometown, and when the predicament in which the Buick company had placed both was explained
to him, Billy returned home from New York to look into the situation.
On September 4, Dr. Hills took him for his first ride in the Buick.
"Durant kept firing questions at me about how the car ran and if I liked
it or not," Hills recalled. "We didn't talk about anything else the whole
time." The conversation did not distract Billy from noticing that the
good doctor had chosen only Flint's best paved streets for the ride, so
he asked Whiting for another demonstrator in which to conduct his
own testing.

The Buick that Billy borrowed from the factory would be returned a
very used car. Day in, day out, week after week, Durant drove over
every conceivable road surface, the worst conditions he could find in
the area. Often, his daughter accompanied him. "I came to know where
all the good-natured farmers with the strongest mules lived," Margery
Durant remembered. When the way was lost or something broke, the
nearest farmhouse was found, and Durant often asked if they could pay
for a meal. When a hotel was necessary, Margery blushed as the desk
clerk asked suspiciously about their lack of luggage.

As the mileage on his borrowed Buick increased, Billy began spreading the gospel. The automobile was the future, he proclaimed to

townspeople, to those encountered along country roads, and to farmers at whose kitchen table he sat. Finally, in mid-October, Durant asked James Whiting to join him on a drive around Flint. Pulling up in front of the latter's house, the two men talked for an hour. "Billy's sold," Whiting announced to his family with undisguised relief as he walked through the front door, late for dinner.

On November 1, 1904, the leadership of the Buick Motor Company passed to Durant. Capitalization was increased immediately from $75,000 to $300,000, within weeks to $500,000, and within ten months to $1.5 million. For years, Billy enjoyed saying that in forty-eight hours, he sold a half-million dollars in company stock just to people in Flint, most of whom had "never ridden in an automobile." That feat paled in comparison to how quickly he sold the Buick to America.

"William has just returned from the 'auto' show in N.Y. where he sold 1,108 machines," Clara Durant wrote to a friend in January 1905. "The Buick is certainly a success." Their marriage was not. Billy had not been the hearth-and-slippers sort in the past; Clara's complaints of neglect would only increase now. Durant became totally committed to the Buick. One evening in 1906, Dallas Dort and Charles Nash, who had started at the Durant-Dort Carriage Company as a cushion stuffer and was now its vice president, joined Billy for dinner at his home. Both men had faith in him, if little in the automobile. Thumping on a player piano, their host rhapsodized that before long, a single company might sell 100,000 automobiles a year. "Dallas," sighed Charlie Nash, "Billy's crazy." That same year when Margery was married, she had to admonish her father that no speed record had to be set in the walk down the aisle. To Billy, the only way to move was fast.

His pace overwhelmed David Dunbar Buick. "There wasn't an executive in the place who ever knew what time it was," lamented the man whose name was on the car. Durant associates had suggested the Buick should be renamed, but Billy pooh-poohed the idea. Although he worried privately to Margery that people might think it was pronounced Boo-ick, he figured time and familiarity would take care of that problem. The immediate dilemma was getting the Buick produced. At first, final assembly was seen to in the Durant-Dort plant in Jackson, which had been vacated when the partners' Imperial Wheel Company relocated to Flint. But this makeshift solution was as inconvenient logistically as it was annoying to Flint businessmen, who wanted the whole of the Buick operation at home. Durant and the city soon came to mutually favorable terms. The increase in capitalization to $1.5 million in September 1905 was part of the deal; less than two years later, Durant had only to mention that he wanted capital increased to $2.6 million, and it was done.

Durant-Dort carriage agencies were convenient outlets for the new Buick, although again, Durant regarded this as makeshift. At the same time, he began a recruitment program for distributors. A little capital and a lot of selling savvy and spirit were the qualifications. Thirteen qualified. In Minneapolis, Harry E. Pence rounded up as many drivers as Buicks allotted him and headed the caravan west, sending a driver home as soon as his car was sold—and returning home himself only after the last Buick had a buyer. In New England, Harry K. Noyes was a one-man caravan as he trekked over a different mountain each trip, sold his Buick and a local man on a dealership, and then returned home by railroad or sometimes oxcart. In San Francisco, Charles Howard's Buick agency was destroyed in the earthquake, but he used the few showroom cars that remained operable to carry the homeless to shelter and the injured to the hospital. His Buick sales increased wonderfully when he was able to reestablish his business in a new location.

But none of the thirteen Buick supersalesmen was any better than Billy. On a one-hour layover in Detroit en route to New York, Durant learned from the local Buick dealership that several prospects remained interested but unsold. Billy got the name of one of those wavering and sold him a Buick before the train left the station. When the Chicago dealership sales proved less than anticipated, Billy took charge personally and broke the agency's previous record by selling ninety-nine cars in five weeks.

On the north side of Flint, on 220 acres, trees were felled, streets were laid out, and buildings were erected. By the fall of 1906, when the Buick automobile plant was completed, Durant claimed that fourteen acres of working space made it the largest in the world. However, more important was the proximity of other component plants—Imperial Wheel, Flint Varnish, Michigan Motor Casting, and the W.F. Stewart coachbuilding works. Durant wanted everything for his Buick close by. When he discovered that the axles ordered from Weston-Mott in Utica, New York, were too long arriving regular freight and too expensive if shipped express, Durant asked Charles Stewart Mott if he would consider establishing a branch plant in Flint. Mott demurred that proper management couldn't be handled long distance but left himself open to an offer to move his entire operation there.

That was all Durant needed. He and Dallas Dort entrained for Utica, toured the Weston-Mott plant, and invited Mott, his associate William Doolittle, and their wives to Flint, where they were feted to a fare-thee-well. Durant was aware this deal would be no pushover. Despite patriarchal urging that he study the chemistry of fermentation, which could be put to good use in the family cider and vinegar business, Mott had chosen mechanical engineering instead. And despite the family connections that got him into the wheel- and axle-making business, Mott had been singularly responsible for deftly engineering the transition from wagon to automobile.

The package Durant fashioned for Mott was irresistible: the real estate plus $100,000 to build a factory next to Buick, and an exclusive contract to make axles for Durant, but with the freedom to sell to anyone else. "All were to cohere as if drawn together like some magnetic force," wrote Alfred P. Sloan, Jr., of the integration of the automobile industry, which he believed began with the transfer of Weston-Mott to Michigan. Charles Mott's metaphor for Durant was "spark plug."

From a 37-car production and the brink of bankruptcy in 1904, Durant surged Buick to profitability and a 750-car year in 1905. "We worked until we had the day's job done and were ready for tomorrow and then we went home—and not until then," said David Buick. How productive Buick's hours were is moot. Durant treated him kindly but leaned on Buick's chief engineer, Walter Marr, to keep things moving. Assisting Marr was Enos DeWaters, who had been associated with Henry Leland at Cadillac the previous year. In his office, Durant often worked until midnight and was always back at his desk at seven the next morning.

In 1906, the three best-selling cars in America were the Ford, Henry Leland's Cadillac, and Tom Jeffery's Rambler. Still gearing up his facilities, Durant increased Buick production by almost half and ranked eighth in the industry. The Association of Licensed Automobile Manufacturers had initially looked upon the Buick operation with as much disdain as it had Henry Ford's. Durant, who had no time for lawsuits, acquired his Selden license the easy way—by buying out the already-licensed Pope-Robinson company, which Colonel Pope had decided to cut adrift from his empire. By 1907, with output tripled over the preceding year, Billy waltzed Buick past Cadillac and Rambler into the number two spot in the industry. The Buick was the best-selling car in the A.L.A.M.

———

In January 1905, the A.L.A.M. negotiated an exclusive two-year lease of Madison Square Garden for the New York Automobile Show, with an option for a two-year extension. This "canny act," Fred Smith said, was "the only outstanding bit of high-handed monopolistic injustice we indulged in." Early the following month, A.L.A.M. manager George Day announced that henceforth the Madison Square Garden show would be a members-only event. Less than two weeks later, a secret meeting was held at the Ford Motor Company to organize the American Motor Car Manufacturers' Association (A.M.C.M.A.). Anyone without a Selden license was invited to join. Charter members would number twenty.

Among them were Charles Duryea's Duryea Power Company of Reading, Pennsylvania (brother J. Frank's Stevens-Duryea belonged to the A.L.A.M.), Ransom Olds of Reo (who wouldn't speak to Fred Smith, much less ask him for a Selden license), and Ben Briscoe of Maxwell-Briscoe (who had never liked the A.L.A.M. crowd much, a feeling that was apparently mutual). The A.M.C.M.A. was hoping to lure Tom Jeffery into the fold, but the Rambler maker from Kenosha wanted no entangling alliances whatsoever. That spring, the new association leased the 69th Regiment Armory, at Lexington Avenue and 25th Street, within spitting distance of the Garden, for its own automobile show to be held at the same time as the A.L.A.M. event.

"We are in this fight for blood," Jim Couzens exhorted, "and we mean to draw it." Henry Ford said his car was the product of his own brain "and no man on earth was entitled to any 'rake-off'." These were sentiments guaranteed to appeal to makers who had either been denied a Selden license or who didn't care to apply for one. But among the reasons the A.M.C.M.A. was so successful in recruiting members was that the Ford Motor Company made clear financial assistance in its litigation was neither requested nor desired. The pressing need for an organization of independents, of course, was to provide a place to get together to display and sell their wares in the important New York market and other major metropolitan areas. That taken care of, the A.M.C.M.A.'s objectives were similar to the worthier aims of the A.L.A.M.: promoting races and good roads, encouraging public interest in the automobile, and exchanging technical information.*

Fred Smith's demurral notwithstanding, turning the Madison Square Garden show into a private party was obviously not the only high-handed injustice in which the A.L.A.M. indulged. Indeed, even Smith admitted that "We undoubtedly were the direct means of influencing capital to pause before backing an undertaking that might be headed for a lawsuit." Some potential producers were intimidated enough not to even try. When Russell Abner Frisbie, who had been experimenting with automobiles in his Connecticut bicycle shop since the turn of the century, turned down an engineering job at Pope-Hartford, he was advised that attempting manufacture on his own would only bring trouble. Consequently, the Frisbie name was never put on a production car. (Decades later, it would become famous after Yale undergraduates discovered the pie plate manufactured by the family was so aerodynamically well designed that it flew.)

In Los Angeles, the Auto Vehicle Company was convinced but could not prove that its difficulty in securing parts in the East was A.L.A.M. related. Less subtly, the A.L.A.M. would insist that American Simplex of Mishawaka, Indiana, change its name to Amplex before being awarded membership, because there was already a Simplex (built in New York City) among member firms. The Smith, built by the Topeka, Kansas, family formerly well known for manufacture of artificial limbs and trusses, metamorphosed into the Great Smith. But when the business was sold to a consortium of Grand Rapids, Michigan, businessmen who planned to move operations to that city, the A.L.A.M. said

---

* The last named would prove the most important contribution made by the A.L.A.M. "Anything that will save shop cost and promote the quality of the goods and the convenience of users," Henry Joy of Packard wrote, "I think we should consider most earnestly." The A.L.A.M. did. Its Mechanical Branch, composed of engineers of member companies, set standards and nomenclature for materials, parts, processes, and machine tools that would become universal in the U.S. industry. A testing laboratory was maintained at Hartford, Mechanical Branch members met monthly to compare notes, and engineering reports were routinely issued to member companies. Granted, establishment of the Mechanical Branch had been largely a legal tactic in the Selden litigation, but motivation did not lessen the importance of its contribution.

no. Geographic distribution of the industry was the reason; Michigan already had enough automobile plants, whereas Kansas had few. So the Great Smith remained in Topeka, the Grand Rapids businessmen lost interest, a very admirable automobile died through neglect, and its factory was sold to a maker of silos.

———

Unquestionably, the hard-to-get Selden license was coveted by many manufacturers, some like Durant buying a freshly defunct member firm just to get one. This was faster than proving worthiness of purpose before the A.L.A.M. high tribunal. In a delicious piece of irony, George Selden himself, after securing the capital to begin gasoline automobile manufacture in Rochester, New York, received the usual infringement notice from the A.L.A.M. This created the curious situation of a patentee, willing to pay royalties to himself, being prevented from manufacture of his own product. Selden solved this by absorbing the already-licensed Buffalo Gasoline Motor Company, which made for another fine irony. The Buffalo firm had been among the earliest sued under the Selden patent, and among its backers was Charles Annesley, who had bought Henry Ford's first experimental car. Properly accredited ("Seldenized," as the press said), the Selden Motor Vehicle Company strode forthrightly into the industry.

The automobile Selden manufactured bore no resemblance to the automobile he patented, of course, although by now, two of the latter had been produced. Because proving that a car built to the original specs was operable would eventually be necessary, George Day had put engineer Henry Cave to work building one at the Electric Vehicle Company in Hartford as early as 1902. The long lead time was a good idea; Cave had his hands full. "Had he not the essence of patience, tenacity, and resourcefulness," wrote Percy Maxim, "he certainly would have failed and brought himself to the madhouse." Maxim called the engine described in the patent "a fearful and terrible affair" and did not care to speculate on the many thousands of dollars spent to make a car that would run. Frederic Coudert, one of the defense attorneys representing the foreign car litigants, described the result wryly, and accurately, as "much Hartford and little Selden."

A few years later, in Rochester, Selden put his two sons to work on a patent car as well. They had the advantage of the uncompleted Brayton-inspired engine Selden had built in the nineteenth century but exercised some creative license in equipping it with twentieth-century parts and devices. In large letters, on the side of both the Rochester and Hartford Seldens, the year "1877" was boldly painted. George Selden had a stickpin made for himself of his patent car—body of sapphires, hubcaps and lamps in diamonds—which he wore conspicuously in the knot of his cravat on all advantageous occasions.

All was fair in this war. Sarcasm and bitter exchanges marked the testimony. University professors and other engineering experts were contacted on both sides of the Atlantic; A.L.A.M. lawyers searched out the widow of George Brayton for details on her husband's engine work. Ransom Olds and Charles Duryea testified on behalf of the defense, and Ben Briscoe made certain that Jonathan Maxwell did, too. Percy Maxim, torn between his private views and his interest in holding onto his job, was a reluctant witness. Although he chose not to testify, Tom Jeffery anonymously sent $10,000 to Henry Ford for his defense fund.

If updating the Selden patent car was a deception the offense hoped would pass scrutiny, the defense was no less willing to try a few tricks of its own. Ford Motor Company advertising had already predated Henry Ford's first experimental car. And at the Maxwell-Briscoe stand at one A.M.C.M.A. show, a very primitive-looking vehicle was displayed with the legend, "This car was built in San Francisco by J.W. Wilkins in 1877. It is believed to be the first gasoline propelled vehicle ever built." Wilkins had indeed built an automobile the same year Selden submitted his patent application, but it was a steamer; his gasoline car was completed in 1899. The New York show car may have been the '77 chassis with the '99 engine. Most definitely, it was effective propaganda for the independents as thousands passed the Maxwell-Briscoe stand and wondered how the Selden forces could possibly think they had a case at all. Publicly tested was a car the Ford Motor Company built using its own 1903 chassis and running gear, powered by an engine that was an artful amalgam of the Lenoir and another French internal combustion unit, both predating Selden's patent.

In his fight against the Selden patent, Henry Ford did not lack moral support from his fellow outlaws in the industry. A certain class consciousness seems to have been involved in the entire affair. Although it has been suggested that the same geographic distribution that kept the Great Smith in Topeka may have been among the reasons for the refusal of a license to Ford, most probably the fact that the Ford Motor

Company backers did not travel in the same social circles as the powers behind Packard and Olds carried more weight. The Northern and Cadillac companies, backed by Detroit money that was agreeably old, had been readily accepted. Similarly, the newly successful Ben Briscoe, who had begun his career clerking in a hardware store, had not attended the right parties in Detroit prior to moving to Tarrytown, New York, to manufacture the Maxwell. The founding members of the A.L.A.M., by and large, were patricians dedicated to the concept of high-quality automobiles for the privileged classes. Most A.M.C.M.A. members were producing middle-range cars. That Ford was beginning to talk about a car for everybody was seen as hopelessly philistine in A.L.A.M. circles.

———

In 1906, of the top ten companies in the industry, exactly half were A.L.A.M. members. Of the other half, three belonged to the A.M.C.M.A., one was with them in spirit (Tom Jeffery), and the remaining company built only steamers (White of Cleveland; Stanley was ranked eleventh). Ford had forged into first place that year as the Smiths phased out the curved dash Oldsmobile and phased in larger and more expensive cars, the new "Palace Touring" and "Flying Roadster" models fully five feet longer and 1,500 pounds heavier than the little runabout that had made Ransom Olds' name famous. The company that bore his initials was doing very well, in fourth place in the industry *vis-à-vis* Olds Motor Works' sixth, with Reos offered in a full model line of one to four cylinders and emphasis on $1,250-range cars. The Rambler's median price range was the same, and Tom Jeffery was producing as many as he wanted to sell. Two-cylinder Maxwells were available for less than $1,000; Ben Briscoe sold well over 2,000 of them. More than 1,500 White steamers were sold at an average of $3,000; more than 900 Packards found new owners at $4,000+. The Ford Motor Company was far and away the industry leader, with its sales of 8,000+ cars, more than twice the second best seller. But Henry was having the same problem Ransom Olds had at Olds Motor Works. He was being told that Ford should claim its share of the higher-priced market.

"The way to make automobiles is to make one automobile like another," Henry Ford had told stockholder Anderson in 1903, "to make them all alike, to make them come through the factory just alike—just like one pin is like another pin when it comes from a pin factory." By early 1905, Ford operations had moved into a new plant on Piquette Avenue, ten times the size of the original Mack Avenue facilities. Jim Couzens informed reporters in April that production was averaging twenty-five vehicles a day. That May, a Detroit paper headlined, "Plan Ten Thousand Autos at $400 Apiece." When asked how he would do it, Henry responded that "It will take some time to figure out." Looking around the spacious and new but already cluttered and disorganized plant, Ford concluded that there must be a better way to manufacture automobiles.

But his immediate problem was Malcomson. For the 1906 model year, Henry was able to sell his little four-cylinder Model N runabout at $600, but he was also stuck with Malcomson's pet, the big six-cylinder Model K, which he hated. "A car should not have any more cylinders than a cow has teats," Henry snorted. At $2,500, the Model K was not a moneymaker; raised to $2,800, it still wasn't. Disagreements between the two men became heated. Finally, Henry concluded, with no apparent reluctance, that Malcomson had to go. Seeing to it was as adventurous an undertaking as the winter's ride across Lake St. Clair that had brought the land speed record to Ford.

Henry had help, unwittingly from Malcomson himself, who had managed to irritate just about everybody in Ford who mattered. John Dodge hadn't liked the man much since the contract renewal in 1904, when Malcomson argued the brothers' price should be lowered because their risk had been reduced. Jim Couzens, who disagreed, had been Henry's staunch ally virtually from the day he had moved over from the coal company. John Gray's fondness for his nephew did not mitigate his belief that Malcomson was better at his original business, and Horace Dodge could always be relied on to support his brother (and vice versa). Thus, Ford could count on support from almost a majority of the company board of directors already and almost half of the stock that could be voted. Ransom Olds would have envied him that position.

On November 22, 1905, the Ford Manufacturing Company was incorporated. Of its $100,000 capitalization, only $50,000 was subscribed and only $10,000 paid in cash. Ford and Couzens were the masterminds; the Dodges were amiable collaborators. Conspicuously absent on the list of shareholders was Malcomson. He was properly enraged, of course. Ostensibly, the purpose of the Ford Manufacturing Company was to produce engines and running gear for the lower-priced Model N, the Dodges to continue supplying same for the Model K. The concerted entry into the low-priced field to which both Ford and

Couzens were committed made in-house production of drivetrain components logical, but that it was embarked on by a new Ford company had a single purpose. When a minority stockholder friendly to Malcomson expressed reservations, John Gray replied that "I have Mr. Ford's promise that when they get things straightened out with Mr. Malcomson, the Ford Manufacturing Company is to be taken into the Ford Motor Company, just as if it had never existed."

Push never had to come to shove, however, because Malcomson deftly jettisoned himself out of Ford by announcing the formation of a company of his own. The *Detroit Free Press* carried the story on December 5 that a new automobile would be produced in town, called the Aerocar. Malcomson was majority stockholder and majordomo. His idea wasn't bad: an air-cooled car to challenge the popular Franklin built in Syracuse, New York. (Franklin, an A.L.A.M. member, was in the industry's top ten.) But Malcomson's timing was awful. The *Free Press* article mentioned a large new factory already under construction, the plan for an output of 500 cars in 1906, and a doubling of plant capacity by 1907. Even Malcomson's friends on the Ford board were appalled. To their thinking, he was using his share of Ford profits to produce a competitor to the Ford car.

Following a meeting at Ford on December 6, Malcomson was asked to resign as treasurer and director of the company. He refused. In an aggrieved letter of reply, he insisted no conflict of interest existed because his ownership of more than 25 percent of Ford stock was an investment he would naturally want to protect. Malcomson was setting no precedent in holding a major interest in two automobile companies at the same time, but that was not an argument he made. Instead, he railed at the Ford Manufacturing Company as an example of "a general tendency to sacrifice the interests of the general body of stockholders to those of some individuals."

The individuals were ecstatic at this turn of events. To Ford and Couzens, Malcomson's Aerocar venture made his threats of a lawsuit over the formation of the Ford Manufacturing Company less intimidating. The Selden patent was the only litigation they wanted on their hands. Malcomson refused to concede, loudly, into the early summer of 1906, but with the Aerocar Company consuming a lot of his time, he didn't have much left to defend his position at Ford. Moreover, the investment he was anxious to protect didn't appear very attractive anymore. Ford profits could be carefully siphoned into the manufacturing company, leaving the parent company virtually broke. Finally, on July 12, Malcomson capitulated, selling his stock to Ford for $175,000. Given his investment thus far, this represented a fine profit; given what the stock would be worth a decade later, it was a pittance.

Ford, who had sunk his savings into the manufacturing company, borrowed the money for the Malcomson buyout. Three of Malcomson's allies on the board—Woodall, Fry, and Bennett—divested themselves of their stock as well. Strelow had earlier sold his to Couzens when a gold-mining venture in British Columbia seemed more promising. (It wasn't.) "The enemy is completely whipped," Henry chortled to Couzens, who took over as treasurer. Ford already had the manufacturing company's presidency; with the death that July of John Gray, the motor company's was his, too. Ford Manufacturing Company and Ford Motor Company merged as soon as the paperwork was filled out. It had been nothing less than a revolution. The Ford destiny was now firmly in the hands of Henry. "We're going to expand this company, and you will see that it will grow by leaps and bounds," he declared to one of his mechanics on the day he became majority stockholder. "The proper system, as I have it in mind, is to get the car to the multitude."

In August, Walter E. Flanders was hired as production manager. To Ford and Couzens, this was a wonderful coup. No one in America knew more about machine tools, plant design, and factory management than this self-taught native of Vermont. A curly-haired giant of a man whose voice purportedly could be heard in a drop-forge plant, Flanders enjoyed boozing and barroom brawling as much as the Dodges did. To straitlaced Henry, such behavior was off-putting, but his moral indignation was subordinated to how efficiently and quickly his new production manager streamlined Ford production. Flanders yanked out old machines, brought in new ones, rearranged the plant, simplified procedures, set up new parts contracts, and began stockpiling a large inventory. He drilled efficiency into Ford workers like a master sergeant and put the fear of God into Ford suppliers about delivery deadlines.

He also scared Jim Couzens, who thought the Ford treasury would be drained before Flanders' ambitious plans for expanded production were fully implemented. Couzens shared his apprehension with Ford. Henry in turn worried aloud one evening to Charles Sorensen, the twenty-five-year-old Danish-born pattern maker who had joined the company the preceding year. "Mr. Ford was pretty well disturbed over the fact that we didn't have enough money to carry on the business...," Sorensen remembered. "I never knew anybody who had such a fear of debt as he had." But then Ford rambled into his dream of producing a family car that his workers could afford to buy. Diplomatically, Sorensen said that was a "magnificent idea." After a few pensive moments, Ford slapped his young employee on the back and said, "Charlie, I'm going to do that job...I'm determined to do it, and nobody, Couzens or anyone else, is going to stop me on it."

Couzens had no such intention. His fears of red ink had been premature. The Model N runabout was a solid hit, and even Flanders' efficient production couldn't keep up with the demand. Planning was accelerated. Dealers, who were clamoring for Ford cars, would help rid Henry of the one tangible reminder he had of the Malcomson era. For every ten Ns allotted, a dealer had to take one K. The Model R followed as "a car of more pretentious appearance" than the N and was in turn followed by a composite of the N and R that was designated the Model S. Henry was only practicing.

One day that winter, Ford took Sorensen to the third floor of the Piquette plant and, pointing to an unoccupied area, asked that a room be put there "with a door...big enough to run a car in and out." The door was to have a lock. Regarding what was to come out, Henry told a reporter only that he hoped it would be "in the nature of forked lightening." Rarely again would Henry Ford be guilty of such understatement.

CHAPTER 18

Sticks and Stones:
Autophobia and the Law

"NOTHING HAS SPREAD socialistic feeling in this country more than the automobile," Woodrow Wilson, then president of Princeton University, said in 1906. "To the countryman they are a picture of the arrogance of wealth, with all its independence and carelessness." A couple of years earlier, *The Churchman* hinted darkly that the behavior of automobilists could lead to a revolution of the proletariat. In *The Horseless Age*, E.P. Ingersoll complained bitterly that "newspapers circulating chiefly among the working class try to make capital out of class hatred and lose no opportunity to hold up the automobile as a means of oppression of the poor by the wealthy."

Henry Ford was preparing to produce a car for the common man. The question was: Did the common man want it? As more and more cars appeared on the road, so did public hostility against them. "The only obstacle in the way of the general use of the automobile in the next ten years," *Outing* concluded in 1906, "is the automobile owner himself." *The New York Times* fulminated about the "worthless sons" of the very rich and other "rowdies having money enough to own [cars] without sense enough to drive them properly." Or to behave civilly. "Don't run away after running down anybody; you'll stand a better chance if you stay" was the admonition in one motorist's handbook. "Don't leave the scene of an accident," read another, "...remember that small country places are connected with each other by rural telephones."

But the automobile was both sinner and sinned against. For years, a routine listing in *The New York Times* annual index was "Automobiles Stoned," and the newspaper estimated that probably not one attack in a dozen was even reported. While decrying "the street arabs who hurled discarded kitchen ware" at stockbroker E.R. Thomas' automobile as it motored sedately into town, the *Times* observed that "The outrage and violence from which Mr. Thomas suffered were the riotous and unlawful reflection of a public sentiment which the reckless drivers and owners of automobiles have themselves created." Another editorial suggested that the motorists whose cars were stoned should be thankful the dents were not on their heads "where, to tell the plain truth, they would usually do most good." The Chicago Automobile Club attempted to combat the problem by taking suspected stoners for rides in member cars. Other clubs in urban areas tried well-publicized good deeds, such as annual automobile outings for orphans, to gain public sympathy for the automobile's cause. In New York, a raffle of a car was held to benefit the Free School of Crippled Children.

––––

Lawlessness in cities could be managed to a degree, but in rural areas, the automobilist remained on his own. Farmers, both individually and in groups, rose up to protest the invasion of their territory. In 1904, *The Breeder's Gazette* stated that speeding motorists were no more fit to be at large than mad dogs. Farm journals routinely referred to the automobile as murderous, deadly, and a menace. Tacks and broken glass were strewn over rural roads; across them, rope and sometimes barbed wire was strung from tree to tree. Particularly effective were saws and rakes buried teeth up. A passing motorist in Upstate New York was horsewhipped. The driver of a Pope-Hartford in South Carolina felt the whiz of pistol shots above his head. Among devices patented on the automobilists' behalf were a giant pair of scissors to be mounted on the front of a car for cutting rope or barbed-wire from the driver's seat, and two fans for mounting at the rear of the car to deflect bullets. Autophobia was widespread in the countryside.

A farmer's club in New Jersey pledged not to support any candidate for public office who owned an automobile; in Chatham Country, Georgia, a small-town mayor made a public apology and an explanation for his purchase of a car. "If we were running for Congress, we would not accept an automobile as a gift," a newspaper editor in Kansas declared. Automobile enthusiast William Lampton lamented that practically every civilized ruler in the world was an automobile owner except the President of the United States, who "has declined to combine his own strenuosity with that of the automobile lest dire disaster follow, to man and machine." More likely, Teddy Roosevelt was not a car owner because he was a good politician. He did drive a White steamer once— while visiting Puerto Rico.*

Newspaper publisher William Randolph Hearst understood the appeal. An auto enthusiast since the turn of the century, he returned from England, enthralled with Lord Montagu's magazine of social motoring, *The Car Illustrated*, and started one in America called *MoToR*. Hearst prided himself on being the first U.S. Congressman to be arrested for speeding, which may have been among the numerous reasons the publisher's political career was so brief.

In New England, non-car-owning "cottagers" offered a reward for apprehension of speed demons. In Oyster Bay, the Long Island Highway Protective Society was formed to assist local authorities in making the roads safe. Among the early violators identified was actress Lillian Russell; among the earliest apprehended was millionaire sportsman Foxhall Keene, who argued that had he been driving as recklessly as

---

* To the President's chagrin, his daughter was an ardent automobilist. Alice Roosevelt was offered cars gratis by several manufacturers and even tried to order one herself in 1903. "Wedded to horse flesh," the *Washington Post* reported, "the President refuses to allow Alice to take possession of a motor car." So the irrepressible young woman, who had already embarrassed her father by rouging her cheeks and smoking in public, did the next best thing. Her friend, the Countess Marguerite Cassini, daughter of the Russian ambassador, owned a large red touring car, and the two of them would pile as many young men as could fit into the tonneau and speed around Washington, exulting in the commotion they were creating. Alice's trek from Newport to Boston in a French Panhard racer brought further tut-tuts. The President's political friends—and perhaps even his enemies—agreed among themselves that Theodore Roosevelt was better at handling affairs of state than daughter Alice.

alleged, the bicycling deputy sheriff would not have been able to catch him. His point was well taken. He was still arrested.

Although a few members availed themselves of the tacks-and-glass approach, the Long Island Highway Protective Society was law-abiding and anxious principally to lobby for stricter road laws. "We recognize that the automobile is the twentieth century vehicle," the organization's 1902 incorporation charter read, "and that it is with us to stay." The problem for local authorities throughout the country was what to do with the vehicle that would not go away.

Legal bridling of this new form of transportation was haphazard. At the turn of the century, the automobile was classified with "wild animals" in the New York Penal Code. In Boston, the board of aldermen sought to ban any vehicle of which it did not unanimously approve. For years, Elwood Haynes carried in his pocket a copy of the 1901 Indiana Supreme Court decision that "highways and streets are not for the exclusive use of vehicles propelled by animal power."

The earliest battle for automobilist rights had been fought in city parks: the South Side in Chicago, Fairmount in Philadelphia, and Druid Hill in Baltimore. Park commissioners routinely barred automobiles. Chicago electric producer Clinton E. Woods defiantly drove his car into forbidden territory in order to be arrested. Similarly, in New York, a veritable flotilla of automobilists motored into Central Park to protest exclusion. Ultimately, the motorists won out, although permits to drive in parks were required for awhile.

———

Legal restraints against the automobile ran a wide gamut. An ordinance passed in Chicago allowed drivers to wear eyeglasses but not *pince-nez*. Nettlesome was the regulation in many areas that gasoline tanks had to be drained before a car boarded a ferry. Driving after dark wasn't allowed in other communities. Certain counties in West Virginia didn't allow automobiles at all as late as 1905.

As late as 1907, a bill was introduced in the Alabama legislature to prohibit the use of automobiles on all public highways of the state. Tennessee demanded a week's notice before the commencement of an automobile trip.

The equine sensibility was accommodated in other legislation. San Rafael, California, required a driver to come to a complete halt within 300 feet of a passing horse; motorists in Iowa had to telephone ahead that they would be arriving in town "so that owners of nervous horses may be warned in advance." In New York State, the raising of a hand by the owner of a horse-drawn vehicle required an automobile driver to pull to the side of the road and stop; another hand signal, and he had to shut off his engine. Vermont carried a law on its books requiring "a person of mature age carrying a red flag" to precede an automobile by an eighth of a mile (obviously cribbed from England's notorious "Red Flag" act). In Belleville, Illinois, a bell had to be rung 15 feet before each intersection. In New Hampshire, if two vehicles approached an intersection at the same time, both had to stop and neither proceed until the other passed, a law that had not been well thought out. In Washington, D.C., the increasing number of vehicles on the streets, and the conundrum of how to deal with them, brought an official request from Congress to the State Department to inquire from consuls abroad about regulations in effect in foreign countries.

Most early laws had to do strictly with speed. Automobilists insisted that the same "reasonable and proper" allowed horse-drawn vehicles should be allowed them. Most automobiles were capable of more than the 15 miles per hour of a horse and buggy. In New England, a "common trot" was a nebulous limit soon replaced by a number. Attempts to arrive at the speed figure scientifically were made in New York City, where the board of aldermen conducted brake testing. "That a motor vehicle running at twenty miles an hour may be brought to a standstill in eighty to a hundred feet is a fact of mechanical interest," *The New York Times* observed, but still did not properly address the traffic situation.

Speed limits were generally made arbitrarily. Some hamlets allowed no more than 2 or 3 miles per hour. In New York State, 20 miles per hour was approved for country roads, and 8 miles per hour for villages and cities. Connecticut okayed 12 miles per hour in cities but put the limit at 15 miles per hour in the country. The Massachusetts state legislature's passing of a 10-miles-per-hour limit sent Brockton automobilists to the record books to complain that "a man can run that fast." One Michigan town allowed bicyclists to pedal 10 miles per hour but kept automobiles to 8. "The speed limit this year is a secret" read the sign leading into another small town, followed by a warning that violators would be prosecuted. No state was more resolute on "scorching" than New Jersey. "The only evil in the state is the automobilists and their deadly machines," one politician said in 1902. "Jersey Justice" was quickly rendered to anyone invading the border who was caught.

Catching the culprits was the problem. They didn't always stop. "The Automobile War on the North Shore" was the title of an article in *The Horseless Age* in 1902, detailing how Chicago area authorities made sure they got their man. Cordwood or logs thrown in the path of speeders proved effective. Speed traps were everywhere. Particularly feared was a magistrate named Kellogg in New York, whom *Automobile Topics* accused of "petty despotism." A mayor named Dennis in Illinois strung steel cables across the main road into his town until he was successfully sued and had to substitute large artificial bumps.

Some motor vehicle statutes held the occupants of an automobile liable for the same penalty as the driver, regardless of the charge. Following the collision of a Winton with a streetcar, chauffeur W. Byrd Raymond gave his own particulars but refused to divulge the identity of the people in the back seat nor who owned the car. He was "railroaded to the penitentiary," said *The Automobile and Motor Review*, while the trolley-car driver went free. Retribution was swift in those days. Recalled pioneer motorist Edward Ringwood Hewitt: "There was no leniency and no tickets; immediate arrest and jail was routine." Bail of $500 was required before Victor Plumer of Fifth Avenue was released from the Harlem police station. Saying that he had been "hurrying to the bed of a friend who was ill in Yonkers" didn't impress the judge after the arresting bicycle policeman said he had chased Robert Goelet's automobile for twenty blocks, and it stopped only after the policeman had yelled himself hoarse. In Vermont, Dr. Nelson Jackson, the first man to cross the country in an automobile, cheerfully pled guilty to exceeding Burlington's 6-miles-per-hour speed limit in the same Winton. In Massachusetts, the Stanley brothers enjoyed confounding the constabulary on Sunday afternoon drives; when one of the brothers was pulled over for speeding, his identical twin would motor past in an identical car, which invariably left the arresting officer scratching his head for awhile.

Motorists detested the speed traps, often justifiably. Guilt was about evenly divided between autophile and autophobe. While some drivers got genuine delight in seeing how close they could come to a pedestrian without hitting him—"close misses are the sweeteners of the automobilist's existence," one editorial explained—it was equally true that many boys found sport in standing in the middle of the road to determine how long they could remain "in the danger zone without getting hit."

Accidents were inevitable. Inexperience was often to blame. Of the 207 cars negotiating a sharp turn on Pelham Road (New York), counted by a reporter for *Outing* in 1906, thirty-one didn't bother to slow down, and five ended in the ditch. Automobilists wrecking their cars didn't bother non-automobilists much. Fatalities aroused their ire. Most deadly serious accidents happened in or near urban areas—collisions with trolleys, runaway horses, and even runaway automobiles. In reporting the death near West Point of F.H. Benedict, whose father-in-law was Selden patent defense attorney Frederic Coudert, pointed mention was made of the young man's earlier reckless driving on Long Island, which had terrified a cousin of the President "and the entire Roosevelt family was arrayed on her side during the controversy." There was a subtle implication that Benedict had reaped his just desserts.

Some rued that the automobile had been invented at all.

CHAPTER 19

Of Ills and Remedies

IN THE ONGOING dialog about the automobile's relative merits, the risk to innocent victims was the number one argument of the anti-auto contingent. The risk to motorists engaged automobile advocates. Some safety requirements for vehicle construction were the norm in Europe, not in the United States. "Government supervision of the matter would be quite to the point," commented *The Horseless Age*. But *laissez-faire* prevailed, and some truly hazardous cars were marketed. Even among exemplary automobiles, there was naïveté as to potential sources of danger. Had Diamond Jim Brady collided with anything, all that curved glass he had ordered in his Baker Electric would have had shattering results, both literally and figuratively, for everyone inside.

And from some quarters came warnings that motoring simply wasn't good for you. It was psychologically unnerving, one newspaper said, because people "will never get used to speeding along the road behind nothing." Predicted a medical journal, "If the machine ever attains the unlikely speed of 80 miles an hour, it will have to drive itself, for the human brain will be incapable of controlling it." Anatomy was considered, too. Some physicians warned of the "decay of the human legs" as people gave up walking for driving; others opined that an automobile's noise had a detrimental "influence on patients with nervous disorders." Circulatory disturbances were foreseen for the delicate female constitution. Even robust men were regarded as inviting sinus problems with exposure to wind currents, and positive havoc to nasal passages as "small winged insects" were inhaled while motoring. Speed was an addiction, one doctor said, not unlike tobacco and alcohol: "It is clear that permission to drive...should not be accorded to anyone who has ever exhibited signs of mental disequilibrium...even healthy persons find it hard enough to keep their balance." The quasi-medical term for the physiological result of habitual speeding was "automobile face," evidenced by a perpetually open mouth which, aesthetics notwithstanding, rendered the motorist more likely to infection.

But each of these arguments could be turned on its ear—and was, by other physicians and enthusiasts. Rhapsodies were written on the benefits of motoring in the great outdoors. "The cubic feet of fresh air that are literally forced into one while automobiling rehabilitate worn-out nerves and drive out worry, insomnia and indigestion," publisher Frank Munsey wrote. "It will renew the life and youth of the overworked man or woman, and will make the thin fat and the fat—but I forbear." The disuse of legs in walking, it was argued, was compensated by their vigorous use in controlling the pedals in the cockpit of a car. The automobile's jolting ride was regarded as beneficial. "It 'acts on the liver,' to use a popular phrase," said one doctor, "which means only that it aids the peristaltic movements of the bowels and promotes the good performance of their functions."

Overwhelmingly, the principal benefit seen for the general adoption of the automobile was ecological. The figures were staggering. In New York City alone, 150,000 horses deposited an estimated 2.5 million pounds of manure and 60,000 gallons of urine on the streets each day. When he was eighty years old, Ransom Olds was asked by a reporter why he had been motivated to develop an automobile. "I didn't like the smell of horses on the farm," he replied.

The situation was far worse in urban areas. Cities smelled like huge stables at the turn of the century. Traffic pounded manure into a dust that flew into trouser cuffs and skirt linings, and into apartment windows to permeate carpets and furniture. Wet weather turned the excreta into soup to be waded through and tracked home. Summer heat waves felled horses in their tracks; others were destroyed right on the streets after breaking their legs. Removal averaged 15,000 dead horses annually in New York City. Rotting carcasses fouled the air more.

"Ideal health conditions cannot prevail as long as horses are in the city," the Chicago health commissioner declared. Two-thirds of a city street's filth was directly attributable to the animals. So, in significant measure, was the routine outbreak in cities of tetanus, dysentery, diarrhea, and typhoid. Inhaling a gasoline car's fumes might be unpleasant, automobile adherents argued, but it paled in comparison to horse droppings. Moreover, while automobiles might be noisy, their sound level in cities was no more than iron-clad hooves clattering over brick and cobblestone streets. Reprised was the humanitarian approach that had prompted Richard Dudgeon to build his steamer during the Civil War era. The automobile would provide emancipation for the horse from his life of travail.

Not surprisingly, none of these arguments was found worthy by harness makers, blacksmiths, and proprietors of livery stables, who saw their livelihood threatened. Others simply preferred hoofed power. "The horse is an intelligent animal," one devoted equestrian protested, "the automobile is a brainless machine." Moral influence was also cited. "There is something noble about a horse," wrote another, "...that humanizes those who love him." Because of ardent devotion to his horse, bicycle maker Adolph Arnold was able to talk partner Ignaz Schwinn out of entering the automobile field.

Automobile makers were perhaps a bit too vociferous in extolling the advantages of their machines. Talk that the horse was "already obsolete and deserved to be" brought widespread protest, even from some automobilists. Vowing that he had no intention of giving up equestrianism, John Gilmore Speed declared in *Cosmopolitan* that "There is room in this wide world for both horses and horseless carriages."

It didn't seem so at first. *Munsey's Magazine* cited 1905 accident statistics—40 percent fatalities by runaway horse, only 5 percent by automobile, and the remainder by railroad, streetcar, or on water—to declare the automobile the "safest means of transit." That begged the question of what caused some of the horses to run away. Asked whether his car ever frightened horses, Henry Ford cleverly said that it "depends on the horse. A low-bred, ignorant horse, yes; a high-born fellow, no."

Proximity accustomed city animals to automobiles more quickly than in small towns. In rural areas, farmers looked upon the situation as one to be solved entirely by the automobilist. Among the ideas suggested by the Farmers Anti-Automobile Association of Pennsylvania was to require automobiles to be equipped with a large canvas depicting a landscape scene for display in front of the car until the horse had passed. If the animal still was not convinced, the automobile had to be pulled to the side of the road, dismantled and its parts hidden in the bushes, to be reassembled only after the horse was safely on its way. Despite the importance of the rural vote, the Pennsylvania state legislature declined to act on these proposals.

Automobile enthusiasts came up with ideas of their own, some equally as ludicrous. Joseph Barsaleux of Sandy Hill, New York, thought the solution was a vehicle that would fool horses into thinking they were meeting one of their own and invented a dummy animal with engine inside (the driving wheel between four stationary legs), which could be hooked up to a carriage and driven by reins. Unfortunately, Barsaleux's automotive horse couldn't run as fast as the animal it was intended to replace. More practical was the "Horsey Horseless" expedient suggested by Uriah Smith of Battle Creek, Michigan: a sculpted horse's head on the front of an automobile. Apparently, a few automobilists tried this during the early years, even Ransom Olds admitting that he had bought a harness maker's dummy for the purpose.

The long-term solution, of course, was simply for horses to become used to automobiles. This doubtless would have happened eventually anyway, but automobilists sought to accelerate the process. Prior to one automobile club meet, horses were invited to the fairground to eat hay out of the rear seats of competing cars. More formal was the establishment of "schools for horses" by enthusiast organizations in various communities. Even livery men found it advantageous to enroll. The course of instruction was free and usually required three mornings. The horse received a diploma upon graduation.

———

"I like motoring," Rudyard Kipling said in 1904, "because I have suffered for its sake." That sentiment could have been echoed throughout America. Unpleasant confrontations with horses, the possibility of being stoned or even shot at, verbal abuse, taunts, and ridicule—all were part of automobiling. And not necessarily even the worst of it.

How much one suffered depended on the degree of preparation, which included what one wore. The dust on country roads dictated that, no matter how warm the weather, a car's occupants be well covered. Full-length double-breasted linen dusters were the norm for both men and women. Fortunately, the bicycling craze had made sporting attire for women socially acceptable because climbing into an automobile in a crinoline or bustle would have been difficult and, if caught up in the machinery or gear levers, a potential disaster. Most women motored in the long skirt and shirtwaist popularized by Charles Dana Gibson, over which the duster could be easily worn. Hats were held on with three-yard scarves, and veiling shrouded the entire face. Hat brims were narrow because, it was said, "a twenty-mile breeze is not compatible with the Gainsborough style of millinery." Only above the neck could one readily distinguish between the motoring sexes. Men eschewed the ladies' veiling for a cap and goggles, and sometime a mask. As women became more daring, they put their veils away and adopted the men's headgear. Gauntlet-like gloves were necessary for drivers to prevent wind riffling up the sleeve.

Cooler weather brought out leather for men, both in jodhpur-type leggings and Norfolk-style jackets. *Scientific American* recommended kangaroo hides because that animal's skin was oily and shed water well. For inclement weather, some motorists opted for a raincoat that spread from the lap over the entire dash of the car. Rubber "rainshirts" were a popular item "to keep always aboard the car for emergency."

When the weather became colder, one just put on more clothing. A.J. Hodson, a Wisconsin doctor who built his own car in 1902, described his winter motoring attire from inside out: a union suit, a suit of perforated buckskin, a heavy business suit, a pair of slicker overalls and jumper, two pairs of socks and one of felt shoes, yarn mittens over kid gloves, and a cap with ears. Such attire provided protection against more than the cold. When playboy Veryl Preston and two female companions were tossed out of a car in a mid-December accident, their cold weather gear cushioned the fall and was believed the reason no bones were broken.

Beaver and raccoon coats came into vogue, but some motorists in the early days wore the fur on the inside. "How to look well when automobiling is a problem which many women are finding a difficult one to solve," a fashion expert commented. Most serious automobilists, male and female, made the decision for comfort. Carrying newspapers onboard to be stuffed under coats when the weather turned suddenly chilly was recommended.

Some automobiles hibernated the entire winter. The sporting proclivity of the owner was usually the deciding factor. There was always the possibility that if you didn't freeze, your car might. Various combinations of wood alcohol, glycerin, and sodium carbonate were advised for the cooling system. Swathing the carburetor in hot-water-soaked flannel or felt and asbestos, and throwing a lap robe over the radiator could help in cold-weather starts. One manufacturer offered a device for heating the steering wheel by means of the exhaust. Winter motoring could be lovely, as could night-time driving, although here the sporting challenge was seeing the road via acetylene or kerosene lamps whose flickering beam illuminated six feet ahead or so. The advantage of driving at night, in addition to the lessened chance of encountering horses, was elimination of the clouds of hot dust that bedeviled automobilists during the day. Ladies could remove their veils, and men their masks.

As important as one's own wearing apparel in motoring was how well one's car was dressed. An automobile was sold practically naked. A top, lamps, extra tires, horn, and spare parts could cost as much as the purchase price of the less expensive cars, which meant that many runabout owners who had scrimped to buy hit the road unprepared for anything but good luck.

Expecting that was expecting a lot. "With new cars, go new operators," explained enthusiast Leon Vandervort, "men who have never handled anything more complicated in the mechanical line than a bicycle or a telephone." Many of them didn't have the foggiest notion of what an automobile was all about. Jim Couzens enjoyed telling about his first drives with boss Alexander Malcomson in the latter's Winton just before their collaboration with Henry Ford. "Frequently he turned something on the dash board, explaining to me that he was changing the mixture," Couzens said. "I thought that he meant he was mixing water with the gasoline and I continued to think so for a long time." In apparent seriousness, C.L. Bangs of Malden, Massachusetts, wrote *Motor Review* of his discovery that running his car into a telegraph pole was an awkward way of bringing it to a standstill "as it sometimes sets the machine on fire."

Being related to someone in the automobile business certainly helped in becoming a skilled automobile operator faster. Florence E. Woods, schoolgirl daughter of electric producer Clinton E. Woods, was the first of her sex to obtain the necessary permit to drive in Central Park. Elwood Haynes' daughter, Bernice, was an accomplished automobilist at sixteen, although her excursions were confined to Kokomo because she couldn't crank the car herself. Cranking required strength; finesse and a good memory were needed for the other chores in starting a gasoline car—turning on the carburetor tap, switching on the accumulator, engaging the brake, disengaging the clutch, putting the gear lever in neutral, opening the throttle, retarding the ignition, and tickling the carburetor float—and those Bernice had mastered.

Without fortuitous family connections, a new motorist had to make do with the instructions provided by the trained factory mechanic who was delivered with the car, but this service was accorded only purchasers of expensive automobiles, and eventually the factory man went home. Most cars were delivered more informally, the dealer and the client proceeding to the railroad yard where the latter climbed into the boxcar to approve his purchase, and the two then going to the bank. Dealers usually offered little more than a demonstration ride, figuring their job was finished once the sale was made. The automobilist's was only beginning.

"No person would expect to become a musician if he did not practice his exercises," *The New York Times* noted, "and the same is true of automobiles." Practice did not always make perfect. "Cases have been known where men have practiced day after day," commented *The Automobile Magazine,* "and have ended by running down fences, innocent dogs in the highways, or colliding with trees, to the great disadvantage of the tree, not to mention the automobile." By 1904, the Y.M.C.A. had opened its first automobile school in Boston, which was so successful that other major cities followed. Perhaps early to sign up in Baltimore was the Stanley owner who tied his car to a stake and let it go around in circles until it ran out of steam because he couldn't figure out the shutoff mechanism.

Manufacturers usually provided extensive manuals for purchasers. In 1899, Edgar Apperson had sought to demonstrate that his Kokomo factory instructions were explicit enough by taking the secretary who had typed them to lunch and then telling her to drive back to the plant by herself. Apperson also wanted to prove to himself that a woman could drive.

"Don't take anybody's word for it that your tanks have plenty of gasoline and water and your cup plenty of oil," Olds Motor Works advised. "They may be guessing." General how-to books were legion. "Steering a car when running backwards is diametrically opposite to that when running forward," L. Elliott Brookes mentioned in *The Automobile Handbook*. "Don't look for gasoline leaks with a candle or a match," Forrest R. Jones noted sagely in *Automobile Catechism*. "Don't use a match for seeing how much gasoline is in a tank." One of the "Things Worth Knowing on the Road" published in *Country Life in America* was that picking up a stick by the side of the road and poking it into the gas tank without making sure it was clean beforehand could lead to carburetor problems. In *The Lever*, the carburetor was described as a device that "mixes drinks for the cylinders."

"In driving, the heel of either foot will be allowed to rest on the floor of the car, with the ball of the foot resting lightly on either pedal, from which position the feet will not be moved so long as the car is in motion" was the instruction from *Harper's Weekly*, "if the feet were taken from the pedals, and it should become necessary to stop suddenly, the novice might become confused and be unable to find the proper pedals with his feet." Any knock in any automobile was a sure sign something was wrong, *Outing* commented, "many troubles begin with a gentle rhythmical tapping." And from everywhere came the advice that one should practice driving regularly for at least a week before inviting friends for a ride, longer if the friends were ladies.

"Never condemn a machine because it won't work properly under your personal management," enthusiast Elliott Ranney wrote. "You are more apt to be at fault than the machine." With that, the automobile manufacturers heartily concurred. One of them, unnamed but probably Alexander Winton, was quoted as saying, "We wouldn't need to repair the machine so often if we could fix the machinery in a man's head." *Country Life in America* queried a number of factories regarding the sins owners most often committed against their cars. H.H. Franklin of Syracuse, New York, listed twenty-two, among them "changing the construction or mechanism of machine to suit some fanciful idea" and "continually meddling with the spark coil vibrators." From Buffalo,

E.R. Thomas complained that "the owner expects his car to run all day, seven days out of every week, with no attention to adjustments." Frank Duryea was appalled that Stevens-Duryea purchasers neglected lubrication, despite being told of its vital importance. The White company deftly inserted a commercial in commenting that its steamer could operate longer without proper care than a gasoline car and therefore was often taken for granted. "An automobile in the hands of some persons is like a valuable watch in the hands of a six-year-old boy," wrote the producers of the Baker Electric. "The same exhilarating joy is experienced in the possession, but they are more liable to use a hammer than judgment in investigations and imagined needed repairs."

Exhilaration was the undoing of many experienced motorists. They took to the road with cheerful abandon. Possibly the most ill-conceived trek in American automobile history was the drive to San Francisco that John D. Davis and his wife, Louise, attempted in a car Colonel Pope built especially for them, in 1899, four years before Dr. Nelson drove from the West in the Winton. They left New York City in mid-July; in September, *The Automobile* reported that "Mr. and Mrs. Davis...have at last gotten out of the state of New York." Detroit was reached twenty-five breakdowns later, and the Davises arrived in Chicago shortly before winter set in, having spent far more for repairs than the cost of the car. They elected to proceed no further. Rather than endure American road conditions, wealthy motorists shipped their cars abroad to tour the splendid roads on the Continent.

Before venturing into the countryside, an automobilist was well advised to equip himself for any eventuality. One enthusiast suggested no fewer than seventy different items of repair; others found such standard household items as chewing gum, rubber bands, strong twine, and two-by-fours useful. Useful, too, for motorists who could afford it was the small sterling silver device marketed by Tiffany & Company to prevent cigar ashes from blowing in the driver's face. Less practical apparently was the venetian blind that was sold by another company for bracketing to the rear of the car to alleviate the problem of blowing dust.

Dust was irksome, but rain was worse. It ruined the trip from Western Springs to Sycamore (Illinois) that Paul Hoffman took with his family in a Pope-Hartford. "In the first few miles I changed four spark plugs. Otherwise everything was lovely," Hoffman wrote, demonstrating the forbearance typical of automobilists of the period. As Kipling said,

"Any fool can wait to buy the invention when it is thoroughly perfected." But then the rains came. Hoffman had to cut brush to provide traction for the wheels; with darkness, the carbide lamps were turned on, flickered, and went out. The car slid into a ditch on the slick road, and a nearby farmer provided accommodations for the night. While the Hoffman ladies were grateful for the bed, they were horrified to learn that a hatchet murder had taken place in the house, which the farmer's wife told them about in grisly detail. The next morning, the car was manhandled out of the culvert and headed for home. Abruptly, the Pope-Hartford just stopped. Grandpa Hoffman gashed his forehead trying to crank it to restart. Paul's aunt and mother began to cry. A gerrymander fix of a part broken during the excursion into the ditch made the car operable again. The two ladies decided to take the streetcar home in St. Charles, and the men limped on fourteen miles to the nearest garage in Aurora, hitting at least fifty deep ruts on the way. "Grandpa used most of his vivid vocabulary," Hoffman wrote. "The car stayed in the Aurora garage about a month and was practically rebuilt." And the Hoffman family was back on the road.

The tenacity of automobilists confounded those who didn't own automobiles. Wrote one horse lover after accepting the invitation of a friend for a country drive and patiently sitting through several stops, "Finally there was a new kind of wheeze, more vicious and portending greater evil than any of the others, and with a gasp we stopped again. I felt sure this was the machine's death rattle. Another rapid exit and removal of cushions, floor and impedimenta, and another ante-mortem statement from the engine. This time the ailment was deeper seated and involved a subterranean examination. Finally my former friend—for he was a friend no longer—crawled out from under, explaining that the 'thing-em-bob' had caught on the 'whatch-call-it...'" The horse lover chose to walk.

Even with all mechanical parts operating to perfection, the pioneer motorist was not home free, for failing with even greater frequency were his tires. Under the best of circumstances, they were good for less than 1,000 miles; on rutted country roads, the number of punctures skyrocketed. Changing the tire was a chore. One automobilist described the procedure: "You unstrap [the spare], lay it by your wheel; then prod, pry and pull at the old tire-casing, pull, pry and prod again at the new; insert its intestinal tubing; and pump, pump, pump in the hot sunlight [to about 70 pounds pressure] till the firm, replete and distended tire encircles your wheel like some gargantuan sausage." Only the unusually skillful could manage the job in an hour.

Repairing rather than replacing an inner tube on the road required dexterity, too. Rubber patches or plugs with a mushroom head often became unglued, and other remedies had to be found. Stuck by the side of the road on a trip to Albany (New York), Edward Ringwood Hewitt wished aloud that he had some electrical tape "to hold the damn plug in." Mrs. Hewitt replied that if silk tape would do, she thought she could find some in the woods. "This seemed a queer place to me to look for tape," Hewitt recalled, "but I was so mad that I didn't pay much attention." His wife returned with the tape, "and I noticed she was not the same shape she had been when she went into the woods." The Hewitts made it to Albany without further incident.

Electric owners, who seldom strayed far from the city, were provided lists of charging stations in "suburban territory" by the various Edison companies. Steamers could usually find water in either town or country. But gasoline was really a problem at first for those whose cars had internal combustion engines. "More than once I had to go to a cleaning establishment for gas," Bellamy Partridge remembered, "and in one town the popcorn stand was the only place where it could be bought." General stores, hardware stores, and blacksmiths soon found it profitable to stock gasoline because, in desperation, an automobilist might grumble but would pay whatever the going rate. Gasoline quality was low; a pocket hydrometer could be used to test it, not that there was much of a choice about purchase. Foolish was the driver who did not filter the gasoline through a piece of chamois into the tank.

If finding fuel taxed the patience of drivers of gasoline cars, finding one's way perplexed all automobilists. Rand McNally published the first road map in 1904 of "The Country Around New York"; the A.A.A. followed with its first Blue Book in 1905 for the same area. Both used buildings, streams, or other visual aids as landmarks. Road signs were few. On the East Coast, the Automobile Club of America, aware that "state and county authorities are not inclined to give speedy attention to the matter," took the initiative and put up signposts along routes most usually traveled by members. In the Midwest, Tom Jeffery spent $25,000 to erect thousands of road signs in Wisconsin and Illinois, which was widely applauded as a public-spirited gesture. But it was money cleverly spent. Each sign indicated the way and the distance to the nearest town or city, above a prominent Rambler logo.

Neither of these efforts helped Carl Fisher, however, when he and two friends motored less than ten miles outside Indianapolis. Because of typical road delays, darkness fell midway home, as did rain. Arriving at a three-way fork in the road, the men were pondering which to take when one spotted a sign high on a pole. "We matched to see who should climb," Fisher said. "I lost." Halfway up the pole, he realized he had forgotten the matter of light, shinnied down, put a book of matches in his hat, put the hat back on his head, started climbing again, and eventually reached the top. "I scratched a match and before the wind blew it out I read the sign," he remembered. "It said: 'Chew Battle-Ax Plug'."

———

Worse than any happenstance on the road was what could happen to an automobilist when he consigned his car to an expert for repair. That Paul Hoffman's Pope-Hartford remained in the garage for a month following his family's ill-fated excursion in Illinois was not unusual. "A job that should take an hour will consume a day, for it takes about eight hours to find out what needs to be done and how to do it," *The Horseless Age* commented. "In many cases when one part is duly fixed something else is thrown out of adjustment, and then comes a puzzling search, sometimes taking several days..." A month could go by very quickly that way.

Garage mechanics were often little more experienced than owners, although fast talking might convince the naive automobilist otherwise— at least until, as happened in one well-known New York garage, the mechanic installed the differential housing backwards, and the owner drove out to discover that he had one speed forward, three in reverse. Even the most ingenious of car owners cringed whenever repairs were necessary in a small town where the only recourse was the local blacksmith. "His equipment of tools consists generally of a forge and anvil, ax, heavy hammer and a cold chisel," one enthusiast wrote, "...the delicacy and accuracy of some of his repairs may well be left to the imagination." *Motor World* complained that even the work performed in repair departments of most factories was "badly done, expensive and altogether unsatisfactory."

One answer was to have a mechanically adept chauffeur in your personal employ, but that was a solution available only to the well-heeled who did not always make a wise choice of whom to employ. Manufacturers of high-priced cars—Locomobile in Bridgeport, and Pierce in Buffalo, for example—established factory schools to train those who would be driving their customers' cars; their customers frequently sent their former coachmen to be turned into chauffeurs. Learning to drive well was possible in a two-week course; learning mechanics wasn't. When Rastus Johnson, chauffeur to former Brooklyn mayor Frederick W. Wurster, found his employer's car begin to shake uncontrollably in downtown Greenwich, Connecticut, he "stuck to the machine as if his mount had been a bucking mule," rode it round and round and into the air, before finally bringing the vehicle to a halt without injury to himself or anyone else. To fix what was wrong, the car had to be sent back to the factory.

Moreover, many coachmen were reluctant to make the change to mechanical horsepower. "Deeply disgusted" was the phrase used by Alva Belmont, hostess of the Newport automobile "obstacle course" lawn party, to describe her coachman's reaction when the Belmonts purchased their first car. "When, as occasionally happened, our auto stalled on Ocean Drive and we had to send for Lewis to come to our rescue with the horses, he was secretly delighted," Alva recalled. "Every such manifestation of the inferiority of the automobile was a source of gratification to him, and in his eyes at least a vindication of his low opinion of our latest acquisition." Lewis never was won over.

Former factory mechanics were the obvious optimal choice for a chauffeur's job, and many were so employed. But for awhile, it was considered much more fashionable to hire someone from France. "March 9th—Engaged incognito Count for chauffeur. We all hope to improve our accent. Maybe he will get us into society," Helena Smith Dayton wrote jocularly in her motoring diary. "...May 29th—Arm still in sling. Count's fault. New man coming to-morrow." The cachet for a French chauffeur abated somewhat when it was discovered that the driving academy certificates many brought over with their accents were forged.

Imported chauffeurs tended to be snobs, refusing menial tasks like washing the car and imperiously looking down their noses at the owners of garages and repair stations. A good number also tended to drink a lot, with predictable results on the road. In opening its New York City chauffeur's school in 1904, the Y.M.C.A. averred that the young men it would train "will have the natural desire to avoid running over Americans."

Chauffeur—from the French verb "to heat"—had become a noun initially to define one who fired up or stoked a fire. This lent itself well to both the motoring chauffeur's reputation for daredevilry on the road and his prowess back at the manor. Heiresses eloping with the family retainer was a staple of society columns for years. That the reason for this phenomenon was the automobile and not its driver was explained, breathlessly, in the pages of William Randolph Hearst's *MoToR*: "That great living, wonderful thing with its passion for motion seemed to call and claim her as a kindred spirit. She wanted to feel the throb of its quickening pulses; to lay her hand on lever and handle and thrill with the sense of mastery; to claim its power as her own—and feel its sullen-yielded obedience answer her will." Concluded the *New York American* succinctly, "The chauffeur is the New Lochinvar of the gasoline steeds. Once the lady is swung up behind him the magic of speed does the rest."

It was more than speed. More even than sex. The automobile brought freedom. "The first radical departure from the bondage of the iron railway," James P. Holland said. "You are the most independent and absolute monarch locomotion ever produced," commented Robert Bruce, "—until something happens." But not all excursions brought breakdowns or flat tires, and not all country hotels bore "No Automobiles" signs. Indeed, welcome mats were at least as numerous. When Missourian H.F. Busse and the car he had built himself arrived in Belleville, Illinois, in the midst of a rainstorm, both of them were invited into the local saloon so the car could stay dry, although probably Mr. Busse did not.

When everything went right, automobiling was a sensual, romantic, and joyful experience. "So obedient is the speeding car that the high and exquisite key of its activity seems...an echo of your mastery," Henry Copley Greene rhapsodized. "A village appears, keen-spired among trees; it sweeps near, sweeps past on either hand; and the road before you flows like a spring freshet down the slope that you surmount." Enthused R.G. Betts, "Think how much more thoroughly Columbus could have discovered America had the good Queen been able to pawn an extra jewel to place an automobile...at his command!" Once introduced to motoring, commitment almost invariably followed. "I can call on friends living thirty miles away who have been asking me to come for twenty years," wrote a converted anti-automobilist who had previously been content with the twelve-mile circle that his horse could do in a day. He planned to keep his stable. "In my case there is a distinct place for both. It isn't a question of horse or machine," he said. "If it were, I am afraid old Charlie would have to go."

CHAPTER 20

Highwheelers and Panic

SIGNS THAT AMERICA wanted to be put on wheels were every-where. Even those harboring "devil-wagon" notions were impressed by the automobile's virtues after the San Francisco earthquake in 1906. A caravan of White steamers brought supplies to the disaster area. Buick agent Charlie Howard sent every available showroom car into the rubble, as did other dealers whose facilities remained intact. Some 200 privately owned automobiles were pressed into emergency service by military and civic authorities who had previously turned up their noses at the vehicle for government use. Other automobilists pitched in on their own. When horses collapsed under the strain, automobiles were hitched to rescue wagons. When the heat of the pavement caused tires to explode, the cars continued rolling on their rims. The esti-mated 15,000 gallons of gasoline donated by the Standard Oil Com-pany provided a measure of the extent of the relief effort. The result was profound. Although the countryside antics of rowdies might con-tinue to cause the automobile an image problem, after the earthquake the utility of the vehicle was unquestionable.

Despite sporadic demurrers, doctors had long been convinced. The sustained and greater speed of the vehicle allowed a physician to get to his patients faster, which was beneficial to them both. The more patients a doctor could see in a day, the more fees he collected. "I never knew what true comfort and safety was in making my professional calls until I purchased a Pope-Waverley," a New Jersey physician wrote the Colonel testimonially. "I have sold all my horses and discharged my stable man. I figure I am saving about fifty percent by my new method of getting around."

That the automobile was cheaper to buy and maintain than a horse and buggy was an advertising claim put forth by manufacturers. For doctors and other professionals for whom an automobile increased business efficiency, this was certainly true. "A hard cold will reduce 'Billy' to a simple figure in the profit and loss column," one commentator noted wryly. But, for pleasure use, the equation changed. Most objective appraisals confirmed that from a dollar-and-cents point of view, the horse won every time—whether the automobile was a $3,000 touring car that could obsolete a stable of four horse-drawn vehicles or a $650 runabout bought by a horse-and-buggy owner who stabled his rig at a livery.

The telling difference was performance; for one-third more, the automobile could carry its owner six times as far. And a lot faster. In Ohio, as a lynch mob approached, the Mount Vernon sheriff bundled an accused murderer into his car and sped twelve miles to the safety of the Centerville jail. To keep his doors open during a run, a Lancaster (Ohio) bank president drove $55,000 in gold from Columbus in record time.

"Yesterday it was the plaything of the few," Winthrop Scarritt told members and honored guests (among them Alexander Graham Bell) at the Automobile Club of America's annual banquet in 1905. "Today it is the servant of many, tomorrow it will be the necessity of humanity." European observers, perpetually bemused by Americans, found it piquant that so many Continental luxuries were regarded as commonplace possessions in the United States. But Scarritt's idea was not new. As early as 1899, Israel G. Howell of Hopewell, New Jersey, had written, "It is the working and middle classes of people, the bone and sinew of the Nation, who want these wagons for everyday use, and the horseless wagon will be the greatest seller...when it is sold at a price within the reach of all classes. The people are just waiting for it."

Price—there was the rub. But already many of those who could not afford an automobile in America had decided they had to have one. The easiest way was to buy someone else's. The Hoffman family's Pope-Hartford, for example, was a used car. In 1906, Marius Krarup, the automotive editor who had accompanied Tom Fetch on the Packard transcontinental, estimated that of the 80,000 automobiles in America, probably 50,000 were runabouts and as many as 30,000 of those in the hands of second or third owners. Among them was Rhey T. Snodgrass of South Orange, New Jersey, who bought a used curved dash Oldsmobile for $100. "In a few rapturous moments I hurdled over from the ranks of the poor and joined the envied fraternity of the rich," he wrote in a prize-winning *Collier's* essay. "For a man with a humble hundred in a savings bank is poor, while he with an auto is rich, even if the auto only cost the same hundred. ...Style I had not, extreme speed I had not, but fun and exhilaration, oh yes!" Snodgrass' only problem was his plump wife, whom he continually elbowed manipulating the curved dash's tiller steering. So he sold the Olds for the same price he paid for it, added another fifty dollars, and bought a car with a steering wheel.

Secondhand cars were traded either from owner to owner or through the middleman of a car broker. The Automobile Auction Company of America advertised itself as "the clearing house for cars that run." Automobile dealers figured that because a milliner wouldn't accept an old hat, why should they be burdened with old cars. Some were willing to take back automobiles from good customers, but on the whole, new-car dealers weren't interested in secondhand sales—and for good reason. They usually had a long waiting list for fresh-from-the-factory versions. In the New World, there were many who wanted only a new car.

By 1907, the banking community became alarmed at the number of people leveraging their homes to finance automobile purchases. In one county in Connecticut, fully 74 percent of the mortgages recorded in 1906 were assumed for the purpose of purchasing cars. In 1908, a New York attorney revealed that over the last winter, his office had handled more than 200 foreclosures of mortgages that had been created for the same purpose. In Pennsylvania, a committee of Pittsburgh club women reporting on the phenomenon noted that "something must be done before utter ruin follows on the wake of folly."

Ardent automobilist Frank Munsey used the pages of his popular magazine to champion the automobile cause and sometimes, inadvertently, to raise hopes falsely. "The cost of making a sixty horse machine and that of making ten horse cannot vary more than a few hundred dollars at most," he said in 1906, "whereas the price of the larger machine is five or six times as great." Automobile manufacturers had to smile at his naïveté. Prevailing wisdom was that to build strong, one had to build heavy. And that was necessarily expensive. There was a world of difference between a big touring car and a little runabout.

The automobile makers' principal problem was grappling with success. Regardless of price class, cars could be sold as quickly as they were made. Granted, the per-unit profit on America's most powerful vehicles was great. To serve the highest segment of the market, luxury makers produced ever more puissant automobiles. In Chicopee Falls (Massachusetts), Frank Duryea introduced a 50-horsepower $6,000 Stevens-Duryea; in Plattsburgh (New York), Harry Lozier's 60-horsepower Lozier had a price tag of $7,000; in Buffalo, the new Great Arrow from the Pierce company was similarly powerful and pricey. For $15,000 or so, purchasers could have replicas of 90-horsepower racers from Locomobile in Bridgeport and the Apperson brothers in Kokomo. "The disease has about eighteen months to run," Packard sales manager Sidney Waldon commented. While allowing that his company, then producing a 30-horsepower $4,500-range car, might be forced to offer a 60 or a 90, he remained convinced that the automobilists *bête noire*—tires—would end the vogue for ultra-powerful machines. And he was right, for the time being. Even automobilists able to afford the colossal tire bills of these giant cars soon grew weary of the aggravation of incessant tire changing.

Although there were warnings that the luxury market might be nearing saturation, makers of the highest-priced cars continued to enjoy increased sales. The middle-class market had barely been plumbed; "touching the fringe" was Alexander Winton's phrase. A four-cylinder touring car offering 20 to 30 horsepower and selling in the $2,000 range was doubtless the car for which many Americans were mortgaging their homes. It was the beau ideal to those an echelon or two below the folks for whom price was no factor at all. Tom Jeffery's Rambler was solidly in that class. And the Cadillac had moved into it by now, too. The Lelands' single-cylinder $800 runabout continued to sell in numbers four times as great, but they clearly took more pride in their line of

$2,000+ fours. Ben Briscoe talked about how the automobile "has been brought within the reach of the man of moderate means." R.M. Owen, Ransom Olds' friend who had followed him to Reo, commented that "from the start of my connection with automobiling I have believed that the medium-price car would appeal to the masses." But by masses, he meant "the salaried man, the small merchant, the lawyer, the doctor, and even the minister and undertaker."

At the turn of the century, one American in 1.5 million owned an automobile. By 1907, the figure was one to about every 800. The population was approaching 90 million. There were more people who wanted cars than there were used cars available. And some people just weren't willing to mortgage their house to get a new one. Not that there weren't many makers anxious to corner this untapped market. The results were usually dismal. "Remember always that a cheap automobile is the most expensive type to buy," Harry B. Haines cautioned in the *Review of Reviews*. "By a cheap car I mean one that is turned out in a careless slipshod manner by a manufacturer who has gone into business with the idea of making a quick 'clean-up' and quitting."

No doubt concurring with Haines' assessment was the owner who got so mad at his Milwaukee-built Superior that he pushed it off the 14th Street viaduct. In Indiana, a disgruntled owner, fed up with yet another breakdown, gathered a crowd, refused fifteen dollars for the beast, set the car on fire, gave the ruins to a bystander, and took the train home. Commented *The Motor World* in 1905, "Quite unselfish in his ambitions, [James] Stanley is endeavoring to form a stock company to supply the poorer people with automobiles at $350 per—or less. No doubt the most worthy of the poor will be allowed to purchase a block of stock." The road to a car for the common man in America was littered with shoddy efforts that survived little longer than the get-rich-quick promoters who foisted them upon an automobile-hungry public.

Sincere attempts were legion, too. The most ingenuous was as American as the Fourth of July: the highwheeler, a genre unknown in Europe. If the first-generation runabout was passé by 1906, the highwheeler was positively antediluvian. It was only one step removed from a horse. Whip sockets on early versions betrayed their carriage origins. Manufacturers bragged about the plagiarism. "It is built as nearly as possible like a buggy," International Harvester declared of its example. "This type of vehicle has been serving country-town and rural people for years, and there is no reason why a simple motor vehicle of this type cannot serve them in the future."

"Mechanically self-effacing...no hazard of new ideas," boasted Holsman, the granddaddy of all highwheelers, whose final drive was initially by manila rope that stretched badly in wet weather and was finally replaced by chain. Belt or friction drive proved popular among highwheeler makers, too.

Most runabouts by now had steering wheels and their engines up front under a proper hood. In highwheelers, the engine returned under the seat, and the tiller enjoyed a comeback. The front end of the highwheeler seemed to beg for a horse to be hitched. This was, makers averred, a real plus for rural motoring because the vehicle's uncanny resemblance to a buggy wouldn't frighten the animal it replaced as much. But what truly distinguished the genre, of course, was its wheels. "High wheels travel all roads," Holsman declared, "because all roads are made to be traveled by high wheels." Most were three or four feet in diameter, shod with solid rubber tires. Highwheeler makers regarded anything smaller as "little casters" and pneumatic tires as "windbags" that were so expensive and troublesome as to be beneath contempt.

Holsman had been building highwheelers since 1903; not until 1906 did that company suffer much competition. Then suddenly, the motor buggy became the thing. "Who will supply them?" Charles Duryea asked rhetorically in *The Horseless Age*, answering with a slam at the kind of vehicle his brother was building. "Not the present automakers, for they have gone daffy over multiple cylinders, racing horse power and parlor car fittings, not to mention a ton or two of weight and so many parts that it takes a chassis ten feet long to hold them." The only people demanding the European-type car, Duryea declared, were a few snobs who wanted to show off that they had been abroad. "A little thing like a market for thousands of motor buggies," he concluded, was "lying fallow every year."

Not long did this field lie fallow. Chicago became the capital of the highwheeler world. Over half of the more than two hundred firms producing these vehicles were located there. Highwheeler sales were highest in the Midwest, principally because it had the worst roads and the most farmers. In the fall of 1908, when Sears, Roebuck catalogued its own motor buggy, the genre's future was made.

In many ways, the highwheeler was admirable. On muddy roads, it could sink farther before reaching its hubs and, if stuck, was light enough to be extricated easily. Ruts and stumps, the bane of low-wheeled automobiles, were no obstacle. Moreover, by removing one of the wheels, the motor buggy could be hitched up to saw wood, cut silage, pump water, bale hay, churn butter, grind corn, or press cider, among other farmyard chores. And best of all, it was cheap. Prices ranged from a low of $250 (the Success of St. Louis and the Kiblinger of Auburn, Indiana) to more than $700 (for models providing such amenities as fenders, a top with fringe, and storm curtains). Highwheelers seldom were sold in showrooms. Most arrived crated: "Simply attach wheels and it is ready to roll."

"The craze for a 'car' will wane," Charles Duryea exhorted, "...the era of buggies for business has only begun." Some business and professional people were turned off by the highwheeler's top speed, however, which was little more than a good horse and buggy. "If the baby had cut a tooth, the doctor would get there in time," one physician wrote, "but if the baby had cut an artery it would be a case for the undertaker instead." Still, by the thousands and then tens of thousands, highwheelers were sold to a car-hungry public.

Arriving at a highwheeler price for a vehicle that could legitimately be called an automobile was the aim of numerous manufacturers. Most failed miserably with a product little better, and often worse, than the motor buggy it was supposed to replace. The most successful cheap car of the period was unquestionably the one designed by Alanson Brush, not surprising given the exemplary engineering he had contributed to the first Cadillac. Also, Al Brush had a helpful neighbor to talk cars with.

The Brushes lived on Harper Avenue in Detroit, across the alley from the Fords. Despite Brush's position in the company that had arisen from the ashes of Ford's own firm, Al and Henry were friends. Brush and the senior Leland didn't see eye to eye. So Brush soon left with $40,000 for use of his patents for two years and the understanding he not enter any business competitive with Cadillac during that same period. This, in essence, meant that if Brush wanted to develop a new automobile, it would have to be low priced. A sponsor was quickly found. Happy to manufacture the car for him was Frank Briscoe, who was tired of tending to the family sheet metal business in Detroit while his brother Ben was having a much better time in New York, producing the Maxwell. As Ben Briscoe said, Frank had "an itch to get into the big tent."

Advertising for the Brush Runabout was clever, explaining the hill-climbing superiority of the little 6-horsepower one-lunger over its bigger brethren by suggesting that potential purchasers reflect on the reason a squirrel can climb a tree better than an elephant. The Brush's 35-miles-per-hour top speed was almost twice that of most highwheelers. Indeed, the car offered more speed for the dollar than any other automobile in America. But to realize a $500 price tag, Brush relied extensively on oak, hickory, and maple. Although instantly popular, the car would be lampooned, unjustly, as "wooden body, wooden axles, wooden wheels, wooden run."

The Brush Runabout was leagues more sophisticated than a highwheeler and vastly improved over first-generation runabouts like the Olds. But the fact was that no car with a single cylinder and horsepower not exceeding one digit could be expected to perform well for long on American roads. Moreover, although some runabouts were offered with a small rear-deck-mounted auxiliary bench, which became known, presumably with affection, as the "mother-in-law seat," the cars were overburdened with more than two passengers.

"The likelihood of poor folks enjoying the automobile seems to be mostly a question of If," Allen Sangree wrote in *Harper's Weekly*. "If roads improve; if we all turn mechanics; if manufacturers can afford to put good steel in cheap machines; and if one is satisfied with a runabout when his neighbor owns a touring car—then there is a chance."

———

On March 13, 1907, New York Stock Exchange prices collapsed. On October 23, the Knickerbocker Trust Company in New York closed its doors and was followed by a run on banks in other cities. Precipitating these events, economists told themselves, were the money drain occasioned by the Russo-Japanese War and the rebuilding of San Francisco following the earthquake, overexpansion by several large railroads, and a late season tying up farmers' cash. At Princeton University, Woodrow Wilson seethed about manipulating financiers; President Roosevelt attacked the "malefactors of great wealth." To many, the Panic of '07 was senseless. But that did not make it any less real.

Sitting none too patiently in his office in Elmira on the day the Knickerbocker closed was automobile dealer John North Willys. On his desk was a pile of unfilled orders. The Overland Auto Company of Indianapolis had $10,000 of his money as deposit on 500 cars for 1907. For months, he had received no Overlands, nor heard from the factory. Inaction of any kind irritated Willys. Since purchasing an Elmira sporting goods store whose owner had caught Klondike fever and was willing to sell dirt cheap, he had built the business into a wonderful success. By 1900, he was grossing $500,000 a year in the sale of Remington rifles, Victor phonographs, and Pierce bicycles. And soon he was selling automobiles, first the Pierce, then Tom Jeffery's Rambler, and the American of Indianapolis.

From none of those factories could he get as many cars as he thought he could sell, however, hence the overture to Overland, a newcomer to the field, presumably backed by a local millionaire. Willys fretted until November and then put himself on a train headed west to see what was the matter. In Indianapolis, he found a deserted sheet-metal shed, assorted machinery, and parts for fewer than three automobiles. The Indianapolis millionaire had lost everything, even his home, in the Panic. "I had no choice, I had $10,000 invested...," Willys remembered. "That factory was going to fill my order before it died."

To bring back the workers who hadn't been paid in weeks, Willys returned to his hotel, wrote out a check for $350, and informed the manager that even though Indianapolis was on scrip, he wanted cash. To forestall receivership, he shot a telegram to the wealthy lumberman who had financed his excursion into the automobile sales field, asking for a loan of $7,500. To avert imminent disaster, he convinced Overland creditors to whom $80,000 was owed that the company was worth saving and to be patient. "I was manufacturer, I was president, treasurer, general manager—everything from Lord High Executioner down," he said. "As assets I had a sheaf of orders, health, energy, enthusiasm, and a factory which was notable chiefly for the things it lacked." For the next year, he produced Overlands in a circus tent, 465 of them, priced at $1,200 each. The year following, his output increased tenfold, and he had a proper factory. But it was not in Indianapolis. In Toledo, Ohio, Willys found a huge, well-equipped, and idle plant available at a rock-bottom price. Previously, it had been the home of the Pope-Toledo.

The Colonel was not happy. News of the receivership of the Pope Manufacturing Company was a bombshell. The Pope assets were nearly $8 million and liabilities less than $1.5 million. But, salvaged from the wreckage of the American Bicycle conglomerate, the company was grossly overcapitalized at $22.5 million, and the Colonel had a lot of his relatives on the payroll.

Editorial columns offered free advice. The first thing to do, said the *Hartford Courant*, was "to squeeze the water out of the stock." The *New York American* commented that "unless the big salary roll is pared down so that those on the list will be paid for duties they perform rather than for looking wise, the big corporation will have difficulty in regaining its feet." The financially sagacious *New York Evening Post* noted the Pope folly in making no adequate provision for working capital and financing a season's production through bank loans.

The inability to renew its loans was one reason for the Pope financial embarrassment. The other was the six-month strike at the Toledo factory, which put deliveries so far behind that nearly 200 cars were left on the company's hands through canceled orders. But the Colonel preferred to vent his wrath solely at the financial community. To a reporter from *The New York Times*, he declared himself "sick and tired" of the way banks were treating him, especially because the Pope debts amounted to only about $2 million. "The banks will get what is due them," the Colonel sniffed, "when the company gets ready to pay them." This was scarcely the time for belligerence.

Still, even in financial straits, the Colonel had clout. He managed to get himself appointed the Pope receiver. Not surprisingly, some creditors and stockholders did not think this was a good idea. Proclaiming "this huge corporation" as a monument to the Colonel, Pope's attorney said that it was inconceivable that he would wish "to destroy that monument for a petty little receivership fee."

No one wanted to save the company more than the man who had built it. And he valiantly tried. Desperately retrenching, he sold off the Hagerstown (Maryland) plant of the Pope-Tribune to the Montrose Metal Casket Company, and the Indianapolis plant of the Pope-Waverley to local businessmen who continued production of the Colonel's car as the Waverley Electric. But his embarrassment was hellish and the strain unbearable. Around the time he was forced to sell the Pope-Toledo factory to John North Willys, Albert Pope suffered a nervous break-down. On August 10, 1909, at the age of sixty-six, he died. All that was left of his empire now was the Pope-Hartford, which fittingly if fitfully remained in production in his beloved Connecticut. It would not long survive the Colonel.

———

Wilfred Leland was on his honeymoon when the Panic of '07 set in. "We are bankrupt," Lem Bowen cried upon his return. "All our money is lost." Among Cadillac directors, Bowen was the most given to pre-mature alarm. Granted, the situation presented cause for concern. Following four years of steady increases, Cadillac sales were down by a third. Previously, the steady plant expansion concomitant to that growth had been financed by short-term loans repaid out of annual sales—which would be impossible in 1907. Bowen's outburst was a hyperbolic reflection of the unease felt by all the Cadillac directors.

The angst Henry Leland suffered that year was largely due to the mar-riages of both Wilfred and his daughter Gertrude, both of whom moved out of the patriarchal home into apartments in the same building on Grand Avenue in Detroit. That the patriarch was distressed is indi-cated by his subsequent purchase of the house next door for himself and the construction of a passageway between the two buildings. Losing his children to marriage provided the most panic Henry Leland felt in 1907. Supremely confident that exemplary engineering was his sole job, he focused on the Cadillac automobile, leaving financial con-cerns to the money men.

Money men generally were worried. As Fred Smith of Olds Motor Works commented, the word along the banking grapevine was "Watch your automobile loans." Going to the wall in Peoria, Illinois, was John L. French, who began building runabouts—"Rigs that Run" was the slogan—with George Dorris in St. Louis at the turn of the century. Disagreement over how quickly to expand had broken up the partner-ship. Both were now producing four-cylinder touring cars. In St. Louis, Dorris, still operating on a small scale, eked through 1907; in Peoria, French was caught in the midst of efforts to become a major producer.

New automobile companies were similarly caught by surprise. In Philadelphia, a bank commandeered the 200 automobiles the Dragon Automobile Company had used as security for a loan—and the

Dragon, a $2,000 four designed by Leo Melanowski, the former Winton engineer, was no more. Another Melanowski design—"The Practical Car Built by Practical Men"—was a panic casualty, too, and one that must have delighted Henry Ford. In Detroit, Alexander Malcomson called it quits with his Aerocar Company.

Among the many firms founded in 1907 that were soon visited by the sheriff were the Earl Motor Car Company of Kenosha, Wisconsin, and the Bethlehem Automobile Company in Pennsylvania, which had been organized by two of Charles Duryea's former managers in Reading. The year 1907 marked the end of Perry Okey's efforts to become a producer, too. A one-man automobile company since before the turn of the century, this Columbus, Ohio, machinist apparently had talent. *Cycle and Automobile Trade Journal*'s Hugh Dolnar, who road-tested Okey's latest effort in 1906, had pronounced him capable of producing "better and lower-cost light cars than any other man can make" and subtly pleaded for someone to finance him.

In Orange, Massachusetts, William L. Grout served a $200,000 attachment on the factory of the Grout Brothers Automobile Company. Like fellow sewing-machine manufacturer Thomas White, Grout had set his sons up in the steamer business. Unlike the White brothers, the Grouts had some rather bizarre automotive ideas (including a coupe that was as tall as a sentry box and a touring car complete with a cow-catcher in front) and had been little more successful in business than they were now in trying to have a conservator appointed for their father because of his advanced age. When William Grout succeeded in taking over the company, his sons left town. Grout Senior died the following year at the age of seventy-five, and the Grout automobile limped into oblivion.

"Come back," the telegram read. "Company in hands of receiver." When he got the wire in the fall of 1907, Charles Duryea was in Chicago en route to California with a carload of his cars. Some of Charles' automotive ideas were as peculiar as those of the Grout boys. The Duryeas he preferred to make were three-wheelers, although he obligingly added a fourth wheel to some models to meet market demand. He had not yet wavered in his belief, however, that an automobile's optimum number of cylinders was three. Although somewhat the odd man out in the industry, Charles had managed to thus far survive the manufacturers' common problems: "Each winter I [was] forced to lay off much of our force because even a fifteen percent reduction in price would not tempt buyers before apple-blossom time and then they wanted delivery yesterday." Banks had refused to lend him even 25 percent on cars nearly completed to tide him over. "Thus the winter passed and more good men found other jobs and greenies had to be trained another spring."

It had been to alleviate this situation that Charles was on his way to the West Coast, where automobiles could be sold year round. Now he returned to Reading to find his situation terminal. His plant was already partially disassembled. Duryea was convinced the receivership was a "move to grab the business." And that happened easily enough; the Duryea Power Company was taken over by Charles M. Middleby of Connecticut, who moved in to produce the Middleby. Duryea sued, slashing prices on his inventoried cars to as little as $300 (a 75 percent discount) to pay legal expenses. "While the lawsuit was in progress, I worked for others," Charles said, "including ninety days in the Selden-Ford suit [brother Frank's Stevens-Duryea company was an A.L.A.M. member, of course], paid my debts, kept the girl in college, and had $2,000 in the bank—$500 of which was all I got from my proved claim of $20,000 against the defunct company." With that $2,000, Charles set up shop elsewhere in Reading and developed his own version of the vehicle he regarded as a sure thing. The Duryea highwheeler was called the Buggyaut. "I soon had one per week coming through," Charles bragged. "The depression of November 1907 was still cursing the land, but my men did not feel it."

Other automakers felt the Panic but did not flinch. In Rochester, New York, the Gearless Transmission Company—whose giant 75-horse-power friction-drive car had two hoods, one for the engine and the other the gearset—avoided receivership with the financial help of local optical manufacturer William Bausch. Surviving receivership in Cleveland was the Royal Motor Car and Manufacturing Company, which had recently moved into a spacious new factory where 400 workers built the Royal Tourist. Royal's plan to introduce a six-cylinder car was scotched, however. In Springfield, Massachusetts, surviving receivership brought on principally by expansion as well was the Knox Automobile Company. Although irritated that creditors were in virtual control, Elihu Cutler could report within months that Knox was "on the fair road to recovery."

The collapse of the Pope empire and Knox's financial predicament made something of a mockery of the A.L.A.M.'s self-styled role as a stabilizer of the automobile industry. More shocking in December 1907 was the announcement of the default on a $2.5 million bond payment and the subsequent receivership of the Electric Vehicle Company. Of its $14 million in listed assets, fully $10 million was credited to the Selden patent. Cash on hand was a mere $12,000. Commented Henry Ford, "I hardly expected there would be anything so tangible as cash."

The Electric Vehicle Company receivership was a joyful relief to makers outside the A.L.A.M., who had been soundly scared earlier that year. Although it had been generally believed that further action would await the Ford suit decision, the A.L.A.M., citing precedence in sewing machine and other major patent litigation, launched a fusillade of lawsuits against independent producers. "Whistles to keep their courage up," scoffed Henry Ford of the individual cases against seventy manufacturers. But the manufacturers weren't so sure.

A quick conference was called in Detroit at the Ford Motor Company. Even Tom Jeffery showed up. Wisely, Ford and Couzens asked Ralzemond Parker to expound on the deficiencies of the Selden patent. Parker did, exhaustively. Even those independents who had been wavering about applying for a license changed their mind. From all around the room came offers of substantial money to assist the Ford defense. Henry smiled and said, no thanks.

The A.L.A.M. would carry on, but without manager George Day, the amicable peacemaker who had so ably held the alliance together. Day died that November. The Electric Vehicle Company would survive receivership, but without the talents of chief engineer Percy Maxim. Recognizing the impending crisis, Maxim had defected that summer.*

---

* Maxim initially had no intention of abandoning the automobile field. In partnership with T.W. Goodridge, former general manager for the Studebaker brothers in Indiana, he developed a new automobile in Hartford. Curiously for the man who had tried to convince the powers at the Electric Vehicle Company that more attention should be paid to the marketing of a gasoline car, the new automobile was an electric that was to be marketed under the trade name of Lenox. But at the same time, assaying the field in which his father had become famous, Maxim invented a gun silencer that he regarded as more potentially lucrative. By the end of 1908, he and Goodridge had parted company, the latter to join the Matheson Automobile

Defecting during receivership were most of the Wall Street promoters behind the Electric Vehicle Company. Rumors spread awhile that Packard would buy the company. That did not happen, but the manufacturing focus of the reorganized firm did change. By 1909, the model lineup was five gasoline models to two electrics, and the firm's name was revised to Columbia Motor Car Company.

Ironically, the Panic of '07 was perhaps the most encouraging event for the automobile industry since the Chicago Times-Herald contest of 1895. Doomsayers visiting Automobile Row in the big cities reported of the scene: "The enormous areas of plate glass generally reveal one or two chassis, a limousine and perhaps a touring model, and in the rear, adding a sort of *dolce far niente* touch to the picture, lounge, recline or sprawl two or three salesmen with plenty of time to spare." But that was not the whole picture. Granted, with money tight, advertising was either halved or abandoned altogether. But industry-wide, more cars were bought: some 43,000 *vis-à-vis* the 33,200 of 1906.

Automobiles sold themselves. If this didn't happen fast enough in an East Coast dealership, an entire showroom of cars might be dispatched to the hinterlands of Iowa, Minnesota, or the Dakotas, where big-name manufacturers did not deign to have dealers and where smaller producers could unload models that hadn't been well received upon introduction. Virtually any car that showed up in Montana was snapped up immediately.

Although failures were rife during the Panic of '07 among firms on shaky footing, the marginally healthy generally held on, and those on solid ground sailed through the year. In Kokomo, both Elwood Haynes and the Apperson brothers did well; in Cleveland, Winton sales reached a new high of 1,100 cars; in Chicopee Falls, Frank Duryea enjoyed a million-dollar year with the Stevens-Duryea. H.H. Franklin's sales of 1,500 cars in Syracuse was nearly 200 better than sales in 1906. The 4,000 Reos sold was a splendid increase of over 1,500 cars for Ransom Olds in Lansing; in Tarrytown, Ben Briscoe and the Maxwell enjoyed

---

Company in Wilkes-Barre, Pennsylvania. Maxim sold the worm drive he had patented for the Lenox Electric to the Waverley Company of Indianapolis and organized the Maxim Company in Hartford for manufacture of his silencer. Hiram Percy Maxim died in 1936, at the age of sixty-six, a very rich man.

similar good fortune. With more than 3,200 Ramblers marketed, even conservative Tom Jeffery increased sales by nearly 500. Go-getter Billy Durant saw to it that Buick sales soared from 1,400 to 4,641. Sources differ as to whether Henry Ford sold more or fewer cars than the 8,000+ he had marketed in 1906. Perhaps even Henry didn't know. He was otherwise occupied.

CHAPTER 21

"There's Millions in It"

PERHAPS HENRY FORD chuckled when he read Allen Sangree's article in *Harper's Weekly*. "Automobiles for the multitude," Sangree declared, "would be possible only: 1) if roads improved, 2) if all owners were mechanics, 3) if good steel could be used in cheap machines, 4) if people would remain satisfied with a runabout when his neighbor had a touring car." Henry was about to turn that "iffy" proposition on its ear. His automobile would be so sturdy it wouldn't matter when roads improved. His automobile would be so simple that anyone with the technical skill to change a light bulb could fix it. His automobile would be a touring car built of vanadium steel.

Ford was a subscriber to *Harper's Weekly* and, indeed, became a first-time author in the magazine in 1907, the same year the Sangree piece appeared. Henry's article was titled "Special Automobile Steel." A British metallurgist had introduced him to vanadium, a light but tough steel alloy. "Fat men cannot run as fast as thin men," Henry would comment years later, "...I cannot imagine where the delusion that weight means strength came from."

Vanadium steel was absolutely essential to the car he wanted to produce. The problem was getting someone to make it for him. Vanadium
required 3000 degrees Fahrenheit, 300 degrees beyond the capacity of
most U.S. steel mills. Finally, he found the United Steel Company, a
small plant in Canton, Ohio. "I offered to guarantee them against loss
if they would run a heat for us," Henry said. "They agreed. The first
heat was a failure. Very little vanadium remained in the steel. I had
them try again and the second time [it] came through." With vanadium, the tensile strength of steel shot from 70,000 pounds to 170,000.

As fascinated with this metallurgical wonder as Ford was Harold Wills,
Henry's long-time right-hand man. Job titles were anathema to Ford;
he preferred to shuffle his people around, depending on the assignment. Once Malcomson was gone, so largely was bureaucracy in the
manufacturing end of the Ford business. Chief engineer had been Wills'
title earlier, but at the same time, he had also "engineered" the graphic
script of the Ford logo after rummaging through his attic to find the
home printing set he used to print calling cards when he was a kid.

Wills and Ford remained as close now as they had been during the lean
days when boxing matches warmed cold fingers during the design of
the 999 race car. "If it's in a book," Wills once replied when someone
directed him to look up some technical matter, "then it's at least four
years old and I don't have any use for it." Henry Ford was similarly
disposed. Thus, he was surprised, when it became obvious the company would need its own metallurgical laboratory, that Wills suggested
a "university man" to run it. "No, make an expert of Wandersee,"
Henry said. It was done. Three months of intense training at the United
Alloy Steel Laboratory, and the company had its metallurgist. John
Wandersee had been hired at Ford as a sweeper.

Wills had the knack of taking Ford's ideas and making them work when
the older man was confounded. Similarly close in wavelength was
Charlie Sorensen who, upon hearing an idea from Henry, often didn't
bother with a blueprint but went directly to a pattern and casting.
Working together on a problem, Henry and Charlie would keep at it
until the job was done, once for forty-two hours straight.

To Sorensen, Wills, and Wandersee was added a small group of men
who were talented and could be trusted by Henry to help him realize
his dream of a universal car: Spider Huff, the mechanic who had

accompanied Henry on his record attempt on frozen Lake St. Clair, a whiz with electrics; Hungarian-born and German-trained Joseph Galamb, a veteran of Westinghouse, who had already proven himself a master draftsman; C.J. (Jimmy) Smith, a Ford machinist who had regarded milling each cam separately as wasteful and on his own initiative began machining eight or ten at a time; George Brown, whose mechanical prowess had also caught Ford's eye; and Gus Degener, whose tenure with Henry dated back to 999 and who had long had a key to the company design room.

For the Model T, a special new room had been constructed, twelve by fifteen feet, big enough for a milling machine, a drill press, a lathe, a few power tools, and one car. Adjoining was a jerry-built cubicle to serve as a drafting room, with a large blackboard at one end and a rocking chair in the middle for Henry. He used it a lot, every day, often until eight at night, sometimes as late as eleven, rocking and talking. Telling jokes. And bantering.

"He'd never say, 'I *want* this done!' " George Brown remembered. "He'd say, 'I wonder if we can do it. I wonder.' Well, the men would just break their necks to see if they could do it. They knew what he wanted." Commented Jimmy Smith, "He brought ideas to us. First, he would think the thing up, then he would have [the draftsmen] draw it up, and then we would make it up." Because he was not adept at reading blueprints, Ford needed a working model of all parts. At all stages, from blackboard to three-dimensional piece, photographs were taken, the Selden patent case having proven to Henry the value of evidence to demonstrate prior art.

Although many hands contributed to the final result, there can be no question that the Model T said Henry Ford as effectively as a signature. This was his car. After two years of epic striving, of solving problems, it was reality. Henry was too nervous to take the wheel on the first road test, but as passenger, he made sure they drove past the offices of Alexander Malcomson. Back at the plant, he gave everyone within striking distance a playful kick in the pants or a punch on the shoulders. "Well," he grinned to his crew, "I guess we've got started."

Started, indeed. Already Ford dealers had been made aware the car was coming. They were alternately rapturous and circumspect. The introductory circular described the car's specifications in detail. One dealer said he had to rub his eyes to make sure he wasn't dreaming. Too good to be true, said another. Another forecast a flood of orders. Quite a few suggested that advance word was a mistake that might make disposing of current models a problem. Joked one dealer, "We have carefully hidden the sheets away and locked the drawer, throwing the key down the cold-air shaft."

Dealer excitement about the Model T was right on target. In late September, the trade press was informed and proved just as enthusiastic: "unique in many of its constructions" (*Cycle and Automobile Trade Journal*), "an entirely distinct design" (*The Automobile*), "a new car all the way through" (*The Horseless Age*), and "a credit to the genius of Henry Ford" (*Motor World*).

On Friday, October 2, 1908, the Model T was formally introduced to the public in a *Saturday Evening Post* ad. Reported the *Ford Times*, "Saturday's mail brought nearly one thousand inquiries. Monday's response swamped our mail clerks, and by Tuesday night, the office was well nigh inundated." The factory couldn't keep up. Dealers who had hid the Model T circular fared best. Ford rationed the new car to agencies that had disposed of all previous models on hand. The demand for the Model T was far more than the 10,000+ that could be produced over the next year.

Artful and artless, the Model T made no pretense to aesthetics. This was an unabashedly practical car. Its body rode high in deference to America's roads; its three-point suspension allowed the Model T to bump and grind its way out of ruts. The four cylinders of the engine, cast en bloc, were enclosed in one case combining the transmission and flywheel with built-in magneto—a neat setup. The transmission was planetary. Tricky at first, except for an organist, was mastering the three foot pedals (one for braking, one for forward, and one for reverse). As novelist John Steinbeck commented, two generations of Americans knew more about "the planetary system of gears than the solar system of stars."

Not all of the Model T's features were new to the industry or even to Ford. The package was the surprise. Some features would soon be widely imitated, most especially Ford's placement of the steering wheel on the left side of the car. Henry Ford's automobile for the family stretched 100 inches between axles, weighed 1,200 pounds, developed close to 20 horsepower, and, with the wind in your favor, was good for about 40 miles per hour. All for $850. "This Ford is a better car, not because it costs less," the company said, "but because it is worth more." Another ad explained, "No car under $2,000 offers more, and no car over $2,000 offers more except in trimmings."

To the inhabitants of that small incubation room in the corner of the Ford plant, the Model T measured up to all expectations. To the man in the rocking chair, only one matter remained. Company advertising was right in proclaiming that the new Ford offered more for the money than any other car on the road. But $850 was more than most could afford. Jim Couzens had calculated that, in order to tap the mass market, the price should not be more than $600. But he had also calculated that $850 was the lowest price at which the Model T could be sold. "In those days J.C. was the entire office management," *Ford Times* related, "...he kept the books, collected, spent, and saved the cash, established agencies, and dictated policy."

All these things he did without a discernible sense of humor. Jim Couzens smiled once a year, it was said, and when he did, the ice on the Great Lakes began to break. He was implacable on the Model T's price tag.

Henry Ford had come up with his ideal car for the multitude. Now he would have to figure out how to make it more cheaply.

———

The call was made from Chicago one evening late in 1907. When William Crapo Durant picked up the phone in Flint, he heard an excited Benjamin Briscoe say, "Billy, I have a most important matter to discuss with you. Don't ask me to explain. It's the biggest thing in the country. There's millions in it."

The following morning, the two men met over breakfast at the Dresden Hotel in Flint. Briscoe explained that George Perkins, a partner in J.P. Morgan & Company, was interested in promoting merger in the automobile industry. Given the success Morgan enjoyed in such activity—most prominently in the creation of U.S. Steel—this interest did not surprise Briscoe who, as Morgan's resident automobile man, was naturally the first person contacted. Which automobile firms might be involved didn't matter much to Perkins. Details like that would be left to Briscoe.

The proposal could not have been made at a more opportune time for Ben. Maxwell-Briscoe was badly overextended. Wary of the insecurity of renting, he had purchased the Tarrytown facilities in 1906. For a million dollars more, he added plants in Pawtucket, Rhode Island, and Newcastle, Indiana. Jonathan Maxwell continually complained they were moving too fast and taking too many risks. When sales plummeted the following year, Ben found his usual money sources "as helpful as a busted crutch" and survived the crisis by selling debenture bonds to Maxwell-Briscoe dealers in exchange for favorable discounts on the vehicles they bought. Until the overture from Perkins, Ben Briscoe had been testy all through the Panic of '07.

Billy Durant, on the other hand, was neither testy nor did he panic. Production might be curtailed in other factories, but it was full-speed ahead at Buick. When cash-poor dealers curtailed orders, Durant stuffed the cars in warehouses and barns throughout the Flint area. And he introduced a brand-new Buick that November. A $900 four-cylinder runabout, the Model 10 was marketed for "men with real red blood who don't like to eat dust," in the company's phrase, and was the sensation of the New York show. Further, *Motor Age* predicted, this Buick would be the first automobile to provide "real competition to some of the low-priced four-cylinder unlicensed cars" (as indeed it did to the then-current Ford Model S). Few knew that Billy was ordering supplies one moment and staving off creditors the next. His balancing act was sublime. Charles Stewart Mott, whose Weston-Mott's cash flow was so dismal that he had to beg off paying his attorney's $250 annual retainer awhile, never could figure out how Durant had managed it. Said Mott, "He was one hell of a gambler."

Desperation had been among the reasons Ben Briscoe jumped at Perkins' idea or, as Ben would later observe defensively, "the history of almost every combination will show that the principal motive comes from being hard up." Certainly there was a case to be made that consolidation might strengthen all concerned by spreading the risks of an undeniably volatile industry. Briscoe was worried that another "silly season" might do in even the healthy and that "having one big concern of such dominating influence...would prevent many of the abuses that we believed existed." Even the "sanest of manufacturers" had been forced down risky avenues, Briscoe averred, "which they would not have entered had they not been fearful that some other concern would gain a few points on them."

Such self-serving altruism probably didn't even enter Durant's mind. He liked Perkins' idea because it promised to be an adventure and because it would make him a more prominent participant in the action. Further, he had very effectively combined companies whose products appealed to various markets during Durant-Dort carriage days. Whether Briscoe was aware of that is not known. Certainly he was well aware of the splendid success Billy had made of David Buick's automobile venture, which Ben had unloaded as hopeless only a half-decade earlier. That Billy was A.L.A.M. while Ben was independent didn't concern Briscoe much because the Durant affiliation with the establishment was strictly a marriage of convenience. Moreover, unlike many auto manufacturers, Billy was at home on Wall Street. He knew how to wheel and deal. Durant was the perfect colleague with whom to make grand plans.

Over breakfast, the two men recapped previous multi-car consolidation attempts, beginning with the then-crumbling Pope empire. The Colonel's mistakes were all too obvious. Two further tries seem to have sprung out of the A.L.A.M. since the detailed reports companies filed with their royalty fees meant members were cognizant of the comparative health of fellow member firms. The first, attempted in 1903 by the Searchmont Automobile Company of Philadelphia to bring itself together with Packard and Northern, among others, was quickly kaput when Searchmont itself went under. The second was instigated by Anthony N. Brady, the traction and utilities magnate and Whitney colleague when the Selden patent was acquired. Hermann F. Cuntz, the former Pope mechanical engineer hired to serve as traveling liaison between the A.L.A.M. and its member companies, was in a perfect position to convey strategic information to Brady about the likeliest candidates for a consortium powerful enough to control prices industry-wide. But Brady sensed the Panic of '07 coming and concluded the timing was not right.

Operating from a defensive posture instead of an offensive one, Briscoe had no difficulty convincing Durant of the merit of his timing. Still, although concerned by the overall health of the industry he had embraced, Billy was probably mesmerized more by the possibility of collaboration with the vaunted House of Morgan. Had not the venerable J. Pierpont Morgan single-handedly averted financial disaster for the entire nation by wrangling pledges of millions after locking up leading New York trust company presidents in his library until they saw things his way? To Durant, who thought he had played the Panic of '07 well himself, the idea of proximity to J.P. was intoxicating.

Billy didn't like the way Briscoe proposed they get there, however. Ben suggested a meeting of about twenty companies, specifically naming Packard, Peerless, Pierce-Arrow, Stoddard-Dayton, and Thomas. A mob scene like that didn't appeal to Durant: too many discordant voices. He countered with a proposal of only a handful of people. He and Ben were two of the nation's top volume producers; why not add just two more—Henry Ford and Ransom Olds. Probably Billy would have suggested the maker of the Rambler, too, except he knew Tom Jeffery would never go for it.

Briscoe approved the Durant plan right away. Billy had only one further suggestion: that Henry Ford be approached first because Ford "was in the limelight, liked publicity and unless he could lead the procession would not play." Briscoe contacted Ford in Detroit and then Ransom Olds at the Reo plant in Lansing. Both agreed to a meeting in Detroit on January 17, 1908. As the four participants shook hands in a public room of the Penobscot Building, Durant concluded that Briscoe had made another error in judgment. This place was too open. A reporter passing by might wonder why four of the country's leading automobile manufacturers were getting together and, worse, speculate in print about it. Nearby, in the Pontchartrain Hotel, Durant kept a suite, and he suggested that each of them leave separately and arrive the same way at his room in the Pontchartrain, where he would treat them all to lunch. That seems to have been the only thing all four of the men agreed on for the rest of the day.

Over coffee and cigars following lunch, the business of the meeting was broached. Briscoe said that a consolidation plan should be prepared to present to Morgan. Then he stopped. Nobody said anything until, finally, Durant turned to Ford and asked that if a value of $10 million were put on his company, would he regard $6 million reasonable for Reo? Henry said he had no idea what Reo was worth. Ransom Olds glared his disapproval but no more so than Briscoe did when

Durant next asked Olds if $5 million would be agreeable for Maxwell-Briscoe. "What about Buick?" Ben demanded. Billy said he would accede to whatever an independent auditor concluded was the value of his company. Everybody muttered that would be okay by them, too.

Nothing much had happened thus far, but at least there would no longer be any painful pauses. The ice had been broken. Discussion moved to the administrative form consolidation might take. Briscoe argued for centralization, with the purchasing, engineering, advertising, and sales departments of the four firms merged into one. Blanching visibly, Durant countered that he preferred a simple holding company with each participant to retain operating control of his own firm. "Ho ho," Briscoe chortled. "Durant is for states' rights, I am for a union." Precisely. Billy didn't want to lose his grip on Buick, and, equally important, he didn't want to botch the deal at the outset with Ford. Industry gossip told of Ransom Olds' frequent absences from his Reo office; he might look forward to retirement to pursue other interests. But Ford? That he didn't like the business of business was evident from the failures of his early companies. At the time, Durant did not know what was going on in that locked room at the Ford Motor Company, but he wasn't at all certain Henry's presence meant that he would acquiesce to any deal that would take him away from his Ford automobile.

The only commitment made by the principals at this meeting was for another one—in New York the following week at 120 Broadway in the law offices of Ward, Hayden & Satterlee. Herbert L. Satterlee was married to Louisa Pierpont Morgan, was a close associate of her father's, and had been appointed go-between for Morgan at this stage of negotiations. Well born, well educated, and well versed in financial and corporate law, Satterlee was apprehensive about any deal with these people because J.P. regarded the automobile business warily and Satterlee was already trying his father-in-law's patience by reorganizing the Knickerbocker Trust Company, whose failure had precipitated the Panic of '07. Bucking J.P. Morgan twice in the same month, if not the same lifetime, was something most tried to avoid. Still, Satterlee thought, although J.P. believed the Knickerbocker's doors should remain closed, he might be open to this idea because Maxwell-Briscoe was returning a pleasant 20 percent on the Morgan investment annually and, of the hundreds of automobile companies in the United States, these four were among the least likely to fail. Moreover, the top figure mentioned thus far was $35 million, paltry by J.P. Morgan's standards.

That first January meeting probed various aspects of a consolidation, the principal negative comment arriving from Henry Ford, who argued that the tendency of mergers was to increase prices, which was the opposite of what he wanted to do. How many more meetings followed is not known; minutes were never taken, and accounts differ in Olds' diary, Durant's recollection, Briscoe's published reminiscences, and the notes Jim Couzens took for Henry Ford. At one point, Briscoe recalled, Couzens suddenly blurted that in addition to the appraised valuation of the Ford Motor Company, Henry wanted an additional $3 million in cash. With that, Ransom Olds said that if Ford got $3 million, so should he. Durant remembered being startled at Henry's declaration that he had told Briscoe at their first meeting in Detroit he was interested only in cash, not stock. Briscoe conceded this was the case, but Ford's continuing interest in the project had led him to believe he had changed his mind. "Mr. Satterlee was quite put out," Durant remembered. Morgan had planned only an exchange of stock for any possible combine, not any payment of cash. Henry Ford departed. So did Ransom Olds.

Durant was not about to give up. "Let's go it alone," he told Briscoe, "we two." But before proceeding further on that pairing, he had a personal one of his own to attend to. On May 27, in Flint, Clara Durant was granted a divorce. The next day, in New York, Billy Durant married Catherine Lederer. She was nineteen years old; Durant's daughter Margery had introduced them. Catherine was not an "other woman" in the accepted sense; that the Durants' marriage had long been over was an open secret in Flint. Propriety was served in Billy's formally asking Mrs. Lederer if he might "call on" Catherine. Because Durant was still legally married, the mother naturally refused, which made not a whit of difference to the daughter. Following the marriage, Mrs. Lederer grew very fond of the son-in-law who was her own age. Interestingly, Durant's own son-in-law was his age. It perhaps says a lot about the relationship of the father and daughter that Billy and Margery found happiness with someone very like the other. For Durant's part, Catherine was the perfect wife: young, beautiful, innocent, adoring, loyal, and undemanding. The last two virtues were most important. Catherine had to be aware already that her husband wouldn't be around for extended periods of time.

Shortly after the honeymoon, Durant was on the express train from New York to Chicago, in the private drawing room of George W. Perkins.

Briscoe had willingly agreed to Billy's taking the lead in further negotiations. Perhaps Ben recognized that the man who was six years his
senior was more skilled in the fine art of persuasion. By now, Satterlee
had departed for Washington to serve as assistant secretary of the navy,
a plum President Roosevelt had awarded for his reorganization of the
Knickerbocker Bank. With the Ford and Olds pullout, Morgan was
officially out of the picture. But George Perkins, J.P.'s right-hand man
and the most powerful of the Morgan partners, remained interested.

The projected output of the Buick and Maxwell-Briscoe factories for
1908 was 20 percent of the industry total. Their consolidation could
form a solid base from which to entice others into the combine. As the
train sped toward Chicago, Perkins became increasingly impressed with
Durant, although he didn't like the designation—United Motors—that
Billy and Ben had chosen for the new company. Because International
Harvester had been the first merger Perkins had successfully engineered
after joining Morgan, he was very fond of that name. Durant had no
problem with International Motors.

But increasingly he had problems with Morgan. The firm's head office
at Wall and Broad streets was known throughout the financial district
as "the Corner"—much in the same way as the C.I.A. became famil-
iarly known as "the Company." To deal with the House of Morgan was
to deal with power, raw and unrelenting. Durant's next meeting was
with Morgan attorney Francis Lynde Stetson, at sixty-two the dean of
the New York bar and a man of exquisite courtesy. In this conference,
Stetson became a man of countless suggestions, not many of which
Durant liked. "A long hot session with our friends in New York...was
pretty nearly used up at the finish," Durant wrote to his Flint attorney
afterward. "If you think it is an easy matter to get money from New
York capitalists to finance a Motor Car proposition in Michigan you
have another guess coming." At another meeting, Durant declared that
before long, a half million cars would be sold each year. Perkins, aware
current industry output was one-tenth that figure, replied that anyone
harboring such outlandish notions best keep them to himself.

Durant bridled at the glacial pace at which negotiations were proceeding. Thinking that a surprise step on his part might move things along
more quickly, he headed back to Flint and phoned a good friend in
Lansing. Olds Motor Works was in trouble, he knew, but people were
still singing about Lucille in her merry Oldsmobile, and the company's

nationwide network of billboards kept the name in perpetual prominence. Landing the company for the proposed consolidation might impress even the Morgan people. Besides, he could conduct this negotiation in his own style. He put in a full day at Buick in Flint, left his desk there that evening, entrained for Lansing, and arrived at Olds Motor Works offices a little past midnight.

"All hours were business hours for W.C.," his friend Fred Smith commented. Fred's brother Angus was on hand, as was their father, Samuel, who recently had to advance Olds Motor Works a million dollars and was pretty much resigned to not getting it back. The four men chatted. "At about 3:00 a.m. I suggested an inspection of our plant," Fred Smith related, "and Billy, rather grudging the time, expended a scant fifteen minutes in galloping down through the dim factory aisles and racing back to the office 'to get down to business'." Selling the Smiths on joining International Motors was accomplished before dawn. "We came to a provisional understanding," Fred said. "Durant did the understanding; the rest of us just thought we understood." Then everybody went out for breakfast.

Happy as a lark in Lansing, Billy Durant returned to New York to undergo yet again the eagle eye of Morgan. Because he was no stranger to Wall Street, the bankers were suspicious that Durant might use the merger to speculate in Buick stock. Of more immediate concern, Stetson was aghast that Durant had made an offer for Olds without bothering to look at the company's books. For Durant's part, he chafed that Morgan was dragging its feet in coming to a decision about underwriting International Motors. Perhaps by this time, Ben Briscoe was becoming fidgety, too, because he did the unthinkable. He talked to a reporter.

"Plan a $25,000,000 Motor Car Merger," *The New York Times* headlined on July 31. "Morgan's Relatives In It." The article was essentially accurate, noting Satterlee's involvement as well as another Morgan son-in-law who had participated in the talks. The House of Morgan rose up in collective outrage. "The people on 'the Corner' are very upset," Briscoe wrote to Durant. "Why they should feel it as deeply as they do I can't quite fathom myself."

Because no project demanded secrecy more than a deal in the making, the Morgan partners declared, this deal was undone. Actually, the *Times* story allowed the financiers an easy out from an entanglement they now regarded as untenable anyway. Durant, all concerned recognized, would not be content to yield the control Morgan routinely demanded in consolidations it underwrote. Now he would not have to be asked to do so. The connection was neatly severed.

Briscoe was embarrassed. He apologized to Durant and said they didn't need Morgan to do a deal: "We have both concluded that a million dollars in cash would be enough to finance the proposition, and I will eat my shoes if we can't raise a million dollars between us." But by now, Billy had cooled on Ben. Apparently no awkward moments followed, because Briscoe had quick second thoughts about doing anything without Morgan approval. The two parted as friends.

Earlier in the year, Durant had developed an affinity for another lawyer at Ward, Hayden & Satterlee. Curtis R. Hatheway was aggressive, ambitious, and hungry, just the sort of man Billy needed for his next move. Walking into Hatheway's office late in August, Durant declared that consolidation was absolutely necessary, now or never. But you're the only one left, Hatheway sputtered, how can you consolidate one company? With that, Durant, who, unlike Briscoe, well knew the advantage of keeping a secret, revealed that he had an option on Olds Motor Works.

The rest was easy. Buick chief engineer Walter Marr had enough patents against which stock could be issued, Durant said, and would be happy to help because Marr liked Billy so much he had named his only son after him. This was enough assurance for Hatheway. Because New Jersey smiled on holding companies, that state was chosen for the incorporation. Only one snag developed. George Perkins insisted on keeping "International" for his own use. Hatheway quickly scanned other names on Durant's list, researched them, advised Billy of one that could be used, and also that "we have seen to it, as far as we were able, that no publicity will attend the filing of the papers."

On September 15, 1908, in Hudson County, New Jersey, with the press none the wiser, Billy Durant's company became reality. It was called General Motors.

CHAPTER 22

The Whirlwind Man

THE $2,000 AT which the General Motors Company (GM) was initially capitalized guaranteed that it would be given no more than a passing glance in the "new incorporations" columns of trade magazines. *Motor Age, Motor World, The Horseless Age, Cycle & Automobile Trade Journal, The Automobile,* and other publications routinely listed newcomers to the field, a dozen or more appearing each week. Some ventures boasting nothing more than a backyard shop, a hope, and a prayer had grander-sounding titles and a more generous stock issue than did GM. Actually, six days later, when GM capitalization was raised to $12.5 million, that news probably didn't provoke much reaction either. Latter-day swindlers were as aware as pioneer con man E.J. Pennington of how often a sucker is born. Multi-million-dollar incorporations of automobile companies were still falling like rain.

A low profile suited Durant's immediate purposes, but he knew it couldn't long be maintained. At every echelon in the Buick plant in Flint, there was talk. For some time, the company had been making a little money on the side by selling engines to small Midwest automobile producers. This had stopped abruptly in 1908. Al Leicher of the

Luverne Automobile Company in Minneapolis went to Flint and asked David Buick why. He replied that "these crazy carriage builders," as he always referred to Durant and associates, wanted the whole production because they were starting a new company to take over Buick.

It happened on October 1. General Motors exchanged its stock for Durant's 20,000 shares of Buick. On October 20, seven directors were appointed to the GM board, Curtis Hatheway serving as secretary/treasurer, Durant as vice president, and the administrative bother of the presidency being given to Michigan businessman William M. Eaton. All proper formalities were served. But there was no question that GM was Billy Durant's show. His first two acquisitive moves were on Flint companies: W.F. Stewart, the builder of Buick bodies, was purchased for $240,000; and a 49 percent interest in Weston-Mott, by now the largest axle manufacturer in the world, was secured in exchange for GM stock. Charles Stewart Mott was pleased to get on Durant's bandwagon. David Dunbar Buick got off by year's end.*

Durant's next acquisition was one he had begun negotiating at the same time GM itself was in the works. In Boston on Buick business one day,

---

* In 1908, his partner's death left Mott the sole ownership of Weston-Mott stock. In 1913, Mott exchanged the 51 percent remaining for General Motors stock. That year, he became a GM director and remained on the board until his death in 1973. At one time, Mott was GM's largest stockholder. He died at the age of 97, one of America's richest men and also one of the country's most generous philanthropists. David Dunbar Buick's life from 1908 was in stark contrast. Because his debt to early investor James Whiting had never been repaid, Buick had to surrender the stock held in his name when he resigned from the company later that year. But he did not leave empty-handed. Durant personally saw to it that Buick was given $100,000, perhaps more; the exact figure is not known. Whatever the amount, Buick lost it, investing in mines that had no gold, land that produced little oil, a carburetor business that went nowhere, and another automobile called the Dunbar, for which production was planned in Walden, New York, a venture that had failed by 1923. A few more business failures later, Buick took on a job teaching mechanics at the Y.M.C.A.'s School of Trades in Detroit. In 1928, Bruce Catton, then a newspaperman, found him there. Now 73 years old, Buick was so frail that he had been transferred to the school's information desk. The streets were filled with cars bearing his name, he told Catton, but he did not have the money to buy one. Indeed, he could not even afford a telephone. "Just the breaks of the game," he sighed, adding, "It's kind of hard for a man of my age to be uncertain about the future." His old friend Ben Briscoe once commented that David Dunbar Buick had made a hundred men millionaires. He himself died impoverished at Detroit's Harper Hospital on March 6, 1929.

he had been visited by a balding mustachioed man with a Parisian accent, who had the good fortune to be born a Champion, the perfect name for just about any automotive product in those days when racing was indulged in by most go-getter manufacturers. (Typically, Durant's Buick factory team was among the most ambitious and successful.) Albert Champion himself had been successively a bicycle, motorcycle, and automobile racer, primarily in his native France. His American competition was best remembered for the drive through a fence that he took with the Packard Gray Wolf at Brighton Beach (New York) in 1903. In 1904, he decided to take up less dangerous work, specifically the manufacture of various ignition devices to aid automobile engine performance. The Albert Champion Company followed in 1905. It was Champion's spark plug that most interested Durant, but Albert's Boston backers were not interested in selling to Billy either the Champion business or the man's name. So Durant took only the man, whom he set up in Flint in October 1908. The following year, Albert Champion's new business, which would carry his initials, was sold to General Motors.

Only a crossing of the t's and a dotting of the i's was necessary to make Olds Motor Works part of General Motors, a deed done on November 12. Considering the $3.75 million that GM paid for thriving Buick, the $3.0 million paid for faltering Olds was exorbitant. Durant acknowledged as much, muttering, "That's a hell of a price to pay for a bunch of road signs." Believing that Fred Smith's preference for more expensive model lines had contributed to the Olds decline, Durant had an easy remedial solution. Shortly after the ink was dry on the Olds deal, Durant directed the W.F. Stewart Company to truck a Model 10 Buick body to Lansing. When Durant arrived there, he told workmen to saw it apart lengthwise and crosswise, then had the pieces laid on the ground a few inches apart from each other and announced the new Oldsmobile Model 20 to the stunned onlookers. Just substitute the usual Lansing grille and other identifying features, Billy said. Priced somewhat above the Model 10 Buick but about half the usual Olds' price, the Model 20 accounted for 5,325 of the total 6,575 Oldsmobiles sold in 1909 and put the company into the black for the first time since 1906. Few ever knew this popular Oldsmobile had been drawn from a quartered Buick.

The Oakland Motor Car Company of Pontiac, named for the Michigan county in which it was located, caught Durant's acquisitive eye next.

It had been organized during the summer of 1907 when Pontiac Buggy Company president Edward W. Murphy realized that his traditional product's days were numbered. Impressed with the new Brush Runabout that Frank Briscoe was producing, Murphy had asked its designer to come to Pontiac to talk. Alanson P. Brush was delighted to do so. The timing was perfect. His two-year restrictive agreement with Cadillac was about to end, and Brush was anxious to join the ranks of automobile manufacturers. He readily accepted a co-founding partnership with Murphy and moved his family from Detroit to Pontiac. But he did not stay there long.

As fellow carriage builders, Durant and Murphy had been friends since the 1890s. As a relative newcomer to automotive ranks, Murphy might be won over, Durant thought, by the tack that placing total product responsibility on one engineer could be disastrous if that engineer misjudged public taste only one time. This was a variation of Ben Briscoe's "silly season" argument, and, with a bit of the Durant soft soap, it worked. Oakland was brought under the protective GM umbrella. Then, at Durant's request, Brush packed up his family again and moved from Pontiac to Flint to serve as acting chief engineer for Walter Marr, who had just contracted tuberculosis.

Murphy's death later in 1909 left Oakland momentarily bereft of leadership at the top, which does not appear to have bothered Durant. In Pontiac, he made a typically lightning-fast trip through the Oakland plant and told general manager Lee Dunlap that expansion was in order and to come to Flint with plans the next day. A frazzled Dunlap had only the night to come up with something to show Billy. He and his staff made a rough drawing of the grounds and cut a piece of paper into various-sized squares to represent possible factory units. In Flint, to Dunlap's utter amazement, Durant declared himself "pleased pink" with the proposal. The two men shuffled the little pieces of paper around for awhile, and then Billy told Dunlap to glue them down and call in a contractor.

What the Oakland general manager could not know was that his GM boss was preoccupied with bigger fish in Detroit. Durant was trying to land the Lelands. Al Brush, who had begun his career at Cadillac, could have told him it wouldn't be easy.

Henry Martyn Leland intimidated people. In a way, he still does. Consider standardization of parts, a concept that can be traced to the remote areas of the American frontier where firearms had to be capable of repair with spare parts or by cannibalizing another weapon. Interchangeability was necessary for survival. The government insisted on it for those firearms it bought. Leland had been introduced to precision manufacture while working for Samuel Colt in Connecticut after the Civil War. And precision had been his byword from the beginning of his automotive development. But interchangeability had been on Henry Ford's agenda from the beginning, too, because the "universal car" he wanted to build depended on it. Still, mention standardization of parts to many automobile scholars, and the Pavlovian response is Leland. Partly this was because of his ferocity on the subject.

"Old Leland's on the warpath," Alfred Sloan remembered his partner Pete Steenstrup phoning him one day in panic. "I'm no mechanic. I'm a salesman. We're not speaking the same language." Sloan hastened to Detroit to interpret and got a stern lecture. "The white beard...seemed to wag at me, he spoke with such long faced emphasis," the lecturee remembered. " 'Mr. Sloan, Cadillacs are made to run, not just to sell.' On his desk were some of our roller bearings, like culprits before a judge." Sloan left the meeting repentant and "determined to be as fanatical as he in obtaining precision in our work."

That neither emery cloth nor file was allowed in the Cadillac assembly room, as rumored to be the Leland decree, was given demonstrable documentation in 1908, when the company's English agent subjected Cadillac to a standardization test supervised by the Royal Automobile Club. Three randomly selected Cadillac runabouts were completely disassembled and their components mixed with eighty-nine parts from stock, again chosen at random. From the resulting pile, four cars were assembled using four tools (wrench, hammer, screwdriver, and pliers) and driven five hundred miles around Brooklands Track. For this achievement, Cadillac received the industry's highest award, the Dewar Trophy, sponsored by English automobile enthusiast Sir Thomas Dewar, whose fortune was in scotch.

The trophy was welcome news for the Lelands. They hadn't cared for the Panic of '07. The overreaction of Cadillac board directors, especially Lem Bowen, was rattling. Leland Senior liked worrying only about tolerances in the ten-thousandths of an inch. Son Wilfred tolerated commercial realities, but grudgingly. Both Lelands had been accustomed to a strong and steady increase in Cadillac sales, so any decline was unpleasant. Ben Briscoe approached the Lelands and Cadillac's directors during this period, about the same time as the post-midnight whirlwind courtship of Durant and the Smiths. Negotiations in this case were more circumspect but led to a similar end. Ben landed Cadillac for the proposed House of Morgan combine. When Durant and Briscoe parted company, Briscoe took the Cadillac option he had secured with him. It lapsed in November 1908.

Knowing that he might not be a welcome sight to the Lelands because his two-cylinder Models F and G Buicks had proven formidable competitors to the one-lunger Cadillac runabout, Durant asked an intermediary to arrange a meeting. The Lelands were cordial but also demonstrated their mastery at precision in deal-making: the price for Cadillac was $3.5 million, cash only, and the offer was good for only ten days. None of this silly option business. Durant replied that he did not want an option, but the Leland price figure seemed excessive "in view of the confused state of the industry," and he would get back to them after meeting with the General Motors board.

If he could swing this deal, GM would command respect in all quarters. Durant wanted Cadillac badly and was disinclined to dicker. Still, the price was high, so he dispatched Buick secretary Arnold Goss to the Lelands to see if they might be willing to settle for less. They wouldn't. Durant then called a meeting of the board of directors at GM's New York office at 101 Park Avenue. Attending were William Eaton, Curtis Hatheway, and the Smith brothers, Fred and Angus. It would be a short meeting, Durant figured, he would explain the deal and everyone around the table would endorse it. Afterward, Billy declared himself "somewhat surprised" when Fred Smith "entered a mild protest," commenting that a million-plus was still owed to his father from the Olds deal. "This small matter I had entirely overlooked," said Billy. The Cadillac deal was off for the moment. Durant wired the Lelands that, "much to my regret," the proposition had to be withdrawn.

Some months later, with the debt to Samuel Smith paid, the Lelands were approached again. They were still willing to sell, but their price had risen to $4.125 million, cash, another offer good for only ten days.

Durant tried the financial community but found no takers. Finally, he had an idea. General Motors might be cash poor, but GM's company in Flint had lots of money. Buick could buy Cadillac. By the time he arranged the logistics, more than ten days had passed. The Lelands' price now was $4.75 million. But they were willing to accept $75,000 of it in stock. On the July 29, 1909, a hot day in Detroit, the deal was done. Cadillac's stockholders were paid off at $300 a share. Because the total cash investment these ten people had made in the company was only $327,000, they enjoyed a handsome profit. The largest shareholder, William Murphy, walked away with close to a million dollars.

Immediately after the payout, Durant asked the Lelands to stay on. Perhaps they thought Billy might blanch at their terms—absolute freedom—but he didn't. "That is exactly what I want," he said, slapping his knee. "I want you to continue to run the Cadillac exactly as though it were still your own. You will receive no directions from anyone." Durant did wince, however, at the press release Wilfred Leland subsequently issued about the arrangement for their continued employment: "Cadillac standards, Cadillac policies, Cadillac methods, and the entire Cadillac organization will be carried on without alteration, and exactly as though the transaction recently consummated had never taken place." Neither General Motors nor Durant were mentioned in the release. "The written assurance of the purchaser," the Lelands said, was being accepted "in good faith, and with the full expectation and belief that the statements above made will be actually carried out."

Durant could accept the Lelands' imperiousness because it suited his purpose. The announcement of the sale created a sensation as the biggest bank transaction in Detroit to that time. With Buick and Cadillac together, General Motors had two of the top five automobile producers in America. With Olds Motor Works, GM had a lot of billboards and a company that had ceased being profitable. Billy Durant had no intention of delving into the management of the various GM companies. That's why it was important to him that the Lelands remain at Cadillac, a factory he had not yet bothered to visit. That's why it was equally important that better management be secured for the Olds Motor Works, much as he personally liked the Smiths. A month after Cadillac became part of General Motors, Fred Smith and his brother Angus resigned from Olds. Doubtless Billy, the master salesman, had applied more persuasion than pressure in easing the Smiths out. Fred Smith remained an ardent admirer of Durant the rest of his life. In memoirs written in 1928, he described Billy as "the most picturesque, spectacular and aggressive figure in the chronicles of American automobiledom" and the creation of General Motors as "a feat more staggering at the time than can be easily appreciated today."

Billy was moving fast. He could easily forget a million-dollar debt, as he had with Fred Smith's father. His mind was elsewhere—his next appointment, the next deal. Because his strategy was to convince prospects that General Motors stock was a worthier commodity than cash—and, except for the Lelands, the strategy worked beautifully—Billy could buy a lot of companies. He did, at the rate of about one a month. Stopping by one of his acquisitions was like "a visitation of a cyclone," in the words of Oakland's Lee Dunlap: "He would lead his staff in, take off his coat, begin issuing orders, dictating letters and calling the ends of the continent on the telephone... Only a phenomenal memory could keep his deals straight; he worked so fast that the records were always behind." He wore out associates in platoons.

Work was Durant's obsession. He begrudged the four hours of sleep he required each day. "No, you're on the night shift," he would laugh when someone suggested that one-thirty surely meant in the afternoon. "No, we'll get to this yet today," he said another time in scheduling a post-midnight appointment. Driven to a business meeting at the Bryant House in Flint one evening just after dusk, Billy got out and told his chauffeur to "wait here." At six-thirty the following morning, he emerged, got into the car, and, without another word, asked to be taken to the Buick plant.

Billy Durant stood a tad under five feet eight and weighed less than 150 pounds. Journalists couldn't resist Napoleonic references; neither apparently could his chauffeur, who vividly recalled dropping him at the train station in Flint one cold winter morning and watching him pace the platform, his arms folded in front of him, his head buried in the fur collar of his long overcoat. Winfred Murphy, Durant's secretary, remembered riding as Billy's passenger one afternoon, headed for Detroit to catch the express train to New York. Coming upon a hay wagon that hogged the entire road, Durant drove into and out of a ditch, breaking a leaf spring in the process. When Murphy asked what the loud snap was, Durant replied, "Never mind, we're still running."

A Detroit reporter in 1909 commented that Durant "is calmest in the time of stress and cheeriest under the heaviest burdens." A friend said that he "is never happy unless he is hanging to a window sill by his finger tips." He liked life on the edge, existence as a perpetual challenge. Wrote *Motor World* in 1910, "He kept one eye on his factories and another on the stock ticker, and the while he dreamed of world conquests."

A number of his conquests were not world caliber. What Durant might refer to as a "peach of a deal" sometimes turned out to be a lemon of a company. And he did buy a lot of odds and ends. In a breathtakingly short period of time, Durant purchased four companies beginning with the letter "R": Reliance of Detroit, Rapid of Pontiac, Randolph of Flint, and Rainier of Saginaw. The first three were truck producers; the last was an upscale automobile described as the "Pullman of Motor Cars" and made by a company that had already been petitioned into bankruptcy. Another top-market automobile purchase was Welch of Detroit—"the super passenger car of its day," a Durant associate said, "as big as a freight train." Companies purchased for the novelty of their engineering included Elmore of Clyde, Ohio, and Cartercar of Pontiac. The former produced "The Car That Has No Valves" and was vociferous in championing the two-stroke engine. The latter was the most popular car on the market sporting friction drive, a system offering limitless gear ratios if one replaced the paper fiber rims every 4,000 miles—a maintenance cost, Cartercar said, that was "at least one-half the amount expended on grease packing in a geared transmission." Heavily publicized in climbing, pulling, and carrying stunts at state fairs throughout the country, the company producing the "Car of a Thousand Speeds" was also available reasonably because of the sudden death of its founder, Byron Carter, the preceding year.

"How could I tell what these engineers would say next?" Billy lamented later when aspersions were cast on some of his purchases. "...I was for getting every car in sight, playing safe all along the line." Many of the Durant purchases did make sense, at least on the surface. The three-cylinder Elmore, for example, was enjoying sustained service in the taxicab field. Likewise was the Ewing of Geneva, Ohio, which had been designed by Louis P. Mooers (the engineer noted for the exemplary Peerless). Besides, these companies didn't cost General Motors much—not in cash, anyway.

Accessory and parts firms were brought into the GM fold with stock, too. Durant sometimes bought patents outright. A team of associates ferreted these out for him. One scout, returning from a patent investigation in Fargo, North Dakota, in the dead of winter, recommended against purchase. But Durant, learning that the patent could be acquired for only $10,000, bought it anyway.

———

Not every deal Durant went after worked out. The first to go awry apparently was with his former consolidation colleague. During the summer of 1909, chatting with Ben Briscoe must have been a welcome diversion for Billy, who was then in negotiation with the Lelands and doing most of the listening. The deal the two men hammered out was a nice one for both. For $5 million in General Motors stock, Ben was willing to sell to Billy not only Maxwell-Briscoe, but the Briscoe sheet metal business and brother Frank's Brush Runabout Company.

From Durant's viewpoint, the deal was super because it would bring to three the number of automobile producers in the top five belonging to GM, add one of America's most popular truly cheap cars of the year, and provide a thriving company that manufactured something every car needed. For Briscoe, ever fearful of a "silly season," joining General Motors would provide the safety in numbers that he believed would ultimately be necessary for survival in the automobile industry. Unfortunately, Morgan balked on a stock-only exchange. Should $2 million of the purchase price be provided in cash, the Morgan interests said they would be delighted with the deal. Having just agreed to the Lelands' demand for money, Durant couldn't hope to come up with another $2 million with a snap of the fingers. So he told Ben he had to beg off.

Just before Labor Day, Briscoe was approached by a New York reporter. Rumors continued to be spread that General Motors was about to acquire Maxwell-Briscoe. The usually loquacious Briscoe was terse in his reply. It was more likely, he said, that Maxwell-Briscoe would be doing the acquiring. He provided no further details.*

---

* Ben Briscoe was learning. Part of his difficulty in failing to understand Morgan's ire at *The New York Times* article that put the kibosh to the first Briscoe-Durant combine was the fact that Detroit and Flint papers had previously mentioned the merger possibility. But the Morgan interests weren't specifically cited in those accounts, and the Eastern establishment wasn't much concerned about gossip

No details were provided to Billy Durant a few weeks later when he heard through a reliable source that the one company capable of propelling General Motors into industrial orbit might be available. Henry Ford was willing to talk.

published on the other side of the Appalachians anyway. This time, Briscoe was more circumspect. In 1921, however, Ben could not resist a public and wistful "I told you so" in calculating that the $5 million in GM stock that Morgan turned down was by then worth $100 million.

Ransom Eli Olds was earliest to experiment among the major figures in American automobile history. News of his 1892 steamer (right) was published in *Scientific American.*

Race winner J. Frank Duryea with "umpire" Arthur Wright (below) before the start of the 1895 Chicago Times-Herald race, which launched the Duryeas as first in America to manufacture a gasoline car.

Photos courtesy of the Oldsmobile Historical Center (top) and the National Automotive History Collection, Detroit Public Library (bottom), hereafter NAHC.

America's best-selling car in 1899, the Locomobile steamer (left) with a welded bicycle-like frame, was soon overtaken by other automobiles of more sturdy build.

A landmark event in Madison Square Garden, the New York Automobile Show of 1900 (below) brought together thirty-four gasoline, steam, and electric vehicle makers.

Photos courtesy of the NAHC.

To prove it could be done...tackling the continent in 1903. E.T. "Tom" Fetch with *Automobile* editor Marius Krarup (above) was photographed while taking on the desert in a Packard.

L.L. Whitman and Eugene Hammond (below) ford a stream in the Midwest in the curved dash Oldsmobile.

Photos courtesy of the NAHC.

The automobile's first "captain of industry," Albert Pope (above, in top hat, surveying the competition) was headquartered in Connecticut and had factories in Massachusetts, Maryland, Ohio, and Indiana.

Air-cooled Franklin of Syracuse, New York, lampooned the "plumbing" of water-cooled cars. L.L. Whitman is behind the wheel, following his second cross-country drive.

Photos courtesy of the NAHC.

A "Stick-Seat" Stanley (top) joined the traffic mix in Boston, 1903.

What one wore while motoring depended partly on how rapidly one planned to travel. Sportsmen intent on "scorching" (center, right) used heavy equipment.

The minimal face covering was a veil (below) to ward off insects.

Photos courtesy of the Stanley Museum (top) and the NAHC (center and bottom).

"Get a horse" often became a literal fact for a motorist in trouble (above).

Sometimes, a horse couldn't help (center, left); accidents often left an automobile in pieces along-side the road.

For awhile, auto-hating farmers provided obstacles like smoke bombs (below) to impede automobilists venturing into the countryside.

Photos courtesy of the NAHC.

The 1906 San Francisco earthquake demonstrated the automobile's utility when hundreds were pressed into service (above) as the only mode of transport that could do the job.

In 1904, George Selden posed with the patent car (below) his sons built for the court case against Henry Ford.

Photos courtesy of the NAHC.

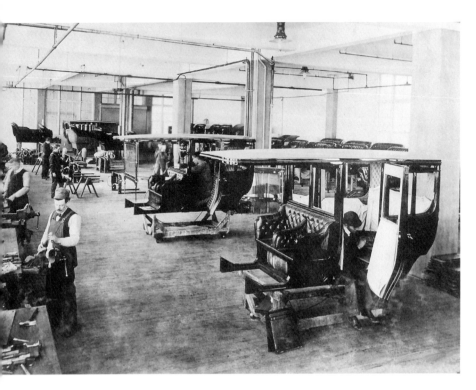

In Buffalo, New York, the Pierce-Arrow was hand-built by craftsmen (above).

In Dearborn, Michigan, the Model T Ford was mass produced on an assembly line (below).

Photos courtesy of the NAHC.

The highwheeler was an automobile pared to its essentials. The Zimmerman of Auburn, Indiana (above, circa 1909), put its engine under a hood. Usually, it was under the seat, betraying its buggy origins.

The cyclecar was an early try at minimal transport, the Imp (below, circa 1913) also built in Auburn. Both genres were killed by the Model T Ford.

Photos courtesy of the Auburn Cord Duesenberg Museum.

Doctors were the earliest professional group to adopt the automobile, this physician favoring Cleveland's Broc electric (above, circa 1911), which continued a tiller when the industry had long since converted to a steering wheel.

The introduction of a new model line was cause to celebrate with a parade and a photo opportunity; Hudson (below, 1910) made it a fashion event.

Photos courtesy of the Beverly Rae Kimes Archives (top) and the NAHC (bottom).

The industry's most charismatic player of the pre-World War I era, William Crapo Durant (right, with grandson) founded General Motors, lost it, organized Chevrolet, and got GM back, only to lose it again in 1920.

The automobile liberated women before the Constitutional amendment, although their taking to the wheel had not been universally acclaimed by the male gender. Harry Stutz was said to have made his clutch too stiff for a woman to use. A decade later, a woman (below, 1921) posed with her new Bearcat outside the dealership.

Photos courtesy of the Beverly Rae Kimes Archives (top) and the NAHC (bottom).

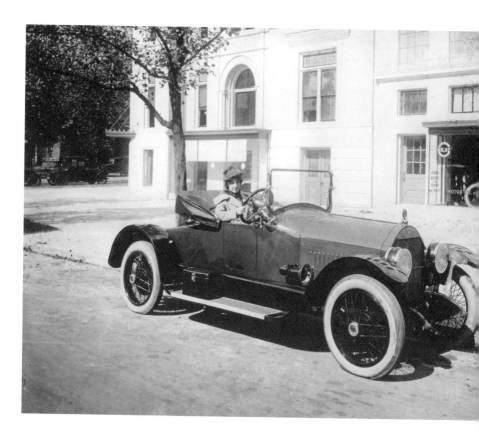

A white-bearded Henry Martyn Leland posed with Packard's Alvan Macauley during World War I Liberty engine testing (above).

The end of World War II saw the industry celebrate its first fifty years; Charlie Nash (below, left), who began as a cushion stuffer in a carriage factory, posed with production genius William "Big Bill" Knudsen (right) and his old boss, the man who put the world on wheels, Henry Ford (center).

Photos courtesy of the James A. Wren Archives (top) and the NAHC (bottom).

CHAPTER 23

The Race for Empire

IN THE SPRING of 1909, the Selden patent matter was put on the calendar of the U.S. Circuit Court of the Southern District of New York. At last, after six years of legal maneuvering, the case would be heard. Both sides publicly expected victory, but the anti-Selden forces had the greater confidence.

The Pope and Electric Vehicle Company receiverships during the Panic of '07 had put a sizable chink in the armor of the A.L.A.M. There were no outright defections from its ranks, but non-compliance among member companies was no longer abjectly feared. Fred Smith, the A.L.A.M.'s first president, stopped sending in Olds' royalties. The association's largest volume producer, Billy Durant, after being told by his attorney that "the Selden patent does not mean anything," did likewise. Around the time Durant incorporated General Motors, the A.L.A.M. brought suit for back royalties against both Buick and Olds. Around the time Durant and the Smiths were at the paper-signing stage, Olds Motor Works was expelled from the A.L.A.M. There is no evidence that Durant gave other than passing notice to either of these events.

Alone among the anti-Selden forces, Ford attorney Ralzemond Parker expressed concern. This followed his learning that Charles Merrill Hough would be hearing the case. "Hough is said to be cranky," Parker wrote to Henry Ford, "and I *know* he is *not* a patent judge." Parker became more concerned just before the first argument was to be heard when Judge Hough remarked that somebody had best explain to him what a gasoline engine was.

The trial began on May 28, 1909, and lasted six days. Sitting in the spectator section were Henry Ford and Tom Jeffery. On day four, the two men left the courtroom and walked across City Hall Park to wish Godspeed to the contestants of the New-York-to-Seattle race, an event sponsored by mining magnate Robert Guggenheim to promote the Alaska-Yukon-Pacific Exposition in Seattle. The failure of the A.L.A.M. to bestow official sanction and the Automobile Club of America's unnecessarily strict rules had kept most manufacturers away. Cognizant of the publicity that Winton, Packard, and Olds enjoyed following their transcontinental treks, Henry Ford had entered two Model Ts. On the starting line as well were an Acme, manufactured in Reading, Pennsylvania; a Shawmut from Stoneham, Massachusetts; and one foreign car, an Itala from Turin—all of them having more than twice the horsepower of the Model T. A Stearns entered from Cleveland was late arriving.

Thousands looked on as Mayor George B. McClellan, son of the Civil War general, raised a gold-plated starting pistol. Court was adjourned for a few moments so plaintiff attorneys, defense attorneys, and the bench could watch the start from the window. "Your Honor, there is something that puzzles me," Ford attorney Frederic Coudert said, with as straight a face as he could manage. "I don't see a Selden car. I see a Ford car, two Ford cars, but I see no Selden car!" Gentle laughter filled the courtroom. Ralzemond Parker, noticing that Judge Hough was chuckling, too, began to breathe a little easier.

Compared with his opponents, Parker's brief was as "chess to checkers," in historian Allan Nevins' fine phrase. It had been exhaustively researched; the scholarship was meticulous. From the other side of the aisle, plaintiff attorneys Samuel Betts and William Redding hammered away at only three points: that Selden was a great pioneer, that he designed an operable vehicle, and that his patent was the first for a gasoline car. When both sides finished, Judge Hough had the massive record sent to his summer home in Rhode Island where he would deliberate. And Henry Ford took the train to Seattle to watch one of his Fords cross the finish line first and hear Robert Guggenheim praise him for coming up with "the solution of the popular automobile."

Because he had been as confident of victory in the Selden case as he had been in the New-York-to-Seattle race, Ford was devastated on September 15 when Judge Hough returned from Rhode Island and found for the plaintiff. *Motor World* described the industry as "fairly stunned." Others were merely appalled. "By what miracle that flimsy patent was ever sustained I know not," Fred Smith wrote, although doubtless relieved that the Olds' license problem was now Durant's. Few, even among the A.L.A.M. faithful, truly believed George Selden was the inventor of the gasoline automobile. In *The Horseless Age*, E.P. Ingersoll noted sarcastically that Selden's luster was somewhat dimmed by Judge Hough's admission that the inventor "contributed little to motor car advancement in the United States, and nothing at all abroad." But that was academic. The patent was valid.

The winning side accepted victory with varying degrees of grace. "Radical members of the association," *Motor World* said, "favor a general hurling of firebrands" into the nether regions. "Every American automobile manufacturer was warned years ago not to infringe upon the Selden patent," Alexander Winton exhorted. "The patent has withstood the assault of the ablest legal talent on this continent; it emerges from the court triumphant, and nothing now remains but to exact from the trespassers a share of that income which they have enjoyed for years without legal right..."

The executive committee of the A.L.A.M. got together to decide what to do about those independent manufacturers already sheepishly begging for membership. Worried that industry overproduction was almost a reality and saturation would be reached soon, Herbert H. Franklin argued for a policy of strict exclusion. Hayden Eames, the former Electric Vehicle Company executive who had recently joined the Studebaker brothers in South Bend, favored the "exercise of broad-gauge liberality." With only three years until the expiration of the patent, this approach made more sense. Why not line the A.L.A.M. coffers as handsomely as possible?

With mass defections, the independent American Motor Car Manufacturers' Association's days were numbered anyway, but the A.L.A.M. hastened its death by welcoming Alfred Reeves, the general manager of the A.M.C.M.A., with open arms and giving him the same position in the pro-Selden group. The office of the A.L.A.M. general manager had been vacant since its previous inhabitant, M.J. Budlong, had accepted Henry Joy's offer to manage the Packard sales branches two years earlier. So, ostensibly, Reeves would not have much to do. Actually, he completed his real job for the Selden people on February 9, 1910, when he declared the A.M.C.M.A. dissolved and made arrangements to distribute its $60,000 in cash among member companies.

Ultimately, the A.L.A.M. would boast eighty-four member firms. The new arrivals paid a $2,500 initiation fee and 0.8 percent back royalty on all cars produced since 1903. Gritting his teeth, Ben Briscoe moved Maxwell-Briscoe into the A.L.A.M. promptly. So did Ransom Olds with Reo. The lone holdout among the major producers was Tom Jeffery's Rambler. But, sadly, this was not the decision of the avuncular carmaker from Kenosha. While vacationing with his wife Kate in Italy, Tom Jeffery had suffered a fatal heart attack. He was sixty-five. Kenosha grieved. So did the industry. Everybody loved Tom Jeffery. "To the end that his name may remain in the memories of men," his son Charles would announce a few years later, the Rambler automobile was renamed the Jeffery. In the immediate aftermath of his father's death and because of his father's views, Charles Jeffery could not commit the company to the A.L.A.M. Wisely, the association did not publicly press the issue. It had lots of other power plays to ponder anyway.

Basking in its newly won authority, the A.L.A.M. told new member firms the maximum number of cars they could produce annually and decreed that changes from list prices could be made only with A.L.A.M. consent. Licenses were summarily denied to any companies organized after the Hough decision.

To make peace with the A.L.A.M., Billy Durant paid a purported $1 million in back royalties, which sum negated the Buick lawsuit and reinstalled Olds as a licensed member company. At the onset of the Buick case, Durant had countersued, charging restraint of trade. Publicly, that unpleasantry was forgotten now, as Billy put on a charming prodigal-son-is-happy-to-be-back face. Privately, he remained unrepentant. Doing something about it was as easy as A.B.C., literally.

One of Durant's close colleagues from carriage-building days was Alexander Brunnell Cullen Hardy, who preferred using initials to his unwieldy trio of given names. An automobile enthusiast even before Billy, Hardy had left Durant-Dort in 1901, when he was serving as president, to produce the Flint Roadster. After putting together fifty-two of the cars, A.B.C. Hardy voluntarily folded his company after a visitation from the A.L.A.M. because he was opposed to paying Selden royalties and could not afford a lawsuit. His experience as an automobile manufacturer had convinced him the carriage business would remain viable for about a decade longer, so he returned to it until 1909, when Billy Durant called and asked him to take charge of the Welch factory in Detroit. Hardy was also prevailed upon to revive his old Flint Automobile Company for the sole purpose of suing the A.L.A.M. for restraint of trade and damages ensuing from that firm's failure. Had he been asked, of course, Billy would have feigned total innocence.

———

Like Durant, Henry Ford sported two faces in the wake of the Selden verdict. Publicly, he was defiant. "We will fight to a finish," he telegraphed a dealer the day after the decision. Privately, he wavered. The mood at the Ford Motor Company was somber. "We thought we were in great jeopardy," John Anderson remembered. "We were feeling very blue indeed." Commented another, "It seemed like the end." Then came another blow. New-York-to-Seattle race judges discovered a rules violation and took the trophy from Ford and gave it to Shawmut. The company had already advertised the victory extensively in newspapers and magazines; tens of thousands of copies of a company booklet, "The Story of the Race," were on their way to Ford dealers. Henry was sorely embarrassed.

Charles Sorensen said he knew his boss "better than did members of his own family, but it was useless to try to understand Henry Ford. One had to *sense* him." Even Sorensen wasn't sure what the man was thinking now when he let it be known again that he was willing to talk to Billy Durant about Ford joining General Motors.

Durant didn't dally. On October 5, 1909, in GM's Park Avenue offices, Billy met with Jim Couzens. Ford would have been there, too, his associate explained, but was "sick in body and disturbed in mind" and preferred remaining in his room across the street at the

Hotel Belmont. Couzens had complete authority to negotiate at this preliminary stage.

In the deal negotiated by the two men, the Ford Motor Company would become part of General Motors for $8 million, Couzens to remain on to manage, and Ford to retire. The only aspect of the business Henry was adamant on retaining was the Ford tractor, which was then in the experimental stage. There may have been a poignant reason for that. William Ford had died four years earlier, without ever truly approving of what his son was doing. Perhaps Henry Ford had visions of revolutionizing agriculture by creating a "Model T" for the farmer. That would allow Henry the satisfaction of doing something that certainly would have won paternal approval. And, of course, a tractor did not require a Selden license.

When Couzens returned to the Hotel Belmont, he found his boss lying on the floor, forced there to try for some relief from lumbago. When Henry was told of the $8 million offer, he replied, "All right, but *gold on the table*," meaning cash, and he directed his associate to tell Durant that "I'll throw in my lumbago."

The option to buy the Ford Motor Company—as agreed by all three men—included $2 million immediately, as down payment, the remaining $6 million to be paid over two years. On Sunday, October 24, Durant was given a secret tour of the factory by Ford and Couzens, which might have been insisted upon only by the latter two men. Durant, at least perfunctorily, checked the company's inventory. Two days later, Billy received formal approval from the General Motors board to implement the purchase agreement.

The only thing necessary right away was the $2 million kick-off money. The National City Bank of New York seemed amenable to a loan, the officers to whom Durant spoke indicating the necessary authorization would be sought from the bank's board of directors. The $3 million profit the Ford Motor Company had earned the previous year boded well, Billy was told, so he confidently returned to Flint by train. The bad news came by long-distance telephone. A sizable transaction with a copper company had turned sour, Durant was informed, and the board of directors thought it unwise "to have it understood that they were sponsoring an automobile venture." The National City Bank was controlled by J.P. Morgan.

Knowing he was licked, Durant didn't even attempt finding another source. But he did arrange an interview—unusual for him—with a *Wall Street Journal* reporter to try to educate the financial community about the automobile industry. The journalist went away impressed by Billy's proselytism and his projected production by GM companies for 1910 which, the reporter noted, "was the total output of the [entire] country in 1908."

———

Henry Ford's reaction to Durant's message that the deal could not be done has not been recorded. If he was dismayed, it was not for long. Possibly his lumbago was better. But because the Ford Motor Company remained his, so did the Selden problem. Colonel Charles Clifton, treasurer of Pierce and president of the A.L.A.M., had sent emissaries to Ford, bearing inducements for Henry to sign up. Capitulation would give the association unfettered freedom to rule. Uncertain what to do, Ford showed up unannounced one day at the New Jersey laboratory of the man he revered more than anyone else. He had last seen Thomas Edison in 1896, but the advice the inventor had given Ford about his first experimental automobile was all the encouragement he needed then. Now Edison advised him to stay out of the A.L.A.M. and to appeal the court decision.

Again, Ford did not hesitate to follow Edison's advice. John Anderson was directed to write to Colonel Clifton, declining "to entertain [the A.L.A.M.] suggestion as to a settlement." A new defense was prepared. To try it, Ralzemond Parker recommended Edmund Wetmore of Wetmore, Gifford & Crisp. Now sixty-eight, Parker was dog tired from his years of prodigious work on the case and thought New York savvy would be advantageous in arguing the appeal. Back home in Detroit, he prepared a new brief of thirty-one pages for Wetmore's use and remained intimately involved with the proceedings.

By the spring of 1910, Henry Ford released an official reply to Colonel Clifton. Bonds totaling $12 million had been arranged, indemnifying all Ford purchasers. "It is said that everyone has his price," Henry wrote, "but I can assure you that while I am head of the Ford Motor Company there will be no price that would induce me to permit my name to be added to those of the seventy-two licensees."

The Ford declaration would not staunch the tide of automobile companies taking up the Selden banner. But newspapers across the country were impressed. "There's a man for you, a man of backbone," enthused the *Detroit Free Press*. "As a human figure he presents a spectacle to win the applause of all men with red blood; for this world dearly loves the fighting man."

Thomas Edison was right again.

———

Like Ford, Durant did not long rue the collapse of the GM/Ford deal. Unlike the moody Henry, Billy was eternally optimistic. If the banks were reluctant to dispense money, he would dispense with cash. There were many available companies happy to accept stock in order to join General Motors. Durant went on buying them. Soon he had competition.

"I was in the frame of mind to make a deal," Ben Briscoe said. It smarted that Durant was having all the fun with an idea that he had first. Through the American Motor Car Manufacturers' Association, Briscoe had come to know Alfred Reeves well. Now that the A.M.C.M.A. was breathing its last and Reeves' new job for the A.L.A.M. was largely titular, he had time on his hands. Public relations was Reeves' forte, something in which Briscoe had never excelled. Theirs was a marriage of considerable convenience.

In late September, shortly after the Selden decision, Briscoe and Reeves met with Ransom Olds. Ben thought that Olds, earlier amenable to retiring to a life of leisure and civic pursuits, might be especially anxious to do so now that the Selden decision would necessarily move Reo into the A.L.A.M. camp. To Olds, any mention of the A.L.A.M. brought to mind Fred Smith, whose existence Olds took pains to ignore. Briscoe was right; Olds was ready to talk seriously, but only if the subject was cash. Reeves couldn't budge him. Likewise, the Ford Motor Company was momentarily available for the same terms offered Durant. Briscoe didn't even bother calling Jim Couzens back.

Ben's salvation was a phone call made to him about a month later. Anthony N. Brady was on the line. A self-made man, Brady had found consolidations both effective and profitable in traction lines and utilities and was a bit irked that he had allowed the Panic of '07 to dissuade him from an automobile combine. He knew how hungry Briscoe was for one; Brady hadn't become Brady by not knowing what was going on—or being involved one way or another. Most biographical dictionaries of the day gave up listing his board directorships after a dozen or so, begging off with "about thirty more." Brady promised Briscoe $1 million to play with if Ben would do something to help the Columbia Motor Car Company (*nee* Electric Vehicle Company). Because Maxwell-Briscoe was on its way to a record 10,000 units for 1909 (more than double 1908), Brady was not throwing his money away. Briscoe knew automobiles, and he knew manufacturing.

With the Brady overture, Briscoe became a more attractive proposition to Morgan. And both of those parties' involvement interested investment banker Eugene Meyer, Jr. By February 1910, Ben Briscoe found the United States Motor Company floating around him, capitalized at a cool $30 million. Offices were taken initially at 505 Fifth Avenue, but these proved too confining for Ben, who soon moved U.S. Motor to a big seven-story building on 61st Street between Central Park West and Broadway that had originally been a riding academy. His own company was the first for the new combine, of course, which left Jonathan Maxwell flabbergasted. Why Briscoe would want to fool around with other automobiles when the demand for Maxwells was straining the Tarrytown factory was beyond him. Briscoe tried to mollify Maxwell by making him U.S. Motor's vice president, but to little avail. To avoid lengthy argument, Maxwell didn't come into Manhattan much.

From his grand presidential offices, Ben began making grand plans. Bringing the Columbia Motor Car Company into the fold wasn't particularly desired—the car had been "engineered to death," in Ben's phrase—but naturally had to be done. Amusingly, the Knight sleeve-valve engine was among the ingredients that were hoped would restore panache to the Columbia, so the company that controlled the Selden patent began paying Charles Yale Knight license royalties for it.

Talking kid brother Frank into coming aboard with the Brush Runabout Company was a breeze. Ben put Alfred Reeves to work concluding negotiations for the Dayton Motor Car Company in Ohio, producers of the Stoddard-Dayton, a solid middle-class car that was advertised "As Good As It Looks." This deal did look good; Stoddard-Dayton sales had tripled or better each year since introduction. With production surpassing 2,000 units in the Panic of '07, John and Charles Stoddard had moved ahead with dispatch, adding new models as soon as they could be developed. As Briscoe wistfully remembered, "The matter of what obligations for material the company had contracted for seemed to have been overlooked." The figure ran into the millions.

Ben was frustrated. Here he was with a company that, on paper anyway, was three times bigger than his friend Durant's, but Billy had already beaten him to a lot of the desirable automobile firms. With the Brush Runabout, Maxwell, and Stoddard-Dayton, Ben ostensibly covered the market well from the lower end through the middle. Acquiring a company to put on top proved a problem. Most luxury car manufacturers, doing quite nicely with their high-profit margins, weren't interested in talking. Alexander Winton was willing to listen for a short while, but one suspects only to find out what somebody else thought his company was worth. The ornery Scotsman didn't come close to signing anything. Instead of an automobile at the prestige end of United States Motor, Ben had to settle for a truck. At $8,000, the Sampson, produced by the Alden-Sampson Manufacturing Company of Pittsfield, Massachusetts, was certainly a luxury vehicle; so cost-no-object was its construction, in fact, that the firm was losing money on each one it built. That was a matter Ben would have to look into.

Meanwhile, Briscoe kept buying wherever he could. Working capital quickly consumed, $6 million in debenture bonds were issued through Eugene Meyer & Company. Ostensibly, this would last awhile because Ben's *modus operandi* was the same as Billy's: a stock exchange was preferable to a cash sale. Thus was Providence Engineering Works of Rhode Island (earlier famed as the first company to develop the Corliss steam engine) and the Gray Motor Company of Detroit (noted for its marine engines) brought under the United States Motor umbrella.

Because he was striking out so often with automobile manufacturers, Briscoe put Alfred Reeves on the lookout for accessory or ancillary firms—any product that conceivably might have an automobile in its future. Forthwith, Reeves announced with appropriate fanfare the acquisition of the Motor Maintenance Company of New York City and the Westchester Appliance Company a few miles to the north. Others fell, like dominoes. Reeves did Briscoe's bidding all too well. As many as 130 allied firms would eventually be brought into the United States Motor empire.

During the autumn of 1910, Ben Briscoe sailed to England on the *Lusitania* for the purpose of setting up the United Kingdom Motor Company, although his advisors there would eschew the tidy correlative designation and opt for United International Motors Ltd. instead. This was the first time Ben had one-upped Billy. Durant had cast an acquisitive eye across the border to the north, buying both McLaughlin and Bedford in Ontario. But he had not yet thought of crossing the Atlantic. Not that he could now.

Because Billy Durant was in big trouble.

———

No question, it was Billy's fault. Perpetual optimism can be dangerous. Durant was a gambler; he thought he was on a roll. His basic instinct, as usual, was good. With increasing use, automobiles would be driven day and night. They were to some extent now, but acetylene, kerosene, and other gas lamps were difficult to keep lit under the best of conditions and practically impossible in wind and rain. Durant thought he knew the man with the answer: John Albert Heany had developed an electric lamp operable in an automobile and sturdy enough to stay lit on the worst roads. Unfortunately, his patent application was fudged to give a false priority of date. General Electric noticed, and so did the U.S. Patent Office. The former sued, and the latter turned the facts over to federal attorneys. Heany, his attorney, and a Patent Office clerk were indicted. Only the lawyer and the clerk went to jail; Heany was cleared, free to lament the fate of the innocent independent inventor against the malevolent corporate giant. Meanwhile, Durant had bought Heany's manufacturing operation.

The price paid was astronomical: only $112,759 in cash, but $7 million in GM stock, more than Olds and Buick combined. That the deal was an elaborate stock-watering scheme engineered by Heany's major creditor, Anthony N. Brady, who had earlier supported the company against Morgan-backed General Electric, has been suggested, the idea being to bring General Motors stock closer to parity with United States Motor for the purpose of merging the two combines into one mega-colossus for the profit of all involved, most especially Brady. Durant's attorney John Carton said that what his client liked best were "large stock issues in which he, from an inside position, could dicker and trade."

But this scenario overlooks several aspects of the Durant persona. The fact that, unlike Briscoe, he had pulled off General Motors without the aid of a Wall Street sponsor was a source of supreme satisfaction to Durant. That he would have allowed himself to become a foot soldier in Brady's army doesn't ring true.

Moreover, since his days as a cigar peddler, Durant had pride of product. He was a super salesman who reveled in the virtues of what he had to sell. From the beginning, he referred to General Motors as "my baby." His bad judgment notwithstanding, the companies he bought for the corporation were hedges against where an industry still in its infancy might be headed. He was planning long-term.

What Durant had accomplished thus far had made him cocky. When Billy wanted something, price was secondary, particularly in a case such as Heany's when little cash was involved. If the Heany lamp had been everything its inventor said it was, the cost for the company would not have loomed so large. Even after the patents were declared worthless, Durant continued to insist that Heany's tungsten filament was more "elastic" than General Electric's and thus more suitable for automotive use. Perhaps his trip through the manufacturing plant had been as whirlwind as his wee-hours jaunt through Olds Motor Works. Whatever the reason Durant bought Heany, he carried it to his death. In 1910, the Heany deal carried Billy to the brink of disaster.

None of this was evident early in the year. Indeed, overall the figures looked good. For less than $33 million, only $6.2 million in cash (and most of that for Cadillac), General Motors had bought properties valued at $54 million earning profits of $10 million annually. But Billy had stretched himself woefully thin. Being cash poor wasn't a negative to Durant as long as the cash there was continued to flow. Operating expenses were paid from sales—simple as that. And expansion money was easy to get in Flint. For a new Buick engine plant, Durant floated a $1 million stock issue in March. Buick employees subscribed $122,000 in two weeks; the remainder sold in the next three days.

To Durant, bankers lacked vision. He never forgot the afternoon when one of them pointed to a large vacant space on a factory blueprint and asked what it was. His reply that the workers would park their cars there brought the gasp, "Do you mean to tell me, Mr. Durant, that ordinary factory employees will drive automobiles?" In 1910, Buick production would double to 30,000 cars. The industry had nowhere to go but up.

Then, suddenly, as spring approached, there was a downturn, one of Briscoe's "silly seasons," blessedly short for the industry as a whole but, for Durant, living on the edge, disastrous. To bolster public confidence in GM, Durant anonymously published a circular listing the production figures for all A.L.A.M. companies; Buick headed the list, Cadillac was second. Furious, the A.L.A.M. censured Durant for divulging confidential information, confident of the culprit because all of the GM companies on the list had been printed "in heavy type."

Many of those GM companies were, as A.B.C. Hardy said, "head over heels in debt." With each operating independently, there was no way to easily gauge GM's financial condition. But when Buick was stricken, Durant had an inkling. Because the cash for Cadillac had been siphoned from the treasury in Flint, Durant couldn't sail through this short recession by stockpiling Buicks as he had done so successfully during the Panic of '07. Indeed, Buick's bills couldn't even be paid. The Durant-Dort Carriage Company advanced some funds, and Boston distributor Harry K. Noyes helped meet the payroll by shipping suitcases of cash to Flint. On another occasion, Noyes wrote a cashier's check payable to GM after depositing Buick money in his own account because going through the usual banking channels would have seen the money used to pay Buick's overdrawn account. New plant construction in Flint ground to a halt; more than four thousand workers were laid off.

Because much of Buick's expansion capital had been borrowed in dollops of a couple hundred thousand dollars each from banks all over the Midwest, Durant was surprised to find the company that was the rock upon which General Motors had been created, now had an indebtedness of nearly $8 million.

Because these same banks had earlier financed his carriage dealers, Durant was confident of "accommodation"; instead, many began to call in their loans. So he tried other banks. So did A.B.C. Hardy and Arnold Goss. One evening, the three of them met at the depot in Chicago, each at the end of a long, fruitless day of bank hopping. Their train headed back to Flint in the midst of a downpour; Durant remained awake while his companions dozed. At one station stop, he glanced out the window. Far down the dismal black street, a single electric sign shone. "BANK," it read. Durant chuckled. "Wake up, Goss," he said, nudging his seatmate. "There's one we missed."

The Lelands were aloof to the GM problem early on. Durant's lavish spending had caused them some unease, but it was assuaged by Billy's assertion that raising money would never be a problem. Thus, during the summer of 1910, Henry Martyn Leland joined the American Society of Mechanical Engineers on a junket to visit European industries. This left Wilfred alone at Cadillac when the crunch came. The son had been content to bask in his father's shadow in the past. Now, Durant brought him center stage—to lend Cadillac cachet on trips to the banks. At first, it didn't help much.

The lack of centralized accounting at GM meant Durant wasn't sure how much money he needed. One bank seemed willing to lend $7.5 million. But then Billy determined he needed $9.5. When that figure loomed as a possibility from another source, Durant looked again and realized $12 million was required. Shortly after Labor Day, the GM directors met and decided to sell (or, more accurately, sacrifice) three of General Motors' weaker links including, upon A.B.C. Hardy's advice, Welch-Detroit. Durant's discomfort was palpable. He had spent two years building General Motors; now it was being chipped away. But the worst was yet to come.

Probably Wilfred Leland was not the haloed savior of General Motors that he painted himself to be. But because no one else at the meeting commented afterward, history shall never know. What is known is that an afternoon meeting later in September at the Chase National Bank in New York ended with the bankers telling Durant to return the following morning. Leland said he was pulled aside and invited to a private evening session at the Belmont Hotel, during which he was told that Cadillac was worthy of saving but the rest of GM should be scuttled. Until the wee hours, Wilfred Leland said, he urged the financiers to reconsider, that General Motors was not so bad off, that the automobile industry held grand promise, and that it would be better to ponder how GM might be saved rather than dissolved.

At ten the next morning, Durant was informed of the terms of salvation. A $15 million loan would be organized by J. & W. Seligman of New York and Boston's Lee, Higginson & Company. For this, the banks would be paid more than $8 million in cash and securities. Further, for the five-year life of the loan, General Motors would be a banker-run operation with voting power vested in five people: Albert Strauss for Seligman; James Storrow for Lee, Higginson; James N. Wallace of Central Trust of New York; Anthony Brady, who, via his Heany holdings, had become a major stockholder in General Motors; and Billy Durant. The bone thrown to the creator of GM was lean indeed.

"If ever a man exhibited a divine forbearance toward other men it was my father in those months of late 1910 and early 1911," Margery Durant Campbell said. "He accepted the inevitable gracefully; helped when and where he could; kept quietly out of the new working of the machine he had so carefully built."

But privately, Billy Durant was furious. "Outrageous" was the word he used to describe the terms forced upon him "to save my 'baby,' born and raised by me, the result of hectic years of night and day work. ...[The loan] having been accomplished, we notified our dealers that we were again doing business as usual, and the first week we received orders for 13,886 Buick cars having a money value of $13,886,000."

The financial community was convinced it had tamed the wild man of the industry. "The meat of the situation is this," concluded Lee, Higginson in a letter circulated to potential GM bond purchasers. "Here is a concern which got into trouble, not from lack of earnings but from lack of management. We now take the business up..." Even *Motor World*, staunch Durant supporter on his way up, was happy to twist the knife now that he was down: "The feeling is...that an element of real peril to the entire industry has been circumvented and chastened."

Chastened, yes. Circumvented? Not for long.

CHAPTER 24

Selden Undone, Hooray

ALFRED REEVES SWITCHED allegiance with aplomb. The energy he had expended on behalf of the anti-Selden forces he now turned to expounding the A.L.A.M. gospel. He decided to tackle the association's bogeyman image first. "The industry has reached a stage where precautionary measures are necessary," he said. "Men are starting factories on blueprints and nerve. They will never be able to meet the demands made upon them and it is only right that the public should be protected." Praising Henry Ford as a pioneer of the industry, Reeves insisted that "the association only desires that he enter the A.L.A.M." and emphasized that "no cut-throat methods" would be employed against Ford.

Instead, those methods were directed toward automakers who had not rushed lemming-like to join the A.L.A.M. following the Selden victory in court. Emboldened by Ford's avowal to mount a rigorous appeal, some fought back. After the association reneged on the granting of a license to the newly organized Carharrt Automobile Corporation of Detroit, the company took its case to the press. A substantial investment in equipment and materials had been made only after being assured a license, the company spokesman said, and bankruptcy loomed if operations had to be suspended until expiration of the Selden patent. The Velie Motor Car Company of Moline, Illinois, took its case to court, asserting that the $17,000 in fees and back royalties demanded for a license was usurious, the restriction demanded on output (2,500 cars in 1910 and 2,000 in 1911, about 1,000 less than the Velie norm) was injurious, and the A.L.A.M.'s pressuring of advertising agencies to boycott the Velie account was unethical, if not illegal.

With briefs already filed, the hearing on the Ford appeal began on November 22, 1910, before three sitting judges of the U.S. Circuit Court of Appeals. Henry Ford and Jim Couzens sat in on every session—and Henry smiled broadly at least once. Having elicited the admission from the Selden lawyers that much of their case was based on the testimony of English engine expert Dugald Clerk, Ford attorney Frederic Coudert waved aloft a copy of Clerk's recently published book on the internal combustion engine. Afraid of what was coming, Samuel Betts objected that the volume was not in evidence. The objection was overruled. Allowing that the hefty fee paid Clerk for his testimony was beyond reproach, Coudert suggested that what Clerk had to say about Selden without "a retainer in his pocket" might be of interest. The answer was precisely nothing. "The man who for six years was their retained expert," said Coudert with a flourish, "...has not a word in his book, not a single syllable, about Selden."

The unanimous opinion of the court was read on January 9, 1911, by its author, Judge Walter Noyes. Adroitly written, the decision acknowledged that "the patentee had ideas ahead of the times and appreciated many aspects of the problem to be solved in creating a practical motor vehicle." The Selden patent was declared valid but only insofar as it pertained to the Brayton-type engine that George Selden used. Subsequent pioneers, beginning with Gottlieb Daimler in the mid-1880s, had developed their engines along Otto-type principles. Thus, the patent had not been infringed. With its careful, comparative examination of the Brayton and Otto engines, the decision was heavily weighted in technical talk. But, in an era of trust busting, obviously the public interest had been considered as well.

The verdict arrived propitiously, in the midst of the New York Automobile Show. "The decision came like a clap of thunder," reported

The Automobile. "The whole atmosphere seemed to take on an electric quality after the announcement." Presidents of A.L.A.M. member companies saw the result as good-news/bad-news. On one hand, the A.L.A.M. was doomed, and everyone recognized the need for an industry association.* On the other hand, there now would be no royalties to pay. The telephone wires from New York burned with calls to auto company treasurers to ask whether the current quarterly payment had yet been sent out—and if not, don't send it.

George Selden took the defeat philosophically. "I went into this enterprise hoping to make a little money out of it," he remarked. "I have succeeded much better than I expected." But his philosophy changed. A decade later, on his deathbed, Selden declared that "morally, the victory is mine." Likewise, Alfred Reeves announced initially that, because of the judicial difference of opinion in the two verdicts, the A.LA.M. would take the case to the U.S. Supreme Court. But that idea was quickly reversed as a waste of money, given the brief time left of the patent's life.

Instead, the A.L.A.M. invited Henry Ford to its annual banquet at the Hotel Astor on January 12. His was the only business suit at this very formal affair, which was explained away by a Ford spokesman as the result of Henry's being "kidnapped" at the last minute. Actually, Ford had entrained from Detroit for the event the preceding day. Asked at the station by a *Free Press* reporter for a comment on the court verdict, Ford demurred, "Whatever I say now might sound like boasting. I think the decision speaks for itself." At the A.L.A.M. banquet, he overlooked his distaste for tobacco long enough to smoke the peace pipe proffered by Alfred Reeves as the audience of his former adversaries lustily cheered, "Ford, Ford, Ford." Tributes for the patent slayer were fulsome. To the wild applause, Ford bowed in appreciation. He never uttered a word.

---

* Any fears that anarchy would reign in the industry were ill-founded. The Automobile Board of Trade, the A.L.A.M.'s immediate successor, became the National Automobile Chamber of Commerce in 1914. To avoid another Selden situation, a cross-licensing agreement was instituted that year, which allowed a general sharing of patents among automakers. Typically, Henry Ford refused to sign it, but he abided by its rules. The agreement was largely responsible for the phenomenal strides made by the industry in the decades ahead.

Henry Ford was a shy man. He was also astute. Within twenty-four hours of the court decision, the Ford Motor Company was deluged by more than 1,000 telegrams of congratulations. "Hurrah for Henry Ford!" wired his old friend Charlie King. Charles Duryea lauded Ford for "a plucky, hard and above all, HONEST fight." One message was especially poignant. Wrote Charles Jeffery, Tom's son, "Your determination and courage have surely won for you the admiration and respect of the whole automobile industry." And the adulation of the public.

Henry Ford became a folk hero. Modestly declining to gloat in public added to his appeal. But his plans were anything but modest. At the Ford victory party on the evening following the A.LA.M. banquet, Henry sat on the sidelines, smiling. Finally, he broke the silence. "Nobody can stop me now," he said almost defiantly. "From here on, the sky's the limit."

———

"My Farewell Car...," the ad for the 1912 Reo read. "Embodied here are the final results of my 25 years of experience. I do not believe that a car materially better will ever be built. In any event, this car marks my limit." Ransom Olds read the copy to be carried over his signature and frowned. "But I don't intend to retire," he told copywriter Claude Hopkins. Hopkins replied that Sarah Bernhardt had made seven farewell tours, so Olds was surely entitled to at least a few: "Every farewell is subject to reconsideration."

That mollified Olds, and the extraordinary ad ran. But the fact was that Olds had long vacillated about retirement. Some thought he had started Reo only to prove to the Smiths that he could do it and outdo them. Reo had quickly outsold Olds, which the Smiths took personally. The bitter rivalry had amusing moments, as in 1907, when President Roosevelt announced he would travel by automobile while in Lansing for a visit. Both Reo and Olds sent emissaries to Washington to win the President's favor. The lobbying was fierce; T.R. diplomatically chose to motor to the campus in a Reo (with Olds as chauffeur) and return via an Oldsmobile.

Of all the manufacturers enjoying prominence in the industry, Ransom Olds had been plugging away at the automobile idea the longest. Designing cars still held interest for him, but running a company didn't. Day-to-day decisions were left to vice president Reuben Shetler, the

Lansing friend who had helped establish Reo. Emory Olds served his brother as private secretary and kept Ransom aware of what was going on during his winters in Florida and his increasing vacations elsewhere in the country and abroad. Had Ford not insisted on cash during the first merger talks with Durant and Briscoe, Olds would have sold out. But, an intensely proud man, Ransom would not be one-upped by his rival in Dearborn.

That Olds was willing to sell had infuriated Shetler, who attempted a coup which would have put Ray Owen, whose firm handled Reo sales, in charge of Ransom's company. Owen and Olds had been friends since curved dash days, but now the two men locked horns. The coup failed, Shetler was booted out, and Owen bowed out, "an event fraught with significance to the automobile business," as *Automobile Trade Journal* reported. Reo taking over its own sales effort from Owen's company eliminated the middleman and made sense. The rift between Ray Owen and Ransom Olds became the talk of the town.

Although unnerved by the takeover attempt, Olds did not change his management-in-absentia style, installing his loyal superintendent Richard Scott, who was an ardent proponent of the Anti-Saloon League, in Shetler's vice presidential post. Olds left no doubt whose company it was and made it clear—as in his remark to adman Hopkins—that he did not intend to relinquish power under any terms except his own. The terms Ransom Olds demanded for Reo in January 1912 were simply stated: $7 million cash. The meeting between Olds and John North Willys ended quickly. That was an exorbitant price, Willys thought, for a company with an output one-third his own.

Willys had come a long way in the four years since he began building Overlands in a circus tent. By year's end 1912, only Ford would be producing more cars. "Where there's a Willys, there's a way," *Collier's* punned in describing "one of the most remarkable industrial enterprises of our times." John Willys' success, the magazine concluded, was attributable to his being "supremely a salesman, a manufacturing Cyclops, because he is a Brobdingnagian merchandiser." He was also a consummate public relations man. At a press luncheon early in 1910 to announce plans for the doubling of Overland production, Willys said he did not expect "free reading notices" from the press to sell the increased output but was inaugurating an advertising budget of about $50,000 per month, an extraordinary sum. Reporters, accustomed to

the heavy hands other manufacturers used to wheedle favorable stories, applauded appreciatively. At the conclusion of the lunch, each of
the journalists was presented "a thermos bottle in a leather case filled
with good intentions and best wishes for the New Year."

Willys' new Overland was a $1,000 car slightly larger and more pow-
erful than the Model T Ford and, the company claimed, the first automobile "completely equipped" (meaning lamps, windshield, and top)
at that price. "She is a pretty little boat," wrote an Overland dealer,
"...the only thing I don't like is the front appearance, the hood is too
short, the fourth cylinder comes under the toe boards." Magazine
articles about the new model usually used the "first completely equipped
$1,000 car" in the lead paragraph, and reporters didn't find the hood
too short at all.

When various additions to the Toledo complex were finished, Willys
boasted the largest automobile factory in the world (which it would
remain until Henry Ford bought a marsh and turned it into the River
Rouge). In 1912, Willys increased the capital stock of Willys-Overland
to $25 million, selling two-thirds of the new issue outright to William
Salomon & Company. Cash surpluses and extra dividends were
declared. So pleased were the denizens of Wall Street with John Willys,
they threw him a lavish dinner at Sherry's, the first automobile man to
be so honored.

Willys was also the first to vigorously promote Charles Yale Knight's
sleeve-valve engine, which was used in the first car to bear his name.
It was the salesman in him that recognized the sleeve valve's novelty
and promotional possibilities. Quite possibly, Willys was the first as
well to try to do away with demonstrator models. "Many a person has
entered a showroom feigning an interest in a car when the sole object
was to secure a ride," he argued. "...The demonstration has become
'graft' on the part of joy riders and a drainage on the dealer."

But if Willys wanted to undo a fake customer's good times, he was
equally anxious to make the *bona fide* customer's buying of an Overland or Willys-Knight as painless as possible. That the automobile
business could long flourish on a cash-only basis had been a subject of
debate in trade circles for some time. Mortgaging their homes indicated the cheerful willingness of ardent automobilists to go into debt
for a car. In 1911, Studebaker had begun assisting dealers who sold

cars on the installment plan. But Willys wanted a bigger piece of the action and in 1915 started the Guaranty Securities Company. Customers loved being able to purchase a car for one-third down and eight relatively modest installments. Dealers loved being unburdened of the drudgery and possible risk of financing time payments themselves. And Willys loved depositing the interest earned. The Willys idea spread like wildfire in the industry.

In June 1913, Willys reduced the weekly hours of his workers from fifty-four to fifty, with no decrease in pay. The press was impressed, which delighted Willys. He liked the notion of being a benevolent emperor. Empire building was very much on his mind. When negotiations with Ransom Olds went nowhere, Willys went to Elyria and bought the Garford Company (which had previously made cars for Studebaker), and to Lima, where he purchased the Gramm Motor Truck Company; back home in Toledo, he picked up the Electric Auto-Lite Company.

Among the few deals he could not pull off was one with the man he was plainly emulating. For a while, the press pondered whether "an amicable understanding" could be effected between John North Willys and William Crapo Durant. It could not.

In 1910, just before General Motors came crashing down around him, Billy Durant had chatted briefly with Willys about buying the Toledo company. The discussions in 1912 doubtless were initiated by Willys, who saw himself as a better Briscoe for Durant. Billy agreed to the meetings to learn more about the ambitious Willys' plans. He had no intention of allying with anyone.

Nor did he now intend to sit quietly in his GM director's chair, making a modest suggestion every now and then that was likely as not to be ignored by the bankers in charge. "With no idea of being disloyal, it seemed to me that it would be better to let the new group handle the business to suit themselves," he wrote, "and if I ever expected to regain control of General Motors, which I certainly intended to do, I should have a company of my own, run in my own way. In other words, another one-man institution, but taking a leaf out of Henry Ford's book—No bankers."

This self-assurance that GM would again be his was startling from a man who had been brusquely and publicly humiliated, who had been soundly and excessively pilloried, whose motives had been questioned, and whose abilities had been slandered. But it was not surprising. One New York banker described him well: "Durant is a genius, and therefore not to be dealt with on the same basis as ordinary business men. In many respects he is a child in emotions, in temperament and in mental balance, yet possessed of wonderful energy and ability along certain other well-defined lines. He is sensitive and proud; and successful leadership, I think, really counts more with him than financial success."

To his genius, Billy could add one further valuable asset: the adulation of an entire city. Durant was Willie to his mother and his wife, Pops to his daughter, and Billy to his friends. To Flint, Michigan, he was "The Man." On November 28, 1911, ten days before his fiftieth birthday, Durant was feted by 150 of Flint's leading citizens at "The Wizard's Banquet" held in the Masonic Temple. Locally made cigars were passed around in boxes bearing Durant's portrait and labels touting "El Capitan de Industria." Flint was grateful to Billy Durant for favors past—and anticipating favors future. "While he has declined thus far to disclose his plans," the *Flint Journal* reported, "they appear to have been so framed as to take particularly good care of his home town." Said "The Man" himself at the banquet, "Do not think that I have left Flint and am coming back. I never have been away from this city." Ironically, even as he was pledging undying devotion, Durant was moving away from Flint, at least physically. His beloved mother Rebecca would begin to complain of his infrequent visits. Clara Durant got the house in Flint in the divorce settlement. The city was large but perhaps not large enough for Durant's new, young wife, Catherine, to feel comfortable living there.

Detroit would be the new Michigan home for the Durants. While house hunting, they stayed with Durant's daughter Margery and her husband, Dr. Edwin Campbell. Unlike her younger brother Cliff, who had chosen to live with his mother following military school graduation, Margery was shamelessly devoted to her "Pops." Staying at the Campbell home was enjoyable for Catherine because she had been a friend of Margery's long before being introduced to Margery's father. For Billy Durant, the proximity to Margery's husband, who was close to his own age, would result in his gaining a valuable assistant and confidant in his project to get General Motors away from the bankers.

"He was planning a comeback and told me, 'We're going to need a car.'" That was how the French-speaking son of a Swiss clockmaker remembered the incident. Now the star of Buick's factory racing team, the race driver was thinking of retirement and trying his hand at automobile design. Billy Durant knew that before he stopped by the garage at 3939 Grand River Avenue in Detroit and asked to see Louis Chevrolet.

CHAPTER 25

■

From Lawn to Dust

NOTHING ILLUSTRATES THE democratization of the automobile in America better than what happened to racing. Within a decade from the social frivolity of Mrs. Belmont's lawn in Newport, the sport had become serious business and livelihood for the likes of Louis Chevrolet. Motor sport was arguably the first organized activity in America that drew all social classes together. It happened on a beach. Given the condition of American roads, racing on sand was an attractive alternative, and between Ormond and Daytona in Florida stretched miles of it, lapped solid and smooth by the pounding waves. Each winter, the population of the area mushroomed as society en masse took the train south to the sun.

Joining New York's 400 in ever increasing numbers were dozens of Midwesterners who had made their money in automobile manufacturing. In 1902, Ransom Olds and Alexander Winton were persuaded by the proprietor of the Ormond Hotel, at which both were staying, into driving their respective cars in a short impromptu race along the ocean for the enjoyment of fellow hotel guests. From this, an annual speed carnival grew.

These races quickly became very important. The *raison d'être* varied. Alfred G. Vanderbilt, hoping to defeat his more celebrated cousin Willie K., commissioned a French automobile designer to build a 200-miles-per-hour racer, and followed with a lawsuit when the car did not perform as expected. ("I met many Frenchmen on the beach" was François Richard's excuse for submitting a $1,400 bill for personal expenses.) For automobile entrepreneurs, the advertising value of victory was tantalizing and the reason that practicality overcame ego as manufacturers gave the wheel to those who could better show off the product. Thus commingled on the beach were the rich and the infamous, gentlemen drivers well known to society pages and tough guys whose names had previously graced only an occasional police blotter. They got on surprisingly well. First to congratulate Willie K. Vanderbilt on his 39-second flying mile that broke Henry Ford's record in 1904 was Barney Oldfield. Vanderbilt had been practicing on the beach since dawn, about the time the carousing Oldfield had called it a night. Even nursing a hangover, Barney was sure his Winton Bullet was faster than Willie K's Mercedes, but he arrived late on the beach when neither the winds nor the tide favored a record attempt.

For manufacturers, racing was dollars and cents. As convinced of its value as Winton or Ford was Billy Durant. High on his agenda in Flint after taking over Buick had been organizing a race team. Louis Chevrolet was soon on the payroll. Chevrolet had emigrated to Montreal at the turn of the century, then headed south to Brooklyn to work as a mechanic for the U.S. branch of the French De Dion company, and then into similar work for Fiat in Manhattan because that company was prominent in motor sport. As a substitute racer in local events, Chevrolet showed a daredevil style ("the most audacious driver in the world," one journalist wrote) that attracted the attention of Carl Fisher. An Indianapolis entrepreneur whose automotive ideas thus far had been that city's Automobile Row and the Prest-O-Lite Company, Fisher latched onto Louis as a worthy adversary for Barney Oldfield in his latest venture: the promotion of match races at county fairs and dirt tracks across the land.

Chevrolet stayed with Fisher until enticed by J. Walter Christie to help him build a race car, Louis having already developed a hankering to design automobiles. Unfortunately, Christie had no skills as an entrepreneur and was unable to convince anyone that front-wheel drive was a good idea for automobiles. "It's no shame to be poor," he once observed, "but it's damn inconvenient." Eternal underfinancing meant Christie's front-drive cars were not properly developed. His Ormond racer performed dismally.

Fortunately for Chevrolet, behaving even worse in 1906 was Victor Hémery, tempestuous driver of the French Darracq. Recognizing the Stanley brothers as his fiercest competition, Hémery had nudged the Darracq ahead of the steam car at the starting line and revved his engine furiously, hoping his exhaust flames would set the Stanley's canvas-and-wood body afire. After disqualifying Hémery, the American Automobile Association shrewdly avoided a ticklish diplomatic situation by turning the Darracq over to French-speaking Chevrolet. Both Louis in the Darracq and Fred Marriott in the Stanley exceeded two miles per minute for the first time in history. Watching were Ransom Olds and Henry Ford, whose own cars performed little better than Walter Christie's. And Billy Durant.

Durant's first recruit for his Buick race team had been Bob Burman, a Michigan farm boy whose racing philosophy was simple: "It either holds together and I win running wide open, or it breaks and I lose." Durant wanted more like him. By now, Louis' younger brothers, Arthur and Gaston, who were as motor mad as he, had arrived from France. Billy invited the trio to Flint and gave them three Buicks for a match race on a horse track near the factory. At its conclusion, Durant hired the most cautious, Arthur, as his personal chauffeur. Winner Louis was incredulous until Billy told him of the other job he had open. Gaston was hired for the new Buick factory team, too.

As race manager, Durant procured the services of William H. Pickens, who had been guiding Barney Oldfield's fortunes and whose character was already regarded as somewhat shady. But Pickens was a mover, which was all important to Durant. The last driver hired specifically by Billy was Lewis Strang, a nephew of Walter Christie's whose competition career had begun as chauffeur and race driver for sugar king H.O. Havemeyer. All remaining drivers and all mechanics were signed on by Pickens. The team was among the largest in the industry.

The Buick team traveled from race to race on the railroad—and in style. Durant leased a baggage car and had it fitted out as a complete machine shop that allowed a quick-response capability not enjoyed by other factories. After a lantern-light look at an underslung Benz that had crashed fortuitously close to the Buick camp, engineer Walter Marr telegraphed what they learned back to Flint, where new components were engineered and loaded onto the boxcar; by the time the train arrived at its next race destination, mechanics had transformed the Buicks from overslung to underslung. Reporters marveled at the Buick ingenuity, the clever sleight of hand, the wizardry—words that gladdened the heart of Billy Durant.

Durant's directive to his team manager had been simple: make Buick look good. A $100,000 annual budget gave Pickens ample wherewithal to do it. The problem initially was finding enough places to take Buick racing.

———

Prior to the Florida speed weeks, most automobile racing in America had been on short dirt tracks built for racing by horses. Ormond-Daytona, while physically ideal between tides, was found limited by manufacturers desirous of a larger demographic audience to show off their wares. Ironically, the solution was provided, not by one of the industry's own, but by one of the industry's critics: "I felt the United States was far behind other nations...and I wanted the country to catch up," Willie K. Vanderbilt said later. "I wanted to bring foreign drivers and their cars over here in the hope that America would wake up." (In another irony, the race that had spurred Europeans to build better race cars was inaugurated by American expatriate James Gordon Bennett, Jr., editor of the Paris edition of his father's *New York Herald*. Only two Cleveland manufacturers—Winton and Peerless—had traveled to Europe thus far to represent the United States in the Gordon Bennett Cup. Given the results, neither should have bothered.)

The races Vanderbilt organized on New York's Long Island were the first international motor sports contest America had ever seen. The Vanderbilt Cup itself was designed by Tiffany. "Chain your dogs and lock up your fowl" was the pre-race admonition in 1904 to Nassau County residents upon whose roads (nearly thirty public miles of them) the race was to be run. Local objection disappeared after the first year's autumn event proved how much money could be made. "Land in Nassau County is expensive," reported *The New York Herald* in 1906, "but it never will sell for what some of it brought in rent yesterday." Ten dollars for a parking place along the circuit was a lot of money. Hot dogs on the Island cost more than the posh "Vanderbilt breakfasts" served at the Waldorf and other grand hotels in Manhattan where spectators gathered pre-race. Hawkers, pitchmen, gamblers, pickpockets, and wily farmers offering a log seat and a warming fire for a price—all were sure of a profitable day. And no wonder. A quarter of a million spectators showed up for a Long Island Vanderbilt, compared to the several thousand who watched the races on Florida's beach.

America's automobile manufacturers reacted variously to the Vanderbilts. Aware that Willie K. was exactly right in declaring the Europeans leagues more sophisticated in race car design and hands-down winner of the horsepower race, Packard regarded mere participation in the international event as sufficient promotion. Its venerable Gray Wolf was entrusted to engineer Charles Schmidt, who was waving to friends at the start and had to be politely reminded that the race had begun. Manufacturer E.R. Thomas, on the other hand, was deadly serious and set up an engineering office in Paris to design the race car that would be built in his Buffalo, New York, factory.

"I learned a lot from them," Edgar Apperson said of the Vanderbilts. In trying to keep up during practice, George Robertson wrapped the Kokomo car around a telephone pole. "I mean he wrapped it!" Apperson emphasized. "Front and rear ends almost touched." From the outset, Locomobile of Bridgeport signaled its intention to become a *bona fide* competitor with an all-American car and finished third in 1905.

While challenging the best of Europe made sense for an upper echelon luxury builder such as Locomobile, mid-range manufacturers assayed a less taxing course. Durant's policy was typical: rather than build a racing Buick, a racer was made out of the production Buick. Class rather than overall victory was the aim. By 1908, the Long Island Vanderbilt success had spawned road races in Lowell, Massachusetts, New York's Westchester County, and Philadelphia's Fairmount Park. The new international Grand Prize in Savannah included a curtain-raiser "light car" race for vehicles just like the Buick. Elsewhere, races within races, even at the Vanderbilt, allowed median-range cars to bask in the glory of their mega-powered brethren while competing in a concurrent event among their peers. The big boys drew the crowds; once at the races, the little fellas were cheered on just as lustily. Soon major road races sprang up in the Midwest as well—in Crown Point, Indiana, and in Elgin, Illinois, where the watch company provided a handsome trophy.

For awhile, American road racing was wonderfully egalitarian. Equal exuberance was exhibited by wealthy amateurs who raced for the sport of it and the professionals whose job depended on performance. Well-born Foxhall Keene didn't stop immediately when his Mercedes caught fire but—one hand on the steering wheel, the other snuffing out sparks in his mustache—drove valiantly on to the pits.

Some pros did their best to stop their opponents from driving on, carrying a broom aboard to stir up dust behind and even throwing an occasional wrench at a pursuer. Never, replied George Robertson when accused of the latter, adding that a bunch of bolts was cheaper than a wrench and worked just as well.

Even more dangerous than the driver's seat was the position of the riding mechanic. His help during a race was invaluable: pressurizing the fuel tank, serving as the driver's eyes to the rear, warning of potholes and other hazards ahead, and seeing to roadside repairs and tire changes. His reward for all this was sometimes a flattering obituary. After sharing a pit-stop beer with mechanic Charles Miller in one Vanderbilt, Louis Chevrolet charged back into the fray, lost the steering on his Buick, and vaulted onto the porch of a farmhouse. Louis hung on, but Miller was thrown to his death, one of two mechanics killed in the race.

Editorial outcry on the dangers of motor sport was generally subdued until a spectator was killed, a tragedy that had been inevitable since the first Vanderbilt. In the exultation surrounding the inaugural race, one reporter declared Willie K. "a bully good democratic fellow who isn't to blame for being a society swell and a millionaire." But his first real experience in democracy appalled Vanderbilt. The masses were unruly. Anxious for better proximity to the action, the crowds edged ever closer to the race cars. Some drivers insisted they had been slapped on the back by spectators as they sped by.

A cousin of Willie K.'s was the driver responsible for the spectator fatality in 1906. Vanderbilt was despondent. By commercial standards, the Vanderbilt Cup was a roaring success, proving beyond argument that automobile racing was a huge crowd pleaser, a most viable new sport. But Vanderbilt had inaugurated his race to spur American manufacturers to action, and thus far, an American car had not won. Now, in the wake of the spectator death, press comments turned ugly.

A racing automobile on a public road, said *The New York Times*, was "as much out of place...as a Gatling gun introduced into a hotel for the purpose of killing cockroaches."

After cheering himself up with a trip to Europe, Vanderbilt decided not to abandon his race but to make a new place for it. With friends like Harry Payne Whitney and August Belmont, he created the Long Island Motor Parkway Corporation. His partners were not being altruistic. In addition to providing Willie K. with a site for his race, these new roads would be operated as a private tollway for those who liked the idea of taking a fast spin on the Island without the local constabulary infringing on their fun.

———

In Buffalo, E.R. Thomas was having no fun at all. A former steamboat captain who, typically, had entered the automobile business by way of the bicycle, Thomas was atypical in being a manufacturer who never bothered to learn how to drive. Still, "Uncle Ed," as he was known in later years, was obsessed that his cars be the best and the best known everywhere. A pleasant success was already his; 1,400 workers in his Niagara Street factory produced nearly 1,000 high-priced Thomas Flyers a year. And in a plant in Detroit, two Olds Motor Works veterans— engineer Howard E. Coffin and super salesman Roy Chapin—were overseeing the manufacture of a lower-priced companion car called the Thomas-Detroit.

But thus far, Thomas had been thwarted in another goal. Hard as he tried, he could not come up with a competitive Vanderbilt Cup car. Some in that situation might have thought smaller. Not Uncle Ed. He decided to take on the world. What better way to become internationally famous than by winning a race around the globe?

Incredibly, such an event was in the offing for 1908: a 20,000-mile run from New York to Paris by way of Siberia. A newspaper stunt that rivaled the search of Stanley for Livingston, its sponsors were *Le Matin* of Paris and *The New York Times*, the latter aegis perhaps surprising for a journal most often described as grey, not yellow. But if the *Times* was, as advertised, a newspaper that would "not soil the breakfast cloth" as did its sensationalist New York brethren, it was also a newspaper that publisher Adolph S. Ochs wanted to sell. Ochs deemed news of a contest that defied the imagination fit to print and a good circulation booster that would promote automobilism and engender international good will at the same time.

The 1908 race from New York to Paris was heaven-sent for E.R. Thomas. Nor was he the only American manufacturer to be interested in racing around the world. The Moon Motor Company was quick to enter from St. Louis, as was White from Cleveland. Ben Briscoe considered the event a great way to promote Maxwell but soon thought better of the idea, as did the dozen other American manufacturers who sent in entries. Everybody but E.R. Thomas. He championed the contest as proving American cars superior to their European rivals, whose motoring experiences were on the "billiard table" roads of the Continent.

The automobile industry of Europe had misgivings, too. "Is such a journey possible?" the *Daily Mail* of London asked rhetorically and answered, "Theoretically it is, but it must be borne in mind that the motor car, after woman, is the most fragile and capricious thing on earth." No British producer volunteered trying to demonstrate otherwise. But from the Continent, Züst of Italy, Protos of Germany, and three French firms (De Dion, Sizaire et Naudin, and Motobloc) signed on.

More than 50,000 people thronged Times Square and upper Broadway to see off the racers on February 12, 1908. A huge banner draped across the Thomas showroom proclaimed "America Against the World." Driving for the United States was Montague Roberts, a twenty-five-year-old who, as a demonstrator for the New York dealership, had delivered a Thomas to the Roosevelt family in Hyde Park and taught young Franklin how to drive. His riding mechanic and relief driver was George Schuster. In pre-race news releases, Roberts had expressed his hope of averaging 30 miles per hour (which was faster than the speed limit in most U.S. states) and his prediction that the Thomas Flyer would reach Chicago in seven days (which a late-season snowstorm increased to two weeks). So impossible were the roads that the Indiana Railway Company patriotically offered a thirty-mile stretch of its track for the Thomas Flyer to drive over, an invitation gratefully accepted. Denied the same permission, the European teams cried foul and took to the railroad ties, too.

Conditions didn't improve significantly west of the Mississippi, but the timber wolves pursuing the Züst across much of Wyoming were said to have hastened the travel of the Italian team. In Pocatello, Idaho, the Germans, fed up with weather-caused delays, sent their Protos on to Seattle on a flatcar. The Thomas Flyer, which by now had a nine-day lead, had been shipped to Valdez, Alaska, to be greeted by fifteen-foot-high snow on the roads—and shipment back to Seattle. Crossing the tundra was beyond sanity.

E.R. Thomas was furious. He demanded disqualification of the Protos for its comfortable ride on the railroad, while his Flyer was being flogged unmercifully in the Pacific Northwest. Because two of the French cars had already given up, the race committee in Paris was reluctant to thin the field further, deciding instead to penalize the German team fifteen days for its transgression and to allow the U.S. team fifteen days for its trip to Alaska.

Vladivostock was the continuing point for the race. The Protos, Züst, and De Dion were shipped there direct. Visa problems with the Russian consulate put the American car on a steamer to Yokohama, where proper documentation was waiting, followed by a drive across Japan to catch another steamer to Vladivostock. Count Albert de Dion, believing the 8,000 miles ahead would be more formidable than the trip thus far, bowed out, commenting that the rules changes and violations had made a mockery of the race. More to the point, the poor performance of the De Dion was poor public relations. The German, Italian, and American teams soldiered on.

Siberia was horrendous. Manchuria defied description. In rural Russia, a telegrapher balked at accepting the Züst driver's wireless because sending messages in code was against the law of the czar. The driver screamed that Italian wasn't code, but the bureaucrat wouldn't budge until a local pharmacist was bribed five rubles to swear to it.

The Protos crew spoke Russian. The Americans did not and got lost more often. The Germans were first to arrive in Paris. The Thomas Flyer motored in four days later, on the evening of July 30, with a bicycle wedged between the front seats. A by-the-book *gendarme*, unimpressed by the Thomas Flyer's mission, insisted that its broken headlamps prohibited the car on the streets of Paris. A passing bicyclist offered his headlight and, when it wouldn't be removed, handed over the two-wheeler and hopped aboard the rear of the Thomas Flyer for its triumphal procession to the offices of *Le Matin*.

Because of the previously imposed penalty/allowances, the American car was overwhelmingly "winner" of the race by twenty-six days. The Protos basked in the immediate glory of being first at the finish line. New York's famous Luchow's Restaurant on 14th Street saw this as a win-win situation: "The race could hardly have been more successful from the German-American point of view," said the manager. "The German car has got in first, and the American car wins on time allowance."

Fearful that the public might not appreciate the distinction, E.R. Thomas grabbed the offensive, boasting that so unscathed in Paris was the Thomas Flyer, it could be turned around and retrace its way back to New York. Wiser heads prevailed.

Probably unwise was Thomas' shotgun approach to further competition that same year. Buoyed by the ongoing world-stage performance from February through early summer, the factory was emboldened to enter the French Grand Prix, successor to the Gordon Bennett Cup. The result was as unfortunate as poor Walter Christie's attempt in the same race the previous year. In U.S. races as well, the Thomas Flyer star did not shine brightly in 1908. But the New-York-to-Paris victory was so epochal that also-ran finishes elsewhere didn't matter. Better press was garnered when the 'round-the-world car was used ceremonially, as a pathfinder, for example, to the New-York-to-Seattle race of 1909 that was won, then lost, by the Model T Ford.

Not surprisingly, Billy Durant, now in the midst of buying up companies for General Motors, cast a covetous eye toward Buffalo, but an ebullient E.R. Thomas wasn't interested enough to even discuss it. The Thomas Flyer feat had received better press than either the formation of General Motors or the introduction of the Model T Ford. Euphoria put blinders on Thomas' good business sense. Taking advantage of the New-York-to-Paris victory remained effective marketing so long as the Thomas Flyers in the showroom remained worthy. But the new Model L was a dud, in the words of Montague Roberts (with the agreement of George Schuster), "noisy, underpowered and literally leaked oil." Sales plummeted, and by 1912, the E.R. Thomas Motor Company was gone.

Poignantly, when the firm went under, nearly 6,000 of the 7,000 Thomas cars built were still on the road, an achievement almost as worthy as the epic New-York-to-Paris race.

———

The Vanderbilt Cup was back in the fall of 1908. The Long Island Motor Parkway beckoned, a nine-mile stretch of concrete so velvet smooth that people drove out just to see it. Once they knew where it was. Deliberately sited in the rural center of the Island, the new Parkway seemed as remote as Siberia, especially to those trying to find it in the dead of night. Save for Willie K.'s perennial boxes for the likes of the Duchess of Marlborough among other titled guests, grandstand seats were first-come/first-served, so arriving well before the early morning start was the plan of many. In the inky darkness, guided only by the flickering headlamps of their touring cars, race-goers trudged over plowed meadows toward light, sometimes finding themselves at the campsite of another race-going group or face to face with another touring car whose occupants were just as lost as they were.

Rather than the grandstand, others preferred an advantageous spot along the Parkway or the fourteen miles of public highway that completed the circuit. A good many spectators still opted for the middle of the road; only when hoses were turned on them was the way cleared for the race cars to get to the starting line. Willie K. had hired Pinkerton men to assist Nassau County deputies in crowd control, but once at their appointed posts, most of them paid more attention to cheering on their favorites and keeping their scorecards straight.

This was perhaps the most wildly cheered Vanderbilt of all, for by the halfway point, it was obvious that a native car had a real chance. Fresh from victory in Philadelphia's Fairmount Park, George Robertson was driving masterfully. While leading by 2 minutes 22 seconds on the last lap, however, his Locomobile shattered a tire, news that was megaphoned to loud moans from the grandstand. In just over two minutes, Robertson and his mechanic had the tire changed and were back on the road. Again, the grandstand was informed. "I'd give five hundred dollars to see that American car win," Henry Ford shouted.

There is no record that Henry paid up and, if so, to whom. But driving like a demon, unaware of how much time he had to make up because of the staggered start, Robertson vaulted to the checkered flag—winner by more than a minute and a half, a photo finish in those days. The Locomobile's 64.3-miles-per-hour average was a Vanderbilt Cup record.

Unlike E.R. Thomas, Samuel T. Davis knew how to handle success. Having skillfully moved Locomobile from steamer to the gasoline car field, Davis made sure chief engineer Andrew Riker translated the Vanderbilt Cup experience into an improved production car.

———

America triumphed in the 1909 and 1910 Long Island Vanderbilts, too. But all else was different. By now, the success of Willie K.'s cup race had not only spawned look-alikes, it had changed the character of the sport. Acutely aware of the benefits to accrue from racing, manufacturers began calling the shots. The long-smoldering feud between the socially prominent Automobile Club of America and the democratic American Automobile Association was resolved in a truce that saw the Vanderbilt transformed from an international event for special-built race cars to a stock chassis contest restricted to production models of no more than 600-cubic-inch engine displacement. Previous cup races specified only a maximum overall weight, which had seen ever bigger engines stuffed into chassis that were drilled with enough holes so the scales wouldn't tip during weighing in. Structural integrity was sacrificed, of course, and resulted in a Simplex that was literally driven into the ground by Frank Croker (son of the Tammany Hall boss) in 1904. No racer would buckle under in 1909.

Attendance that year was paltry: 20,000 spectators, 10 percent of the gate of the previous year. This was less the result of change in the character of the contest than its being moved to the seemingly more amenable hour of 9:00 a.m. Apparently, the Vanderbilt crowd preferred leaving at midnight to see a race with a daybreak start, to rising at daybreak for a race that began mid-morning. The latter smacked of getting up and going to work. The 1910 Vanderbilt was moved back to dawn, and the crowd mushroomed to 300,000.

Winning both years was the same car and driver: Harry Fortune Grant on an American Locomotive Company Alco. Declaring in 1909 that "milk is my toddy" and that approximately 63 miles per hour would win the race (his winning speed was 62.81), Grant was a breed apart from the hard-drinking hellion that Barney Oldfield had made the public stereotype of the professional driver. Indeed, Alco was criticized "for not securing a more sensational pilot for its cars" after the 1909 Vanderbilt. No one suggested the same when Grant won again in 1910 at 65.18 miles per hour, the fastest Vanderbilt ever.

American Locomotive handled its Vanderbilt success with Locomobile-like assurance. The Providence, Rhode Island, company seemed to have done everything right thus far, entering the industry in 1905 by manufacturing the famed French Berliet under license until the firm's own engineers were sure they could do as well or better. A high-priced luxury car, the Alco was among the most respected makes in America and, with American Locomotive gross earnings in the $30+ million range annually, its future seemed secure. The Alco demise in 1913 was a shock, until it was revealed that in five years, American Locomotive had produced 5,000 cars in fifty-four models—and lost an average of $460 on each one of them. Upon discovering that making an automobile profitably was a different proposition from making locomotives, the company announced its intention "to sever as completely and as soon as possible all connections with the automobile branch of the business."

Less rude was Willie K.'s awakening that he was no longer a power in motor sport. From 1904, when, as one journalist noted, "Mr. Vanderbilt takes snuff [and] the racing board sneezes," racing now belonged to the people who built the cars. The millionaire was sanguine. Appalled in 1910 that souvenir hunters had divested Louis Chevrolet's mechanic of his coveralls before the ambulance arrived and that twenty-two people were hospitalized after being struck by racers or trampled in the mob, Willie K. gave up democracy and the automobile except "to get there and back"—and went off to sail his yacht. The Vanderbilt Cup moved off Long Island, first to the site of the Grand Prize in Savannah, then Milwaukee, and ultimately to the West Coast, where it would die in 1916.

For every event that ended, another began. Mt. Washington's "Climb to the Clouds" in New Hampshire had spawned competition ascents wherever there was a steep grade and an enthusiastic local automobile club—and culminated in Pikes Peak. And, for a rollicking while, there was a concerted return to the short dirt tracks for events variously referred to as "twice-around-the-clocks," "mad marathons," and "grinds."

Packard had launched the basic concept at the Grosse Point track in 1904 when a corps of workers from the factory shops joined chief engineer Charles Schmidt to try out the new Model L. A "non-engine-stop" run of 1,000 miles was the goal; company president Henry Joy was behind the wheel for the first five miles. This first attempt ended during the moonless night when the Packard's driver, his own lights faltering, was momentarily blinded by the headlamps of cars parked at trackside and crashed through the fence. Some weeks later, with a full moon, the run was successfully completed and touted by Packard as a performance that "stands without parallel in any branch of engineering history." Hyperbole notwithstanding, the record did not stand for long.

Peerless of Cleveland did a continuous 1,000 miles next in just under twenty-six hours, lowering Packard's mark by four. Next, the full-day barrier was breached, and, with a certain inevitability, someone figured out that twenty-four-hour races among a whole bunch of cars might be a profitable venture. He was Buick team manager Bill Pickens, who was having problems coming up with enough events to enter to suit Billy Durant and was confident other manufacturers would agree that winning a race of twenty-four hours better demonstrated a car's durability than the less-than-four-hour comparative sprint of a Vanderbilt. The U.S. Motor Racing Association (U.S.M.R.A.) was organized for the purpose.

Given the duration of the contest and the shortness of the track, Pickens anticipated shunts aplenty and astutely positioned repair stations directly across from the main grandstand. Each team would have its own tent for supplies and driver/mechanic relaxation during off-hours. Three dozen or so arc lights were positioned around the track so spectators might have a better look at the whole show. In the clubhouse, they were assured non-stop conviviality because the bar, unlike most entries, would function for the full twenty-four hours.

Point Breeze (Philadelphia), Harlem (Chicago), Brighton Beach (Brooklyn), Morris Park (Bronx), Empire City (Yonkers), Ascot Park (Los Angeles), and the horse tracks in Detroit and Milwaukee saw most of the twenty-four-hour grinds from 1907 to 1910. Attendance ranged from 10,000 to 20,000, depending on venue. Spectators generally had a good time, which to Pickens was paramount. Showmanship was all.

Overlooked were several factors that impacted less happily on the manufacturers. Driving at the limit for a full day put a severe strain on the cars, and, although desperate efforts to repair parts and get the machine rolling again made for great theater, it was good promotion only if the car made it to the finish—and finished respectably.

Strain was no less severe for the race course itself, the track literally disintegrating as the hours of relentless pounding wore on. With inclement weather, it was even worse. Commented driver Ralph Mulford of the 1907 Point Breeze, which saw steady rain for thirteen hours, "We drove our three-hour shifts with chains on all four wheels, and what with the rain and the cars throwing up mud it was impossible to drive with goggles on and pretty painful to drive without them. So most of the race we drove with one hand and peeked between the fingers of the other." Corners on a few tracks were paved, which helped some in foul-weather races. Even so, a grind remained brutal on tires; a two-car team could use well over a hundred of them in a single event.

Then there was the human factor. Scoring in these events was haphazard after dark because the dirt thrown up on the track and the inadequate lighting combined to make visual identification of the cars impossible; therefore, they were timed instead by the sounds of their individual exhausts. Many scorers spent their off-hours in the clubhouse, which further impaired acuity.

Of all the cars contesting the grinds, the most successful was the Lozier produced by the Lake Placid (New York) family of the same name. Ralph Mulford was the Lozier star. Thomas Flyer star Montague Roberts added an element of suspense to the 1907 Brighton Beach grind by announcing beforehand that he would attempt to drive the entire event himself. When the Jackson from Michigan broke a timing gear after leading the race for nineteen hours, Roberts romped home the victor. In 1908, E.R. Thomas entered the Flyer that had just won the New York to Paris at Brighton Beach but then withdrew when he found out the U.S.M.R.A. had neglected the formality of applying for A.A.A. sanction. Because the Brooklyn track had already been leased, the tickets printed, and broadsides plastered everywhere, Pickens decided to go ahead with the race. Hoping to lend an aura of legitimacy to it, he announced that President Roosevelt would start the race and hired a Teddy look-alike.

Hewing to the legal was not high on the priority list of a grind. In Detroit in 1907, a decision was hastily made to allow not only the usual change of drivers during the race but, if necessary, a change of car as well, so long as it was an identical model. This last-minute rule revision obviously favored those who could take advantage of it. When the record-setting pace of the victorious Ford was advertised without mention that the feat had needed two cars to accomplish it, there were protests far and wide.

The grinds were equally fierce for both race car and race driver. For small entries, as many as five relief drivers were required for a single race. Even drivers of large cars had to bandage hands, arms, and torsos to help absorb road shock during the final stages of a grind. Those with high pain thresholds—such as Bob Burman and Louis Chevrolet—often broke their cars. The Buick team was notorious for trying to win a grind from the starting flag. Records fell virtually every lap in the early hours, but a Buick seldom survived the full day of racing. That was probably the reason Billy Durant enlisted his personal chauffeur, Arthur Chevrolet, for several events.

A variety of factors killed the grinds, some of them already obvious. Further, spectators became bored once the novelty of a twenty-four-hour race wore off. For sheer thrills, the sands of Ormond-Daytona beckoned again. Nowhere better could the ultimate speed be attempted than along that long, smooth Florida beach.

———

Being the fastest man on earth had been an irresistible challenge for Willie K. Vanderbilt, who wanted to prove himself, and for Henry Ford, who wanted to prove his car. Their speed marks were made during the first month of 1904; the record was broken four more times that year. As time went on, however, the ultimate speed was attempted less often. Building a single car capable of the job was enormously expensive; fielding a factory race team used the same money to better promotional effect.

The Stanley's better than 2-miles-per-minute mark of 1906 went unchallenged until 1909, when Benz of Germany built a hairy bolide named the Blitzen; at the steeply banked Brooklands track in England, Victor Hémery broke the Stanley's kilometer record but couldn't manage the mile. The Blitzen was sent back to Mannheim for further streamlining and then to Florida, but Hémery wasn't sent with it—to the relief of the A.A.A.

Barney Oldfield and the Blitzen Benz were made for each other. Breaking records was Barney's game, and he played it well. Carl Fisher had taught him, prior to moving on to other ventures, and Bill Pickens had honed the technique before doing likewise. Oldfield's manager now was Ernie Moross. At every fairground he worked, Barney won races (some officially sanctioned, others match races with stooges hired to finish second) and broke the local track records (invariably saving that feat as a finale). But he had never been the fastest man on earth.

Oldfield put on a spectacular show with the Blitzen on the beach. "Me and the Benz here, we're gonna warm up the sand a little," he shouted in February 1910 as he stuck cotton in his ears and a cigar in his mouth. A straightaway mile later, the Benz was clocked at 131.724 miles per hour—"as near to the absolute limit of speed as humanity will ever travel," declared Barney. Kaiser Wilhelm wired congratulations, and Moross began accepting invitations from fairgrounds all across the country for Barney and the Blitzen to come visit that summer.

Another invitation got Oldfield into big trouble. Whenever upbraided for flimflam or other dubious practices, Bill Pickens would respond that he was in the business of entertainment, pure and simple. The entertaining idea he engineered for his former client (for whom he still moonlighted on occasion) was a match race at Brooklyn's Sheepshead Bay with heavyweight champion Jack Johnson. It was a fiasco and, because the boxer was not an accredited race driver, illegal, too. "So who needs the stinking A.A.A.," Barney snorted when told about his suspension. He barnstormed the Blitzen in Mexico awhile, and then decided to retire from racing and open a saloon in Los Angeles.

Startup money for the bar was provided by Ernie Moross, who bought out Barney's investment in all of his competition cars, including the Blitzen, and latched onto Buick's "Wild Bob" Burman to drive it. A teetotaling non-smoking Baptist, Burman was the antithesis of Oldfield off the race track but the fearless equal of Barney with foot on accelerator. Burman's beach speed record with the Blitzen in April 1911 was 141.732 miles per hour, an embarrassing 10 miles per hour faster than Oldfield, who, at his manager's insistence, had not driven at ten-tenths to leave room for the profitable promotion of another record run. Barney was so mad at Moross that he un-retired to seek vengeance.

The Burman land speed record would stand for eight years, however, because no one in the industry cared to expend the development money necessary to come up with a faster machine, not even for Oldfield. But one auto builder was willing to sell his race car: Walter Christie, who needed the money. "Barney Oldfield is back again! More daring, more chance-taking than ever!" Bill Pickens wrote to county fair secretaries across the nation. "...Select the day you usually have the poorest attendance—and let Barney Oldfield turn it into the BIG day at your fair. Don't wait to write—WIRE the moment you get this circular." Barney was back in show biz.

For all his bombast and braggadocio, Oldfield was a consummate race driver. Only Ralph De Palma—who combined the controlled ferocity of the seasoned professional with the class and civility of the gentleman driver—exceeded him in talent. Both lived well past their retirement from motor sport. Many more race drivers of that era died in their cars and often took others with them. American La France of Elmira (New York) initially thought campaigning a race car would be a fine way to call national attention to its impending conversion from horse-drawn to motorized apparatus—but canceled those plans after eleven spectators were killed in a race at the fairgrounds in nearby Syracuse. After the spectator accidents attending the last Long Island Vanderbilt, the governor of New York banned racing on the roads of the state.

There had to be a better way.

———

The Indianapolis Motor Speedway was the first track in America built specifically for automobile racing. It was Carl Fisher's best idea to date. To help him realize it, he latched onto a group of fellow Indianapolis businessmen, including Arthur Newby, president of the National Motor Vehicle Company; Frank H. Wheeler of Wheeler-Schebler Carburetor; and James Allison, at the moment manufacturing fountain pens but soon to be in the aircraft engine business. Each of them was a race enthusiast and easy to convince. Fisher was also able to persuade Newby and Allison to join him in organizing the Empire Motor Car Company for production of a saucy low-priced runabout that was advertised as "The Little Aristocrat." But this new make in the marketplace was quickly ignored as problems mounted with the new Speedway.

Because of construction delays, the inaugural had to be moved ahead six weeks, to mid-August of 1909 from the original planned Fourth of July weekend. Many came just to see the track that was being touted as the latest eighth wonder of the world: a gently rounded and gently banked dirt oval a full two and one-half miles long. It was impressive. Quickly, it was also proven quite dangerous. Junior team members handled the Buick cars in the five-mile curtain raiser; the Buick stars— Chevrolet, Strang, and Burman—were in the eight-car field for the ten-miler and finished smartly in that order. Feature race of the day was the 250-mile Prest-O-Lite Trophy, which began splendidly for Buick, with Chevrolet charging into the lead and relinquishing it only twice (to teammate Burman) in the first 130 miles. But then Chevrolet pulled into the pit area. Blinded by the dust, he had to be led away from the track. His Buick was withdrawn. Worse, the dust had killed a Knox driver and his mechanic who failed to see where the track curved. Burman won the race. Fisher and friends tried to dampen news of the tragedy.

Day Two saw further Buick triumphs. Day Three saw three more deaths—and the racing was stopped. The disintegrated track resembled a Civil War battlefield, with spectators and mechanics lying injured, waiting for first aid. Rumors spread that the A.A.A. would sanction no further events at the Speedway. Before this could happen, Fisher and company got together with the National Paving Brick Manufacturers' Association. Sixty-three days, $155,000, and 3.2 million bricks later, the Indianapolis Motor Speedway was reborn.

The second inaugural of the track was a three-day carnival of events on Memorial Day weekend of 1911. Preoccupied with keeping the banker wolves from General Motors' door, Billy Durant wasn't on hand as he had been the previous August. Sixty thousand other people were. They saw some spirited racing by a small Buick team. Strang had gone on to another factory; Durant had fired Pickens for a breach of sporting etiquette, the nature of which history has not recorded. Louis Chevrolet was Buick team manager; his brother Arthur was the team.

Independence Day weekend brought another three-day meet. Both Louis Chevrolet and Bob Burman raced well for Buick, but Durant, in deeper trouble, wasn't on hand again. Fisher and company had a problem with their Speedway, too; the crowd was half that of Memorial Day. By the Labor Day meet, attendance was down again.

Concluding that "too much racing" was being offered, Carl Fisher and company decided the Speedway should see year-round use only as a test track leased to manufacturers and a single annual race to be held on Memorial Day. They pondered the sort of race it should be. A 24-hour grind was discussed, as was a 1,000-miler. Finally, 500 miles seemed the ideal solution.

CHAPTER 26

Cheap, Reliable, Saleable

MEMORIAL DAY 1911 dawned cool and bright, with just enough cloud cover so the brick surface would not become oppressively hot to tire or touch. Forty racers faced the starting flag for the first Indianapolis 500. Carl Fisher drove the pace car, a Stoddard-Dayton.

Except for the gentlemen drivers with their European racers, and two Benzes entered by Ernie Moross, the inaugural Indy 500 was an all-American show. Fisher had worked tirelessly to bring manufacturers to the Speedway. The East Coast was represented by Knox, the turn-of-the-century producer from Massachusetts; Simplex, the sporting car from New York City; and a brand-new marketplace entry, Mercer of Trenton (New Jersey), backed by the Roebling and Kuser families, whose previous endeavors had included the Brooklyn Bridge.

The Indy 500 provided a curtain call for such automotive celebrities as the Pope-Hartford (longest-lived of the cars in the Colonel's empire) and the Alco (just before the locomotive company accountants began totting up the figures of their automotive department). And it provided a Midwest showcase for Lozier, recently relocated from Upstate New York to Detroit to battle Packard in the luxury car field.

Midwest entries were numerous. In Moline (Illinois), Will Velie saw the Indy 500 as a way to broaden national awareness of the automobile then being sold through John Deere Plow Company dealerships. (Velie's mother was the former Emma Deere.) And in Racine (Wisconsin), the J.I. Case Threshing Machine Company enthusiastically sent a team of three of its brand-new cars.

Little persuasion had been needed to entice entries from Joseph J. Cole and Howard Marmon, whose Indianapolis factories were within spitting distance of the Speedway. Asking for an entry from the National Motor Vehicle Company wasn't necessary at all because president Arthur Newby was Fisher's partner in both the race track and the Empire Motor Car Company. Earlier in the year, Harry C. Stutz had been hired to change the Empire runabout from chain to the more progressive shaft drive to make the company more attractive to sell, which the partners would do by year's end. The Empire assignment gave Stutz, an auto parts maker, the ready cash he needed to build a car in only five weeks' time to introduce to the nation in the Indy 500.

The 1911 Indianapolis 500 was won by a Marmon nicknamed the Wasp because of its bright yellow color and long stinger tail. Its rear-view mirror was driver Ray Harroun's innovation and was necessary because the slim single-seater wouldn't accommodate a riding mechanic. In 1912, victory went to a National in the two-seater configuration that would remain standard at Indy until after World War I. That the first two Indy 500s were won by Indianapolis-built cars was not entirely happenstance. The Speedway's easy accessibility to local manufacturers meant those teams were the most familiar with the track. They also enjoyed the encouragement of about 90,000 or so largely partisan fans.

After two years, the character of the Indy 500 changed. The victory of a Peugeot driven by Jules Goux, who filled up with both gasoline and champagne at pit stops, began a five-year European takeover of the American event. In part, this was because Carl Fisher, with the Speedway a success, turned his powers of persuasion and spirited press agentry into stimulating interest in a south Florida jungle that he was carving into a winter playground called Miami Beach. Without the Fisher cajolery, most manufacturers had second thoughts.

The Appersons decided to stay home after a single appearance. Their car came to grief in the pits during a tire change when a runaway

Westcott smacked it in the rear. Ed Apperson's yell alerted the driver to jump out, but the mechanic, in the front cranking, sailed over the retaining wall with the car, somersaulted, and landed, miraculously, upright in the driver's seat. "Word spread through the stands that all three of us had been killed," Ed Apperson said. "My wife Inez heard it and believed it...We quit racing right there."

Continuing on was Harry Stutz, whose in-the-money finish in 1911 produced the slogan "The Car That Made Good in a Day." He named his new model a Bearcat. For a few years, Maxwell entered a team of cars designed by the first Indy 500 winner, Ray Harroun. But these were the exceptions. Some industry stalwarts had ignored the Indy 500 altogether. Alexander Winton's ardor for competition had cooled by now. Henry Ford remained interested but was preoccupied with trying to make enough Model Ts to meet the demand. A perfunctory entry of two Buicks showed up for the first Indy 500 and, driven by lesser talents, didn't finish. Buick stars Bob Burman and Lewis Strang had switched allegiance to Benz and Case, respectively. Louis Chevrolet was preoccupied designing a car for Billy Durant.

———

Interestingly, it was on the day of the first Indianapolis 500 that the industry was made aware of the collaboration. A Detroit paper leaked the news of a "Durant-Chevrolet car" to be produced in a new Detroit factory.

Unlike Henry Ford, who had used partner Malcomson's intention of Aerocar manufacture to maneuver him out of the Ford company, the General Motors board gave Durant's new venture little notice. Perhaps the association with Chevrolet was seen as a welcome diversion that would keep Billy out of its hair. Margery Durant Campbell said her father "enjoyed the amusement the bankers got out of...his insignificant property...his hobby [that] had to be satisfied." Billy had been appalled that one of the new regime's first acts was elimination of the Buick Model 10, which left GM without an under-$1,000 competitor to Ford's Model T. He planned to produce that competitor himself as a Chevrolet. But Louis wasn't cooperating.

By the end of 1911, Durant had incorporated three companies: Chevrolet, Mason, and Little. The latter two were named for Arthur C. Mason, a Buick engineer whose new job was to make motors for Durant, and William H. Little, the big bear of a man who had been Buick's general manager and would now manufacture a small stopgap car while Louis was laboring to come up with a world-beater Chevrolet. Both Mason and Little shared quarters in the Flint Wagon Works, which Billy purchased from James Whiting, the pre-Durant financial backer of Buick who wanted to retire.

Before Little could set up shop in Flint, however, Durant dispatched him to Detroit to hurry Chevrolet along. Louis was dawdling, according to Durant. To see to the manufacture of the Little car, Billy looked up A.B.C. Hardy, who arrived to find that Arthur Mason had already commandeered the best part of the plant, consigning Little to a hovel littered with such horse-drawn age paraphernalia as wooden wagons and whip sockets. Sell the stuff, Billy commanded. He was heading east and could use a little extra cash.

With a smile and a small down payment, Durant bought an entire New York City block—56th to 57th streets on Eleventh Avenue in Manhattan. *Motor World* described it as "one of those immense projects which seem essential to Durant's happiness." This was the first of ten assembly plants that Durant planned for Chevrolet. "Grown-up people are very much like children in many respects," Billy said. "They like to see the wheels go 'round." Dotting plants around the country meant no customer would have to travel far to see his own car being built, and opening these places for public guided tours would be effective advertising. Most important, Durant believed the industry bugbear was less production than distribution, which would be neatly solved with a nationwide assembly system.

But so far, the only product Durant could assemble was the Little. This did not bode well. Durant had set aside one Little for staff use in an informal road test. The car, in Durant's words, was "driven to its death in less than 25,000 miles." Several years or more might be required for the average motorist to put that kind of mileage on his car, but durability was obviously not the Little's long suit.

"From the standpoint of appearance, not satisfactory," Durant said of Chevrolet's first efforts, "...from the standpoint of cost, impossible." To help him design the new car, Louis had latched onto Etienne Planche, like himself an *émigré* from France. Planche had plenteous experience. One of his U.S. cars—designed for William Walter's American

Chocolate Machinery Company in New York City—had metamorphosed into the Roebling-Planche, predecessor to the sporting and highly respected Mercer. Louis was thinking performance, but a Mercer was not what Durant had in mind. When Chevrolet told Billy with delight that the pre-dawn road test of his completed prototype had resulted in his being nabbed for speeding and impersonating a race driver, Billy was not amused. The light car "of the French type" that he had asked Chevrolet to design was *de trop*—but at last, Louis had come up with something to build. And so the car was ordered into production.

Chevrolet made himself available to test-drive reporters around Detroit and, when critical reviews of his car were uniformly congratulatory, considered his job done and rewarded himself with an extended vacation in France. Louis' absence provided all concerned a chance to assess the situation. The Little was making a profit but would no longer, once cars on the road reached their life expectancy. The Chevrolet, which could be driven in perpetuity, was not profitable. To Durant, the answer was obvious: make one car out of the best features of both.

A.B.C. Hardy agreed, noting that the Chevrolet name, in addition to being famous in motor sport, did not carry an in-built pejorative. Salesmen were already complaining that people didn't like being reminded in capital letters that they were driving a little car, even when they were. Hardy also recommended moving Chevrolet from Detroit to Flint, where he had finally made a fine factory of the old wagon works. Durant was regarded as a demi-god in Flint, another good reason to relocate there.

So the Little was buried without so much as a eulogy. Ending about the same time, after more than a quarter century, was the association of Billy Durant and Dallas Dort. Neither ever said why, but most probably, Dallas had wearied of dwelling forever in his flamboyant partner's shadow. He hired Etienne Planche to design a car that he would market as a Dort.

Thus did Louis Chevrolet return from his holiday in France to find everything changed—and none of it to his liking. He didn't relish his car being put on a level with the Model T Ford. He didn't care for the move to Flint. And, most of all, he detested Durant's incessant attempts to make him into a proper business executive. Finally, when Billy told him to give up cigarettes for cigars, Louis hit the ceiling. "I sold you my car and I sold you my name," he screamed, "but I'm not going to sell myself to you." According to Catherine Durant, her husband did not object so much to what Louis smoked as to how he did it, the "cigarette hanging on his lower lip...it used to annoy Willie to tears." Chevrolet huffed and puffed and departed, never to return.

Louis' leave-taking didn't bother Billy much. Of more concern was his factory in New York City, which was proving to be a mixed blessing. Its convenient location to Wall Street provided Durant an easily accessible visual aid should he wish to scout for fresh capital (although sincerely hoping he could emulate Ford in staying away from bankers, Billy also wanted to keep all options open). But the neighborhood was awful, and vandalism was a real problem.

Ben Briscoe came to the rescue, inadvertently. Durant learned there was a "for sale" sign outside his old friend's Maxwell-Briscoe factory just north of the city in Tarrytown.

——

"One of the worst failures in the history of the automobile industry" was *The Horseless Age*'s verdict on the receivership of the United States Motor Company in September 1912. Given the salvation from near disaster of General Motors, the business community was surprised. But Brady and Morgan, who had backed Briscoe, weren't able to agree on a rescue. And there had been other ominous signs.

Unlike GM, which had several strong lines, U.S. Motor was saddled with mostly losers. The Brush Runabout became irrelevant with the introduction of the Model T. The Selden patent verdict put the kibosh on the only bankable asset of Columbia. Alden Sampson lost money on each truck it built. Fourteen thousand U.S. Motor employees were producing fifty-two different models in eighteen factories. Ben Briscoe struggled valiantly to keep his empire together, but simply keeping tabs on it was difficult enough. Its crazy-quilt pattern geographically— companies in New York, Michigan, Connecticut, Rhode Island, Ohio, and Massachusetts—was a matter he planned to address, but only after he saw to the acquisition of the one product he lacked: a high-priced car. He bought Thomas of Buffalo—barely a month before the firm made famous by the New-York-to-Paris race went into receivership.

Briscoe quickly followed. As his colleague Alfred Reeves put it, "Ben just plain ran out of money."

Having his Stoddard-Dayton selected as the pace car for the first Indianapolis 500 was about the only salutary news Briscoe could savor in more than a year.

Sensing the impending doom, U.S. Motor executives began an early exodus. One of the last to go, a month before receivership, was Frank Briscoe, who resigned his vice presidency to "study automobile engineering abroad." A month into receivership, his brother joined him. "I am going away for a rest and one of the main objects will be to regain the correct perspective of things," Ben told the press. "I believe that some other man, unhampered by any of the old influences and traditions of the company can carry it through successfully. I have been asked to remain but I feel that it would be better for me to go."

That Briscoe had been asked to stay on is unlikely. He hadn't the heart to dismantle what he had worked so hard to put together, in any case. His successor, Walter E. Flanders, would have no such compunction. U.S. Motor creditors—led by chief bondholder, Eugene Meyer, Jr.—had known little of Flanders personally because he had been calling Michigan home since early in his career. But his resumé looked good. It was widely acknowledged that Flanders had put Henry Ford on the road to orderly and profitable production. The bankers assumed he was available because Flanders, having fallen victim to the ego gremlin, had unwisely put his name on a bad car and was himself plunged into receivership.

The bankers were right about his availability. But Flanders put a steep price on his services: $1 million in cash, the sale of his own beleaguered company to U.S. Motor, and $2.75 million in stock in the new company he would create. A quick look around convinced Flanders the only thing of value left in U.S. Motor was Maxwell. So he scrapped everything else. Jonathan Maxwell, who had been leery of Ben Briscoe's buying spree optimism, was just as disturbed by Flanders' pessimistic demolition derby. So he drifted away and got into the auto parts business. The Tarrytown plant of the former Maxwell-Briscoe company was put up for sale as Flanders moved the new Maxwell Motor Company to Detroit, a comfortable distance from meddling by the New York bankers. Actually, the bankers didn't care what Flanders did, so long as regular dividends were issued to recoup their losses.

Ben Briscoe did not witness the dismemberment of his empire. After taking a few French lessons, he joined brother Frank in Billancourt on the Seine, where they started a new company called Briscoe Frères and proceeded to be very coy about what they would do next. Trade publications on both sides of the Atlantic wondered whether a French car made of American parts for the European market was planned, or an American car made of French parts for the European market. Finally, Ben revealed he would be making both—with a simultaneous introduction on both continents.

The onset of World War I in Europe ruined these grand plans. Briscoe Frères was forced, as one U.S. journalist put it, to "come back to God's country" and relocate its "international" headquarters on 42nd Street, just off Fifth Avenue in New York City. The inconvenience of European politics meant that, for the moment, Ben had only one product to offer, the car that in France had been called the Ajax. In America, Ajaxes were as numerous in the automobile industry as Smiths were in the telephone book, so Ben grabbed a dictionary to find another mythological reference and didn't proceed far before happening upon one he liked. Ergo the Argo. It was a cyclecar.

———

Like the highwheeler, the cyclecar was an answer to motoring for the millions. Unlike the highwheeler, which was generically American, the cyclecar was spawned in Europe. Henri Bourbeau's Bédèlia is credited as the progenitor. Being present at the creation, Ben Briscoe thought, would give him a leg up in marketing the genre in America. Not so. His Ajax-*cum*-Argo was one of more than 200 different cyclecars offered for sale in the United States. American entrepreneurs had been quick to recognize an opportunity.

The cyclecar defined itself as an automobile developed with the simplicity of a bicycle in mind. Further parameters varied. In Europe, the rule of thumb was that any vehicle, the front end of which could be lifted from the ground by a man of average strength, was a cyclecar. In the United States, the American Cyclecar Manufacturers' Association decided on four wheels and an engine no bigger than 71 cubic inches as the criteria.

Innovative engineering, while not precluded, was seldom among the chief virtues of a cyclecar. Economy was paramount: the vehicle was priced from $300 to $400 and was generally good for 45 or 50 miles per gallon. (Comparable figures of the full-size Model T in 1913 were $550 and 20 miles per gallon.) "Built like a watch" was the slogan for the Woods Mobilette of Harvey, Illinois, "...ownership will not cause tuberculosis of one's wallet." "One didn't even need a garage. A cyclecar could be driven through the garden gate and stored under or beside one's porch—or even on it, with a little help from a friend.

Engines were generally air-cooled vee twins provided by a variety of proprietary manufacturers who had previously supplied the motorcycle industry. Most makers put the engines up front, but the Real's was rear-mounted, and the driver of a Cricket had his right alongside. Shaft or chain drives were rare; most cyclecars transmitted power through leather belts. The DoDo was front-wheel drive. Brake systems ranged from nothing more than hardwood blocks pressing against the wheels to the internal expanding rear drum brakes of the Scripps-Booth.

Less diversity was possible in seating arrangements because the cyclecar held no more than two. They might sit side-by-side, as in full-size cars, or staggered, as in racing practice. Makers choosing one of those two arrangements invariably mentioned the "sociable" advantage that the third option, tandem seating, lacked. But only with the latter could the ideal of a 36-inch tread be easily achieved. A cyclecar more than a yard wide ran the danger of one or both of its narrow tires falling haplessly into the ruts of standard 56-inch tread cars. Tandem seating provided makers one further option: where to put the steering wheel. Most chose the front, although a few, citing better balance of the engine, elected for a rear-seat driver.

Cyclecar names ran a wide gamut from the self-explanatory (the Economycar from Providence, Rhode Island) to the vainglorious (the Ritz from New York City). The Cycleplane suggested it was a somewhat faster machine than the usual. Mythology was plumbed for variations to join Ben Briscoe's Argo. But, more aptly, a diminutive was chosen—and sometimes delectably, as in the Sprite (Aurora, Illinois), the Gadabout (Newark, New Jersey), the Daisy (Los Angeles), and the Baby Moose (St. Paul). Imp was the name selected by the W.H. McIntyre Company of Auburn, Indiana, erstwhile makers of a highwheeler. The Peter Pan arrived from Quincy, Massachusetts.

As quickly as the cyclecar arrived in America, it departed. The genre survived longer in Europe, where vehicles were taxed on size and minimalist motoring had cachet, in addition to real effectiveness, the Bédèlia serving as a motorized stretcher during World War I. But in the United States, the cyclecar carried the seeds of its own destruction. Such small and whippy machines were not equal to road conditions, and many literally fell apart over the course of one season's motoring. Because they were so easy to make, many get-rich-quick hustlers who would not have attempted a full-size automobile believed themselves equal to this task. A lot of truly bad cyclecars were produced and ruined the reputation of the entire type.

————

The fate of the cyclecar seemed sealed, but that was not assurance enough for Henry Ford. In the garage at his Edison Avenue home, he had a three-quarter-scale version of the Model T built. "Now you take it and park it in front of the Pontchartrain Hotel," Henry told his son. Just turned twenty, Edsel Ford had been working for his father since graduation from a Detroit prep school. (The Ford Motor Company was the only higher education Henry believed his son needed.) Edsel's appearance at the Pontchartrain with the mini Model T had the desired effect. Rumors that Ford was about to launch a cyclecar persuaded major manufacturers so inclined not to enter the field and discouraged many others who had been thinking about it. Henry Ford wanted the low-priced field all to himself.

In 1913, Model T production, at 200,000 units, was more than the rest of the industry's top ten put together. Henry had not outflanked his competitors. His competition had chosen not to fight. Certainly what transpired at General Motors following Durant's ouster was encouraging to Ford. Although the bankers were, in the retrospective words of one GM director, "too skeptical about the future of the automobile industry [and] didn't take advantage of the opportunities," there was reason at the time to practice prudence. And no more prudent practitioners were there than James J. Storrow, chairman of the voting trust, and Charles W. Nash, who, upon Durant's recommendation, was made president of Buick and soon thereafter, on Storrow's recommendation, president of GM.

Storrow and Nash hit it off immediately, although a more unlikely pair of close friends could not be imagined than the Harvard-educated

Boston Brahmin and the youngster abandoned and bound out at the age of six to a farmer in Michigan. Charlie Nash had run away at age twelve to get a paying job on another farm. His first capital expenditure was for ten sheep, which soon became a flock of eighty, and wool sales were brisk. Before the turn of the century, he had learned carpentry, clerked at a grocery, and began work as a laborer at the Durant-Dort Carriage Company. Said Dallas Dort, "That Charlie was a mighty good and fast [cushion] stuffer is evidenced by the complaint of many of his fellow workers that he might upset the standard production requirements on the piecework price in effect. But Charlie had his eye on bigger things. He needed the money, so he kept right on stuffing." He and Jessie, the farmer's daughter he had married, were starting a family. Charlie's rise through the ranks at Durant-Dort was spectacular. Recommending him for the Buick post was Billy's last official act before the bankers took over. "We were great friends," Charlie Nash said of Durant. "His policies and mine, of course, were absolutely opposed to each other."

Indeed. Scarcely was Charlie through Buick's door before he began phasing out the racing department. Then he reduced inventory, eliminated models with low profit margins, and ordered development of a six-cylinder car because automobilists were demanding more "oomph." The Buick Model 10 Durant had been grooming as a Model T competitor was among the cars sacrificed. Because of its popularity, this move might have been a power play by the bankers to show Durant who was boss. But the fact was that the safest path in the automobile industry was straight down the middle. Charlie Nash, the carriage man who did not yet know automobile manufacturing, was taking it.

Before long, Storrow, whose weekly commuting between Boston and Detroit was tiresome, had become convinced Nash was the man to take on the GM presidential chair he was anxious to relinquish. This would not leave Buick bereft, however, because Storrow had come up with a wonderful candidate for Nash's job in the meantime: the assistant works manager who had made a moneymaker of the long-unprofitable Pittsburgh branch of American Locomotive, another company for which Storrow sat on the board. A casual meeting was arranged, during which Storrow asked Walter Percy Chrysler if he had ever given any thought to automobile manufacturing.

The thought had crossed Chrysler's mind. He was in the locomotive business principally because he had grown up in the railroad town of Ellis, Kansas. His father was an engineer for the Union Pacific. His own first job was as a roundhouse sweeper at ten cents an hour. Chrysler taught himself mechanics and took the hands-on approach to learning about automobiles. Captivated by a big Locomobile phaeton at the 1908 Chicago Automobile Show, he sweet-talked both his wife and his banker into purchase—and happily joined the ample ranks of those willing to wipe out their savings and mortgage their homes for an automobile. But Chrysler hadn't bought the Loco to use; instead, he tore it apart and for several months studied the workings of every component. After he put the car back together, he didn't bother to teach himself how to drive before taking wife Della and their children for a ride, and they ended up in the neighbor's yard.

Chrysler probably would have continued working on the railroad—his salary of $12,000 in 1912 was double his starting pay of only two years earlier—save for the Storrow inquiry. Eagerly accepting the invitation to discuss the matter further over lunch, Chrysler found Charlie Nash rather cool until the coffee arrived and both pulled out the same brand of panatelas. Things warmed up after that. Charlie was drawn to anyone who liked a cigar that was both robust and modestly priced. After a tour of the Flint plant, all that remained for Chrysler to join Buick was agreement on salary. Informed what American Locomotive was paying, Nash replied that he couldn't afford more than $6,000. Chrysler accepted immediately.

"I saved the Buick Motor Company my first year's salary the first week I was in Flint," Chrysler said. Establishing a register to log completed chassis in and out on test drives meant Buick didn't routinely "lose" up to ten Buicks per month. Told that the sheet metal plant had to be enlarged to alleviate congestion, he staggered the working hours and achieved the same thing. Except for Nash himself, Buick had never had as cost-conscious an executive as Chrysler. "Wally and I made a great team," said Charlie.

"Charlie," Chrysler would implore whenever Nash turned thumbs-down on a Buick expenditure, "please show me the first nickel you ever earned. Mr. Storrow says you've got it hidden somewhere." After a couple of years without a raise, Chrysler walked into his boss' office one day and demanded $25,000 a year. Nash almost fainted. Finally, convinced this was no joke and that his friend was prepared to resign, Charlie sputtered that he would have to check with Storrow. Informed that his raise was approved, Chrysler replied, "Thank you and, by the way, next year I want $50,000."

Charlie Nash ran a tight ship and a straight course at GM. Oldsmobile was steered away from the luxury leviathans of the Smith era but not back to the low-priced models of the Ransom Olds years. Only with the Lelands was he sorely vexed, and then only because he was "unable to make any progress in learning of Cadillac affairs." Father and son were conducting design work in rented offices on the twenty-second floor of the new Dime Building and sending individual experimental parts to various shops in New England for machining to ensure secrecy. When Charlie Nash was finally informed that the Lelands were planning a V-8 engine for the Cadillac, he blanched. The rest of the industry had been content to go from four to six cylinders. When the Lelands told him they could offer the new V-8 for the same price as the former Cadillac four, Charlie smiled.

In five years, Nash turned General Motors from a "wreck into a concern having $25,000,000 in the bank," in Jim Storrow's words. With figures like that, who could argue the corporation's prudent median course? So long as Charlie Nash was in charge, Henry Ford didn't need to fear GM producing a competitor to the Model T.

In Toledo, Willys-Overland didn't seem to be a threat either. Empire building remained on John North Willys' mind. He bought more auto-related companies and sold some of those he had. His personal pet project was the Knight-engined car that bore his name. Overlands were being offered in a staggering array of models, the cheapest several hundred dollars more than the Model T. There was no compelling need to lower prices because people who couldn't afford to pay cash for an Overland could buy one on installments through Willys' Guaranty Security Company. Living the good life absorbed John North Willys. Already he owned several homes and a million-dollar yacht.

The competitive surprise for Henry Ford would come from the corner he least expected. Henry had cast no more than a passing glance at Louis' Chevrolet. But with Louis gone, Billy's Chevrolet was on the way.

As with Buick, Durant liked the name Chevrolet as much for its sound as its significance. Concerned those not aware of the race driver might pronounce the last syllable to rhyme with pet, he spelled the name phonetically on early billboards, as he had done with Buick.

With Louis' departure, Billy gave the Chevrolet the bowtie emblem he had been planning for some time. The wallpaper in a hotel room in Paris had given him the idea, Billy said, and he had snatched a small piece from an inconspicuous spot that he put in his wallet for safekeeping. Catherine Durant remembered him spotting the motif in the rotogravure section of a Sunday newspaper he happened to read during a vacation in Hot Springs. Billy's was the more romantic story, and he stuck with it to the end. He was obviously very pleased with himself for having thought of the simple but effective logo because some early Chevrolet advertisements used only the emblem with a legend above it, reading, "By this sign ye shall know it."

————

The year 1914 was a busy year for Durant. He established New York City as the headquarters for Chevrolet. His daughter Margery moved to town with her family and took an apartment at 635 Park Avenue on the corner of 66th Street "to be near my father who lived a little farther up the same avenue." Rebecca Durant lived in Billy's apartment much of the year to be near her grandchildren and ostensibly to see more of her son. But Durant still spent much of his time on the road.

With little angst, Billy ripped out the leaf he had only recently taken from Henry Ford's book. He became cozy with a banker. Durant had little choice given his plans, and he was lucky in the money man he chose: Louis Graveret Kaufman, president of the Chatham & Phenix National Bank. Michigan born, Kaufman grew up in the Upper Peninsula iron mining town of Marquette, shoveled ore on the first rung up the ladder to mine superintendent, then took a job in a local bank, was its president by age thirty-five, and parlayed that into a successful plunge into New York banking circles. Self made and very proud of it, Kaufman considered audacity and daring fine character traits. Durant could supply those in spades. He brought along A.B.C. Hardy to fill in the details about production, should the subject arise. Lunch was in Kaufman's splendiferous suite in the Ritz-Carlton. "How much money can you use?" Kaufman got right to the point. Without hesitation, Billy replied "The entire amount controlled by all of the Chatham and Phenix banks" —but $5 million would do for openers.

The deal done, purchase of the Tarrytown plant was finalized, the Manhattan factory was put on line, and assembly operations were begun by old buggy-making friends Russell Gardner and Norman de Vaux in St. Louis and Oakland (California), respectively. Durant's son Cliff was installed as a sales executive in the Oakland branch. The Chevrolet company financed its own assembly plant in Fort Worth, and Durant's friend Sam McLaughlin quickly agreed to build Canadian Chevrolets in Oshawa.

For once, Billy was not moving too fast. With his new Chevrolet, he could not move fast enough. Royal Mail and Baby Grand were the charming names Durant selected for the four-cylinder models to replace Louis' Classic Six as the first Chevrolets to sell for less than $1,000. The big surprise came at the end of the year.

Durant was obviously anxious to spring it. He announced the new model a full six months before it would be put on sale. The new car's designation lacked charm but not import: Four-Ninety. Anybody who knew anything about automobiles knew that 490 represented the number of dollars needed to buy a Model T in 1914.

Billy Durant was challenging and tweaking Henry Ford at the same time. "To build a satisfactory car to sell for $490 is quite an undertaking," Billy noted pointedly. "Cars ordinarily sold for $490 are not satisfactory because they are built in enormous quantities and under great pressure, lacking refinement of detail..." Billy's $490 Chevrolet was "good-looking, easy-riding, well-made...," its proud maker said, and capable of 50 miles per hour "if you care to drive that fast."

The Chevrolet Four-Ninety was introduced at the New York Automobile Show in January 1915 and was placed on sale on June 1. The following month, Billy wrote a letter to a friend in Flint, which was published on the front page of *The Flint Journal*. The wizard had done it again. Said Durant, "At the close of business June 19th, the Chevrolet Motor Company had accepted orders from dealers and distributors—

with every contract secured by a cash deposit—for 46,611 [cars], valued at $23,329,390—a fairly good record for seventeen working days. Since June 19th, we have orders for more than 1,000 cars per day."

Two weeks later, Henry Ford lowered the price of the Model T to $440.

CHAPTER 27

Henry and Lizzie

MASS PRODUCTION DIDN'T happen overnight. It happened over centuries. Henry Ford apparently coined the phrase, although it is not known precisely when. Certainly he was thinking about the concept as early as 1903, with his comment to stockholder John Anderson about automobiles coming out of the factory "one like another...all alike." And it was obviously on his mind during the early years of the Model T, when he groused that "It takes us too long to make cars."

Reduced to essentials, mass production required interchangeability of parts, simplification of manufacture, an orderly flow of materials, and continuous movement. It is satisfying that the first documented use of a conveyor in production happened in 1787 in the grist mill of Oliver Evans, the first American to envision the automobile. Interchangeability, by definition, can be traced back to Gutenberg; standardization made great strides with Eli Whitney and Samuel Colt before Henry Leland. By the dawn of the horseless age, machine tools were becoming increasingly sophisticated.

To meet the demand for his little curved dash runabout, Ransom Olds had systematized production at Olds Motor Works in Lansing. To build their steam car in Cleveland, the White family constructed a long 600-foot central hall, branching various departments out from it. When Packard moved from Ohio to Detroit, it was into a brand-new factory designed by Albert Kahn, whose favored material, reinforced concrete, was cheaper and more flexible than brick or steel, allowed vast open manufacturing areas, and was virtually fireproof—in a word, an automaker's dream.

Since 1907, when he eased Alex Malcomson out of his company, Henry Ford had been thinking about a new factory. With Malcomson gone, he had no trouble convincing directors to purchase the fifty-seven acres that had been a race track at Highland Park. When not absorbed in final details for the Model T, Henry closeted himself with Albert Kahn or took long walks with the architect at the site. By year's end 1909, one-quarter of the Highland Park factory was completed. The transfer from Piquette was made department by department. Reinforced concrete allowed 50,000 square feet of windows—so many that the factory was dubbed Detroit's "Crystal Palace." The claustrophobic gloom of the pre-Kahn automobile plant was replaced by glorious sunlight, an apt metaphor for the new motoring day Henry Ford was planning for America's millions. Thousands of new machines were set up in Highland Park, each numbered and identified by a brass tag that had been young Edsel Ford's job to affix during summer vacation from school. If a better machine was devised, the former version was summarily yanked out, even if only a month old. Cost-conscious Jim Couzens cringed.

But even Couzens recognized the ultimate cost savings of efficient production, although just how efficient Henry Ford would be doubtlessly surprised him, as perhaps it did Ford himself. Elsewhere in the industry, other automakers were striving to make cars better and faster. Walter Chrysler quadrupled production at Buick from 45 to 200 cars per day by updating finishing techniques that, in his words, had previously treated "metal as if it were wood" and installed a pair of tracks made of two by fours to push chassis along from worker to worker.

"Henry Ford had no ideas on mass production," right-hand-man Charlie Sorensen said. "Far from it; he just grew into it like the rest of us." The orderly progression of work, while not new in manufacturing, was new to Ford when, as Sorensen said, Walter Flanders "showed us how to arrange our machine tools at the Mack Avenue and Piquette plants."

The Ford Motor Company was blessed with awesome talent, the right people at the right time. Possibly the magnetism, the fierce sense of purpose, of Henry Ford drew them. That same ferocity of ego might send them away, but he was lucky to latch onto someone else to move production to the next plateau. Walter Flanders' exit was followed by William Knudsen's entrance.

Knudsen, as big as Flanders if not quite as loud, was a Danish immigrant who never lost his accent. In 1911, Ford bought the parts-manufacturing John R. Keim Mills, Inc., of Buffalo, and got "Big Bill" with it. Asked if Keim could assemble automobiles, Knudsen said he thought so but wanted to check out how things were done at Highland Park first. He caught on quickly. It was to Knudsen that Ford complained about the length of time necessary to build a car. Coordinating the flow of materials with sequence of operation—"All noses pointed in one direction," as Knudsen said—would speed things. Big Bill picked up where Flanders left off.

Edsel Ford introduced his father to another key player: Clarence W. Avery, a manual training teacher at the Detroit University School. Sorensen recognized Avery's talent right away and sent him off to learn how things were done in each Ford department.

How pervasive the thinking of Frederick Taylor was is moot. Taylor, whose nickname was "Speedy," was the prevailing guru of the stop-watch approach to manufacturing. His book, *The Principles of Scientific Management*, was in every progressive factory in the country. That he lectured often in Detroit is documented; following a speech of more than four hours to Henry Joy and associates, Packard was persuaded—or perhaps numbed—into being "Taylorized." Scientific job analysis was the rage. Jim Couzens, ever anxious to save a penny, loved it. But, as time passed, the people at Ford could have told Frederick Taylor as much as he told them.

To the newcomers in the company were added the efforts of those who had long been with Ford. Master metallurgist and amateur pugilist Harold Wills contributed machine tool designs to improve production methods. The burly and jowly P.E. "Pete" Martin, a French Canadian hired by Wills in 1903, was a whiz at time studies. William Klann, a Ford veteran since 1905, had the knack of operating machine tools at amazingly high rates of speed. Sorensen said mass production "resulted from an organization which was continually experimenting and improvising to get better production."

The final element fell into place in 1913. That it should be the work and not the man proceeding from operation to operation was recognized. The stockyards held the key. Because slaughterhouses had shown how to take apart a pig's carcass on a moving disassembly line, it followed that an automobile could be put together on a moving assembly line—one in which the motion was machine, not hand, operated. Mechanically operated conveyors in a Pittsburgh brake company and a Chicago caster of valves were inspected. Then all concerned got to work at Highland Park.

Baptism was an endless belt to move factory sand to the core molders, then molds past pouring ladles. Elsewhere in the factory, slides and conveyors were rigged to carry parts from one process to the next. "Don't take him too seriously," Henry Ford advised Sorensen when Couzens went "on the warpath" over the costs involved in setting up a magneto assembly line. The Ford business manager almost smiled thereafter. Whereas one man had needed twenty minutes to assemble a magneto in the past, thirteen man-minutes now saw to the same task. With refinements, the time would be reduced eight minutes more.

With the magneto success, Henry Ford was encouraged to try more complicated operations—the engine, the transmission, and then finally the chassis itself. An electric motor with capstan and heavy rope moved the first assembly line in August 1913, as six workers added parts while the chassis passed. Further down the line, the Model T's engine swung overhead to mate with the Model T chassis. It was crude, but it was marvelous. From more than twelve hours, a Model T Ford now needed fewer than six hours to be born.

By year's end, with practice and an endless chain replacing rope, chassis time was cut to a bit more than an hour and a half.

There were the inevitable glitches. "We had our chain going and some fellow forgot to open the door where [the chassis] go out," William Klann recalled. "...We buckled up three of them." But such mishaps were rare. By February 1914, 1,000 Model Ts per day were being built. A giddy Sorensen declared that the number of Fords made depended only on the number they wanted to make. All they had to do was "speed up the line...just make the belt run faster." One presumes he was kidding. It was almost with a sense of marvel that Henry Ford described the process: "Every piece of work in the shop moves. It may move on hook or overhead chains going to assembly in the exact order in which the parts are required; it may travel on a moving platform, or it may go by gravity, but the point is that there is no lifting or trucking of anything other than materials." The man who made the process work might call it mass production. For well over a decade, to most of the world, it was called "Fordism."

———

Had there been no pre-planning, the first thousand-car day at Ford would have caused a monumental traffic jam in Detroit. How could that many cars be dispatched out of town efficiently? Fortunately in 1912, the Dodge brothers, who would have preferred the dividends, grudgingly joined other Ford stockholders in agreeing to reinvest 15 percent of annual company profits into production facilities. Most of the money was earmarked for branch assembly plants.

Jim Couzens didn't blanch. Indeed, one of his people was mastermind of the plan: Norval Hawkins. A certified public accountant and auditor of the Ford books since 1904, Hawkins had been hired by Couzens in 1907 as company sales manager. Henry Ford, a fan of neither titles nor compartmentalization, put him to work scheduling production, too. Proud that every Model T built was already spoken for, Hawkins told Ford he could sell every car the company could produce. As increasing manufacturing efficiency began to indicate that would be a sizable number, Hawkins spent six weeks at a Detroit railway siding, loading and unloading a boxcar to find the best way of getting Model Ts to dealers. Usually completed automobiles were shipped, three or four per boxcar. Knocked-down, Hawkins could cram in twenty-six. Because railroads charged by weight whether used or not, the freight savings realized by 10,000 knocked-down pounds versus the 6,000 pounds of three complete Model Ts was palpable. Couzens was ecstatic.

Shipping knocked-down was predicated on having some place at the opposite end to put together. Bill Knudsen was given that chore. After setting up Keim in Buffalo for assembly, Knudsen helped in the installation of machinery in Detroit for mass production. Then he was sent into the field to supervise establishment of more than a dozen branch assembly plants from coast to coast. Returning to Detroit when the job was done, Knudsen was summoned to Couzens' office, a sign usually of an impending dressing down. Instead, Ford's business manager complimented him on a job well done and handed him an envelope. "How much are we paying you?" Couzens asked. Six hundred dollars per month was Knudsen's reply. Couzens raised it to a thousand. Leaving the office, Knudsen tore open the envelope. Inside was a check for $5,000. Buffalo would be home to the Knudsens no more; Big Bill packed up his family and moved to Detroit.

With the branch assembly plants on line, Norval Hawkins was vigorously back to his principal job: seeing to Model T sales by setting up a vast national (then international) network. Prior to the final disposition of the Selden patent case, potential dealers had been leery of being drawn into litigation, Ford reassurances notwithstanding. Since 1911, the ranks of Ford agencies had swelled, by 1914 to 7,000 dealers. Hawkins imposed rigorous conditions. Dealers could handle only Ford cars in meticulous showrooms and provide immediate assistance to any Model T owner requiring it. Parts stock at dealerships had to be complete, and parts could be priced only by the factory. Dealers were given strict repair work standards. Hawkins counseled against glass partitions between showroom and shop as intimating something might go wrong with a Model T and even suggested that disabled Fords be towed in the dead of night. He preached the Ford gospel with the fervor of a fire-and-brimstone preacher, admonishing dealers to forego "social affairs, amusements and the theatre" for unswerving allegiance to the cause of the Model T. No matter how many rules he laid down, Hawkins' biggest problem remained whom to allow in among the numberless applicants—mayors, congressmen, and ex-governors among them—who were sure they were the personification of the "live wide-awake hustlers" required. Their anxiousness to please was understandable. In exchange for heavy supervision, the Ford dealers were given a virtual get-rich-quick-and-then-get-richer guarantee.

Becoming richest of all was Henry Ford. From 1912 to 1913, company net profits doubled to $27 million. With the time necessary to build a Model T continually shaved, future profits promised to be even grander. From 450 employees in 1908, Ford's workforce increased to nearly 15,000. "The man who places a part does not fasten it," Henry Ford would say proudly of his mass production technique. "The man who puts in a bolt does not put on the nut; the man who puts on the nut does not tighten it." These men quickly became disenchanted. Laboring on an assembly line was both dull and stressful.

One day, as Henry Ford toured a machine shop with Edsel, a violent fight broke out between two workers. That his son was shaken by the event bothered Ford, as did the look of hatred in the men's faces when they sighted him. What would it cost, Henry wondered to Jim Couzens, to make his workers "glad to see us when we come along?"

Ostensibly, the Ford Motor Company was already a model employer in an industry not noted for largesse toward labor. But it didn't seem to matter. Ford wages were high, but labor turnover was not commensurately low. Generous year-end bonuses were not matched by notable productivity levels through the year. During the summer of 1913, Ford employment director John R. Lee, like Knudsen a veteran of the Keim mills, was asked to diagnose the problem and offer solutions. The sweeping reforms Lee recommended included establishing an employee credit union, instituting a job hierarchy, defanging foremen and superintendents (who could hire, fire, and promote at will), and raising the number of factory shifts from two to three by reducing the workday to eight hours. (A few months earlier, John North Willys had "established a precedent" by cutting the usual six-day week from fifty-four to fifty hours.)

The big news came on January 5. That morning, reporters gathered at Highland Park to hear Jim Couzens, with Ford behind him, read a press release announcing "the greatest revolution in the matter of rewards ever known to the industrial world." Henceforth, the basic wage at the Ford Motor Company would be doubled—to a five dollars a day.

Only in retrospect would the self-interest of this policy be fully realized. Henry Ford was creating customers for his Model T. "At that time industry's practice was to set wages low, the lower the better," Hyatt Bearing's Alfred Sloan wrote years later. "Reduce when you could, increase when you must. The power of an economic wage rate to stimulate consumption had not been realized." At the time, Henry Ford himself spoke only of "profit sharing and efficiency engineering."

Who came up with the five-dollar figure? Authorship would ultimately be claimed for both Ford and Couzens. Both men certainly agreed to the plan. But of all the scenarios offered for how it came about, the most plausible has Henry Ford closeted with his key associates, covering a blackboard with figures—the lowered price to the public for the Model T, the anticipated profits for the company, and the bounty for executives and management. The only people left off the blackboard were Ford workers. John Lee's report of the dismal living conditions of the average working man was fresh in mind, as was the incident in the machine shop with Edsel; Ford's wife, Clara, had been moved by letters from workers' wives, detailing how hard their lives were. The total chalked in for wages seemed pitifully low compared to the other figures. Henry started playing with the minimum—when three dollars brought no response, he added fifty cents to it. At four dollars, Pete Martin objected vociferously, Harold Wills sided with Ford, and Charlie Sorensen and Norval Hawkins murmured noncommittally. Jim Couzens sat like a stone. Henry kept erasing and chalking in new figures, as the room grew silent. Finally, Couzens exploded, "Well, so it's up to $4.75. I dare you to make it $5.00." Thus was it done.

"You know, when you pay men well," Henry Ford said wistfully a short while later, "you can talk to them." That combination of pragmatism and idealism was part of his motivation. But the five-dollar day was much more than that to Henry Ford. Ringing in his ears were the words of the man he admired above all others. "Our production, our factory laws, our charities, our relations with capital and labor, our distribution—all wrong, out of gear," Thomas Edison had declared. "We've stumbled along for a while, trying to run a new civilization in old ways, but we've got to start to make the world over." To Henry, the five-dollar day was a good place to begin.

Concocted in secret and announced without fanfare, news of the Ford minimum wage detonated like a bomb. "An epoch in the world's industrial history," said the *New York Herald*. A "magnificent act of generosity," said the *New York Evening Post*. The initial public response was overwhelmingly favorable. But there were naysayers. *The New York Times* asked Henry Ford point blank if he was a socialist, and a mass meeting of socialists concluded the plan was a "detestable trap." The *Wall Street Journal* was horrified that anyone would raise wages when not compelled to do so by a strike and suggested that Henry had applied "Biblical or spiritual principles" in a field where they did not belong.

Industry reaction varied. Hugh Chalmers said Ford should not have taken such a radical step without first consulting his colleagues. Alvan Macauley of Packard phoned Charlie Sorensen to seethe sarcastically that "We are not running a philanthropic business like you." John and Horace Dodge fumed that the real reason for the five-dollar day was to thwart them in the introduction of their own brand-new car by denying proper Ford dividends and creating turmoil in the labor market.

Studebaker's Albert Erskine remarked that the five-dollar day "contravenes all economic laws and must in the end fail." Others called it treason. The International Workers of the World assumed the Ford wage plan was a calculated attempt at union busting. Ford was a word not spoken with cheer in labor circles, and in Detroit social and country clubs, heads often turned the other way when Jim Couzens walked in. Henry Ford wasn't the clubby sort.

One widely bruited fear—that the five-dollar day would decimate the labor pool in Detroit—was quickly quashed. Obviously, most Ford workers were not about to change jobs; indeed, it was said some of the more motivated had to be slowed down because they got ahead of the assembly line. Many Detroiters not yet employed at Ford wanted to be, of course, but their number was swelled by the hordes now arriving in town. Not since the gold rush had there been such a fever. Applicants stormed the Ford plant, blocked the streets, and jammed the gates. The crowd of 10,000 turned into a mob. When factory fences threatened to give way, fire hoses drove the screaming throng back.

The Ford home on Edison Avenue was open to the street, and Henry and Clara's telephone number was in the city directory. Intruders knocked at their door until late at night; the phone rang incessantly. Moving out of town seemed the wisest course. Grosse Pointe had become the suburb of choice for Detroit industrialists; Ford considered it awhile, but finally decided he would feel less comfortable among the social elite than in the town of his birth. Some years earlier, Ford had bought a large parcel of land in Dearborn along the River Rouge where a bungalow had been built for use as an occasional retreat. Now a glorious mansion, Fair Lane, was designed for the property, sited far from the road, hidden by trees, protected by a wrought iron fence, and guarded twenty-four hours a day. Henry Ford was becoming a captive of his success.

The tumultuous reaction to the five-dollar day was only one factor of the new Ford wage that had been overlooked when the figure was chalked on the blackboard. Office workers weren't included initially, a discrimination that didn't bother Henry when informed of it because of the gender of most stenos. Jim Couzens anticipated problems, however, and implored Clara to intercede. "I consider women only a temporary factor in industry," Henry harrumphed in announcing they would receive five dollars a day, too. "Their real job in life is to get married, have a home and raise a family. I pay our women well so they can dress attractively and get married."

The five-dollar day wasn't admired by everybody seemingly lucky enough to be hired to earn it. A lathe operator named Charles Madison quit Dodge Brothers for Ford, found the quota system (the number of parts to be finished per day, as determined by an efficiency expert) to be too rigorous, and returned to Dodge, where he could earn three dollars or so in peaceful piecework. Others discovered that, although five dollars was the minimum, it might also be the maximum—and more than a few ex-Ford workers ended up at automakers such as Cadillac or Packard, where skilled craftsmanship brought higher wages.

Skilled workers had important roles in mass production, but in sheer numbers, their ranks were overwhelmed by untrained recruits who could quickly learn a simple assigned task. Ford factory notices were posted in at least eight different languages, Arabic and Greek among them. It didn't matter a lot whether a man on the line could talk to the fellow assembling next to him.

Regardless of the language they spoke, new workers at Ford were made aware quickly that the five-dollar day was not automatically awarded upon being hired. Six months on the job was required, and the worker's personal life had to meet certain standards of acceptability. Determining eligibility was the newly organized Sociological Department, headed by John Lee, followed by the Fords' Episcopalian pastor, the Reverend Samuel S. Marquis, who changed its name to Educational Department. "We receive every man on six months' probation," the Reverend said, "and we make a careful study of his habits." Drinking, smoking, and wenching—all of which Henry Ford abhorred publicly—were habits guaranteed to violate probation.

Cigarettes were forbidden in Ford factories, although thousands of workers smoked anyway, flushing butts or even swallowing them when a security guard happened by. At home, liquor and tobacco could be easily hidden from inspectors during visits, but removing from view all vestiges of a live-in lover was more difficult. Inspectors provided advice on the family budget, proper diet, life insurance, personal hygiene, and church attendance. It was a good idea to follow the advice. Anyone not doing so was summoned to the Marquis office where, in the Reverend's words, "his destructive habits are pointed out to him. His profits are taken away until he reforms. If he reforms in sixty days, he gets seventy-five percent of them. If he does not reform, he is allowed to go elsewhere." If dismissed, the employee's profits went to charity. In Henry's view, the money above the standard industrial wage provided by Ford was profit shared in advance of being earned; thus, rigorous standards for its dispersal were wholly warranted.

"Help the Other Fellow" was a factory motto, under which on one placard Henry Ford penciled "to help himself." On motoring trips into the Michigan countryside, whenever he spotted a tramp, Ford would stop and ask if the man wanted honest work—and, if the answer was yes—hired him immediately. Ex-convicts were given a second chance, and the disabled, who were seldom given any chance to work, were welcomed into the Ford factory. There were many meritorious aspects to the company's Sociological/Educational Department, but its patent paternalism won few plaudits. Libertarians were outraged by the unabashed fervor with which Ford invaded an individual's right to privacy. The department survived but a half-dozen years, its educational aspects, including courses in the English language, continued in the Henry Ford Trade School, which was established in 1916.

The budgeting advice provided Ford families by Marquis and his inspectors generally included mention that investing in a Model T was proper use of their increased income. Many among the company's 15,000 employees would—and minions more across the land. In 1914, the first full year of the moving assembly line, more than 300,000 Model Ts were sold, as many cars as were marketed by all the rest of the American industry put together.

The single-mindedness of Henry Ford's purpose was not fully compre-hended by his associates—frequently to their peril. No one learned this more emphatically than Harold Wills, who took the time afforded by a Ford family trip abroad to design an updated version of the Model T, incorporating improvements and design features introduced generally in the industry in the four years since the car's debut. The boss would be pleased, Wills thought, that his time away had been used so productively. Ford returned in good spirits, following fruitful talks with Sir Percival Perry about the formation of an English com-pany and a visit to Ireland to show Edsel the house in which his grand-father had been born. Highland Park was his first stop upon arrival back. The prototype was in the executive garage, ready to be shown off to him as soon as he entered the offices where Wills, Charlie Sorensen, and Pete Martin awaited.

Because it was after hours, just about everyone else had gone home except George Brown, the former Winton treasurer who worked in accounting and who was returning from an errand through the garage just as Henry, taking the back way, walked in. Upon being asked, Brown told Ford what the new car was and that "it's just going into production." Ford walked over to the prototype, then around it slowly, three or four times, with his hands in his pockets. Finally, he stopped, grabbed the left door, and jerked it off; he did the same to the right, hopped up on the hood, and kicked in the windshield. When he jumped into the back seat and started attacking the canvas top, Brown quietly left for the offices. "I guess we're in for it," Harold Wills murmured to his colleagues after being warned of the scene in the garage. Brown stopped at his desk before departing for the night, passing by Wills' office again on the way out: "Mr. Ford was in there, and his hands were going, and his feet were going, and you talk about cussing! It was the first time I had ever heard Mr. Ford cuss and, oh, the other fellows were just taking it. He was going to it, and I kept right on going."

When Brown returned to work the next morning, he was informed by accounting manager Frank Klingensmith that all tooling orders made for the new car had to be canceled. That cost a small fortune. "We got the message," Harold Wills said. As far as Henry Ford was concerned, "The Model T was God and we were to put away false images." Not long afterward, Henry Ford publicly declared there would be no changes in the Model T because it could not be improved.

When William Knudsen came to him with dealer complaints about brake linings, Ford advised, "You have them appoint a committee from among themselves to decide what brake lining they want. Being a committee, they will never agree, so that will take care of that." Only once during the early years did Henry backtrack on his no-change policy, and that was in 1914, when instead of a choice in paint, he pronounced "You can have any color you want, so long as it's black" because black enamel dried the fastest on the assembly line.

During the summer of 1915, after purchase of another large tract of land near River Rouge, Henry Ford announced his intention to build a complex there to make steel, tires, glass, and everything necessary for the Model T. Already he had stopped buying engines from the Dodge brothers and had brought other manufacturing in-house. Vertical integration, everything for the car from the basic raw materials upward, was his aim. When told that the ultimate plan was to congregate all manufacturing at River Rouge, William Knudsen worried aloud that the projected 100,000 workers in a single location could mean a flood of Biblical proportion with so many "flushing at once." Ford just laughed and said, "I want the Ford business all behind one fence so I can see it."

Certainly he did not want any more surprises such as the one that had greeted him in the company garage. Henry Ford's new sole aim was to provide average Americans a well-built car they could afford—no more, no less. The Model T's vitals—engine, transmission, and chassis—had, in one memorable phrase, "the toughness of original sin." More than half of its 5,000 separate parts could be replaced at the dealership for less than fifty cents.

Authorized parts weren't even necessary often. Anything could fix a Model T: baling wire, fish line, stove pipe, waxed twine, chewing gum, a clothespin, a coat hanger, a paper clip, or a bent nail. Drop a raw egg into a leaky radiator, and the hot water would hard-boil it into a leak sealer. Ford did not envision, nor probably approve of, all the Rube Goldberg contrivances to repair an ailing Model T, but he most definitely planned the car for unprecedented ease of maintenance. His number one customer, he believed, would be the farmer, who had long regarded an automobile as the natural enemy. "Mr. Ford always had it in his mind to make the farmer's lot easier," remarked Fred Seeman, a Ford engineering veteran from the early days. Winning over the rural population was important to Henry because of one farmer he had not been able to win over to the automobile—his father.*

People in rural areas were largely self-sufficient, with enough tools and mechanical skill to fix farm machinery. The Ford owner's manual was in question-and-answer form, delineating in sixty-four pages the simple tools and procedures that would right any of the 140 things that could go wrong in a Model T. Interestingly, sometimes the car fixed itself; there were many authenticated cases of a Model T being restored to health after just being parked in the shade awhile. Farmers accepted this readily; they usually had an old mare who behaved the same way.

Assigning gender to inanimate objects is usually risky. Not with the Model T Ford. She was Tin Lizzie. One did not merely own her; one was involved. The automobile in which most members of an entire generation learned to drive, the first car for more millions of Americans than any other, was possibly the most individualistic ever built. Everybody's Tin Lizzie was different, every one the owner's own, with her own set of peculiar quirks and idiosyncrasies. John Steinbeck's car knew exactly the number of cranks he would endure before kicking her radiator—and always started on the last one. Cranking a Model T required practice. Said Lee Strout White, "It was a special trick, and until you learned it (usually from another Ford owner but sometimes by a period of appalling experimentation) you might as well have been winding up an awning." When Floyd Clymer's Lizzie began to hit on two, three, and then four cylinders, she sounded "like a thresher trimming the nap off an acre of barbed wire."

Some Lizzies liked to advance at the first explosion, pinning their owners against the garage wall. Others would have to be chased down the street by drivers who didn't get behind the steering wheel in time. When they aged, some Lizzies listed to port, others to starboard. On the road, the Model T was a white-knuckled 40 miles per hour on the level, a mile a minute on long downhills, with long uphills often taken in reverse

---

* William Ford had died in 1905, before his son's success in the automobile business. "There's just one thing I regret," Henry Ford said near the end of his own life. "I wish my father could have lived to see it happen."

because of the gravity fuel system. Some Lizzies performed a side-to-side sway like a Conestoga wagon, others a fore-aft rocking-horse motion, and still others a cunning combination of both. Some Lizzies were given to sudden inexplicable lurches. Others had a shimmy that would shame the most accomplished belly dancer.

Driving a Model T meant one was reduced to the essentials. There were no gauges, so the owner didn't know how hot his engine was, how fast he was going, or how much gasoline he had left. Lifting the seat cushion and sticking a ruler in the fuel tank gave him the last measurement, but for about a dollar, he could buy a gas gauge; more money would purchase a speedometer. A huge industry grew up to provide Tin Lizzie what she didn't have. Entrepreneurs everywhere rushed to market with anti-rattle devices, shock absorbers, single-shot lubricators, faux hoods, and vee radiator shells. Sears, Roebuck listed no fewer than 5,000 accessories for the Model T. Many owners succumbed to these attempts to make Lizzie more of a lady. Others couldn't afford to, or regarded it a badge of honor to accept her the way she was.

Equal in number to the Ford accessories were the Ford jokes. Model T owners accepted these so long as they were in the spirit of fun. Mean-spirited aspersions were taken personally. The first jokes were about the way the car was built: Model Ts were shipped in asbestos crates because they came off the assembly line so quickly, the metal was still smoking; or a Ford assembly line worker dropped his wrench, and before he could pick it up, twenty Model Ts had passed by him. Some Ford jokes were genuine compliments: the fellow who wanted to be buried with his Model T because it had got him out of every hole he ever got into (Henry Ford's personal favorite), or the Cadillac, Pierce-Arrow, and Packard owners who had Model Ts in their toolboxes for the same purpose.

But most were knee-slappers, taking fun at Lizzie's foibles. Why is Henry Ford a better evangelist than Billy Sunday? Because he shakes the hell out of more people. "Flivver"—another nickname for the Model T—is believed to have been bastardized from what another rattle-and-shake joke suggested the Ford was good for: "for the liver." Tin Lizzie's social status was lampooned. Why is a Model T like a bathtub? Because you hate to be seen in one. When a Model T ran over a chicken, it got up saying "Cheep, cheep, cheep." Henry Ford was delighted. "The jokes about my car sure help to popularize it," he once remarked.

"I hope they never end." He told as many as anyone, and publicly, which let Lizzie owners know that a laugh at their car's expense was just fine.

Model T jokes were unpaid advertising. But, to Henry Ford, even better advertising was provided by price cuts. "Every time I reduce the charge for our car by one dollar," he said, "I get a thousand new buyers." The price cuts were generously reported in the press. If 300,000 cars were sold in 1914, Ford advertised, every Model T buyer would share in the profits with a check for up to $60—a Norval Hawkins idea and the cleverest rebate in history. *Harper's Weekly* said that Ford had "made the deepest, most sensational appeal to human nature he could have made." His appeal in 1916 was sensational, too: another price cut, to $360. What Ford didn't comment on was that these cuts were being largely paid for by his dealers, whose per-car profit was reduced to as little as five dollars. Some dealers defected, but most stayed on. If one sold enough Tin Lizzies, five dollars per car still accumulated into a tidy annual sum.

CHAPTER 28

Games of Mix, Match, and Hatch

THE BAR AT THE Hotel Pontchartrain was packed by 11:30 each morning. Visiting salesmen and parts manufacturers insisted on having their drinks on East Coast time. Tiffany Studios designed the room—mosaic floor, gilded mahogany ceiling beams, and a great marble clock overlooking a massive green marble bar behind which a half-dozen bartenders worked feverishly. At the Pontchartrain, the automobile industry got together to drink and to gossip.

Nobody ever saw Henry Ford there, nor the teetotaling Lelands. Walter Flanders was a regular, and the Dodge brothers practically called the place home. Albert Champion first demonstrated his spark plugs at one of the tables at the Pontchartrain. Carburetors, magnetos, brakes, and steering gears were tested, wheels were rolled in, and tire vulcanizers were tried. Nothing automotive was too bizarre for the Pontchartrain. At times, the place looked more like a machine shop than a barroom. At times, there seemed to be enough components on the tables to build an entire car.

"New models customarily had debuts there," remembered Alfred Sloan. "As word spread that So-and-So's new Whizzer was parked at the curbstone, the crowd would flock outside to appraise the rival of all existing cars." New companies were formed at the Pontchartrain; old partnerships were broken. Contacts were made; contracts were finalized. Tablecloths were littered with chassis sketches, mechanical drawings, and facts and figures. The locals often stayed on when the East Coast contingent left, or returned after working hours to continue an argument that might finish across the square at John's Night Owl Lunch Cart when the Pontchartrain bar closed.

Bankers were welcome at the Pontchartrain but seldom seen. The ambiance at the bar—which one patrician observer likened to a mining camp—was not their scene. Two-fisted drinking types predominated. Detroit "first families" sought to civilize the industry's more rambunctious elements. Henry Joy of Packard came up with one workable idea: another place to go besides the Pontchartrain and "the saloons of Woodward Avenue." The Detroit Athletic Club was chosen, a grand new clubhouse was built, and the motor industry moved in. Hugh Chalmers was the first president.

That Detroit had already become the motor mecca was incontrovertible. Why is obvious. How it happened is interesting. Other cities had as strong an industrial base and as many carriage-making, bicycle, and machine shops. Other cities preceded Detroit into the field. "New England had the chance," said Olds' Fred Smith, "but lacked the financial courage; lacked the one vital thing we describe by a short and ugly word of four letters." ("Guts" was uttered often in Woodward Avenue saloons but not in the rarefied circles in which Smith moved.) From his gun silencer factory in Connecticut, auto pioneer Percy Maxim took another tack: "For every plan to make a big success of automobile manufacture, the New England businessman counters with a plan for making a bigger success in finance or insurance or in some of the old established industries."

By the turn of the century, the shift toward the Middle West was in full swing, with Winton in Ohio and Haynes-Apperson in Indiana enjoying an advantage over their more remote New England counterparts in reaching the important automobile markets nationwide. (As early as 1900, California ranked second in motor vehicle registrations; in 1910,

Los Angeles was the most automobile-populous city in the nation, its preeminence, according to *Munsey's Magazine*, because "many wealthy people from all over the United States go there for the winter.") The serendipitous confluence of the most dogged and ambitious automakers in the nation—Olds, Durant, and Ford—switched the automobile industry's center to Michigan soon afterward.

In 1913, more cars were built in Detroit than in the entire country the preceding year. Michigan companies produced more than 75 percent of America's automobiles, the overwhelming majority of them Model T Fords. But Michigan also led the nation in the number of companies producing cars: a total of seventy-five. Billy Durant's old partner, Dallas Dort, was one of the last carriage makers in Flint to get into the automobile business; his cross-town colleague, William A. Paterson, had pre-empted him by a full half decade. Henry Ford's old buddy Charlie King had returned from engineering study abroad to start a car company bearing his name. Both the Dort and the King—and the Paterson, too—were medium-priced cars.

"Within a few years Olds, Hupp, Buick and E-M-F got out of my way, one by one, in somewhat that order," Henry Ford reminisced years later. "All of them went into larger cars after making a success of small ones. I recall looking at Bobby Hupp's roadster at the first show where it was exhibited and wondering whether we could ever build as good a car for as little money." Ford was awry on chronology but right on target otherwise. The industry did leave him alone in the low-priced field.

Bobby Hupp's car had debuted at the Detroit Automobile Show of February 1909. A veteran of both the Olds and the Ford companies, Hupp had been joined by Charles D. Hastings, former office manager/sales executive for Olds and Thomas-Detroit, in establishing the Hupp Motor Car Company. A coterie of others put up the money. Hastings remembered, "Never will I forget the night we finished working on that exhibition car. I think it was the coldest night I ever saw. Working as we were, in cramped positions, thoroughly tired out and continually racing against time, with the wind blowing through the crevices of that shack and chilling us to the marrow, it took all the courage we had to stick."

Ford, by then a wealthy established manufacturer, admired the grit of Hupp and Hastings, which was very like his own from his threadbare days. The Hupmobile that he admired, at $750 for the roadster, was wonderfully priced. But the good times were short-lived. The four-seater touring Hupmobile introduced two years later couldn't be marketed for less than $900, and the Model T was already underselling it by more than $100. Moreover, tempers had flared in the executive offices over what to do next; Bobby Hupp wanted to emulate Billy Durant, not Henry Ford, and scared the wits out of Hastings and colleagues with his expansionist ideas. The upshot was Hupp's acrimonious departure. Taking a cue from Ransom Eli Olds' Reo, Robert C. Hupp's next car bore his initials; the RCH was not a success, however, nor was the Hupp-Yeats (an electric), the Monarch, or the Emerson, among the other automotive ventures in this talented but ill-starred automaker's career. The Hupmobile moved into the middle-priced field and prospered.

Not until 1914, several years later, did Billy Durant attempt his head-on challenge to the Model T with the Chevrolet Four-Ninety. As we have seen, Ford's checkmate was another $50 price decrease. Try as he might, Durant could not hold to $490 anyway. For 1915, he kept that price tag only to advertise "the lowest-priced electrically lighted and started automobile in the market today," then quietly increased the price to $550. Henry had given the Model T electric lights. The self-starter was a costly installation Durant was convinced the Chevrolet needed just to offer something the Ford didn't. A survey taken about this time by Curtis Publishing Company indicated thousands of buyers were willing to pay $100 more than the Model T for a more stylish car. Producing it was the hard part—and became even more difficult once Ford had his assembly line humming. Thereafter, as the Model T's price was lowered, the Four-Ninety's price was raised, and the price differential between the two cars grew into a chasm.

Possibly a few sour grapes were involved, but most manufacturers insisted they didn't want to build a car like the Model T anyway. James Scripps-Booth, scion of the newspaper publishing family, referred to his little $775 staggered three-seat roadster as a "luxurious light car." Purchasers included Reggie Vanderbilt in America, Winston Churchill in England, and the reigning monarchs of Holland and Spain. As company sales manager (and erstwhile Imp cyclecar designer), William

Stout commented, "The only one who did not have the idea that he was in the luxury business was Henry Ford."

Although scarcely to the manor born, even the Dodge brothers—whose idea of *noblesse oblige* was providing free beer and sandwiches at lunchtime—were almost contemptuous of the Model T. "Just think of all those Ford owners who will someday want an automobile," John Dodge snorted when he and Horace became carmakers themselves. Their car was called the Dodge Brothers, uppercase acknowledgment of the closeness of John and Horace. At $785, it was in essence a grown-up version of the $450 Model T, with nearly twice the power (35 horsepower versus 20), a standard transmission (versus the T's planetary) and the first mass-produced all-steel body in the industry. Worried that its welds wouldn't hold, the brothers added rivets "just in case." The Dodge Brothers was, like its namesakes, sturdy, dependable, and rather homely. More than 45,000 were produced in maiden year 1915—a splendid start in the industry. The brothers chortled that they no longer had to be "carried around in Henry Ford's vest pocket." An irked Ford, believing the Dodges had financed their automobile company with his company's profits, stopped paying dividends.

———

Walter Flanders never took "no" for an answer. Midnight was the hour an ordinance insisted Detroit bars be closed, and the Pontchartrain followed the law to the letter. One evening, however, Flanders would have none of it. Unwilling to join cronies at John's Night Owl Lunch Cart, he stormed the Pontchartrain and pounded in one of the tall mahogany panels separating the bar from the barroom. When aware of what he had done, he insisted on paying for the damage.

Flanders and the Dodge brothers were alike in being hell-raising carousers who were always sorry afterward. They also had Henry Ford in common. In setting up Ford's factory, Flanders had earned his boss' respect. But Ford also feared the man whose personality was as outsized as his physique. A 275-pound bull-necked goliath with a bullhorn voice, Flanders had an awesome power of persuasion—and made Ford wonder whether employee might overwhelm employer in his own company. Moreover, Henry expressed moral outrage that, in addition to being a big drinker, his production manager was renowned in Detroit as a womanizer. In April 1908, Flanders celebrated his resignation from Ford Motor Company with a divorce from his third wife.*

Ford was happy to see him go but probably not surprised. A detective had been following Flanders for some time. Engineer Joseph Galamb found the investigator's report when he changed desks after Flanders' departure. "Mr. Ford had an idea that he [Flanders] was trying to get some information about starting another company," Galamb remembered, "and he didn't like that." Henry Ford was right. Flanders did start his own company, and he took Thomas Walburn and Max Wollering, two exemplary production men Flanders had brought to Ford, to help.

Ford competitors were equally happy with Flanders' departure because, in their view, without him, Ford was heading downhill. Miscalculating what the loss of one of Henry's key people would mean to Ford Motor Company became routine in Detroit. This first significant defection, or possibly the industry buzz about it, nettled Henry Ford mightily, however. "If you say the word," he said to Jim Couzens, "I will have his head knocked off." Couzens asked what he meant. Ford replied that he knew a couple of men who, upon request, would beat up Flanders. Couzens replied that was not a good idea.

———

What happened next demonstrates how monumentally more effective the fanatical zeal of one man was in the early industry over the combined wisdom and resources of several of the industry's most stellar players. For, if any automotive venture pulsated with the promise of success, it was the E-M-F. The initials stood for the people involved. Joining Flanders were Everitt and Metzger.

Canadian born, Byron Forbes Everitt had been "Barney" to everybody in Detroit since the turn of the century when he began a successful

———

* Flanders' wives would number five. This presented a difference to the Dodge brothers, who displayed the same loyalty to spouses as they did to each other. Horace was devoted to his Anna. Following the tragic death of Ivy, John entered a marriage of convenience with the housekeeper hired to care for his three young children but was soon quietly divorced from her in order to marry Matilda, the company stenographer whom he loved but whose youth (she was twenty years his junior) had made him initially apprehensive.

body-building business. Among his first orders were big ones from Ransom Olds and Henry Ford. Among his first employees were Fred Fisher and Walter O. Briggs (rather like Olds Motor Works, the B.F. Everitt Company was the school from which a number of prominent body men graduated). By 1908, Barney Everitt had built, painted, and trimmed more automobile bodies, twice over, than anybody else in the industry.

William E. Metzger was no less renowned as Detroit's pioneer automobile dealer, the organizer of the first automobile show as well as the first races in the area (which showcased Winton and Ford), and the man who made a sales success of the Lelands' Cadillac.

This triumvirate appeared to be a mismatch: Everitt was short, squat, and jovial; Metzger was tall, distinguished, and aristocratic; and Flanders was just plain large. But their credentials blended perfectly. And the cake was iced when LeRoy Pelletier joined. A New Englander possessed of a small body, a large head, and electrifying nervous energy, Pelletier had covered the Klondike stampede for *The New York Times* and served as Henry Ford's first private secretary and "publicity engineer." "Watch the Fords Go By" was his coinage.

The Everitt-Metzger-Flanders Company was launched in June 1908 in a blaze of publicity, the likes of which the industry had not seen since Colonel Pope announced to the world that he was about to build an automobile. The E-M-F announcement was made at the Cafe des Beaux Arts in New York City (for maximum national exposure) during a gala banquet to which wives and sweethearts were invited (for social page coverage, as trade dinners were generally stag). Everitt and Metzger personally transported the frog legs from Detroit, Flanders saw to it that sufficient libation was on hand, and Pelletier told the after-dinner jokes.

Ready-made facilities for production were at hand back in Michigan because E-M-F was realized in essence by the merger of two companies that had been in business for a half decade: Northern (whose alumni included Charlie King and Jonathan Maxwell) and Wayne (like Northern, begun by a stove manufacturer, Charles L. Palms). Metzger already had a financial interest in Northern, and Everitt was involved with Wayne. Neither company was doing well, but that didn't matter because both the Northern and Wayne automobiles were scrapped right away. Designing the new E-M-F was Wayne chief engineer William Kelly.

"We have the talent, the capital, and we will have the factory facilities," Walter Flanders said in announcing the planned plant expansion. "We can manufacture more automobiles of a better quality at a lower cost than any other concern now in existence." Everitt was president of the company, Flanders general manager; Metzger took charge of sales, Pelletier advertising. The 30-horsepower E-M-F was introduced as a $2,500 car available to the public at $1,250—twice the car for half the price. A few months later, Henry Ford announced his new Model T at $850, but the triumvirate didn't care. Everitt, Metzger, and Flanders had no desire to produce as proletarian a vehicle as the Ford.

The new car was entirely meritorious. But its designation was double-edged. That Detroit school children learned both their "A-B-Cs" and "E-M-Fs" was a phrase toastmasters and would-be professional wits used incessantly, but the initials could just as easily be lampooned into "Every Mechanical Failure," "Every Morning Fix-It," "Eternally Missing Fire," and "Every Mechanic's Friend," among others. "Oh, they were awfully peevish," LeRoy Pelletier lamented. Henry Ford saw Model T jokes as effective advertising. Late in 1908, no one at E-M-F was laughing.

Soon they were not even smiling. In New York for the automobile show, William Metzger fretted, "We have been building plants which has taken a lot of time." And a lot of money. Flanders wanted the E-M-F factory to be state-of-the-art and to offer a runabout model of 20 horsepower closer to the Model T's price in order to crack the popular market. Ford may have been right about Flanders' propensity to dominate, for both Metzger and Everitt were cowed. Their partner began making decisions without asking, among them contracting Studebaker to market a substantial part of the E-M-F production. This trod into Metzger's territory, which the company sales manager didn't like. With most sales going to a single buyer, there wasn't much incentive to build a national sales organization, so Metzger took time off for a trip to Europe. Everitt was left to argue alone and urged the E-M-F board to decide "once and for all that we are through with the Studebaker outfit."

For Studebaker, the E-M-F contract was heaven-sent. The California gold rush had made the South Bend wagon-building brothers prosperous, and supplying the Union Army during the Civil War had made them famous. Even the British contacted Studebaker during the Boer War. The family became fabulously wealthy. While riding in Harry Payne Whitney's palatial railroad car on one occasion, John M. Studebaker had to admit his dinner jacket pockets were empty because he had just lost $200,000 in cash in a friendly game of roulette.

But being a high roller in a social setting was quite different from gambling on risky business ventures. The Studebakers had generously offered warehouse space to the Chicago Times-Herald contest organizers in 1895 but wanted no part of the new-fangled horseless carriage business themselves. Had not Frederick Fish, a lawyer and New Jersey politician, married John Studebaker's daughter Grace, the South Bend company's bowing to the automotive age would have been longer in coming. But Fish eased the four brothers into it, with the manufacture of electric cars in 100-unit batches beginning in South Bend in 1902, and in 1904 the purchase of 200 gasoline car chassis annually from Garford of Elyria (Ohio) that were bodied at the Studebaker plant. The E-M-F deal increased the South Bend company's commitment to the automobile.

On the face of it, the liaison benefited both parties. To E-M-F, it brought 4,000 sales outlets immediately, although even Flanders had to admit dealers accustomed to the horse trade did not necessarily know how to sell cars. That detriment was outweighed in Flanders' view, however, by the money the liaison freed, which could be poured into improving production. From the Studebaker viewpoint, Frederick Fish saw a dilemma. "I recognize that you have the whip end in the entire transaction," he wrote to Flanders in April 1909, "...the more we exploit your car, the more we build up your business...and make a strong competitor in the future."

Merger would neatly solve that problem. Totally opposed to the idea, Everitt and Metzger needed little persuasion to sell their shares to Studebaker for $800,000. This gave South Bend one-third of E-M-F stock, directorships for Clem Studebaker, Jr. and Hayden Eames (a Studebaker man whose automotive experience dated back to Colonel Pope), and a contract to market the entire output of E-M-F cars. Fish did not plan to be a minority stockholder for long, but he did not recognize how formidable a foe he faced in Flanders, who took Everitt's place as E-M-F president.

Both sides maneuvered for position—and ended up in a lawsuit. Flanders accused Studebaker of purposely curtailing sales (by forcing a Garford chassis on every dealer ordering an E-M-F) to drive E-M-F's stock downward. Studebaker countercharged that Flanders was deliberately forcing up production beyond what South Bend could handle. Flanders took steps to set up his own dealership network. The first round in court went to him, and he immediately went to Fish to open secret negotiations. As Max Wollering noted, "Studebaker had to buy the E-M-F company to save face." The face-saving was expensive: $5 million. The stove-manufacturing E-M-F stockholders retired from the automobile business, having quintupled their investment of less than two years earlier.

Walter Flanders cleared $1 million and was given a three-year contract to serve as E-M-F president and general manager for $150,000 annually (which would be doubled in today's dollars). LeRoy Pelletier, who had no stock, was awarded $200,000 for "negotiating services" and kept his $20,000-a-year sales manager job. By now, a 20-horsepower runabout to be sold as a Flanders—not an E-M-F—was on the market, the moribund DeLuxe Motor Car Company factory purchased for its manufacture. Other properties were acquired for production of bodies (Everitt remained resolutely miffed), axles, crankshafts, and other parts, and a factory in Windsor, Ontario, was picked up to produce cars for the Canadian market.

In a single year, Walter Flanders had moved the company to fourth in the industry—behind Ford, Durant's Buick, and Briscoe's Maxwell. Studebaker dealers arriving in town to look over the E-M-F and Flanders cars were entertained lavishly at the Pontchartrain. Walter Flanders stationed associates with megaphones around the banquet room to lead a cheer when he entered. Dealer meetings were pep rallies.

There was a lot to cheer about. A front-page story in the *Detroit Journal* during the summer of 1910 announced that the Flanders 20 and the Model T Ford were almost neck-and-neck in sales. A year later, when Flanders bought the Ford Piquette plant following Henry's move to

Highland Park, the E-M-F factory facilities were the largest in Detroit. Flanders knew Piquette well, of course, having set up Ford's manufacturing there.

But this time, Flanders had miscalculated on the prowess of Frederick Fish, who became president of the newly designated Studebaker Corporation as his father-in-law John Studebaker settled into the board chairmanship. Studebaker owned 100 percent of E-M-F; Fish began treating Flanders like an employee and bringing in his own people, most prominently Albert R. Erskine, the Alabama-born vice president of the Underwood Typewriter Company. "I have been given very little to do around the Studebaker plants lately," Flanders complained to a reporter in announcing that he was leaving despite the year left on his contract. "They claim the right to use my name...I do not believe they have the right, and this difference of opinion may result in some entanglements." It did not. Flanders was congenially released from his contract. His name, as well as E-M-F, was promptly dropped. Henceforth, all cars from Studebaker Corporation would be called Studebaker.

This did not, however, leave Walter Flanders out in the cold, because his old partners wanted him back by now. They had started their own automotive venture and were finding the going rough without his production expertise. The equal-billing problem had been solved by calling the product an Everitt produced by the Metzger Motor Car Company. With their friend Walter back, Barney Everitt and William Metzger agreed to change both their car and company name to Flanders. His ego was easily the equal of theirs combined. What Everitt and Metzger didn't realize was the trouble their old friend was already in.

During his waning Studebaker days, when he hadn't much to do, Flanders had bought for a song a huge Chelsea (Michigan) plant that was described by one cynical reporter as "a large imposing structure originally built on an idealized scale with the funds of the taxpayers of Michigan by a defaulting state official." It included a library, a theater, a gymnasium, and a swimming pool, among "other things to make the workmen happy," but none, apparently, to make the workmen productive. Everyone who tried had lost their shirt on the place. Flanders was sure he could make it work. Because he was still employed by Studebaker at the time and wanted to avoid a conflict of interest, he let

LeRoy Pelletier talk him into producing an electric car and a motor-cycle. The Flanders Manufacturing Company was in receivership by December 1912.

The new Flanders Six (revamped from the Everitt) was introduced in January 1913. Its future did not bode well. Walter Flanders, who had always enjoyed a fawning press, was now soundly lambasted for his "thirst for millions." This was not exactly true. As an acquaintance remarked, "He asked nothing better than a gambler's chance to play for big stakes." No one ever accused Flanders of not being resource-ful. He outdid himself this time. He exchanged one company in receivership for another company in receivership. Setting Flanders Manufacturing adrift, he took on a fiasco someone else had created that was even bigger than his own: Ben Briscoe's United States Motor.

As we have seen, New York bankers had readily agreed to Flanders' terms. The purchase of Flanders (*nee* Metzger) Motor turned a tidy profit for Everitt and Metzger, who went their merry ways. The Flanders Six (*nee* Everitt) became a Maxwell. For a price, even Walter Flanders could submerge his ego.

———

Ego was partly the undoing of Hugh Chalmers. In a breathtaking four-teen years, he had risen from office boy to general manager of the National Cash Register Company. In 1907, he was thirty-four years old and making $72,000 a year. In 1908, he was in Detroit, part owner of an automobile company.

Roy Chapin, whose epic drive to New York in 1900 in the curved dash Olds had already become the stuff of legend, was responsible for convincing Chalmers to switch fields. Chapin had left Olds Motor Works in 1906 to become general manager of the Detroit factory of the E.R. Thomas Motor Company of Buffalo. Earlier, Thomas himself had approached Chalmers about becoming his sales manager in Upstate New York, an offer Chalmers declined, saying, frankly, he would not give up his good-paying job except to work for himself. And that was the opportunity Chapin offered. His overture was well timed. NCR's John Patterson was notorious for the abrupt firing of high-salaried execu-tives, and Chalmers had just been given the sack. Thomas, increas-ingly preoccupied by matters at home (soon to include preparation for the New-York-to-Paris race), was amenable. Chalmers bought part of the Buffalo automaker's interest in exchange for Thomas-Detroit being renamed Chalmers-Detroit. In 1909, only a year later, the company declared a 100 percent cash dividend and paid off the mortgage on its factory. Hugh Chalmers was a super salesman.

The problem became the cars he wanted to sell. The Chalmers-Detroit was medium-priced. Chapin and his partner, engineer Howard Coffin, wanted to invade the under-$1,000 field. Chalmers was thinking luxury. An impasse was avoided by Chapin and Coffin taking their automotive idea elsewhere and selling their interest to the newly designated Chalmers Motor Company.

Unfettered by opposing opinion now, Hugh Chalmers made the Chalmers grander. As a contemporary put it, he "wanted to build the type of car—the big one—that he himself would like to drive." His clientele would include Vanderbilts, Rockefellers, and John Herreshoff of America's Cup fame. Ferrying wealthy customers in a Chalmers to lunch at the Detroit Athletic Club, of which he was president, was a source of pride.

A source of frustration was the keen competition in the luxury field. "It doesn't seem to make much difference to our good friends, the Cadillac, how much six-cylinder 'hollering' we do," he lamented after adding a six to the Chalmers line of fours, "because they seem to be able to ship in the neighborhood of 2,000 of their fours a month." That was nearly twice the Chalmers output. And when Chalmers went six-cylinder across the board, the Lelands trumped with the V-8 Cadillac.

Trying to beat Henry Ford at his own game didn't work either. Chalmers installed his ad manager as president of a company that he established across town to produce the low-priced Saxon, but his heart wasn't in it, even at a distance, and he sold out to his ad manager two years later.

What Hugh Chalmers did best was create innovative ways of merchandising. In 1910, he announced that he would present a new Chalmers annually to the best baseball player in both the American and National Leagues. Although irked that the first winner, Ty Cobb, sold his car soon after receiving it, he had some vengeance the year following when Cobb again won and Chalmers made a splashy presentation of also awarding a car to second-place "Shoeless Joe" Jackson.

An associate once marveled at how facilely Chalmers had sold 13,000 of a new model to his distributors in only three hours in 1916. His voice trailed off, "if Hugh had been as fine a manufacturer as he was a salesman..."

———

Although he never pretended to know anything about sales, Howard Earle Coffin was well aware from the moment he entered the field that no automobile could ever be marketed under his name. As a University of Michigan student working part-time as a letter carrier, Coffin stole what hours he could to design and build a gasoline engine, and then a steam car that he used on his postal route. His widowed mother ran a boarding house in Ann Arbor. One of the boarders was Roscoe B. Jackson. An *habitué* of the place was Roy Chapin. In automotive circles, they became known as "the boarding house gang."

Like so many motor-mad Michigan youngsters, Coffin, Jackson, and Chapin began their careers at Olds Motor Works. There the trio became a quartet with the befriending of George W. Dunham of Cleveland. Coffin and Chapin left Olds in 1906, together with two other company veterans, Frederick O. Bezner and James J. Brady (the timekeeper who dragged the curved dash out of the famous Olds fire of 1900). Their plan was to market a small Coffin-designed runabout that Fred Smith had turned down for Olds. The problem was the money necessary to start a new company: $150,000 to $200,000. About $2,000 each was all they could muster.

Thomas-Detroit was the result; Chapin and company were convinced E.R. Thomas wouldn't interfere much from Buffalo. But that same distance meant that Thomas, as an absentee landlord, might not be eternally enthralled with his subsidiary. Hence, Hugh Chalmers was persuaded to enlist.

Meanwhile, the remaining duo of Olds veterans, Jackson and Dunham, began promoting a car Dunham had designed, which nicely met the under-$1,000 specification Chapin and Coffin were after. Again, after Hugh Chalmers reacted with a yawn, the sextet was faced with a lack of funds. This time, help arrived from Jackson's wife's uncle, owner of one of Detroit's most prosperous department stores, J.L. Hudson. All concerned were delighted to put Hudson's name on the car in exchange for the money to proceed.

One of those curious cases of musical chairs with which automobile history is replete occurred next. Dunham, who designed the first Hudson, signed on as chief engineer for Hugh Chalmers and took Brady with him. Everybody else divvied up the executive positions in the new Hudson Motor Car Company, Chapin as president, Jackson as general manager, Bezner as purchasing director, and Coffin as chief engineer. Temporary home for the company was the abandoned factory of Aerocar, the ill-conceived automotive venture that Alex Malcomson used to inadvertently catapult himself out of Ford Motor Company.

The first Hudson advertisement appeared in *The Saturday Evening Post* on June 19, 1909; the first car left the factory on July 8; by the following July, more than 4,000 Hudsons had been sold for the biggest first-year business recorded to date in the automotive industry. Albert Kahn was already overseeing the construction of the new 223,000-square-foot factory on the corner of Jefferson and Conner, which he had designed as the Hudson's new home. And already the people in charge at Hudson knew that were they to try to challenge Henry Ford in the low-priced field, they might as well name the car after their chief engineer. Wiser it was to find a niche of their own, which was accomplished with alacrity.

In 1913, Hudson introduced its first six-cylinder car, promising 65 miles per hour for $2,450, followed in 1914 by a light six offering the same performance for $1,550. Prior to Hudson, fast-paced sixes had been largely the preserve of luxury-car manufacturers. By 1915, Hudson was advertising itself as the "world's largest manufacturer of six-cylinder cars."

CHAPTER 29

Whoa: Beyond Motor Mecca

PRACTICALLY NOISELESS. Silent as the Foot of Time. All That It Is Cracked Up To Be. The Feel of Quality. The Logical Car. The Car of Absolute Exclusiveness. The Gem of the Road. King of All Weather. Distinctive Transportation. No Waiting for Repairs. All the Troublesome Junk Left Out. Miles of Smiles. Any Road— Anywhere. It's a Glutton for Hills—It Eats 'Em Up. Climbs Hills Like a Squirrel and Eats Up the Road Like an Express Train.

The foregoing slogans extolled the virtues of the Stoddard-Dayton, Mitchell, Searchmont, Dorris, Dixie Flyer, Norwalk, Columbia, Cameron, Cunningham, Sellers, Adams-Farwell, American, Crow-Elkhart, Crawford, and Gale.

These cars were built in factories located in Ohio, Wisconsin, Pennsylvania, Missouri, Kentucky, West Virginia, Connecticut, Rhode Island, New York, Kansas, Iowa, New Jersey, Indiana, Maryland, and Illinois.

The predominance of Detroit has obscured one of the most distinctive aspects of American automobile history: its broad geographical spectrum for more than a generation. Of 48 states, 43 boasted automobile companies. In 1911, the comparative number of manufacturers in the top five states were: Michigan, 75; Ohio, 63; Indiana, 61; and Illinois and New York, tied at 54 each.

———

Ohio's industry was strongest in Toledo, home of John North Willys, number two in the industry through World War I with an annual production that peaked at more than 140,000 units. But if more cars were built in Toledo, more carmakers were located in Cleveland. Pioneering the local industry, of course, was Alexander Winton, whose production in 1913 was more than 1,600 cars, which was quite enough for him. Consistently above 2,000 cars annually was Peerless, despite price tags of about $1,000 more than its cross-town competition. Exemplary engineering was a hallmark of the Peerless—one of the luxury "Three Ps" with Packard of Detroit and Pierce-Arrow of Buffalo—but so was frequent corporate upheaval. President Lewis H. Kittredge was strong enough to survive two company takeovers, by National Electric in 1913, and in 1915 by a secretive New York consortium led by Harrison Williams, purportedly at the behest of General Electric.

Outside influences had not intruded at the F.B. Stearns Company since its founding in 1898 by Frank Stearns and Ralph and Raymond Owen. Although the brothers didn't stay long, the Owens' decision to throw their lot in with Ransom Olds in 1901 didn't stall the Stearns effort. Most of the venture's money had come from Frank's father, who had made a fortune in stone quarries. For a decade, production did not exceed 500 cars per year until 1909, when a "baby Stearns" was added to the firm's sporting luxury-car lineup; in 1912, Frank Stearns adopted the Knight sleeve-valve engine with the same verve as John Willys had in Toledo. Stearns-Knight sales topped the 2,000 mark in 1913, and the 3,000 mark in 1915. The factory of the defunct Royal Tourist was acquired to cope with the increased production.

Especially quick to market in Cleveland was the Chandler Motor Car Company, which was incorporated in January 1913, had a prototype ready for the Chicago Automobile Show by February, a factory being outfitted by April, and the assembly line rolling by July. Within a year, production was nudging the 4,000 mark. This success was due largely to the octet of industry veterans, led by Frederick C. Chandler, who had rebelled against the new management at Lozier and chose to desert rather than fight.

Add to these such Cleveland stalwarts as the White family, who had found automobiles as profitable as sewing machines, and the exemplary electric that Walter Baker had been producing since the turn of the century—"It outsells all other electrics because it outclasses them," the company said immodestly in 1910—plus the electric produced by Jacob Rauch and Charles E.J. Lang that was almost as nice, and it's small wonder that Cleveland was not overawed by Detroit, no matter how many Model Ts Henry Ford was building.

Cincinnati wanted to be another Cleveland but never could manage it. Ohio's Queen City had been a noted carriage-making center but was luckless in the automotive age. Cino was one of a half-dozen automobile factories established there in 1910, and its sponsorship by the long-successful carriage-building Haberer & Company boded well. But by 1913, Cino was no more, Al Haberer explaining that the Ohio River had flooded his plant away that spring. Still in business were Gustav and William Schacht, but what Gustav described that year as a "lack of good business system in all departments" persuaded the brothers to give up car manufacturing and concentrate solely on Schacht trucks.

That left only the Enger Motor Car Company among prosperous Cincinnati automakers, with production surpassing 1,000 units in 1916. But, on January 4, 1917, Frank Enger, in ill health, shot himself. Although he left a note that gave full instructions for his vice president to continue, his widow elected to bail out to protect her investment.

Cincinnati was crestfallen. Just the preceding year, the city had made a concerted effort to lure the Westcott Motor Car Company from Richmond, Indiana, but lost out to Springfield, Ohio. (Perhaps more than financial inducement was involved because a few years later, Burton Westcott was Springfield's mayor.) Spurned and desperate after the Enger suicide, city fathers convinced the hearse-producing Sayers & Scovill Company into adding a car for the living so Cincinnati would have a piece of the automotive pie.

Dayton's slice was ample awhile, some thirty companies giving the industry a go there from the turn of the century. The Speedwell Motor

Car Company was carefully nurtured by founder Pierce D. Schenck, who never followed one mistake with another. When his enthusiasm got the better of him in 1909, he leased one of his new factory buildings to Orville and Wilbur Wright to build their flying machines until his sales caught up with his facilities. John Stoddard and his younger brother Charles hadn't made a mistake in 1904 when they turned their farm implement plant into an automobile factory, but a lulu followed in 1910 when the brothers let Ben Briscoe talk them into joining U.S. Motor. Neither the Stoddard Dayton, nor its lower-priced Courier companion, survived Walter Flanders' axe. After Pierce Schenck departed in 1912, the Speedwell languished.

Columbus sailed a smooth course awhile. The Columbus Buggy Company graced the town with both an electric (which was unusual, most carriage-builders starting off with a highwheeler) and a gasoline car named for the company president. But both the Firestone Columbus and the Columbus Electric were doomed in early 1914 when Clinton Firestone was found dead of apoplexy in his apartment at the Vendome Hotel. A few months later, the company was sold to a couple of veterans of Thomas from Buffalo, who never could get the hang of things in Columbus.

Doing fine with the Great Eagle, ostensibly, was the United States Carriage Company, whose cars were huge and expensive and whose clients included the conservatively rich as well as funeral directors. The recession in 1913 interrupted the favorable cash flow, however, and Katherine Myers, who held a $6,000 note against the company, petitioned it into receivership to protect her money, she said, before other creditors had the chance to do the same thing. Mrs. Myers' husband Fred was the United States Carriage president.

———

Ninety-one cities in Ohio boasted automobile manufacturing companies prior to World War I. Seventy-eight was the count for Indiana. Like Ohio with Winton in Cleveland, the Hoosier state had its pioneering Elwood Haynes and the Apperson brothers in Kokomo. But Ohio had no city that threatened to rival Detroit in its automotive diversity. And Indiana already did. In fact, Indianapolis had as many flourishing car factories as Detroit for awhile.

Consummate engineer Howard Marmon had used the considerable coffers of the Nordyke & Marmon Company, one of the world's leading manufacturers of flour-milling machinery, to launch the Marmon, which gained national prominence after the victory in the inaugural Indianapolis 500. The National, winner of the second Indy 500, was selling well in a wide variety of models. Harry Stutz was prospering both on the racetrack and in the showroom.

Elsewhere in Indianapolis, the Premier had earned a fine reputation after completing three Glidden Tours with a perfect score and weathered receivership in the 1913–1914 recession with a change of ownership and an interesting new feature: the Cutler-Hammer electric transmission operated by a steering-wheel-mounted lever. The Pathfinder, an upper-middle-class car, was known for its styling innovation (covering the spare wheel and concealing the roadster's top in a paneled recess), its bright and captivating color schemes, and its haughty advertising: "The family equipage is as true an index of culture and taste as the home itself," one catalog read. "When Pathfinder the Great rules the garage, the family is well worth knowing."

An especially savvy Indianapolis automaker was Joseph J. Cole, who enjoyed tweaking the Lelands' Cadillac. His Cole was an assembled car, and with grace and humor, he bore the inevitable scoffs of those producers who manufactured their parts in-house. The Cole slogan— "Standardized Car"—deftly lampooned Cadillac's "Standard of the World." With justification, J.J. Cole argued that companies making their own components could scarcely specialize in all of them, and he bought only the best from specialists. Cole's V-8 was designed in Indianapolis but manufactured by General Motors' Northway Division, which also produced Cadillac's V-8. Billy Durant had tried to buy the Cole Motor Car Company at least twice, but J.J. Cole turned him down, worried that his company might be moved to Detroit, lose its identity, or both. Instead, he pursued a "GM of Indiana," a conglomerate of ten Hoosier companies bookended by his own and Inter-State of Muncie. It failed when favorable terms could not be negotiated with the banks.

Statewide, the Hoosier industry was healthy. In Kokomo, the Appersons were winning renown with their sporting Jackrabbit, and Elwood Haynes was making vast additions to his factory complex to build more "Cars of Character." Elkhart was proudly proclaiming "The New

Thousand-Dollar Class Car at $725" (the Crow-Elkhart). In Connersville, priced several thousand dollars more, was the huge McFarlan. In Auburn, the Eckhart brothers, former carriage builders like McFarlan, were producing the Auburn automobile. In South Bend, Studebaker was converting its vast wagon works into an automobile plant.

John William Lambert, who had preceded the Duryeas with a gasoline automobile and who tried first with the Buckeye and Union, was now manufacturing a car bearing his own name in Anderson. Expanding into the Westcott plant when that company ignored Cincinnati to relocate in Springfield was George W. Davis, another long-time wagon builder who had successfully made the transition to motorcars and needed more room to manufacture in Richmond. Another erstwhile Richmond buggy builder, George Seidell, called his automobile the Pilot because he had always wanted to be a river boat captain. He advertised it as "The Car Ahead."

———

Illinois and New York were tied with fifty-four automobile companies apiece in 1911. The cars produced could not have been more dissimilar.

Chicago was America's highwheeler capital until the Model T was reduced to the price of the motorized buggy and rendered the genre irrelevant. The Windy City did not see widespread automobile production after that. Southern Illinois produced some interesting cars, however.

"Ride in a Glide and Then Decide" was the confident slogan of J.B. Bartholomew, a Peoria maker of peanut and coffee roasters, who began manufacture of a car that looked a lot like the Leland Cadillac in 1904. Bartholomew confined production to a couple of hundred annually, when he could easily have broken into the couple-thousand range, saying his conservative policy kept him out of trouble and made him enough money to live well in Peoria.

Halladay in Streator was the training ground for such later industry notables as Eddie Rickenbacker and three of the Fisher brothers (Frederick, Charles, and Lawrence). A company slogan was the cheerful "Every Day a Halladay," which amiability was not reflected behind closed doors. Internal strife brought receivership in 1911 and the admission that the firm's policy heretofore had been "to operate on credit and not enough cash." A new day for Halladay was forecast when the company was bought by Albert C. Barley of Rutenber Motor, the successful proprietary engine company, but Barley was never beloved in Streator. Quite the opposite. His idea for making Halladay profitable was rather Dickensian—working employees up to eighteen hours per day with no overtime—and was bound to get him into trouble eventually.

The trouble that gossips in Moline whispered Will Velie might get himself into had nothing to do with employee relations. Velie treated his workers well—and himself even better. Once car sales passed the 3,000 mark annually, he built himself a forty-six-room mansion, the grandiose likes of which the local citizenry had never before seen. Two dozen Italian stonemasons and artisans were imported for carving and fresco painting. Southern France sent twenty-one varieties of grapes for the Velie vineyard. A conservatory was built to grow bananas for Will's breakfast. Villa Velie was queen of the Quad cities, and Will came to be known as Jay Gatsby on the Mississippi.

By contrast, in New York State, success never changed Herbert H. Franklin. A prominent Syracuse industrialist, Franklin became an automaker after being given a ride in the prototype built by Cornell University engineering graduate John Wilkinson. In production by 1902, the H.H. Franklin Company was the industry's most ardent and long-lived proponent of air cooling. Only reluctantly, in 1905, was the car given a fan because Wilkinson regarded it as superfluous. Absolutely anathema was a radiator; the forward end of the Franklin was a one-piece hood hinged at the front and easily removable. Despite a research budget among the industry's highest—computed as a percentage of income—H.H. Franklin was loath to change unless a compelling need arose. Franklins were so stingy on tires—20,000 miles was the usual life—that detachable rims wouldn't be offered until 1922. Franklin's light wooden frame endured for better than a decade after Dodge Brothers went to steel. The company began championing the sedan body style as early as 1913, when most closed cars were sedate electrics, and variations of the open phaeton were *de rigueur* for gasoline automobiles. Despite a fine road performance, Franklins were regarded as stodgy in some quarters.

In no quarter was that said of the Simplex, the New York City make created principally because it was more profitable to design one's own European-type sporting car than to manufacture a European one under license. A good many buyers of this $5,000 car resided on the Upper East Side of Manhattan where the car was built. Some cachet was lost in 1913, however, when the sons of company founder Herman Broesel sold out following his death, and the new owner moved Simplex across the Hudson to New Brunswick, New Jersey.

The death of George Pierce in 1910 did not alter the course of the Pierce-Arrow Motor Car Company in Buffalo. Two years earlier, son Percy had declared his preference for bicycles over cars and ensconced himself in that phase of the business, leaving the automobile department in the capable hands of Colonel Charles Clifton. Company progress had been steady since the turn of the century when the cars were simply Pierce and the most popular model was the little Motorette; the first luxury model, which arrived in 1904, was called the Great Arrow—and created the market niche in which Pierce would spend the rest of its life. After winning the Glidden Tour an astounding five years in a row, the Buffalo firm celebrated by changing its corporate name to Pierce-Arrow. "Great" was dropped as redundant.

More than any other manufacturer in America, Pierce-Arrow was responsible for adding aesthetics to the merchandising of automobiles. Guided by pioneer adman Ernest Elmo Calkins, the company hired many of the nation's top illustrators (N.C. Wyeth, J.C. Leyendecker, Edward Penfield, and Adolph Treidler among them) to portray the Pierce-Arrow in advertisements that were literally works of art. In 1913, staff engineer Herbert Dawley designed and patented the integral fender headlights that would differentiate the Pierce-Arrow from any other car on the road (although illegal on some roads, even those of New York State awhile, a situation Pierce-Arrow alleviated by continuing to offer drum headlights for those who wished or were required to use them). By 1915, Pierce-Arrow had built its twelve-thousandth automobile and was preeminently in the highest echelon of the market. Only Packard built more luxury cars.

The luxury market by now was almost entirely satisfied by native automobiles. The occasional social grandee might still buy European, but by the teens, imports trickled to insignificance as exports steadily increased.

In 1912, only 868 cars were brought into the country, while 23,720 (about 6 percent of total production) left for overseas markets.

Whenever the importing association trooped to Washington to lobby for a reduction in the 45 percent tariff, the native industry sent its big guns, Billy Durant and Ben Briscoe among them. Some importers responded by establishing their own factories in the United States, with varying success. Daimler produced the American Mercedes in Long Island City until the factory burned down during the Panic of '07; the German company did not rebuild, concluding that anyone who could afford a Mercedes could afford the tariff.

———

Unquestionably, Henry Ford's Model T opened new markets for all automobiles. There was no excuse for not having a car now, no matter what your social class. It became embarrassing not to own a car. Some handwringing in the trade press prophesied saturation in the luxury field, but luxury-car makers continued to flourish.

The wealthy themselves also continued to have flings in producing for their own kind. In 1907, Edward Ringwood Hewitt, who had begun driving a Locomobile steamer in the nineteenth century, tried to market a luxury car that shared first American V-8 honors with Buffum of Massachusetts but discovered it was too costly to produce even for the top market. Eight years later, of course, the Lelands had their competitive V-8 for Cadillac, by which time Hewitt was engaged in his new career as a consultant for Mack trucks. In Springfield, Massachusetts, Otis of elevator renown made a few luxury Sultan automobiles (under license from the French designer) but soon confined production to vehicles solely for its own use. More successful was Charles A. Singer, who used sewing machine money to launch a New York City company that turned a fine profit on a 200-car-per-year output. In Main Line Philadelphia, a Biddle did the same.

In Massachusetts, J. Frank Duryea remained in prosperous association with the Stevens armaments people. In Rochester, New York, the renowned funeral-carriage-producing Cunningham company ventured successfully into the luxury automobile field. The luxury S.G.V. (built in Reading, Pennsylvania, by Herbert M. Sternbergh, Robert E. Graham, and Fred Van Tine) found its way into such royal garages as the King's in England, the Kaiser's in Germany, and the Czar's in Russia—

and was bought at home by Drexels, Vanderbilts, Astors, and those Biddles who found it scandalous that anyone in the family would pursue so undignified a trade as building cars. Irritated that Mercer in Trenton (New Jersey) had chosen to revise his engine design, Finley Robertson Porter left for Port Jefferson on Long Island to produce his $5,000+ F.R.P.

Among those expensive makes renowned for sporting machines was Chadwick of Pottstown, Pennsylvania, the first in the world to use a supercharger. The Vanderbilt-winning Locomobile of Connecticut was in the same league, as was New York City's Simplex. The Lozier was the pride of Plattsburgh, New York, until Harry A. Lozier listened to the call of the Midwest.

Packard envy was rampant in Detroit. Watching the Newberrys, McMillans, and others flaunting the latest showroom models at swank Detroit parties was irksome to those who could not do likewise. Importing a competitor worthy of giving the Packard a run for the money in its own neighborhood would neatly solve that problem. The Lozier oozed East Coast class with such evocative model designations as Briarcliff, Knickerbocker, and Larchmont, and a race record superior to Packard's. Harry Lozier was building 600 cars per year, the Plattsburgh capacity, and wanted to increase production by 500 more. He was paid a call by stellar members of the Detroit Athletic Club, who strove to convince him of the soundness of their logic, the color of their money, and the honor of their intentions.

"At first Mr. Lozier turned them down but they kept at him," factory racing ace Ralph Mulford recalled, "and he finally agreed, provided he could retain fifty-one percent ownership." The Detroiters immediately summoned Albert Kahn to design a factory that would rival Packard's on a 65-acre site at the junction of Mack Avenue and the Belt Line. One million dollars later, Loziers were being built in Detroit. Another million, financed through Wall Street, was expended for a new six-cylinder model.

The following year, 1911, the Lozier was America's premier sporting car, and Ralph Mulford was A.A.A. National Champion. The rest of the news was bad. "[Sales manager] Charlie Emise told me that Lozier was getting out of racing for good," Mulford reflected sadly. "After their move to Detroit and the bankers soaking up all of Mr. Lozier's money, we just couldn't afford it anymore." The Detroit folks calling the shots were despised by Lozier veterans. Emise and a number of others left to start the Chandler Motor Car Company in Cleveland. Harry A. Lozier departed, too, for the same city, to produce another car called the H.A.L. He was immediately unsuccessful. In Detroit, the fellows from the Athletic Club who had thought having a prestige car of their own was such a great idea struggled on.

The foregoing indicates that the ultra-luxury car was essentially Eastern by definition. The geographic rule had exceptions—including Austin ("The Highway King" from Grand Rapids, Michigan), but generally Midwest automakers dwelled most comfortably at a $1,500 median (down about $500 from Cadillac in the upper middle range). Interestingly, Wisconsin, which ranked eighth in the industry in 1911 with twenty-two factories, had no fewer than four exemplary and successful $1,500 cars.

In Hartford, George and Will Kissel, whose previous endeavors had included the hardware and grocery businesses, lumber quarries, sand pits, real estate, and homebuilding, were manufacturing the Kissel Kar. Its worthiness was owed to two people: engineer Herman Palmer, who had been playing cello in a small orchestra passing through Hartford when he saw the Kissel factory from the train window and dropped in for an interview, and coachbuilder J. Friedrich Werner, who had worked with Opel in the old country. Annual production was in the 1,000-unit range.

Twenty-five hundred Cases were produced annually in Racine, the J.I. Case Threshing Machine Company participating prominently both in motor sports to counteract its agricultural image and at county fairs because every farmer there would already be aware of the name.

The Mitchell name took a little longer to become well known. Genesis was in 1903, four decades after William Turnor Lewis (a telegrapher from Utica, New York) joined Henry Mitchell's wagon works and wed the boss' daughter. He was the automobile man. By 1907, Mitchell built 1,000 cars. In 1910, Lewis' son William Mitchell Lewis took over from his retiring father. By 1912, annual production stood at 6,000 cars. Some dissatisfaction at the board level caused Lewis to leave the following year with French engineer René Petard and Mitchell veteran James Cram to set up shop across town as the L.P.C. Motor Company for manufacture of a new car to be deliciously named the Lewis VI, "Monarch of the Sixes." It did not long survive. Mitchell weathered the L.P.C. departure handily. The car seems to have been especially favored by Cook County felons, who regarded it as the best getaway car available in Chicago. Subsequently, hit men would become enamored because the Mitchell's offset windshield provided an area where a machine gun could be hidden until the opportune moment.

In Kenosha, which Tom Jeffery had changed "from a prairie to a city," his son Charles continued to produce the Jeffery in more than 10,000 units per year, aided by evocative prose written by advertising manager Edward S. (Ned) Jordan. Born in Merrill, Jordan had worked his way through the University of Wisconsin as a reporter and married Charles' sister. The marriage would last long enough for Ned Jordan to learn the automobile business.

There were less risky ways than a marriage of convenience to enter the industry. It has been widely believed that by 1910, the era of unfettered competition was waning, and that the capital necessary to begin even limited production had mushroomed past $1 million. This was not the case. The presence of a large number of small manufacturers, each producing automobiles totaling only in the hundreds or even less from birth to death, remained among the seminal aspects of the American industry up to World War I.

The principal reason for the attractiveness of the automobile industry was the unsatiated appetite in America for cars. Even Henry Ford in mass production couldn't make as many Model Ts as the market demanded. Middle and upscale makers found the same felicitous situation. The big factories ignored the hinterlands. Others strode into the breech. In 1909, Onida, South Dakota, proudly declared itself America's most populous automobile town (250 inhabitants, 12 vehicles); most of its cars would have been unknown on the other side of the Mississippi. Testimonials in catalogs of the Luverne Automobile Company of Minnesota reveal that virtually its entire output for twelve years was sold in Montana, Idaho, the Dakotas, and its home state. One model was proudly called the Big Brown Luverne.

Every medium-sized city in America seemed to want its own automobile factory. Chambers of commerce were relentless in their pursuit.

Muskegon (Michigan) built a factory for the Gary Motor Car Company, which failed even before coming to town, so the Henry Motor Car Company, named for designer David Henry, moved in. Henry left Muskegon early following an argument and headed for Iowa, where Mason City beckoned with a job to engineer the Colby. In Muskegon, the Henry limped into 1912 and died. In Mason City, the Colby survived until 1914, although David Henry had been booted out before that and headed to Nebraska and another new automobile called the Omaha.

Ambition ruined many automotive ventures. If the car was good, success was immediate, and many entrepreneurs didn't know how to cope with it. Luverne's longevity was the result of that company's conscious decision to stay small. Others tried to grow too quickly. Virtually every manufacturer in business for several years or more went to the wall with orders on its books.

———

Waiting patiently for delivery, often unaware of any problem at the factory, were the dealers. They did not have an easy time. Granted, switching allegiance was a comparatively simple process, and having many competing cars to sell wasn't unusual. One particularly ambitious dealer in Reading, Pennsylvania, had a daunting lineup: Pratt, Chalmers, Buick, Oakland, Marathon, Cadillac, Apperson, Rambler, Franklin, Auburn, Marion, Pullman, Mitchell, Crawford, Cole, and Abbott-Detroit. His paperwork must have been horrendous. The Hampton, Iowa, dealer who marketed his own Hobbie Accessible carried nine other lines in 1908, but by 1910 began selling Willys and Overland cars exclusively.

The number of cars a manufacturer made was not as important to a dealer as the number he was allotted. Often, a better-known line (Buick, for example) would be given up for a lesser-known make (such as Paterson) that promised a more favorable allotment. Selling the cars was less the problem than getting them. Dealers were pretty much at the mercy of automakers. John Willys became a manufacturer, it might be remembered, because his Elmira (New York) dealership had not received the cars he ordered. Factories did not deliver as promised either, because of innocent miscalculation, plain ineptitude, or downright fraud.

The cost of taking on an agency varied, the minimum being one-half the price of one car. Some entrepreneurs sold franchises to get operating capital—before a single vehicle was built. Any dealer signing on under such circumstances might be regarded as deserving what he didn't get, but such deals often worked out better than those delivering at the outset. Franchising fees, when levied, varied from $200 to $1,000 and were not refundable if the agent chose to break off the relationship when cars were not delivered on time. Automakers were careful not to pin themselves down to absolute deadlines, and dealers frustrated into giving up one franchise for another forfeited the fee.

Selling franchises became a profitable sideline for manufacturers such as Great Western, Lambert, and Crawford, who contracted for more dealerships than they could possibly satisfy. Great Western was even selling them while in bankruptcy, money that neatly found its way into the pockets of the company president and his wife. Champion was even better at the franchising game, arriving at a town's best hotel with a contract and a couple of cars, and leaving with a name on the dotted line and a franchise fee. The dealer had two Champions, for which he had fully paid, and never saw another car from the company.

"Dishonest practices did much harm during years when support was most needed," Alexander Winton would write in the *Saturday Evening Post* in 1930. Grousing about the "forces working against those of us who were honestly trying to succeed," he argued that "we pioneers had to be conservative."

It was like Winton to come up with a perfectly logical excuse for his loathness to change.

CHAPTER 30

■

Electrified, Gentrified, and Politicized

OF ALL THE automobile's components, one disrupted more lunches at the Hotel Pontchartrain than any other. "When the need for a self-starter became apparent," LeRoy Pelletier wrote, "the place took on the aspect of a disorderly and diabolic laboratory rather than a respectable, well-behaved barroom. Electrical starters would spit sparks; air starters would emit shrill whistling sounds; mechanical starters would frequently go off with a bang, filling the air with springs and gears liberally mixed with profanity."

Hand cranking remained the gasoline automobile's *bête noire*. Most manufacturers preferred to believe the problem was one of gender exacerbated when, as Charles Duryea commented in 1910, it became apparent that women would no longer be content as merely passengers. Getting out of the vehicle was "an annoyance which the ladies do not forget lightly," Duryea observed; a self-starter would obviate "a very disagreeable trip around to the front of the engine in a street which more often than not is far from clean."

Granted, a long skirt sweeping over horse droppings offended delicate sensibility. But had that been the only disadvantage to hand cranking, fewer hands at the Pontchartrain would have been enlisted to attempt a solution. "Starter's arm" was a syndrome doctors diagnosed in both sexes, although admittedly some women didn't have the strength to start a gasoline car at all. Experience didn't always prove a good teacher; a half-dozen workmen at Cadillac broke their forearms trying to start recalcitrant company engines.

Solutions were many. Few worked. The Harrison from Grand Rapids tried a pneumatic multi-purpose device that could ostensibly start the engine, pump the tires, test the plugs, light the lights, and dust off the whole car. More singular in his approach in Chicago was Vincent Bendix, although he had to admit that the Triumph was not, as advertised, "a car to direct—not to labor with."

Compressed air absorbed most would-be solvers of the hand-cranking problem. The car that bore Barney Everitt's name after he and Bill Metzger left Walter Flanders was advertised as self-starting, although LeRoy Pelletier advised against overplaying the feature when the E-M-F partners reunited. It didn't measure up well to the description. Alexander Winton had no such qualms about the starter he began installing on his cars in 1909. "We had an air starter that took pressure from the cylinders, stored it in a tank, and kept it ready for use," Winton said in 1930. "[It] was the forerunner, in a sense, of the present electric starter." A broad sense, to be sure. A Winton was still equipped with a crank handle, which owners had to use as often as not.

The impetus to develop a self-starter that would really start began, as the story goes, on a cold winter's day in 1910, when a woman stalled her car on a Belle Isle bridge in Detroit. Cartercar manufacturer Byron T. Carter happened by and offered to assist; the engine backfired, and the crank handle flew off, violently striking Carter in the face. Next by were two Cadillac engineers, who got the woman on her way and her good Samaritan to the hospital. But he died shortly thereafter of complications. Henry Leland was devastated. Byron Carter had been a good friend of his. "The Cadillac car will kill no more men if we can help it," Leland exclaimed as he brought his engineering team together. "Lay all the other projects aside. We are going to develop a fool-proof device for starting Cadillac motors."

The only problem with the story, which one occasionally hears even today, is that Byron Carter had died two years earlier, at home, of pneumonia. Henry Leland was in his late sixties and might be forgiven the mis-recollection some years later. He was so good at moral indignation that no one bothered to check the details. Certainly the incident described could have happened with another good Samaritan. Cranking a gasoline car *was* potentially dangerous. No matter the motivation, Cadillac engineers got to work. But neither they nor Leland were able to come up with the answer themselves. They needed the help of the inventor who would become known as "Boss Ket."

Among the many remarkable facts in the remarkable career of Charles Franklin Kettering is that he left the employ of the National Cash Register Company (NCR) under congenial circumstances. NCR's products no longer challenged him; the automobile did. Setting up shop in a disused Ohio barn under the grandiloquent title of Dayton Engineering Laboratories Company (Delco), Kettering and crew—most of them friends from NCR who prudently kept their day jobs—began developing products to make the automobile better. Hearing about Kettering's work, Leland sent his engineers to investigate, and the result was a collaboration.

Kettering's NCR experience had taught him that an electric motor did not have to be of the theoretical size and power needed to crank an automobile. Just as in a cash register, a small motor subjected to an overload for a short time could do the job. Further, unlike others who experimented with electric cranking, Kettering did not stop there. His vision was an integrated electrical system for starting and lighting, a combination motor and generator. The unit was introduced on 1912 model year Cadillacs. Kettering gave Leland a one-year exclusive contract, then put the device on the market. Automobile manufacturers rushed to his door.

Not among them was Alexander Winton. He thought his compressed air starter was good enough. Even his dealers arriving in Cleveland to squawk in unison didn't change his mind. Plummeting sales finally did. By then, Kettering had long since moved out of the barn, and his NCR friends had given up their day jobs. In 1915, Dayton Engineering controlled one-quarter of the automotive electrical market.

Practically all cars had self-starters now. Billy Durant had felt compelled to put one on his low-priced Chevrolet because Henry Ford didn't have one on the Model T. Into that breach strode accessory manufacturers, happy to provide Tin Lizzie owners the benefits of self-starting for ten to sixty-five dollars. Hand-cranking substitutes for the Model T were generally marketed as aids for the ladies.

———

That the self-starter opened a brand-new market by putting women behind the wheel of the gasoline automobile overstates the case. Likewise, the self-starter did not single-handedly sound the death knell for steam and electric cars.

Steam carmakers did themselves in. By 1911, the Lane brothers of Poughkeepsie had decided the manufacture of barn door rollers was easier. That same year, the White Company of Cleveland, after producing more than 9,000 steamers, went to gasoline car production exclusively. The White brothers (Windsor, Rollin, and Walter) were publicity savvy and had heartily endorsed the promotion department's idea in 1910 to offer a White gasoline car to Jack Johnson and a White steamer to Jim Jeffries, for pacing road work prior to their world's heavyweight championship fight. The company's first gasoline car couldn't have been introduced more cleverly than with a tie-in to an impending boxing match that was the talk of the nation.

By 1912, only the Stanley twins remained to spread the steam car gospel. They had never been much interested in either excessive propaganda or production. Output did not exceed 800 units annually. Customers paid cash and waited for the Stanleys to build their cars. If the brothers didn't like the demeanor of someone stopping by the factory, he wasn't allowed the privilege of buying a Stanley. If a prospective client asked for a written guarantee, he was shown the door. The Stanleys regarded their word as their bond. Their obduracy would have done Alexander Winton proud. In 1917, in their late sixties, the Stanleys turned over their business to Francis' sons-in-law; Freelan was spending most of his time in semi-retirement in Colorado anyway. The new owners found themselves with a famous name and lots of problems.

The future for the electric seemed much brighter. Indeed, an article in *Collier's* in 1915 noted that, unlike the "superseded" steamer, the electric had won "a definite place for itself in the automotive world." Since 1912, electric makers had banded together to produce their own automobile shows; overall sales of 34,000 electrics that year indicated their continuing appeal. In a test in Boston, an electric and gasoline runabout were dispatched over a route with twenty stops in the downtown business district, and the electric was back a full three minutes faster. The coachbuilding Healey & Company of New York City built an experimental electric that easily made it to Philadelphia on a single charge. In *Harper's Weekly*, the electric was extolled as the most viable type for commercial use. And industry commentator H.L. Barber said point blank as late as 1917 that the electric was "a perfectly balanced piece of mechanism and the one type of the automobile with the least fits and starts."

On a per capita basis, there were more electrics in Denver than in any other city in the nation. Local engineer Oliver P. Fritchle had leased a mammoth roller-skating rink for production of his $2,000–$3,000 "100 Mile Electric." Fritchle sold the rights to the hybrid gas-electric he had also developed to Chicago's Woods Motor Vehicle Company which, having just lost the number one spot in the electric field, decided to diversify.

In 1914, by which time E-M-F had become Studebaker and Walter Flanders had wrestled Maxwell out of U.S. Motor, LeRoy Pelletier parlayed himself into the Tiffany Electric Car Company, announced a Bijou roadster at $750, and proclaimed his "ambition to become the Henry Ford of the electric automobile industry." LeRoy was too ambitious. Better fortune was enjoyed by the Milburn Wagon Company of Toledo, which began producing electrics about the same time and sold more than 2,500 even before launching a national ad campaign. Building electrics on a custom basis awhile was C.P. Kimball & Company, the piano makers of Chicago. Hoping for a larger share of the market, Baker and Rauch & Lang merged their operations in Cleveland.

Ironically, the most famous electric and the new number one in the industry arrived from the center of gasoline-car country. Long-time carriage-builder William C. Anderson chose to name his product by the city in which it was built. The Detroit Electric was a favorite of industry V.I.P.s. Henry Ford and associates Jim Couzens and Harold Wills, Packard's Henry Joy, Cadillac's Wilfred Leland, Chalmers' George Dunham, Hupmobile's Walter Drake, Frank Duryea, and

Howard Marmon all purchased electrics—some for their own use, others as gifts to their wives. Henry Ford bought one for wife Clara, another for his friend Thomas Edison.

The world's greatest inventor and worst businessman—in Ford's apt description of his mentor—was still striving to improve his alkaline battery. William Anderson was Edison's best automotive customer. "There will be a hot time in the Electric Vehicle biz in advertising," the inventor promised when the contract was signed for the Detroit Electric to be powered by Edison batteries. It was a beaming Anderson who heard Edison exhort that "gasoline-driven cars have no legitimate place in city traffic." That was advocacy and good public relations from someone so renowned. But when the inventor boasted that he would develop a charger that could fit in a suitcase and charge a battery in five minutes, Anderson hit the ceiling. How many sales of today's electrics would be lost if Edison continued to promise a revolutionary version tomorrow?

———

Nor did the gasoline automobile escape revolutionary thought. In Dubuque, Iowa, the Adams Company, manufacturers of grave markers and park benches, was persuaded by Fay Oliver Farwell to produce a car with a rotary engine that spun like a carousel. From Los Angeles came the Hydromotor, an amphibian car. Winters in Clintonville, Wisconsin, suggested the development of four-wheel drive to Otto Zachow and Bill Besserdich, as it did to candymaker Ernest Rosenberger of Mankato, Minnesota. Bad roads everywhere convinced Milton O. Reeves (who had designed the Aerocar for former Ford partner Alexander Malcomson) to try the Octoauto. When four front wheels complicated the problem of turning sharp corners, Reeves revised to the Sextoauto.

Nobody was better at the *extravagante idée*—the gimmick, if you will—than Ben Briscoe, who sought to stay newsworthy by diversion: two engines for the same car. "Buy the Four. Use it a month," Briscoe ads declared. "If then you decide you want the Eight, simply pay the difference and a small charge for installation work."

The assumption was both engines would perform. The issue was how much performance the owner wanted. More was expected of automobiles now. They had to do more than just run. Turn-of-the-century advertising emphasized the basics: "If you go out on a Desberon [from New Rochelle, New York], you will come home and on the machine"; "Buy a Bates [from Lansing, Michigan] and Keep Your Dates." Although a facility for avoiding breakdowns was not an advertising strategy for long, promotion departments seemed compelled to retain the negative: "No Hill Too Steep, No Sand Too Deep" (Jackson); and "No Clutch to Slip, No Gears to Strip" (Metz). But gradually, gentler and more positive qualities came to the fore. "Have You Tried to Hear It Run?" Matheson of Wilkes-Barre asked. "The Full Jeweled Corbin" was the phrase from New Britain, Connecticut. In Adrian, Michigan, "The Lion Forty Runs Like Sixty." "Built on Integrity," OhiO (sic) of Carthage crowed, "Guaranteed for Life." Death for that company was swift.

But, if not immortal, cars were better. One of four patents granted in the United States revolved around the automobile. With so many hands at work, the product had to benefit. Harrison Boyce marketed an engine temperature gauge that also doubled as a radiator ornament. Although a tacit admission that cars could run into things, the addition of bumpers was welcome. So, too, was the lengthening list of features included as standard equipment: top, windshield, horn, and head- and tail-lights. A hand-operated windshield wiper arrived by 1910. The following year saw front doors adopted throughout the industry, a move that followed the relocation of the gear and brake levers from outside to the center of the car, and the shift of the steering wheel from the right to the left. Not until 1914 would Alexander Winton go to left-hand drive, however, Pierce-Arrow would wait until 1920. In 1913, Goodrich had the best news: the replacement of fabric with cord in tire casings, tripling tire life and eliminating the fear of sudden blowouts that often happened when the fabric layers rubbed together. Better tires made for a more comfortable ride that was enhanced by improved devices to cushion road jounce—except for the Model T. What shock absorbers does the Ford have? The answer was "The passengers."

Nearly a half million cars were produced in the United States in 1913, ten times more than France (which ranked second). Seventy-five percent of the world's cars were American. Hooves hadn't been completely replaced, however. Rural horses remained at 20 million; the urban equine population was large (140,000 horses in Manhattan alone). Well into World War I, industry proponents were still arguing that a horse "consumes the production of five acres of land" annually and multiplied by all horses to an area "as great as Ohio, Indiana and Illinois combined," which could instead be used for human "food stuffs of which the world is in such sore need."

That argument didn't impress horse lovers like William Allen White, who waxed nostalgic from Emporia, Kansas, that "Old Tom...will go longer on a forty-cent bale of hay than these new-fangled vessels of wrath fitted into destruction with a bucket of gasoline and a cord of rubber." *Country Life in America* reported in 1912 that "physicians are now announcing that the opaque smoke exhausted from the rear of some automobiles is not only nauseating, but that large quantities of it are actually dangerous to the health of the community." The following year, the same magazine had to concede that "considerations of hygiene and sanitation are conspiring with those of speed and economy" to completely eliminate the horse. Learned and lengthy treatises were published to prove scientifically that horses were harder on roads than cars.

Automobiles were everywhere. To a question by a financial writer about when car sales would reach the saturation point, Billy Durant's quick answer was "When they quit making babies." Already in 1911, magazines were talking about a move to the suburbs by millionaires and professionals, "and the reason for this condition rests upon the automobile." Architects found new work designing a substitute for the automobilist's barn and livery stable, "which will be an ornament to his place as well as mere housing for his machine."

Bankers had moneymaking ideas, too. Horace M. Kilborn started a cooperative of 100 financiers similar to himself to build a like number of cars (called Orson after Kilborn's son), but at about $8,000 apiece, the vehicles were exorbitantly priced, and Daniel M. Brady (brother of "Diamond Jim") claimed to have spent another $1,000 on repairs before his Orson "blew up." Kilborn's company blew up soon afterward. The Club Car Company of America was another of the financial community's short-lived attempts to cash in. As Durant often said, bankers just didn't understand the car business.

———

Business and industry were not alone in realizing the money to be made with automobiles. Governments at every level now recognized the potential windfall. Registration and taxation of vehicles had begun at the turn of the century, if haphazardly. Naming one's vehicle as one did a boat was quickly discovered as unworkable. New York State stipulated that the owner's initials be painted on the car, another short-lived idea. Numerical identification was the logical solution and the owner's responsibility at first. But when the more artistically inclined surrounded the number with landscapes, sunsets, and other scenes painted on the car, New York State stepped in and required the number be on a tag or plate affixed to the vehicle, which again was the owner's responsibility initially.

Alabama required only that automobilists sign in with the probate judge of their county to receive a number, not that they display it. Chicago was plagued by inveterate speeders using bogus numbers that were "judiciously changed at frequent intervals, in order that no one number might become fixed in the minds of the police." With indignation, *The Horseless Age* declared that "speed traps and the practice of convicting automobilists on mere 'seconds' and 'mathematics' should be abolished."

By 1910, automobile registration was the law in thirty-six states, and states had taken over the making of license plates. Only twelve states required all drivers to be licensed, however; seven more demanded it only of professional chauffeurs. In 1911, a book of 1,200-plus pages was published, detailing "all the reported cases decided during the first ten years of the use of motor vehicles upon the public thoroughfares." Conformity was nowhere. One judge might equate possession of a car with possession of a dog (the owner responsible for all damage caused by either). Another might regard the stealing of a half-dozen chickens (ninety days in jail) more heinous than the heist of a Model T (sixty days)—a genuine case that sounded like a Ford joke.

No laughing matter to automobilists was the practice of states to require registration of anyone driving within its borders. Particularly reluctant to give up these lucrative licensing fees was New Jersey, long the bane of motorists, which regarded itself as the convenient thoroughfare that speeders used to get from New York to Philadelphia and vice versa. The White Company of Cleveland sent one of its unregistered cars to Trenton as a test case, declaring the tariff unconstitutional. New Jersey finally gave in. Intramural rivalry among the states posed an onerous solution. "The spectre of Federal registration has vanished for the nonce," *Automobile Journal* reported in 1911. "Like Banquo's ghost, 'twil rise again..."

At last, Washington officially recognized the automobile. Endorsement arrived in 1909 when the U.S. Post Office made its first substantial commitment to motor vehicles in city collection and began encouraging its utilization in rural free delivery. That same year, the U.S. Army used automobiles in its annual war games, and William Howard Taft became the first U.S. president to order an automobile for the White House.

Unlike his rough-riding predecessor, Taft was a car enthusiast. "These buzz wagons are the finest things in existence for the enjoyment of the open air," he said one day as he maneuvered his 300-pound bulk behind the wheel. At a White House reception, his mention to a New England mayor that he had driven through his town brought the reply, "Yes, Mr. President, and the dust hasn't settled yet." Once Taft drove a Packard nearly 60 miles per hour around a race track. Prior to his inaugural, Taft's personal car was a White steamer. For the White House garage, he added a Baker Electric, two Pierce-Arrows, and a couple of motorcycles for the Secret Service.

President Taft made cars politically correct. No longer did politicians feel it necessary to apologize for owning one. Woodrow Wilson, who as president of Princeton had decried the automobile as promoting socialism, was now governor of New Jersey and driving an electric. (He became a Pierce-Arrow fan upon arriving at the White House.) Ohio Senator Warren Harding enjoyed making the trip from Marion to Washington in his fast Stevens-Duryea. In Massachusetts, a rising politician named Calvin Coolidge was a motorist, too, but his driving pace was moderate to slow, and he observed all speed limits. Even Teddy Roosevelt was converted. Elwood Haynes was ecstatic when the former President ordered one of the Kokomo cars to be ready for him when he returned from an African safari.

The advantages of campaigning by car were manifest. Ambitious Michigan politicians used the Jackson a lot because of the symbolism of its logo (a photograph of "Old Hickory" himself). But time was a more vital factor in campaigns. One Indianapolis mayoral contest was described as "literally a political battle of automobiling, the two men speaking at four, five and six places in as many portions of the city in a single night." Conversely, the automobile also meant that more people could get to the places where politicians spoke. A rally for William Jennings Bryan was said to be good for forty acres of parked Model Ts.

No campaign used the automobile to better effect than the movement for women's suffrage. The American car symbolically liberated women long before they could vote. The automobile defined autonomy. Suffragettes found that equality was effectively demonstrated behind the wheel—or, prior to 1913, with a crank handle in hand. All over the country, women hell-bent for emancipation organized local auto tours to spread the word.

Alice Huyler Ramsey was a role model for many. In 1909, she became the first woman transcontinentalist. The wife of a Hackensack lawyer who never learned to drive, Alice was, in her words, "a born mechanic" and loved automobiles. That she handled them well was noticed by Cadwallader Washburn Kelsey at an endurance contest on Long Island. Then sales manager for Maxwell-Briscoe and a wily concocter of publicity stunts, Kelsey proposed that Mrs. Ramsey cross the country in a Maxwell. To his surprise, Alice agreed. With two sisters-in-law and a friend—Nettie, Maggie, and Hermione, none of whom could drive—she motored from Hell's Gate to the Golden Gate in forty-one days. Kelsey enjoyed a publicity bonanza for Maxwell.

A few years later, Kelsey was gone (having resigned in horror when Ben Briscoe started his U.S. Motor empire), and Walter Flanders (who could scarcely be accused of empathy for female emancipation) found it expedient to pick up where Kelsey left off. "Maxwell Takes Up the 'Feminist Movement'," the trade press headlined in announcing the company's plan to hire saleswomen on an equal basis with men for its dealerships. One hundred prominent suffragettes gathered at the Broadway showroom in New York to celebrate the new policy as Maxwell's first automobile saleswoman dismantled and assembled a Maxwell engine in the window. The policy lasted as long as the publicity did.

Women automobilists were widely scorned by their male counterparts. When Vivian Prescott announced her plan to compete in the Indianapolis 500, Speedway officials hurriedly declared that "under no condition" would women be allowed to race. They would not even be allowed in the pits. In Cincinnati, after an automobile accident involving a female, the mayor opined that women should not be allowed to drive at all. The prevailing attitude was nicely summed up in a letter to the editor, signed by "One Who Likes Ladies in the Tonneau" (perhaps the first published admission of someone's fondness for a back-seat driver): "I always give them all the room and run my own car into the ditch or anywhere to get out of their way."

It was Harlan Whipple who didn't get out of Joan Newton Cuneo's way during the first Glidden Tour. Swerving to avoid his Peerless on a bridge in Connecticut, she drove into a river bed and was pinned underneath her White steamer, but got both herself and the car out and back on the road. "The fastest driving I ever did in my life was from Bridgeport to Hartford after that accident," she told a reporter. Thirty-two of the thirty-three Glidden contestants attended the official banquet that night. Mrs. Cuneo was shuttled to another dining room to be "entertained by a special committee of Hartford ladies."

—

The Glidden Tours were reliability events of up to approximately 300 miles conducted from 1905 to 1913, each year over a different route in the East or Midwest. His fortune already made from lacing New England with wires for colleague Alexander Graham Bell's telephone, Charles J. Glidden had needed a hobby and chose motoring because he thought it might help him lose weight. Photographs indicate that did not happen, but in less than a decade, with his wife and a chauffeur, Glidden traveled 46,000 miles in thirty-nine countries and saw more of the earth than anyone else on wheels.

Glidden's purpose in inaugurating his tours was to promote cross-country motoring in the United States. He anticipated manufacturers might regard them as promotional tools and tried to avoid commercialization by stipulating that each car entered had to be driven by its owner. Manufacturers could easily get around the rule, of course, by signing up their executives to drive the newest cars off the line. The inaugural tour in 1905 had seen Ransom Olds in a Reo, conspicuous as a Midwest producer among a field of Easterners including Ben Briscoe and Jonathan Maxwell on Maxwells, Walter White for White, Percy Pierce for Pierce, and a flock of Popes on various hyphenates (-Hartford, -Tribune, and others) in the Colonel's empire, which was then still going strong. The lavish news coverage that event received swelled entrants to seventy-one by 1906 and included Billy Durant for Buick and Elwood Haynes on one of his cars amid a wide Midwest showing in a run that began in Buffalo, wended its way to Montreal, and ended in Bretton Woods, New Hampshire.

A complicated penalty system and the five-year victory run of Pierce of Buffalo served to dampen manufacturer interest in the Gliddens. The year 1911 saw a record number of eighty-six entries, but that was perhaps because the event was moved to mid-October with a Florida destination, which proved more enticing to industry V.I.P.s than the summer tour that had ended in Chicago the preceding year. The last Glidden was held in 1913.

One tour official explained the decline as the result of manufacturers "enjoying too much prosperity." During the life of the Glidden, the automobile truly came into its own. Its reliability didn't have to be proved anymore. Its demand could not be met. With promotion less essential, manufacturers became reluctant to submit their cars to a grueling tour that might turn counterproductive. Later Gliddens had found photographers and reporters finding news principally in those contestants who came to embarrassing grief attempting to ford streams, slog through quagmires, or traverse ruts so big that, in one entrant's immortal phrase, "You could bury a hog in them." Automobiles had improved vastly. The roads on which they traveled had not.

———

The Gliddens did promote motoring, as Charles Glidden hoped. Yankee innkeepers were persuaded to offer "The Ideal Tour," a booklet outlining a scenic route through New England with noonday and night stops at member hotels. B.F. Goodrich inaugurated a travel bureau in 1910, and the Automobile Club of America and A.A.A. became more travel conscious. Gulf Oil began giving away road maps in 1913.

Finding one's way remained difficult in the countryside. Few roads were marked, except for those direction signs that automakers and others used for advertising. Studebaker published a leaflet showing the route from South Bend to Chicago, as did other manufacturers in other cities. Garages and businesses with an automotive affiliation provided customers with local road maps of their own. Accurate mileages and detailed counsel were provided in the Blue Books, which had begun in the East at the turn of the century and by now blanketed much of the country. But "turn left at the watering trough" obviously would not be good advice forever.

In Pottstown, Pennsylvania, Lee Chadwick took time away from producing the automobile carrying his name to invent the Automatic Road Guide, a dashboard instrument geared to the front wheels with a calibrated disc that told the driver where to turn and in which direction. At its 1911 New York Automobile Show introduction, Thomas Edison, whose phonograph had inspired Chadwick, was impressed but saw a potential problem: "What about wear on the tires throwing you off?" Chadwick had anticipated that with a "tire wear compensator." But all this ingenuity was useful only if a disc was available for the two cities between which a motorist wished to travel—and at more than $50, the Chadwick Automatic Road Guide was expensive.

"Uncertain is the outcome of all automobilists," wrote Theodore Dreiser about getting lost on the trip back to his home state that he celebrated in *A Hoosier Holiday*. A New Yorker, Dreiser hadn't been in the countryside much since leaving Indiana as a teenager and eagerly accepted his friend Franklin Booth's invitation for the trip. Booth's car was a Pathfinder, his chauffeur was nicknamed "Speed," and the A.C.A. mapped out a meandering scenic route that took the travelers through Upstate New York before heading west. By Elmira, Dreiser was agog. "I was beginning to get the idea of the magnitude of the revolution which the automobile had effected," Dreiser wrote in comparing horse-and-buggy days to the scene before him. "On this Saturday morning the ways were crowded with farmers coming to town in automobiles, or as Speed always put it, 'in autos and Fords.' Why this useful little machine should be sniffed at is a puzzle to me, for it seems to look nearly as well and to travel quite as fast as any of the others." As a new automobilist, Dreiser lacked discernment. Never would the Model T be more extravagantly complimented, but one doubts the prudish Henry Ford read much that was written by the author of the scandalous *Sister Carrie*. The journey continued to open Dreiser's eyes to the realities of the new age—and how brusquely progress had stalled. "There are no good dirt roads as you know, if you've autoed much," said a grizzled old-timer at an A.C.A. office directing the travelers to a less scenic detour. "There ain't no such thing."

Outside most city limits, roads were dust bowls in summer, snow banks in winter, and mud holes in spring and autumn. Glidden participants in 1907 had joked sardonically that a fund should be taken up for the widows and children of the non-survivors. As motoring increased in popularity, increasing pressure was put on politicians to do something.

Oklahoma Governor Haskell declared that he would ask for all his state's prisoners back from Kansas (there was no penitentiary in Oklahoma) to begin a new highway system. Then he organized a committee and attended a conference. Little more than that had happened anywhere in the United States since 1903—nearly a decade earlier—when the National Good Roads Convention convened in St. Louis.

Finally, Carl Fisher had enough. Bricks would still be being laid at the Indianapolis Speedway if he had worked at the pace of the government. "The highways of America are built chiefly of politics," he would say, "...the proper material is crushed rock or concrete." He knew a better way. The automobile industry would undertake the job of building a grand highway from coast to coast. Carl Fisher was sure he could sell manufacturers on the idea with a good dinner and "then a good cussing."

CHAPTER 31

Roads and Recession, Other Battles Loom

CARL FISHER CHEERFULLY admitted that he "loved to see the dirt fly." Stirring a crowd to fever pitch was a favorite pastime for its own sake; when he had a cause, Carl's zeal increased exponentially, and his enthusiasm knew no bounds. In September 1912, 300 industry leaders were treated to unfettered Fisher *à la carte* during dinner at the German House in Indianapolis.

Why wasn't there a paved road all the way from the Atlantic to the Pacific, he exhorted? The Panama Canal was a bigger engineering challenge and a whole lot more expensive, and it was almost finished already. If the automobile industry pledged a mere one-third of 1 percent of its gross profits for three years, $10 million could be put to work right away. "Let's build it before we're too old to enjoy it," Fisher pleaded. His target date for completion was May 1, 1915, so that "a corps of 25,000 automobiles can be taken over this road" for the opening of the Panama-Pacific International Exposition in San Francisco. What a grand mind's-eye parade that was. And it all seemed so simple. Before coffee cups were filled and cigars passed around, Fisher collected several hundred thousand dollars in pledges.

Within two weeks, he had pulled in more than $1 million. Goodyear president Frank Seiberling offered $300,000 without even asking his board. Packard's Henry Joy pledged $150,000, and John North Willys the same. Roy Chapin chipped in with $100,000 from Hudson. Of all automobile and accessory manufacturers, only one balked, but he was the most important of all. Henry Ford's cooperation was crucial.

Aware of the likelihood of a Ford stumbling block, Fisher had enlisted emissaries such as Elbert Hubbard, Thomas Edison, and even the President of the United States, to intercede on the project's behalf. To no avail. Finally, in front of the pig exhibit at a Midwest county fair, Fisher lobbied Ford himself. True to his reputation, Carl was able to convince the manufacturer to come onboard. But Ford's subsequent action proved typical, too. He reneged and told Jim Couzens to write his regrets.

"As long as private interests are willing to build good roads for the general public, the general public will not be very much interested in building good roads for itself," Couzens wrote. The Ford Motor Company believed its money was best spent in lowering the price of the Model T. Taxes should build good roads, and the public should be educated to their importance. Such was the official word from Ford. Unofficially, and quietly, Edsel Ford sent in a personal contribution.

The Ford rebuke notwithstanding, Henry Joy voiced qualms that "the enterprise has strewn in front of it almost insurmountable difficulties" but did not waffle after succumbing to the Fisher enthusiasm. Indeed, he embraced it with equal verve. A national highway had long been a Joy cause. He was furious that Congress appropriated nearly $2 million to build a Lincoln Memorial along the Potomac, when the money might better be spent building good roads "in the name of Lincoln." Congress didn't back down on the memorial in Washington, D.C. But Lincoln now became the name for the national highway project, too.

Carl Fisher was gratified by Henry Joy's support. Joy was as measured as Fisher was mercurial, as deliberate as Fisher was daring. The project needed a stabilizing influence, someone to keep it literally and figuratively on the ground. Joy had recently recruited Alvan Macauley—

a National Cash Register veteran who had turned Burroughs Adding Machine Company into an efficient moneymaker—as general manager for Packard. This freed Joy from daily administrative duties, time he could now devote to being president of the new Lincoln Highway Association (LHA). Joining Joy on the LHA board were Roy Chapin of Hudson, Frank Seiberling of Goodyear, Emory Clark of Detroit's First National Bank, and, of course, Carl Fisher.

But Fisher soon backed away from total involvement in the project. Still committed, he changed his will to bequeath one-third of his estate to the Lincoln Highway Association "before my knuckleheaded relatives get their hands on it." But, as he told A.G. Batchelder of the American Automobile Association, "I think it's time to pull out personally and take away from our possible subscribers the idea that this road plan is mine. If any particular noise is made for any particular person or small clique of persons, this plan is going to suffer."

Prudent Henry Joy had concluded that the LHA should not build the road itself but should assist the nation in building it. Major funding was to be the responsibility of the government, with LHA-donated dollars used to plan the route and educate the public. Joy had bought the Couzens-*cum*-Ford line. Fisher, the man of soaring vision, was brought crashing down to earth. Appealing to individuals and civic groups for $5.00 donations that bought a certificate, a membership card, and a radiator emblem (giving more rewarded one with a paperweight) wasn't his cup of tea. But he was a team player.

On the day of the first meeting of the Lincoln Highway Association, Carl Fisher was on the road in a Premier, leading a parade of Indiana cars across the country to San Francisco. Every major Hoosier manufacturer was represented: Marion, Pilot, American, Pathfinder, McFarlan, Henderson, and Empire. The first Indy 500 winner, Ray Harroun, drove a Marmon. Elwood Haynes was in his glory. Whenever the caravan stopped, crowds gathered to listen enthralled as the "Father of the Automobile" told the gripping story of how he built the first car. His Kokomo rivals rued that they had sent but not driven the two Appersons. An English observer along for the ride lamented the Haynes preference for "William Jennings Bryan cocktails" (nothing stronger than milk) and telegraphed back another perspective: "Have been able to gather numerous impressions of American roads, chiefly in the shape of bruises on various parts of my anatomy. Rockies fine—Salt Lake City ditto. The lake smelly. The desert beastly. Reno ripping..."

When Carl Fisher announced the tour, more than 100 communities from Indiana to California asked the caravan to stop by. With Lincoln Highway banners flying, the Hoosier cars came to town like heroes. Every day was the Fourth of July. The nights were not always as pleasant. Fisher slept on top of a chicken coop once to escape "the biggest bedbugs known to man" and enjoyed telling about the crony who smashed a mandolin on the wall of a bunkhouse because he thought it was an insect. Everywhere the caravan motored, enthusiasm and support for the Lincoln Highway project followed. Fisher thought he had done well.

Perhaps too well. Although he never specifically said the Lincoln Highway would pass through the towns visited by the Hoosier Tour, Fisher's standard stump speech on behalf of the project energized the local citizenry. Civic-minded merchants who offered free gasoline to the caravan generally expected consideration in kind. Fisher wrote the LHA board that intramural rivalries within states would be "quite a factor to straighten out, but I believe it can be done." Then he decided competition should be encouraged among local governments and states, with the prize of Lincoln Highway routing delivered to those communities promising to build the best roads. Henry Joy was horrified. Political promises could not be the bedrock of the Lincoln Highway. Common sense dictated the route be the shortest distance between two points, concomitant to amenable terrain and other geographic factors.

This would not be easy. The railroad boom of the nineteenth century had proven a bitter object lesson for rural America. Many towns bypassed by the railway had deteriorated; being ignored by the Lincoln Highway could be their death knell. Utah's Bill Rishel, whose road experience dated back to William Randolph Hearst's turn-of-the-century cross-country bicycle race, felt shortchanged because Joy's quickest way across the desert had the highway heading due west from Salt Lake City out of Utah and across the entire width of Nevada. Large motoring organizations weighed in, too. The Automobile Club of Southern California was livid that the Lincoln Highway would terminate in San Francisco and not Los Angeles.

From Illinois came word that, because of the road's name, bypassing Springfield would be tantamount to sacrilege. Linton, Indiana, offered to change its name to Lincoln to get the highway. "Fort Dodge, Dubuque and Other Towns Sore," the *Boone News Republican* headlined when that Iowa town made it to the preliminaries and the others did not. So furious was Colorado at being bypassed altogether that Henry Joy relented and inserted a dog leg to Denver. Then from the White House came a request for a loop below the Mason-Dixon line into the District of Columbia to "symbolize a united North and South." The symbol would require 172 extra miles, so Henry Joy extended regrets to the President and rued the Denver dog leg.

The Lincoln Highway Association had decided on the Conference of Governors to present the Lincoln Highway route and to plead for national unity. In 1913, this annual get-together was in Colorado Springs. On August 26, at the Antlers Hotel, in a meeting closed to spectators and the press, the Lincoln Highway map won general gubernatorial approval. Two weeks later, the public announcement was followed by a barrage of letters to the association, asking for route changes. Henry Joy quietly removed the Denver dog leg as a dangerous precedent. Colorado never forgave him.

For every blotch, there was a bright spot. The Portland Cement Association donated 2.35 million barrels of its product to the cause, which added up to $3 million of concrete, all of it used for the construction of "seedling miles." In this instance, the Lincoln Highway Association did become a road builder to exercise total control. Seedling miles were sited in areas where the contrast between a concrete road and unadulterated mud would be most graphic and at least six miles from the nearest city, to coerce the community to fill in the connecting stretch. The first seedling mile was built in Illinois, west of DeKalb, in the fall of 1914.

Because good roads were in their best interest, automobile manufacturers, Ford excepted, had supported the Lincoln Highway from the beginning. Whether the support was tangible or moral depended on how they were faring. A good many were in deep trouble. In 1913, as Carl Fisher was reaching crescendo in his Lincoln Highway aria, U.S. business moved into recession. There had been signs earlier that the rose-colored glasses through which most automakers viewed their future might begin to cloud. Urged onward by crusading journalists ("muckrakers," in the parlance of the day), state governments boldly legislated factory safety and workmen's compensation laws, only to be thwarted by organizations such as the Employers Association of Detroit, founded by Henry Leland, who believed paternalism was the better way to meet all working-class needs, no matter how old the workers.

But child labor laws were winning wide public support, and if the handwriting on the wall was not yet legible, the portent of the scribbling was chilling for any labor-intensive business. Faced with the prospect that manufacture might soon become costlier, the immediate reality of an economic downturn plunged the automobile community into gloom. Only Henry Ford's five-dollar day, editorialized the *Cleveland Plain Dealer,* "shot like a blinding rocket through the dark clouds of the present industrial depression."

Hundred of manufacturers looked for any silver lining anywhere. For Charles Metz of Waltham, Massachusetts, salvation followed the flawless running of the three-car Metz team in the final Glidden Tour of 1913. No other team finished with a perfect score, a performance Metz parlayed into his best sales year ever. Metz had always been good at seizing opportunity. Saddled with a gigantic inventory five years earlier, he had cleverly turned his parts into profit by advertising "$350 Buys This $600 Car." The only catch was the owner had to put the car together himself through the "Metz Plan," fourteen packages priced at $25.00 each, the purchaser buying each installment of parts as his pocketbook permitted (with the car's starting handle in the last package). Until its price tag moved dangerously close to that of a ready-made Model T, the Metz Plan was popular and profitable. When it ceased to be either, the Metz decision for the Glidden helped keep the wolf from the door of the former Governor Gore mansion, which served as company headquarters in Waltham.

Others gave up. Charles Frederick Herreshoff of the boatbuilding family and the Bergdoll brothers of Main Line Philadelphia found more congenial pursuits than automobile manufacture. Montgomery Ward & Company discontinued its car. (Sears, Roebuck already had.) Companies new to the field didn't stand a chance, like Henderson of Indianapolis, begun by veterans of Cole in 1912, or Cadwallader Washburn Kelsey's three-wheel Motorette, which he launched in Bridgeport, Connecticut, after leaving Ben Briscoe's sinking ship. Some really fine automobiles were killed by the recession. "It was an excellent car and would take an awful beating," Harry Truman said of his 1913 Kansas-built Stafford. "You can be sure of that if one lasted me as long as three years..." Stafford was gone by 1914.

Gone that year, too, were several companies in the forefront of the early industry: Columbia (descended from the Electric Vehicle Company), Selden (whose patent had launched industrial war), and Thomas (whose Flyer had won the 1908 New-York-to-Paris race, still the most grueling contest any automobile has ever survived). The number of casualties of the 1913–1914 recession was staggering: Alpena (Michigan), Atlas Knight (Springfield, Massachusetts), Colby (Mason City, Iowa), Cutting (Jackson, Michigan), DeTamble (Anderson, Indiana), F-A-L (Chicago), Keeton (Detroit), Luck Utility (Cleburne, Texas), Marathon (Nashville, Tennessee), Michigan (Kalamazoo), Midland (Moline, Illinois), Palmer-Singer (Long Island City, New York), Spoerer (Baltimore, Maryland), Staver (Chicago), Vulcan (Painesville, Ohio), and Wahl (Detroit), among many others.

American Motors Company of Indianapolis had hoped the Hoosier Tour might be its salvation. This expensive "Car for the Discriminating Few"—famous for its sexy underslung model and such evocative designations as American Scout, American Tourist, and American Traveler—was "oohed" and "aahed" all the way to San Francisco in 1913. But in 1914, after a dozen years in the field and a lifetime production of 45,000 cars, American was no more.

———

"The highway is open to traffic now," Henry Joy exulted early in 1914. "It already connects 42nd Street, New York, with Market Street, San Francisco." That spring, a Packard ceremoniously dipped its wheels in the Atlantic en route to doing the same ten weeks later in the Pacific. It was the start of a stampede. Previous coast-to-coast treks by automobiles numbered fewer than 100. As many as 5,000 cars took to the Lincoln Highway in 1915 alone, bound for San Francisco and the Panama-Pacific International Exposition.

That same year, the Lincoln Highway Association published its first complete road guide. Already the route was marked well for its full length, with a capital "L" set against red, white, and blue stripes stenciled on telephone poles and whatever else would not move. The LHA membership rolls continued to swell; paperweight sales remained strong. The association made a movie of the entire highway in 1915, its costs underwritten by Fisher, Joy, and colleagues, and its profits donated to the cause. Packard, Studebaker, and Stutz provided the cars. Rare indeed was the autoist who had not heard of the Lincoln Highway.

Among cross-country travelers in 1915 was a New York socialite who dabbled as an occasional writer and would later become famous for establishing a modern code of etiquette. In 1915, Emily Post accepted an assignment from *Collier's* to report on the Lincoln Highway, provided she was not expected to "rough it"—no sleeping bags under the stars, and no canned beans baked over a campfire. Emily demanded hotels and dining rooms. *Collier's* said fine. Son Ned took leave from Harvard to serve as chauffeur because his mother couldn't drive, and she proceeded to prepare for the trip. There does not appear to be a mistake that Emily failed to make.

For her car, Mrs. Post chose a low-slung custom-built four-seater sporting Mercedes. Her luggage included a steamer trunk, a collection of hatboxes, and a picnic basket complete with silver tea service. Most of these amenities didn't make it beyond Albany. In their stead came objects of practicality. Emily even shopped at F.W. Woolworth's for saucepans, utensils, cheap plates, and a breadbox to put it all in. She became a sport, about everything except the Lincoln Highway. "If it were called the cross continent *trail* you would expect little, and be philosophical about less," Emily complained, "but the very word 'highway' suggests macadam at the very least." She grew to dislike her slinky European car. "If it was only a Ford or a Cadillac, I could fix you up right away," one mechanic said when the Mercedes needed help along the way. "But a bearing for that car of yours'll like as not have to be made." The big surprise for Emily was how much she enjoyed herself: "It is your trouble on the road, your bad meals in queer places, your unexpected stops at people's houses; in short, your misadventures that afterwards become your most treasured memories." Had she to do it over again, she would, but in an American car "that needs little care and can be jolted without injury."

Henry Joy's choice for such a trip was a Packard, naturally, and he was a seasoned traveler by now. For a half-dozen years, he had trekked west for his annual summer vacation, shedding business suit for chaps, ten-gallon hat, and spurs. Henry looked the complete cowpoke and reveled in the great outdoors. He used his 1915 trip to road test the brand-new twelve-cylinder Packard Twin Six. Meanwhile, Carl Fisher led another Hoosier Tour, its ranks recession-thinned to fifteen cars, to trail-blaze the Dixie Highway to the resort he was creating in Miami Beach.

Forty-two of the forty-eight states had highway departments now, and thirty of them had actually appropriated money for road building. On the federal level, the difference was dramatic. Despite sixty proposed bills, only a half-million dollars had been allotted to road building in 1912. In 1916, the Federal Aid Road Act would earmark $75 million to be spent during the next half decade. The Lincoln Highway Association had made a big impact.

Henry Joy continued as its champion, writing articles for any magazine that offered space. One editor expressed surprise "at how much juice could be squeezed out of...a somewhat dry subject." Joy cautioned colleagues against hyperbole about how good the nation's highway was; granted, New York to Chicago could be driven in thirty-five hours, but from Illinois to Wyoming, much of the Lincoln Highway remained a mud hole that might take weeks to cross. Still, as Joy pointed out, "with the doors of Europe shut with a mailed fist in the face of American pleasure seekers," traveling one's own land had fresh appeal. World War I was raging.

———

On May 7, 1915, off the Irish coast, the British liner *Lusitania* was sunk by a German U-boat. Among the 1,153 passengers lost, 128 were Americans. Isaac Trumbull had been en route to close a 300-car deal with an English concessionaire; the Trumbull Motor Car Company of Bridgeport, Connecticut, died with him. When the torpedo struck, Alfred G. Vanderbilt, who had made a career of trying to own a faster car than his cousin Willie K., shouted to his valet, "Come and let us save the kiddies"—and they did so silently to the end.

Charles Jeffery was among the 761 survivors. Sales of the four-wheel-drive four-wheel-steering Jeffery Quad his Kenosha company had developed for the U.S. Army Quartermaster Corps increased so dramatically with the onset of war that Jeffery had already farmed out production to Hudson, National, and Paige. The likelihood was that he would have to enlist the assistance of other auto factories after this trip. The torpedo changed his life. "The ship heeled over so much that passengers were clinging to the deck rail," he remembered. "It was a terrible sight—their helplessness with the great ship steadily going down from under us. I knew there was no place for me in the boats, so I stayed on the navigating bridge waiting for the final plunge." He was in the water four hours before being picked up by a trawler.

The *Lusitania* sinking raised a furor in America. Claiming the ship had been carrying war matériel, spokesmen for the German government insisted their placement of advertisements in American newspapers warning U.S. citizens not to sail in Allied ships had absolved them of responsibility. Informal assurances were given to President Wilson that such an attack would not recur. National defense became a national issue.

"Preparedness" was the new watchword and a philosophy espoused vigorously by Hugh Chalmers, Harry Jewitt, and John Dodge. From Hudson, Roy Chapin declared he and Howard Coffin were "heart and soul behind the movement." From Packard, Henry Joy took on the opposition as "loud-mouthed bleaters for peace at any price [who] ought to be shot or punished in some proper manner."

Loudest of the bleaters—and the specific object of Joy's increasingly vituperative attacks—was Henry Ford, who saw war as the result of capitalism, greed, and "the dirty hunger for dollars," and who vowed to burn down his factory rather than convert it to war production. Again, Ford was a one-man bandwagon. But he did have one ally in spirit. Billy Durant was not keen on preparedness. He had his own war to wage.

That Billy had not been able to challenge Henry Ford head-on was a battle lost but did not change Durant's overall strategy. With production nearly tripled between 1914 and 1915 (from 5,000 units to more than 13,000), and profit margins averaging $100 per car, Chevrolet was heaping cash into Durant's coffers. Billy had plans for the surplus. He began buying General Motors stock. The bankers made it easy for him.

"Your board does not believe in running into debt," GM's 1915 annual report noted in declaring corporation profit at $15.2 million. The bad news was General Motors' market share had steadily decreased from the 20 percent when Durant was in charge to less than 8 percent, and the phenomenal success of the Model T Ford had not been the only reason. Watchful stockholders had to reflect on the inroads into the market that Willys-Overland and Studebaker were making at GM's expense. And they had to be miffed that the bankers resolutely refused to pay any dividend until the corporation's $15 million loan was fully repaid.

General Motors stock prices fell, the more disgruntled shareholders bailed out, Eastern bankers cashed in their 1910 bonus stock, and Billy Durant bought up. He even snagged some of the holdings of Lee, Higginson that James Storrow, his eye ever fixed on the bottom line, let go. Even before he started buying, Durant controlled a huge block of General Motors stock: his own original holdings, and those of family, friends, and business associates who had held onto theirs, as Buick president Walter Chrysler commented, because of "faith in his genius" and the belief that "some day Billy would get back on top." To those who had always believed in him, Durant added new allies. His powers of persuasion were formidable; Chrysler's famous phrase that he could "charm a bird right down out of a tree" well described Billy.

The already charmed Louis Graveret Kaufman, who had helped Durant secure the Tarrytown factory for Chevrolet, was Billy's matchmaker in the financial world. An introduction was all Durant required; if the match made was someone who saw the automobile industry as a reasonable gamble for the future, Billy had a sale. John Jacob Raskob was sold. He was treasurer of E.I. du Pont de Nemours and Company, a firm frequently quoted in the press as being "heavily into powder." With the war in Europe, du Pont munition sales had skyrocketed. But even if America became involved, which was no certainty, peace would be the ultimate inevitability—and sure to put a crimp in gunpowder sales. After listening to Durant, Raskob convinced the man for whom he had begun work as a $1,000-a-year bookkeeper that General Motors stock was "easily worth double what it is selling for..." Pierre S. du Pont bought his first GM shares.

There was no time to waste. September 16 was the date of the fifth annual meeting of the bankers' trust; the last $2.5 million installment of the GM loan was to be repaid two weeks later. Heretofore, that loan and the interest it paid had been Storrow's paramount concern. Now, his suspicions aroused about Durant, the idea of the banking syndicate retaining control of a debt-free GM had renewed appeal. Storrow began to buy stock and solicit proxies. So did his banker colleagues.

Durant rushed to preserve his base. With GM stock prices now rising steadily, friends who had held through the hard times might be tempted to take long-deferred profits. "Don't sell any part of your holdings," Billy begged a cousin, "I will protect if necessary." To friends in Flint, he importuned, "Do not let any of our crowd sell any stock. You will hear something that will please you within thirty days." And he sought proxies. Music to his ears was the click of the briefcase clasp that opened to reveal all the GM stock A.M. Bentley of Owosso had received when he sold his Reliance Motor Company to Durant in 1909. Bentley didn't even ask Billy for a receipt.

"Everything coming fine. Proxies galore with some of the nicest letters you ever read," Durant wrote to his son-in-law. "The opposition are out with their hammers and the anvil chorus has already started." Daughter Margery seemed to revel in the intrigue as much as her father. Her husband was plainly concerned that Storrow's control over GM president Charlie Nash was a real problem. Billy Durant found it hard to believe that the go-getting cushion stuffer from Durant-Dort carriage days, the friend he had specifically recommended to the bankers after his ouster, would now be planted so firmly in the enemy camp. But Doc Campbell convinced him and advised, "If you get control and can hold Chrysler, it would not matter about Nash going."

As September 16 approached, Storrow cronies suggested Billy was lying about both the number and identity of his proxies and made "serious representations in regard to Mr. Durant's character." That made Billy mad. "Nash is acting like a baby," he wrote to Doc Campbell, "and Storrow is so disconcerted that he is willing to resort to blackmail to secure even decent representation." The doctor hoped for a payback: "It will be happy days in the village if we ever can get in position where we can even up old scores with some of the sons of bitches."

At this point, no one, including Durant, knew precisely where he stood. Subterfuge could help. Confident the news would get back to Storrow, Billy showed Wilfred Leland a floor safe full of stock certificates and proxies. And he dropped in on Charlie Nash and pointedly asked him to stay on as president of GM "when" (not "if") he regained control. The stage was set.

On the evening of September 15, Durant's long-time and long-suffering secretary, Winfred Murphy, began counting the proxies. He was still counting early in the morning. No matter how many recounts, the answer remained the same: close but not quite enough. At the moment, only Durant and Murphy knew that.

Hours later, as the participants gathered, a nervous Storrow took Durant aside and asked if there would be any problem at the meeting. "There won't be any trouble, Mr. Storrow," Billy replied evenly. "I'm in control of General Motors today." Some tight-lipped negotiation followed. Storrow named six of his people to the board; Durant named six. Neither would accept the other's slate. Pierre du Pont, who had been brought to the meeting by Kaufman and Raskob, seemed confused. Billy had left him with the distinct impression that control was a *fait accompli.*

This meeting before the meeting dragged on and on. Billy kept smiling and kept cool. Finally, an exasperated Storrow suggested a solution: to expand the General Motors board to seventeen members, he and Durant to choose seven each, with du Pont (who was already on Durant's slate) to choose the remaining three. Billy readily agreed so long as du Pont's choices were not "connected with either faction." Du Pont chose Raskob, a brother-in-law, and a long-time business associate. The annual meeting itself was, in one participant's phrase, "a love feast."

Ambiguity remained, the du Pont trio a buffer of sorts between the Durant and Storrow factions. In the sorting out of executive chairs, Charlie Nash was to remain president of General Motors. Pierre du Pont took the chairmanship of the board, and Billy settled into the vice presidential chair. But in press reports, no ambiguity existed as to who had emerged the victor. There was a second-coming tenor to the tales of the Durant triumph—or a royal restoration at least. "Long Live the King," Kaufman jotted on one adulatory press clipping that he sent to Billy.

"The fact that you and I haven't always drilled in the same spread doesn't keep me from sending on my sincere congratulations at carrying thro' what you set out to do...," Fred Smith of Olds wrote. "Your success pleases a whole lot of people who admire a well-scrapped scrap and an ability to bide the time till the other pup has chased himself tired." Harry Shiland, Billy's old Buick service manager, offered to buy him congratulatory chop suey the next time he was in Detroit. "You deserve it all and anything more you want," Arthur Mason wired from Chevrolet. "Please accept my last shirt." A neighbor from Flint enthused, "Five years ago when the gang had you with your back to the wall, I prayed that I might live long enough to see you clean their clocks... My prayer has been answered."

Billy Durant had no intention of awaiting divine intervention to solidify his position in General Motors. With Kaufman's assistance, the Chevrolet Motor Company was incorporated in September to bring together all existing manufacturing facilities and to expand into others in order to rival "within another year or two the Ford and Willys-Overland companies, as to output." That was only half of it. Capitalization was quickly increased from $20 to $80 million. Around Christmas, information was bruited about that anyone holding one share of GM stock could trade it for five of Chevrolet. Then Billy Durant smiled and waited.

———

Henry Ford was not smiling. His only bright spot in recent months had been the visit with Thomas Edison to the Panama-Pacific International Exposition, where the Ford exhibit—a replica of the Highland Park line that saw twenty Model Ts assembled daily in a three-hour demonstration—was the runaway hit of the show. Otherwise, all was gloom.

Cheer would have been difficult, in any case, for a pacifist who saw practically everyone around him rallying to Woodrow Wilson's preparedness flag. Jim Couzens' defection was a particular blow. Because his son's death in the Model T that had been a fourteenth birthday present plunged him into despair, Couzens was in California on extended leave when the October issue of the *Ford Times* was put together. Shown the galleys upon his return, he exploded after reading Henry Ford's suggestion that Lord Balfour and his commission, soon to visit the United States in quest of war loans, be thrown off the dock. Couzens said the piece could not be published. "I own fifty-nine percent of the stock of this company," Ford shot back, "and I guess it can go if I say so." Couzens couldn't argue with that and quit the company.

The breakup had been coming for some time. Both men were responsible for the Ford Motor Company's success, but the one whose name was on the door tended to forget that. Henry admired his colleague's fiscal acumen, although he seldom told him so. Instead, he enjoyed tweaking Couzens about his dour expression and his irascibility—"Old Bear in his den" was Fordese for "Couzens in his office." Moreover, Henry resented the time Couzens spent in California grieving for his son, snorting that he "has been at the plant only 184 days during the past year." Couzens was fed up. Immediately after resigning, his face still red with anger, he told bookkeeper Frank Klingensmith that he "had had enough of [Ford's] goddam persecution." It was time to move on anyway. That Couzens had political ambition was obvious from his next move. He put on his hat, walked out the door, and drove downtown to get his version of the resignation story into the newspapers first.

Couzens' job was parceled out to Klingensmith and Edsel Ford, but Couzens' restraining influence was forever gone. How sorely it would be missed was apparent almost immediately. Henry Ford thought he might be able to end World War I by sending a ship to Europe.

A newspaper story reporting the deaths of 20,000 soldiers in a single day in a meaningless battle had prodded Ford to declare to a Detroit reporter that he would spend half his fortune to end the carnage. Henry had, as Mark Sullivan wryly observed, "a good deal of practical faith in the power of half his fortune." So did a number of pacifists, most notably Louis Lochner, secretary of the International Federation of Students, and Rosika Schwimmer, a Hungarian author on a lecture tour of America, both of whom eagerly latched onto Henry as their personal Nobel peace prize. Ford was a catch for anyone wishing to espouse a cause grandly.

The luxury liner *Oskar II* was chartered for a voyage of Americans to Norway to talk peace with the Europeans. "We're going to get the boys out of the trenches by Christmas," Henry Ford told the press in announcing that such peace-loving luminaries as John Burroughs, William Jennings Bryan, John Wanamaker, Thomas Edison, and Jane Addams of Hull House would be joining him on the transatlantic trip. En route to New York, Henry stopped by the White House to see President Wilson, who was cordial but refused an endorsement.

The press was scathing. Even Detroit papers declared Ford's forth-coming trip "a humiliation to his city and country." New York news-paper cartoonists were wicked: Henry Ford turning a crank in the side of his head (*Herald*), driving a winged Model T into the clouds (*World*), tunic-clad and hurling a Tin Lizzie at the god of war (*Times*). Of hun-dreds of editorials, those favoring the Peace Ship could be counted on the fingers of one hand. Even evangelist Billy Sunday said, "Henry has P.T. Barnum skinned a mile." One by one, the celebrated passen-gers discovered they had previous commitments. Purportedly, Henry offered Edison $1 million to make the trip, but the inventor, as was his wont in compromising situations, turned totally deaf.

In later years, Clara Ford referred to this period as the worst in her marriage. She was furious that the expenses Rosika Schwimmer charged to her husband included a "peace wardrobe" of evening gowns and fur coats. She was sure the Peace Ship would be sunk by a U-boat. Both she and Edsel begged Henry not to go, but even Clara's uncontrollable weeping could not dissuade him. Her only victory was insisting that Samuel Marquis of the Sociological Department and John Dahlinger, a young bodyguard/chauffeur, accompany Henry to protect him against voyagers she was convinced were "after something."

On a cold and gray December 4, from the docks in Hoboken, Henry Ford set sail with his fellow passengers—half of them journalists, many of the others "along for the ride"—in the cause of peace. Fighting broke out halfway across the Atlantic, the ship dividing into factions supporting and opposing President Wilson. By the time the *Oskar II* docked in Oslo, Henry Ford had a cold and quite enough of bickering for peace. When, five days later, he met with the press, he talked about the new Fordson tractor as a more profitable product to manufacture than guns. Then he turned to Lochner and said, "Guess I had better go home to Mother. You've got this thing started and can get along with-out me." Hardly. Without Henry Ford, the peace delegation was no longer news and was shuttled off to low-level government functionar-ies, whose only role was to be courteous.

"I wanted to see peace," Henry said when he returned to America. "I at least tried to bring it about. Most men did not even try." That simple statement touched even the cynical. The same newspapers that had lam-pooned him unmercifully now effusively praised his idealism. Perhaps only Henry Ford could have made such a smashing success of failure.

CHAPTER 32

Gearing Up for War, Other Battles Won

"NO SINGLE EXPERT, either military or automobile, appears to have foreseen the extensive use of automobiles to be developed within a month of the outbreak of war," W.F. Bradley wrote. An Englishman living in Paris who began his career supplying American automobile magazines with French news items, Bradley liked to be in the thick of things. He couldn't have been better placed. He was there as the German army prepared to march on the French capital and General Joseph Gallieni commandeered every taxicab in town to transport five infantry battalions to the front. Back and forth, all night long, Bradley watched the 600 little two-cylinder Renaults ferry their important cargo. The French attack at dawn caught the Germans completely by surprise. Paris was saved.

Although the war would be bogged down for months in bloody trenches and the muddy fields of Flanders, the heroics of the "taxis of the Marne" had immediate impact. A huge demand arose for military cars and trucks. "It is certain that the war authorities had never contemplated having to go outside Europe for their supply of automobiles,"

W.F. Bradley said. But within a month, the French government had sent an emissary to the United States to buy several thousand trucks. Many more delegations would follow.

Because heavier chassis could be easily converted to support two- and three-ton carrying loads, luxury car manufacturers had been early entrants in the commercial field. Except for Stearns of Cleveland, who abandoned trucks in 1914 when Rolls-Royce offered a contract to manufacture aircraft engines, every major U.S. carmaker with a truck model produced for the war effort. Pierce-Arrow in Buffalo built nearly 15,000 two- and five-ton versions. Stearns' neighbor in Cleveland, the White Motor Company, sold 18,000 trucks for $52 million to the Allied governments, an effort so lucrative White elected to discontinue car manufacture in 1918.

Jeffery had a fine head start on military production. Reo smartly named its 3/4-tonner the Speed Wagon and, with heavy government contracts, abolished Saturday half holidays and abandoned the factory baseball team. Trucks accounted for 35 percent of all Reo production during the war. The largest producer was Packard, averaging 6,000 trucks per year.

The only automaker worried that too much truck production might sully its luxury image was Locomobile. Following its spectacular Vanderbilt Cup winning year of 1908, the Connecticut company had quit racing to focus solely on catering to the whims of its well-heeled clientele. Tiffany designed lamps and metal work; Elsie de Wolf added the decorator's touch to interiors. Astutely, Locomobile brought the profits home that had previously gone to independent coachmakers by hiring J. Frank De Causse away from the noted French *carrossier* Kellner et Fils and setting him up as chief designer of its own in-house Custom Body Department. Anxious to capitalize on the war bonanza, but as subtly as possible, the company changed the name of its commercial vehicle to Riker. "The Locomobile is a thoroughbred," an official explained. "The Riker truck is a Percheron." Whether this reference to a draft horse pleased the chief engineer who had been responsible for making a thoroughbred of the Locomobile is something A.L. Riker never revealed.

Not everyone could capitalize. Luxury builders who had traveled dubious avenues to weather the recession were now going under or

selling out. An armaments manufacturer was in the factory of the celebrated Chadwick by 1915, Simplex was acquired by aero engine manufacturer Wright-Martin, and Pope-Hartford's plant was sold to machine
tool maker Pratt-Whitney. The World War I industrial boom saw the
final liquidation of the once-vast Pope empire; creditors received ninety-
two cents on the dollar, which would have pleased the Colonel.

Retiring to a life of financial comfort in Massachusetts was Frank
Duryea. He was only forty-five years old. A nervous breakdown in
1909 had convinced him that living to a ripe old age was more likely if
he reduced life's stresses, and the recession was stressful. In January
1915, despite a "clean sheet on the liability side of the ledger," Stevens-
Duryea ceased car manufacture, citing "the uncertainty of general business conditions." The company had never built a truck. Its plant and
equipment were sold to Westinghouse. Frank lived to be ninety-seven.
His affluence was a source of irritation to brother Charles, who continued his struggle to make a decent living in the automotive field. "The
Biggest Idea in the History of the Motor Car and the Last Word in
Automobile Construction" was his latest effort. It was a triangular-
shaped machine with one wheel in front and two in the rear. Investors
were slow to express interest.

———

Slow to move, too, on maximizing the effectiveness of motor transport
in war was the U.S. government. Immediately after the Renault taxi
caravan to the front, the Society of Automotive Engineers (S.A.E.)
offered its services to the War Department to determine the criteria by
which military vehicles should be built. The offer was accepted two
years later.

By then, the Council of National Defense was in full swing, chaired
by Howard E. Coffin. The Hudson Motor Car Company had made
Coffin rich and itching for a new challenge. President Wilson's dollar-
per-year job to organize the American industrial system for war was
tailor-made for Coffin. Five other S.A.E. colleagues joined him. The
automobile-savvy W.F. Bradley was the French connection, reporting directly to Coffin on modifications indicated by field use of motor
vehicles.

How effective this small cadre was depended on how the observer
looked on preparedness and mobilization for war. "A brave and

pathetic sight," the hawkish Benedict Crowell wrote of Coffin and company, "a pinch of dust amid the serene planets and dead worlds that swam the Washington cosmos." Arguing that the Civil War was "well into its third year before either side really settled down to it," dove-ish Arthur Bullard countered that "There is no reason for us to be ashamed that we do not know how to fight—free people are never prepared for war."

A Mexican revolutionary helped put America in the mood. Early in 1916, a group of U.S. citizens was shot by bandits in Chihuahua, an event followed by a savage raid across the border in New Mexico, which killed more innocent civilians. That Pancho Villa was responsible was doubted by no one. Angered that his military status had waned in Mexico, Villa turned his wrath on the United States, which had officially recognized the legitimacy of Villa's opponent for power. President Wilson retaliated by calling out the National Guard and ordering a punitive expedition against Villa. Chosen to lead it was America's best-known military man, General John J. "Black Jack" Pershing. Capturing the Mexican leader "dead or alive" was the mission's tacit purpose. Villa never would be found, but so well publicized was the effort that, as Henry Ford had discovered with his peace ship, sincerity and zeal can be their own success. Certainly, too, this fray provided at-home evidence of the effectiveness of the automobile in battle.

Pushing the Villa bandits back across the border was easy. Ferreting out those who had retreated to a heavily fortified headquarters 200 miles south was the problem. Devising his own variation on General Gallieni's playbook, Pershing ordered an ambitious young lieutenant and fourteen of his men into three Dodge Brothers touring cars to storm the bandit's garrison. Open countryside sheltered the ranch for more than a mile on all sides. Driving in tight formation with throttles to the floor, the three Dodges were upon the bandits before they could prepare.

The first motorized combat charge in the history of the U.S. Army was a smashing victory. Garrison leader Colonel Julio Cardenas was captured, and two of his aides were killed. Other rebels fell to the guns that blazed from the Dodges, and still others fled half-nude from windows into the countryside. Not one of the American soldiers was hurt. "We couldn't have done it with horses," Lieutenant George S. Patton,

Jr. exulted afterward. "The motorcar is the modern war horse." Pershing placed an order immediately with Dodge Brothers for 250 more of the company's touring cars for use in the Mexican expedition.

The search for Pancho Villa was the best publicity event for the automobile since the San Francisco earthquake. Recognizing that were Jeffery and White, each with a nose for news and a reputation for clever promotion. Both companies saw to it that their vehicles were part of the expedition. Best by far at providing amenities for the press, which arrived on the border en masse, was Packard. His many cross-country camping trips had taught Henry Joy those creature comforts that could be adapted to living in sagebrush, and it didn't surprise anyone that he would want to join this adventure in the great outdoors. The Joy hospitality to journalists was rewarded with lyrical tributes to his product. Wrote Hi Sibley, "It was like riding on velvet when those big Packards laid back their ears and breezed along as though their only ambition was to catch up with the horizon."

————

On the horizon for Billy Durant that spring of 1916 was unequivocal control of General Motors. His offer of five shares of Chevrolet stock for every one of GM traded was an offer few could resist. In fact, so overwhelming was the response that Billy trimmed the trading margin to four to one. Storrow and his banking friends recognized what was happening but could do nothing. From his officially neutral corner, Pierre du Pont watched the internecine struggle until it became obvious who was going to win. Actually, the trading offer had expired by the time du Pont decided to take advantage of it, but Billy let him in on the original five-for-one terms. Du Pont was an important man to have in his corner.

"Chevrolet Buys General Motors" was the way several newspapers headlined the coup when it became history. Storrow didn't bother attending the board meeting in New York. That evening, Durant took his wife to dinner at the local Childs, a popular inexpensive eatery chain. "Well, I took General Motors back from the bankers today," he commented casually. "Oh, Willie," Catherine sighed. "At least we could have gone to the restaurant in the Plaza."

As president of General Motors, now reorganized from a company into a corporation, Charlie Nash found himself in an untenable position.

During the struggle between Durant and the banking faction, he had insisted that "I do not want to get mixed up in any way with this scrap." But in truth, he already was. Temperamentally, he had gravitated toward Storrow as a sunflower does the sun. His quarter-century of friendship with Billy was not as strong as the deep-seated conservatism that told him the man was trouble. "Well, if that doesn't cork it," Charlie reminisced. "Here I spent years putting GM back on financial footing just to have Wild Bill take it back. I had to leave." He said that Durant offered him more "than any man's worth" to stay.

Nash was probably face-saving. Loyalty was paramount to Billy, and Charlie had let him down. Certainly there was a time when he would have done virtually anything to keep his old friend, but not now. There are two other versions of the same event. One has Billy saying quietly to Nash at their last meeting, "Well, Charlie, you're through." In the other, when informed of Nash's resignation, which was submitted to Pierre du Pont as chairman of the board, Durant's reply was a terse "It is the honorable thing for him to do."

The next question was who would take Nash's job. Billy hated titles and was loath to take this one. "Don't make the mistake of putting a figurehead in for president," Doc Campbell implored his father-in-law. "It must be you and you only." Durant was persuaded.

Billy was as anxious to keep Walter Chrysler on as he was to let Nash go. As a factory manager, Chrysler was top-drawer. Durant offered him the Buick presidency. Chrysler long remembered his first visit to Billy's palatial home. "In five minutes he had me feeling as if I owned the place," Walt said of the man with the most winning personality of anyone he had ever known.

But personality alone did not sell Chrysler on the job. Billy offered him $500,000 a year ($9 million in contemporary dollars). Four years earlier, Walt had started at Buick for $6,000. Now he was making $50,000, a figure he had insisted upon to Charlie Nash under the threat of leaving. But with Billy, there was no haggling, no negotiations. The half-million-dollar salary was Durant's idea. "He just sprang it on me that way," Walt remembered about the 7:00 a.m. meeting. "He didn't bat an eye. I couldn't think for a few seconds." His composure regained, Chrysler was bold enough to add a condition: full authority, no interference, "I don't want any other boss but you." Billy drummed his fingers lightly on the table, stretched out his hand, and said, "It's a deal."

Icing on the cake for Durant was knowing that Storrow wanted Chrysler, too. Billy was hurt by Charlie Nash; he hated James Storrow. Maneuvered out of GM, Storrow was looking for other fertile automobile fields. Nash was at liberty, of course, and the banker was hoping Chrysler, with whom both he and Charlie were friendly, might join them. It almost happened. But the board of directors of the Packard Motor Car Company balked. Absorbed with the Lincoln Highway and war preparedness, Henry Joy had been anxious to sell. Within a year, he resigned from the company.

With Packard a miss in Detroit, Storrow and Nash looked in Kenosha. Charles Jeffery was willing to talk. The horror of those hours in the cold Atlantic after the *Lusitania* sank still haunted him. And his father's sudden death reinforced Jeffery's awareness of his own fragile mortality. Five million dollars was a bargain, given the company's facilities and reputation, but it was enough for Jeffery to live luxuriously for the rest of his life.

Chrysler was invited in on this deal, too, but begged off, explaining that he and his wife were settled in Michigan and didn't want to move to Kenosha. That smacked of an excuse. Billy's half-million-dollar offer had arrived in the meantime. Storrow and Nash carried on. The Thomas B. Jeffery Company became Nash Motors, and the partners were in business. An ad headlined "U.S. Marines Adopt Nash Quad" included the *Semper Fidelis* logo and some stirring words encouraging patriotic young men with a sense of adventure to sign up at their local recruiting office.

———

Patriotism became good copy and good business. Henry Ford remained a pacifist. When President Wilson called out the National Guard for the Pancho Villa chase, the *Chicago Tribune* contacted a number of the nation's large employers to ask what provision would be made for those called to serve. Most waved the flag. The Pierce-Arrow policy was typical: full pay for the duration (less the National Guard stipend), and the worker was guaranteed his job on return. When the *Tribune*'s

Detroit stringer phoned the Ford Motor Company, however, the response was negative. Treasurer Frank Klingensmith took the call and said anyone leaving the company to fight forfeited his job.

Klingensmith was wrong. Already numbered M.N.G. (Michigan National Guard) badges had been made for returning guardsmen to get their old jobs back, and guardsmen families in need would be provided for in the meantime. Under the banner "Flivver Patriotism," the *Chicago Tribune* carried the inaccurate story on June 22 and followed it three days later with a stinging editorial that unless Ford modified his policy toward National Guard service, he would "reveal himself not as merely an ignorant idealist but as an anarchistic enemy of the nation which protects him in his wealth." Further, the *Tribune* implied that such a person did not deserve the advantages of a democracy and should move his factories elsewhere.

Henry Ford demanded a retraction. The *Tribune* printed his denial of the Klingensmith statement, but publisher Robert R. McCormick adamantly refused to take back a word of the editorial. Ford sued for libel. In the legal maneuvering that followed, it was concluded that impartial juries would be impossible in either Chicago or Detroit. A new venue was sought.

———

Meanwhile, Henry was embroiled in another lawsuit—with the Dodges. This one had been brewing for some time. In casual conversation, John Dodge had said he was sorry about Jim Couzens' departure, and Ford replied that he wasn't because Couzens often interfered with his plans. These plans, Ford continued, now included doubling the Ford factories, doubling production, and slashing the current $440 Model T price tag in half. Ford's next public act, announced six weeks after the *Tribune* editorial, was to cut the Model T's price to $360.

Worried about the effect millions of $220 Fords would have on their own business, the Dodges asked to meet with Henry but were rebuffed. A registered letter in September brought no reply for three weeks. Finally, Edsel Ford wrote, promising that their views would be fully aired at the next board meeting. The Dodges' return letter, asking further clarification, brought no response. Tired of the runaround, John and Horace concluded that the court was the only remedy left. Their lawsuit was ready October 31, but the brothers waited two days to file it. They had a wedding to attend.

On November 1, Edsel Ford married Eleanor Lowthian Clay. She was the niece of J.L. Hudson, and the wedding took place in the Hudson mansion, formerly the home of Henry Ford's old business partner, Alexander Malcomson. The Dodges and their wives, and Mr. and Mrs. Thomas Edison, were among the hundred guests. Malcomson was not.

The Detroit press played up the marriage as a union of society and money, which was overdoing it. The Clays (the Hudsons, too) were in the country club set but not part of the city's old French aristocracy. Eleanor had not been a debutante. Not that this mollified Henry much about his son's choice of a wife. Clara Ford was charmed by the girl, and her husband liked her spirit. But Henry hated the "swank" prenuptial parties she planned and worried that Eleanor's fondness for jazz and golf might have a bad influence on his son. Apparently, he had chosen not to notice the car in which Edsel had courted Eleanor: a bright yellow Stutz Bearcat.

Detroit evening papers on November 2 carried stories of both the Ford wedding and the Dodge lawsuit. Henry's immediate reaction was to call a friendly Detroit editor who wrote a story for the November 4 editions, stating that the Dodges had already drawn $5.5 million on an investment of only $10,000 and still had Ford holdings valued at $50 million. How could they say that Ford was jeopardizing their stockholders' interest when they had done so well by him? That without the Dodges there might not have been a Ford car went unmentioned. The brothers were made to appear as crass ingrates.

Because the temporary injunction restrained the Ford Motor Company from using its assets to expand the business, this case moved through the litigation process more quickly than the *Tribune* suit. A preliminary hearing was scheduled for mid-November to determine whether Ford could proceed with work at the Rouge while waiting for the actual trial to begin. Testifying for the company, engineer Harold Wills explained expansion was necessary so Ford could make more of its own components because if any one of the roughly 3,000 parts of the Model T didn't arrive on time, the entire line would have to shut down.

Treasurer Klingensmith testified that Ford dealt in cash because the price was better that way and, had the dividend asked by the Dodges been distributed, the company would have required a bank loan.

Most effective of all was Henry himself. Fond of privately referring to his stockholders as "leeches," Ford relished this opportunity to lash out. Elliott G. Stevenson, the Dodges' attorney, had a terrible time. It was the defendant's "duty to earn all the money he legitimately can for his stockholders," Stevenson said, but conscience wouldn't allow Ford to make "awful profits," using Henry's own phrase. Henry said conscience had nothing to do with his decision to lower the Model T price. It was bad business not to lower it. Attorney and witness went round and round. Ford never cracked. He denied Stevenson's allegation that he had called his stockholders parasites and, when the lawyer produced a newspaper clipping with the quote, Henry said that was the reporter's word, not his. He was not asked about leeches. Challenged that he hadn't much regard for stockholders, Ford countered that he had "shown quite a regard" by paying them "lots of dividends."

Court recess for the day was a blessed respite for Stevenson. The next morning, he charged at his witness anew. Following a question about why the Ford Motor Company was in business, this exchange took place.

Ford:	To do as much good as possible for everybody concerned.
Stevenson:	What do you mean by "doing as much good as possible"?
Ford:	To make money and use it, give employment, and send out the car where people can use it...and incidentally to make money.
Stevenson:	Incidentally?
Ford:	That's right. Business is a service not a bonanza.
Stevenson:	Your controlling feature, then, is to employ a great army of men at high wages, to reduce the selling price of your car so that a lot of people

> can buy it at a cheap price, and give everybody a car that wants one?

Ford: If you give all that, the money will fall into your hands; you can't get out of it.

There was silence. A sly smile crossed the witness' face. This smart lawyer had just espoused the Ford philosophy very well. Henry couldn't have done it better himself.

Nonetheless, the smart lawyer carried the judicial day. The court ruled that the Rouge expansion plans exceeded powers expressly granted the company in its charter. That was the sort of legal technicality Ford abhorred. He would appeal. So far as he was concerned, he had won anyway. "Practically gained every point in Dodge suit...," he wrote to Edsel, who was in Hawaii on the last stop of his honeymoon. "Holding up annual meeting until you return."

CHAPTER 33

Hardships of War

BILLY DURANT WAS in an enviable position. The General Motors he took back from the bankers was a lot healthier than the GM he had given to them. Granted, the Nash-Storrow regime's reluctance to assault the mass market had allowed other burgeoning giants such as Willys-Overland and Studebaker to gain in the numbers game, but Charlie had lopped off the deadwood—all those nearly moribund car companies Billy acquired because his policy had been "to buy everything in sight." Nash consolidated the two Durant-bought truck manufacturers (Rapid and Reliance) into one under the GMC banner. With the detritus eliminated and Chevrolet placed alongside the four strong passenger-car companies (Buick, Cadillac, Oldsmobile, and Oakland), General Motors was rock solid. All Billy had to do was hold his exuberance in check.

Durant managed that reasonably well at first. Scripps-Booth was brought into the GM family, but Billy had bought it when he controlled only Chevrolet. "He went to Detroit Sunday to look at Lozier plant," an associate wrote to Doc Campbell. "He turned it *down hard.*" The emphasis was the letter writer's and showed Billy had enough of a critical eye to see the unmitigated disaster Detroit dilettantes had made of this once-thriving New York state company. The first time around, he probably would have bought it.

Durant's first post-coup purchases for General Motors were inspired: Delco, Perlman Rim, Remy Electric, Hyatt Roller Bearing, and New Departure Ball Bearing, all acquired for the usual exchange of stock with the help of his banker friend, Louis Graveret Kaufman. United Motors Corporation was the name chosen for this new consolidation, a natural perhaps, but one wonders what Ben Briscoe must have thought of Billy's purloining a name so similar to his own ill-fated conglomerate's. To this nucleus, Durant would add other component-producing firms to achieve the same manufacturing integration Henry Ford was aiming toward by making more and more of his own parts. In GM history, Durant's next decision was of even greater significance, although it could not have been realized then. The man Billy asked to head United Motors was Hyatt's Alfred Sloan.

One high-rolling mega-deal was attempted in 1916, but Billy Durant was not the principal instigator. John North Willys was. His merger plan involved Willys-Overland, Hudson, and Chalmers, and it made sense. Hudson's Roy Chapin had joined Howard Coffin in war work in Washington, and Hugh Chalmers had taken a dollar-a-year job for the government as well. Neither company was doing well with absentee landlords. The Willys plans also called for the addition of Electric Auto-Lite and United Motors—and the name of American Motors for the whole conglomeration. The ink was scarcely dry on Durant's component consortium, so possibly Billy and John North were making baby steps toward a colossal merger that would have flabbergasted the industry. But they were stopped in their tracks at stage one. American Motors never materialized.

Instead, Willys made big plans to augment his own empire. Because he had been in France when the war broke out, he was perfectly placed to land early European military contracts, and he returned home with a bundle of them. Convinced that America would be in the war soon, he spent $12 million expanding his facilities in Toledo for both military work and to manufacture a new under-$500 Overland to compete with the Model T in the anticipated postwar boom.

In Detroit, Hudson soldiered on without Chapin and Coffin. But Chalmers, with only 12,000 cars produced in 1917 in fifteen buildings covering thirty-six acres of floor space, produced an echo that could be heard as far as Washington. When Hugh Chalmers took time to listen, he decided the only way out was as gracefully as possible. It was "practically a liquidation," one banker noted on the negotiation bringing Chalmers together with Maxwell, which needed additional plant facilities. Maxwell president Walter Flanders added the Chalmers presidency to his list of titles.

On February 3, 1917, following notification from Berlin that its submarines would attack any vessel at will, the United States severed diplomatic relations with Germany. Three days later, Albert Erskine wired President Wilson that "Studebaker's factories, of course, are at the disposal of the government. Any orders given us will receive preference and clear right of way."

Not to diminish Erskine's sense of patriotism, but the emotional Southerner who was Studebaker president seldom missed an opportunity to bring notice to his company. About this same time, he was offering a top-of-the-line Studebaker to the presidents of any car companies in America who would pose with it for their local paper and say a few kind words. A surprising number of America's small manufacturers accepted the proposal.*

Erskine could be persuasive. Neither schooled in engineering nor experienced in the automobile industry, he had been in bookkeeping (American Cotton Company) and sales (Underwood Typewriter) previous to Studebaker. Nonetheless, in 1915, four years after being brought to South Bend as treasurer, he was promoted to the company's presidency when Studebaker son-in-law Fred Fish moved himself up to the chairmanship. Within months, recognizing the wisdom of John North Willys' pioneering of installment auto sales, Erskine introduced a Studebaker credit program. Like Willys, Erskine saw the war as

---

* Among the carmakers willing to smile for the camera alongside a Studebaker were the presidents of Crow-Elkhart, Luverne, Madison, Glide, Douglas, Fritchle, Hatfield, Economy, Seneca, Monitor, Richmond, Woods, Laurel, Austin, Metz, Pullman, Enger, Lambert, and Dixie Flyer. Charles Duryea managed to get a Studebaker, even though not in manufacture at the time. Some company presidents—Messrs. Moon and Davis, for example—sold their cars almost immediately after the shutter clicked.

heaven-sent to add plant capacity for future auto production, and he vigorously pursued military contracts, offering low profit margins and reminding government officials that Studebaker had been a major military supplier since the Civil War. Erskine worked at fever pitch—so fast that colleagues could barely keep up. His board of directors looked on in approving wonder.

With the U.S. entry into the war on April 6, the entire industry rallied to the flag. Willys lent the government his million-dollar yacht nearing completion in Bath, Maine. In early May, Erskine told Studebaker directors they should voluntarily reduce car manufacture by half and expand Plant No. 5 for war work—and was given a fast green light. Upon arriving "Over There" to command the American Expeditionary Force, General Pershing realized the better part of valor included motoring in a staff car equal to those of his French and English counterparts—and wired Locomobile for help. The Connecticut company dropped everything to construct two special limousines, painted khaki, the first of ten such high-command staff cars Locomobile would build for the U.S. Army.

The day after Congress declared war, Wilfred Leland approached Billy Durant for approval to turn over the building just completed for Cadillac closed-car construction. Closed bodies would continue to be purchased from outside sources, Leland explained, so Cadillac could build airplane engines there. Durant said no. Although he had made no secret of his distaste for war and resisted military contracts for GM companies through 1916, Billy had not been as vociferous a pacifist as Henry Ford. Thus, this refusal stunned the Lelands, who were used to having their own way at Cadillac. Margery Durant took pains in her biography to note that because her father believed "war is a stupid thing...there were small minds who doubted his patriotism." For Billy, this war was a distraction and an inconvenience now that he had GM back and wondrous plans for the future. The American entry into the war caught him off guard.

The fastest about-face was Henry Ford's. Likening getting rich on the war to taking blood money, Henry declared he would work on America's behalf "without one cent of profit." He suggested producing a one-man submarine that could attach a "pill-bomb" to the hull of enemy battleships. The Navy was dubious the thing would work and that Ford could build 1,000 of them right away. Some wondered about the carmaker's motivation. Assistant Secretary of the Navy Franklin D. Roosevelt suggested Ford thought a submarine was "something to eat" until he saw the chance to make headlines. Ford would not be making submarines.

Next, Henry proposed to manufacture 150,000 airplanes and asked Percival Perry, who managed Ford in Britain, to send him a downed German fighter to use as a guide. Again, the government said no. His idea for a two-man tank did elicit some Army interest. He could build 1,000 per day, he said. A demonstration of the "flivver tanks" revealed their tendency to get stuck nose-up in the trenches. No matter, said Henry, "we'll have so many of them that we'll use stranded tanks to make a crossing for the following army." The flivver tank never made it to the front.

His patriotic zeal aroused, Henry was miffed at the government foot-dragging on his ideas. The next one, however, came from Washington. The Navy had designed a light and fast submarine patrol boat called the Eagle, which overburdened naval and commercial shipyards had no time to build. Ford leapt at the chance. The perfect place to build them, he said, was along the River Rouge. Within days of signing the contract, Bill Knudsen, who had become a citizen in 1914, was up to his hip boots wading in a swamp, supervising the construction of an all-new idea in shipyards that would rise 100 feet in the air and stretch more than a half mile. Never before had ships been built indoors; Albert Kahn's glass-expansed masterpiece made architectural history. For Henry Ford, Eagle boat building was another triumph—a crafty maneuver around the limitations on Rouge expansion ordered by the court in the Dodge lawsuit decision then under appeal.

"An Eagle a Day Keeps the Kaiser Away," boasted banners waved by 10,000 Ford workers as they marched through Highland Park in patriotic celebration. "Warships While You Wait" was the irreverent line *The New York Times* used to head its story of Ford's attempt to adapt mass production techniques to vessels of considerably more complication than his Tin Lizzie. But it was the very magnitude of the project that played so well to the public. Henry Ford could do anything, folks in the hinterlands said in awe.

The only bad press Ford suffered during this period was because of his son, but Henry was to blame. Edsel wanted to go to France. Henry would not allow it. "I'd rather be in the trenches than holding down a swivel chair," Edsel said. "There is one job in this war that I do not want and will not take and that is the job of a rich man's son." His father insisted Edsel stay home to help with war production, and the local draft board agreed, commenting that the recent birth of Henry Ford II gave Edsel a deferment-qualifying dependent anyway. Buying himself a safe commission in Washington, which many wealthy young men did to avoid the battlefront, would have brought no dishonor. But because saying no to his father was impossible for him, Edsel was forced to live the rest of his life bearing the taint of draft dodger.

————

The night of May 26, 1917, Packard chief engineer Jesse Vincent didn't sleep much. The factory visit of a French and British military delegation that day had set him to thinking. Mention had been made that no U.S. manufacturer produced a combat aircraft engine as good as those already in use. Over breakfast the next morning, as Vincent read the latest issue of *The Automobile,* W.F. Bradley's article practically jumped out at him. Bradley described the chaos caused the French military by reliance upon thirty-four different types of aircraft engine. "As an engineer and manufacturer, I realized the very great importance of this article...," Vincent said, and "immediately jumped in a car and drove up to the residence of the [Packard] president."

Alvan Macauley agreed that Washington should be warned of the danger and put Vincent on the noon train to talk to Howard Coffin, now chairman of the Aircraft Production Board. Standardization was the only way to avoid air war disaster, Vincent said; Packard had an aircraft engine under development, which the company would make available as the basis for a standardized series of engines to be manufactured by the nation's carmakers. The offer was accepted. W.F. Bradley was enlisted as liaison and technical adviser to Washington as the American engine was brought to life. It would be called the Liberty.

Meanwhile, the Lelands chafed at Durant's reluctance to plunge GM into military production. Fiercely patriotic, Henry Leland had been itching to build aircraft engines and to get into war work even before the war started. In 1913, as president of the Society of Automotive Engineers, he had returned from the Continent convinced that Europe would soon erupt and that America should get ready. The old man's patience ran out. In mid-June, he and his son resigned from Cadillac and went to Washington to offer to build airplane engines. While waiting for a government response, they purchased property in Detroit that included several factory buildings, which they commenced to remodel.

Now it was Durant's turn to be stunned. Awakened that, to paraphrase William Jennings Bryan, his country was at war and discussion of peace was closed, Billy asked the Lelands to reconsider leaving Cadillac. General Motors would be in military production straightaway. But the Lelands had already gone too far with their own plans, including a designation for their aircraft-engine venture. Henry Leland made the decision. He named the company after the president for whom he had first voted: Abraham Lincoln.

The Willard Hotel was Washington headquarters for Colonel Vincent, who was given a three-month leave of absence from Packard for the Liberty engine project. Vincent's twenty-five-man engineering team was drawn from Cadillac, Dodge, Pierce-Arrow, and Packard. The white beard of the patriarchal Leland can be spotted in many official government photos of the project.

A month from conception in the Willard Hotel, the first Liberty prototype was completed on the day before the Fourth of July. The final prototype arrived at McCook Field on Thanksgiving, wrapped in an American flag. Then the War Department issued contracts to build the engine to Ford, Buick, Cadillac, Marmon, and the Lelands' Lincoln Motor Company.

Getting the Liberty into production was as frenzied as its creation. Walter Chrysler remembered, "At the plant my own offices were made into a drafting room and we started in on a twenty-four-hour schedule. We had cots brought to the office and slept there until we lost track of time. I remember that we did not go home for two weeks." Cooperation among the factories was exceptional. When Chrysler found out Ford was having trouble making the cylinder heads for the overhead camshaft, which Buick was not, he went to the Ford plant and "made a trade with Harold Wills" for Ford to manufacture the cylinders, Buick the cylinder heads.

As one segment of the automobile industry was striving to put the military in the air, another was working to make transport more effective on land. This idea was Roy Chapin's. The U.S. railroads were taxed, trying to maintain essential civilian services while at the same time seeing to all troop and equipment transport. The Lincoln Highway, while no paved boulevard, was passable most of the time—and Chapin suggested that motor trucks destined for France be driven to points of embarkation, carrying loads of war matériel from factories to dockside. The plan worked wonderfully well. By war's end, some 300,000 trucks were delivered, and long-distance over-the-road transport of freight was recognized as a worthy alternative to rail.

———

Not everything the auto industry produced for the war effort moved. Buick manufactured trench helmets, hospital equipment, and other metal objects. "There was so much work, so many things to be done from day to day, there was hardly time to think," Walt Chrysler recalled. Nor to consult with Durant, for that matter, but Billy never objected to any of the military contracts Chrysler signed, nor the war work he took on.

Durant was preoccupied anyway. His natural inclination whenever stock prices fell was to buy, and when GM stock inexplicably took a nosedive in 1917, Billy found himself in need of a quick $1 million to cover. He asked the GM board for a loan, but the du Ponts preferred giving him a $500,000 annual salary retroactive to 1916. This took care of his immediate problem but also sent Billy a message that came through loud and clear.

Walter Chrysler happened to pass Durant's office during this episode. He saw Billy staring at the wall as if in a daze, and he walked in. "Here was a friend and plainly he was in some kind of trouble," Chrysler said. He wanted to help. Doc Campbell was in the room, Pierre du Pont, du Pont's chief finance man John J. Raskob, and a few others Chrysler didn't recognize. "I seemed to be in a room full of Napoleons at various stages of Napoleonic careers," Walt remembered. "I decided to vanish from the scene. There was nothing I could do."

Shortly thereafter, aware that the end of the war would see a precipitous drop in demand for du Pont's principal product, Raskob suggested the company use its fulsome war profits to acquire a significant quantity of GM stock—specifically, 24 percent of the common, which effectively stabilized the GM price. Merger of General Motors, United

Motors, and Chevrolet was insisted upon by the du Ponts and readily agreed to by Durant. The balance of power had shifted.

———

Rationing of raw materials to nonessential industries was begun in late 1917. The priority circular ranked automobiles in the same category as musical instruments, which infuriated the industry. Trade journals championed the effort to change the designation "pleasure car" to "passenger car" (trucks were "commercial" cars), but Washington continued to look upon automobiles as luxury items on which the same wartime excise taxes could be levied as fur coats, perfume, and jewelry.

Materials shortages hit the small manufacturers the hardest. Regal in Detroit and Abbott in Cleveland went to the wall because they couldn't get parts, as did Pathfinder and Lambert in Indiana. In Maryland, Crawford had to pay its bills with a production cut by two-thirds when parts didn't arrive. In Peoria, Glide ferreted out jobbers for assembled components because raw materials could not be had.

Manufacturers able to get their cars put together were faced with another problem: getting them to market. The railroads were booked solid. Military contracts were no boon to the small manufacturer either, because the government was so laggardly to pay. Cash flow problems at Lozier and Simplex became critical. In Muncie, Indiana, Inter-State directors opted for a going-out-of-business sale to pay off creditors once made aware of the government payment policy.

Although not hit as hard, or as soon, as the small factories, major producers began feeling the pinch by early 1918, when rumor became rife in Washington that the government would end all automobile production. Howard Coffin was able to hold the prohibiting forces at bay by convincing them the automobile industry was much too important to be summarily fiddled with before consulting its leaders.

In March, when Bernard Baruch became chairman of the War Industries Board (W.I.B.), John Dodge, John North Willys, and Billy Durant sat down to talk with the financier and the W.I.B. The meeting was cordial. The automakers suggested a 30 percent reduction, and the W.I.B. seemed pleased. Then everybody went home. The industry assumed the government had guaranteed raw materials for the remaining

70 percent, which it had not. And the W.I.B. belatedly realized the industry had based its volunteered sacrifice on the prospective output for 1918, which was 30 percent more than that of 1917, so its production cut was no cut at all. Relations between the two groups deteriorated—and worsened when the W.I.B., hearing gossip that Willys-Overland had a ten-month supply of steel on hand, began to suspect the industry was stockpiling.

Automakers took the offensive. The first order of business was to determine what the government actually required for war work. "If you will take the materials that you actually need," John Dodge exhorted, "that you can use, not taking stuff and storing it up that wouldn't be shipped in five years...and let us alone, we believe there will be plenty to keep us going." The tack was right; the tone was wrong. To add a more subtle touch to the industry's cause, the president of the National Automobile Chamber of Commerce, super salesman Hugh Chalmers, was enlisted as industry spokesman.

But even the affable Chalmers became exasperated as Baruch and the War Industries Board made ever more stringent proposals. "We are the third largest industry in this country," Hugh cried, "and with all the men we employ and all the obligations we have to our parts people, all the money we owe our banks, we cannot surrender to this." Chalmers prophesied bankruptcy for the state of Michigan if the W.I.B. word became law. Still, by the spring of 1918, as the Kaiser's army advanced toward Paris and the English Channel, Baruch attacked anew, seemingly intent on a manufacturing ban, no matter what happened to the state of Michigan. A W.I.B. memorandum was made public, in which the industry was warned not to expect future supplies of steel, rubber, and other raw materials, and that 100 percent conversion to war work by January 1, 1919, was "in its best interests."

This posture was largely for the benefit of the public then being asked to endure heatless and meatless days. (Self-imposed gasless Sundays had persuaded a lot of people to fill up on Saturday night until many communities banned Sunday driving and appointed local citizens to write down the license plate numbers of any offenders.) More important, Baruch's big stick was meant to bring into line those manufacturers who had been reluctant to take on war production because they didn't believe they could afford to work for the government. This strategy had some effect.

"The Advertisement We Did Not Use–and Why" headlined the Lexington Motor Company, showing the original as an inset with new text revealing Lexington would move into "a 100 percent war base." Hugh Chalmer's personal correspondence indicates that total cessation of car production was never the W.I.B. intent and was furious that what he had understood would be a private memo to carmakers became a public statement that gave the impression the industry was "going out of the car business" by the end of the year.

By the end of the year, the war was over. Already the automobile industry contribution was being autopsied. The Liberty, which Orville Wright called "the finest airplane engine produced up to its time," came under fire because the airplane in which it was installed located the fuel tank between pilot and gunner, a lethal position that gave rise to the DH-4's nickname of "Flaming Coffin." "Tho' I'm not crazy about the bus I'm flying (a Nieuport 28)," Teddy Roosevelt's son Quentin, an A.E.F. lieutenant, wrote, "I'd be much more comfortable in it than I would in a Liberty." Unfortunately, the DH-4 (which had carried other aircraft engines) and the Liberty became synonymous.

The Liberty suffered further when Gutzon Borglum, sculptor of the monument on Mount Rushmore, persuaded his friend President Wilson that the Liberty project was riddled with incompetence, waste, and self-serving extravagance. Congressional investigation followed. Borglum was discredited when it was revealed he intended to start his own automobile company to hopefully take away the military contracts of those firms he was attacking. The Liberty emerged from the process relatively unscathed. Jesse Vincent's neglecting to dispose of his Packard stock when he went to Washington brought the charge that he had profited illegally from the Liberty, but the $55.00 his stock had earned made a practical joke of the allegation.

Some manufacturers with plant facilities at the ready complained that the Lelands were given a huge Liberty contract without a factory, and then the government helped with loans and tax incentives to get one built for them. The Lelands countered, justifiably, that their engine-building expertise was a commodity well worth the purchase. And, too, the Army did dredge the River Rouge for Henry Ford.

Keeping the Kaiser away with an Eagle a day had been grandstanding. The first submarine chaser was ready on schedule, but thereafter, Bill

Knudsen's engineers found adapting automobile production techniques to shipbuilding wasn't as easy as it looked. The two-vessel-per-week projected schedule would not be realized until after the war, with the last of the sixty Eagles completed in May 1919. But the project had begun in a swamp less than two years earlier. "As boats Eagles were not so hot," one Navy man who sailed on them commented, "but as evidence of Bill Knudsen's production ability they were a magnificent achievement."

As America geared up to go to war, expectations had been grand. Using a convoluted equation ("the occupation of a road by a vehicle may be measured by the product of the space actually filled by the vehicle into the time taken in carrying its load from point to point"), the *Quarterly Review* explained how four wheels could win the battle faster than four legs. But more animal fodder was shipped to France than either ammunition or food for the troops. And toward the war's end, there was concern on both sides that the supply of horses and mules might run out.

At the division level, American troops were never moved by American trucks. Although the importance of proper training and repair facilities seems to have been generally understood, implementing such a policy under combat conditions proved impossible. The situation was aggravated by the welter of vehicles sent "Over There," well over 200 different makes and types. The problem had been recognized by early 1917. A Congressional appropriation authorized the U.S. Quartermaster Corps to have standardized truck models designed, but they could not be produced quickly enough. At the war's end, it has been estimated that less than 50 percent of the trucks in the field of battle were operable.

But the proverbial glass was also half full. When the system worked well, it was a marvel. Verdun was saved by motor trucks. "The preparatory organization was so perfect and the condition of the trucks so perfectly attended to that there was scarcely a break in the snake-like procession which moved forward with clock-like regularity," war correspondent Joseph Briker wrote. "Advancing with their capacity loads, the vehicles discharged their burdens at predetermined points behind the front whence the material was carried to the trenches by one- or two-horse carts. The return, empty or with wounded, was made like the advance, with the same military precision."

Less spectacular examples of motorized gallantry abounded, and as often as not involved the Model T. This was partly because Henry was so good at promoting Ford and partly because his car was ubiquitous. Dispatches told of the ten machine-gun-laden Model Ts that drove the enemy out of the trenches along the Marne and the many wounded that Tin Lizzie rescued from the Argonne. Field Marshal Edmund Allenby of the Allied Expeditionary Force said the invasion of Palestine was a success because of "Egyptian laborers, camels and Ford cars." T.E. Lawrence even replaced the camels of his troops with Model Ts to drive the Turks out of Arabia.

"I got the old 'bus' working again with a new motor, new rear construction, new wheels," wrote American Ambulance Corps driver William Yorke Stevenson in *At the Front in a Flivver.* "The chief remains of No. 10 are the frame, body, insects and radiator. As all the replacing parts are old, anyway, the chariot is no ball of fire at that, but she wheezes along somehow."

Determined to get into the war, Gertrude Stein procured a Model T through an American cousin and learned how to use it from a fellow American expatriate (William Cook, a starving artist making ends meet as a Paris taxi driver). Alice B. Toklas recalled with bemusement Gertrude's first test runs when she stalled on the track between two streetcars and ran out of gas on the Champs Elysees. Her technique improved, but she never did learn reverse. Still, friends said Gertrude drove better than she cooked and never had an accident despite being quite aggressive. Her adventures tending to the wounded and carting medical supplies with the Model T, which she adored, were typical. Gertrude nicknamed the car "Auntie" after her Aunt Pauline, "who always behaved admirably in emergencies and behaved fairly well most times if properly flattered."

November 11, 1918, was a day for celebration in America. Europe lay in ruin, but the awful war was over. In Buffalo, a draftsman at Pierce-Arrow, tootling "Yankee Doodle" on a piccolo, marched through the shops and out the door, his fellow workers following him all the way downtown. Some didn't go back to work for several days. In Dearborn, Henry Ford ordered that all tanks be removed from his tractor plant so it could immediately return to its intended purpose. He wanted all war work stopped. "Call Washington," he barked, "and get permission."

Because of its appalling casualties and carnage, the end of World War I was greeted with joy. But for many in the automobile industry, the joy was restrained by hard reality. Having so recently geared up for battle, having just hit stride in armaments production, having committed facilities wholeheartedly to the effort, having stacks of military orders contracted for but not yet fulfilled, what would carmakers do now? From a purely practical standpoint, the only problem with the Armistice was that it happened too soon.

CHAPTER 34

Boom Goes Bust

IN THE IMMEDIATE aftermath of the Armistice, those who fared best were those who could convert back to civilian production quickest. Henry Ford was lucky to have the best man in the industry to do that, and he treated Bill Knudsen with respect because of it. In November 1918, when Big Bill broached the usually volatile subject of a successor to the Model T, his boss didn't erupt but asked instead how long it would take to get the new car into production. No more than six months, Knudsen replied. The same question about the Model T brought a reply of sixty days. "There's your answer," Henry Ford said.

A few months later, however, Henry himself announced not only a new car but a brand-new automobile company. He resigned from and turned the Ford presidency over to Edsel in order to devote all his time to the new venture, which he said would be about five times larger than the one he had originally created. This cataclysmic move followed the adverse decision of the Michigan State Superior Court in his appeal in the Dodge case. The court ordered Ford to pay nearly $20 million in dividends to stockholders. The money didn't faze Henry because as majority holder, he would collect most of it. But by now, Henry hated stockholders the way he did bankers.

Announcement of the new company brought telegrams from chambers of commerce across the nation, suggesting Henry locate one of its many branch plants in their city. They shouldn't have wasted the paper. When Ford stockholders were quietly approached about selling their holdings to an unnamed principal, it didn't take any of them long to figure out who wanted it. Henry had played this game years earlier with Ford Manufacturing. The bidding war didn't last long. The Dodges agreed to $12,500 per share and received $25 million for their investment of $10,000 in 1903. Jim Couzens held out for a little more than $13,000 per share and went home with $30 million.* Henry danced a little jig when the Ford Motor Company was all his. "Of course, there will be no need for a new company now," Edsel replied when asked by a reporter from *The New York Times*.

On January 31, 1919, the city of Flint threw a party for Billy Durant. The banquet, which Dallas Dort called a "love feast," drew 550 of Durant's friends. Billy reminisced about his early days in Flint and praised Pierre du Pont as "one of the fairest and most considerate, one of the most generous" people he knew. John Raskob said pleasant, but not as effusive, things about Billy. That year, General Motors' automobile production increased by 60 percent. The total of 300,000 cars from all GM companies represented less than half the three-quarter million Tin Lizzies Ford produced but was sufficient to raise net profit from $15 to $60 million.

———

The boom was on. Americans, eager to forget the "gasless" years, had $23 billion to spend from wartime purchase of Liberty bonds. They

---

* Ford loathed the man who had been his closest colleague during the company's growing years. Both men had run for public office in 1918. Couzens had won Detroit's mayoralty; Ford had narrowly lost a seat in the U.S. Senate to Truman S. Newberry, a member of Detroit's ruling elite and Packard's board. Ford had run only because he was asked to by President Wilson, for whom he had voted in 1916 "because he kept us out of war" and liked now because of his support for the League of Nations. Ford's campaign was a farce. He gave no speeches and refused to debate Newberry. Nonetheless, he was furious when he lost and managed to persuade the Senate Committee on Privileges and Elections to investigate his opponent for election fraud. Among Newberry contributors called to testify was Billy Durant. Ultimately, citing continued harassment by Ford, Newberry resigned his seat. To Henry's distinct displeasure, Jim Couzens was appointed to succeed him and would serve in the Senate for fourteen years.

wanted new cars, and automakers rushed to assist. Their approaches varied. In St. Louis, Stewart McDonald, not sure of how to proceed, issued revised Moon lineups several times in January 1919 before settling on a model called Victory, whose radiator flattered Rolls-Royce by imitation. The Moon sons had spent the war at the front, leaving Moon son-in-law McDonald in charge, and he inherited the company presidency when patriarch Joseph Moon died that February. McDonald, who looked on frugality even more religiously than Charlie Nash, prided himself on Moon's being debt free, paying vendors almost as quickly as components were delivered, and keeping stockholders happy with dividends. Moon did not have much cash for capital investment, which seemed to be okay with McDonald. The 2,000 new Victory models produced in the eight months from April to November 1919 was more than the company had produced in an entire year earlier, and McDonald was pleased with that result.*

By contrast, in South Bend, Albert Erskine called Studebaker's board of directors together to propose the building of a new plant to produce 100,000 cars annually, notwithstanding the company's peak sales year thus far having been less than two-thirds that many. This staggered a board still puzzling over Studebaker's less than $1 million profit on government sales of more than $17 million. Erskine apparently didn't confide the narrow profit margins of some of his government deals. The man radiated energy, optimism, and confidence, and the conservative Studebaker board bought his proposition. In 1919, he moved the company into the modern age by ending production of harnesses and horse-drawn equipment to concentrate on motor vehicle manufacture exclusively. The following year, Studebaker production was increased by more than 30 percent (to 51,000 units). "This year we went in wading," Erskine said. "Next year we go swimming."

---

* This was curious, given McDonald's relentless attack five years earlier on the Moon's *modus operandi*, which saw supplier components substituted for in-house production of virtually every part of a Moon except the rear axle. "A Moon motor car is put together like a prescription," company ads said, in a variation of the rationale used by Cole. "Every part we buy [is] made by the most famous makers of the best parts." McDonald's rationale for turning the Moon into an assembled versus a manufactured car was to increase company production tenfold to make more money. Possibly the money being made now was enough to satisfy his lifestyle.

Anxious to swim in the lucrative automotive pool, too, were a number of entrepreneurs who had only waded in the past, if that. Luring investors had amusing aspects, most especially Douglas Motors Corporation's try with an ad noting the $1,000 invested in Chalmers that had returned $86,658 in eight years, indicating the Douglas folks didn't read the trades too carefully. Others did; Douglas went nowhere in Omaha.

Prominent Boston capitalists were behind the Northway Motors Corporation of Natick, Massachusetts, organized in January 1918 and named for Ralph E. Northway, whose Detroit engine-building company had been among Billy Durant's purchases for General Motors during his first reign. Hired to design the car was Albert J. Romer, a mechanical engineer who had worked previously for both Ben Briscoe and Otis Elevator.

Hoping to make it big in St. Louis were the Gardners: father Russell and sons Russell, Jr. and Fred. Gardner had made a fortune selling Banner buggies, and he tiptoed into the automotive world by building bodies for and ultimately assembling Chevrolets, which business was sold to General Motors when the boys entered the Navy during World War I. Now back home, the Gardner brothers easily convinced their father they were ready for automobile manufacture. The Gardner was introduced in late 1919, and plans were made for a plant capacity of 40,000 cars annually.

In Elkhart, Indiana, the Huffman brothers, Earl and W.L., launched their enterprise in September 1919. Like the Gardner, the Huffman was an assembled car with a Continental engine (the Gardner's was a Lycoming) in the medium-price range. Another median-price field entrant, Ned Jordan, exemplified a new breed of automaker. In 1916, the Jeffery executive had left wife and Wisconsin to start on his own in Cleveland with the $200,000 he had been able to raise in a day. Ned was both a dandy and a dandy talker. A small sales volume could yield a high annual profit, Jordan said, provided the product had a unique appeal. Convinced sex would sell cars, Jordan advertised accordingly with a memorable series that ran afoul of Anthony Comstock's Society for the Prevention of Vice, most memorably with "The Port of Missing Men" that showed a Jordan Playboy parked in front of a house that was dark, except for one lighted upstairs window. Some magazines used an airbrush to avoid offending readers. Ned said he could make a profit of $750,000 a year with the sale of only 5,000 Jordans.

The remainder of new carmakers aimed high during this period of post-war euphoria. Luxury cars introduced after the Armistice included the du Pont from Wilmington, Delaware (E. Paul, not Pierre S.), which made its debut at New York's Commodore Hotel in 1919, and the Duesenberg from Indianapolis, which arrived at the Commodore in 1920, the Duesenberg name already famous through Fred and Augie's race cars and engine building. Earlier that year at the Commodore, Karl Martin of Bennington, Vermont, had introduced his Wasp, whose price he raised mid-show from $5,000 to $8,500, perhaps after Douglas Fairbanks walked by and bought one for his bride, Mary Pickford.

In Philadelphia, W.D. Morton, whose previous experience included both Mercer and Biddle, introduced the seventh automobile in the industry's thus-far short history to bear the name Meteor, a perhaps ill-advised choice because the only other Meteor still in production was Maurice Wolfe's funeral car in Piqua, Ohio. (Wolfe had a wicked sense of humor, naming a smaller companion version the Mort, which is French for "dead.") Morton's Meteor carried one of the Duesenbergs' engines and a Fleetwood body distinguished by the deep vee of its radiator.

The Ferris evolved out of the Ohio Trailer Company and arrived in Cleveland as "The Car of Character...[for] the man who would not live on a street where all of the houses are alike." The car was named for Ohio veteran William E. Ferris, who was most likely responsible for its aluminum body with a custom-built look; the rest of the car's parts came from supply houses. Most publicity photos were taken in front of Cleveland's posh Union Club. The Leach Power Plus Six was the new entry from Los Angeles. Martin Andrew Leach had long been in the wholesale/retail end of the automobile business and had many contacts in the silent film industry who wouldn't blink at buying a $5,000 car. Leach moved into the former Republic Motor Company factory to build it.

Albert Barley had moved from Streator (Illinois) to Kalamazoo to continue production of "America's Smartest Car." The radiator of the Roamer, named after a famous race horse, was an even more shameless copy of the Rolls-Royce than Moon's Victory; company brochures quoted Oscar Wilde and used tony phrases such as "a certain insouciance" to describe the product. Cloyd Young Kenworthy, who had written Roamer's copy and whose forte was sales, left for Mishawaka,

Indiana, to produce a car under his own name that would boast a straight-eight engine and four-wheel brakes, ideas purloined, although not as successfully, from the Duesenbergs, with whom he was friendly. Among the seven literary giants Kenworthy quoted for his own brochures were Dryden, Conrad, Donne, and Pope.

The new Porter from Bridgeport, Connecticut, was the former F.R.P. from Port Jefferson, Long Island, whose factory had been taken over by the government during the war, with the acquiescence of Finley Robertson Porter, who had become famous with the T-head Mercer. Porter decided to resume automobile production but to leave the work to others, contracting with the American & British Manufacturing Corporation of Bridgeport to make the Porter and New York City's Morton W. Smith Company to distribute it. The chassis price alone was $6,750; with coachwork by Brewster, Fleetwood, and Demarest, among others, a Porter could exceed $10,000.

Looking from the other side of the Atlantic, Claude Johnson of Rolls-Royce became convinced his company's product had a more promising future in the United States than in England. Import duties were high, however, so Johnson bought the American Wire Wheel plant in Springfield, Massachusetts, for manufacture of an American Rolls-Royce.

Most ambitious of all the new automakers was erstwhile Packard vice president Emlen Hare, who left Detroit for the East Coast to organize Hare's Motors. Announced at a press luncheon at the Hotel Claridge in New York City in early 1920, the new venture combined three of America's most stellar marques, two in New Jersey and one in Connecticut: Mercer, which had been put up for sale after death claimed the last Roebling who was interested in automobiles; Simplex, whose owner had found it profitable to sell its New Brunswick factory to Wright-Martin during the war; and Locomobile, whose banks were calling in the loans used to enlarge its plant for military production. Locomobile's A.L. Riker was Hare's vice president and engineering consultant; two of Packard's top engineers joined the venture.

Packard was so rich in talent, these defections were taken in stride. And the company was riding high. "Babbitt as a boy had aspired to the Presidency," Sinclair Lewis wrote. "His son Ted aspired to a Packard Twin Six." Warren Harding, the first president to ride to his inaugural in an automobile, would do so in one of Packard's twelve-cylinder cars. Company profit in 1919 was $5 million.

Wartime production had swelled the Kenosha coffers at Nash, and even careful Charlie was caught up in the euphoria of trying to build enough cars for customers. He bought a half interest in Seaman Body Corporation of Milwaukee to ensure a continuous supply of coachwork and started the Lafayette Motor Company to manufacture a luxury car in a Mars Hill (Indianapolis) factory used to make hand grenades during the war. He stole a number of Cadillac executives for the latter venture, including D. McCall White, who told the press that the new Lafayette was "far ahead of any previous automobile built under [my] supervision."

———

No one was more inclined to expand than General Motors. And it wasn't all Billy. John Raskob was just as big a spender. Fifty-eight million dollars had left the GM treasury in the few years since Durant's return, but by 1919, the company's assets stood at $452 million. "The General Motors Corporation of today is eight times as large as the company the bankers were managing," Raskob wrote to Billy in a note accompanying the balance sheets. "This is indeed a fine tribute to your foresight."

The General Motors Acceptance Corporation was created that year. Pontiac Buggy was purchased to build car bodies for Oakland, and a substantial interest was acquired in Fisher Body. Durant's try to out-Ford Henry in the tractor field with the Samson was a miss, but another of his pet projects hit the target squarely on. Through a friend, Billy became aware of an iceless icebox called Guardian Frigerator in fitful production in an old organ factory in Detroit, was asked to help, visited the place, offered to organize a new company, changed the product's name to Frigidaire, and put A.B.C. Hardy in charge. Once the company was on its feet, Durant sold it to GM for his expenses. "I'd bet my life he did not make a dollar for himself," Alfred Sloan said. At a dinner at New York's Metropolitan Club hosted by Pierre du Pont and attended by fifteen of the city's leading bankers, Durant enthusiastically described the promise of this "unusual and novel household fixture" to a sea of faces as blank as those when he had prophesied the importance of the automobile to the banking community the preceding decade.

General Motors was far too big now to be a one-man show, but Billy behaved as if it still were. He didn't believe in organization charts, and he continued to make most of his decisions intuitively. "I was constantly amazed by his daring...," Sloan said. "He never felt obliged to make an engineering hunt for facts." Durant's desk was a maze of telephones for playing the market. Sloan counted eight; Walter Chrysler thought there were half that many. Billy seemed to be able to talk on several of them at once; Chrysler thought he was "trying to keep in communication with half the continent."

"[He] liked having us around," Sloan said. "We used to go to the offices on Sunday morning, and while his barber Jake was shaving him, we lounged around the room." It was when Durant could not be seen that posed the problem. Often, he would summon executives and keep them waiting for hours, if not longer. Once Chrysler spent four days in New York before returning to Michigan, without ever seeing Durant or knowing why he had been summoned.

Pinning Billy down was practically impossible. Asked by Chrysler what his policies were, Durant laughed that he believed in changing them "as often as my door opens and closes." "That's the kind of fellow he was, though," Walt said. "We'd fight and then he'd want to raise my salary." Interfering with his work infuriated Chrysler, and Billy couldn't stop doing that. Buick was still his "best baby." Finally, there was one fight too many, and Chrysler said he was through. At Durant's urging, Alfred Sloan tried to talk him out of it. But Walt was adamant. At forty-five, he had the money to retire. He told his wife to pack for a trip to Europe to celebrate.

In addition to the presidency of Buick, Chrysler had been made corporate vice president in charge of operations and was concerned that GM was expanding too recklessly. "Buick was making half the money," he complained, "but the corporation was spending much faster than we could earn." By this time, Chrysler had an unexpected ally in his concern: Durant himself. On the GM agenda was a $20 million new headquarters in Detroit, slated to be named the Durant Building. Billy thought the money would be better left as working capital. In October 1919, Durant wrote Raskob about the enormous expenditures against prospective earnings that might "impair our position...in the event of industrial disturbance."

The boom went bust before the leaves turned in 1920. Signs that a day of reckoning was coming had been everywhere, but basking in the rapture of demand outstripping supply, the large automakers ignored them. The smaller producers and the newcomers to the field bore the brunt. Customers wanted cars; getting cars to the customers was the hard part. First there were the strikes. Among the largest was the walkout at United States Steel, but others—machinists in Flint, an axle factory in Detroit, and a bearing plant elsewhere in Michigan—were just as disruptive. And the price of parts soared. Many producers in the process of converting back to civilian production and still waiting to be paid by the government couldn't handle the increases. (In Indiana, hundreds of Auburns sat in a parking lot without instruments because the company didn't have the money to buy them.) And even if the parts could be paid for, they were often agonizingly slow to arrive. The Jackson Automobile Company of Michigan had orders for 3,100 cars but could fill only 1,812 of them. The company's dealers went elsewhere, and Jackson went out of business.

Price increases to automakers were passed along to customers. A Franklin that sold for $1,850 during the war years became $2,450 shortly after the Armistice, $2,650 by June 1919, and $3,100 by 1920. The cost of a Packard zoomed from $3,400 to $5,500 in the space of a year. Even the Model T Ford was no bargain when the same car that had cost $360 four years earlier couldn't be had now for less than $575.

Everyone who had used Liberty war bond money already had their new cars. Others couldn't afford one now without credit. The cost of living skyrocketed; food prices almost doubled. Bolsheviks preaching they had a better way culminated in a "Red Scare" that brought mass arrests of anarchists, communists, and union agitators. The Volstead Act was passed over President Wilson's veto, and prohibition quickly became the most broken law in the nation. Wilson's battle to win Congressional approval for the League of Nations was fought amidst a new call for isolationism. He lost the battle and his health in the process. Taking over the White House was Warren G. Harding, who promised a return to "normalcy."

To curb the runaway inflation and normalize the economy, the Federal Reserve Board tightened credit sharply in a surprise move. Automakers were caught short. Without credit, dealers couldn't sell cars to customers, and automakers couldn't sell to dealers. At a stormy meeting of the National Automobile Chamber of Commerce, Charlie Nash fulminated about the industry's recklessness and vowed never again to allow his enthusiasm to get the better of his judgment. "There have been better times to introduce a motorcar," Charlie rued about his Lafayette as he made plans to move the company from Indianapolis to Kenosha, where it would linger awhile and die.

Everybody was affected by the economic downturn. The only difference was degree. For many new manufacturers, the recession was a death knell. Meteor went to the wall in Philadelphia, Leach in Los Angeles, and Ferris in Cleveland. The Wasp was gone in Bennington, and the Kenworthy in Mishawaka. Charging fraud, stockholders forced the Huffman brothers into receivership, and when the claim was summarily thrown out of court, creditors forced another one, citing debts of about $15,000. The Huffmans finally gave up.

Parts and materials shortages had delayed introduction of the Northway of Massachusetts to January 1921, when it debuted at the Hotel Astor in New York. The Boston capitalists behind the company bailed out almost immediately to look after their other investments. Albert Romer found two financial bankers willing to underwrite a new medium-range car to carry his name, a decision about which they were sorry by year's end. Ralph Northway left to build Maxim fire engines. The Northway was history by the spring of 1922. The brand-new R & V Knight, named for Orlando J. Root and W.H. Vandervoort, whose automobile-building partnership in East Moline (Illinois) traced back to 1904, fell victim to the business slump and World War I plant expansion, the debts for which had not yet been repaid.

Hit hard was another new enterprise. During the summer of 1917, the Lincoln Motor Company had been given a no-cancel contract for 9,000 aircraft engines that the government canceled six months later, leaving the Lelands with a $10 million plant and little to do. "Build us a car, Uncle Henry," company investors had said. Word spread about the new Lincoln by Leland; anticipation was high, and orders were many. But, now in his late seventies, Leland designed a technical *tour de force* cloaked with a body designed by his son-in-law that was an artless afterthought. Worse, parts delays meant production anticipated for January did not begin until September, hitting the business slump head-on. Many who had placed orders took one look at the unstylish car and canceled.

John Willys was in trouble, too. His decision ten days before the Armistice to convert totally to military production could not have been more poorly timed. And his new round of empire building had been Durantian in its ambition. By now, John owned Glenn Curtiss' aviation company as well as Moline Plow of Illinois, which he purchased to get into the tractor business (Moline's automobile, the Stephens Salient Six, was part of the deal) and thirty-five acres in Elizabeth, New Jersey, for new plant construction. He gathered all his enterprises, except Willys-Overland, into a new holding company called Willys Corporation, headquartered in New York.

Willys already had a flurry of fours, which postwar steel shortages had dictated be reduced to two: the popular Willys-Knight, and the Overland, which had been planned as a $500 Ford competitor but arrived as an $845 car when parts prices zoomed. In the Elizabeth plant, a new six was in development. Then the economy went sour. "We had hundreds of thousands of yards of cotton fabrics," Willys said. "We had paid three dollars a yard and the price dropped to thirty cents. It was the same with all materials. This was disturbing to the bankers." So was Willys' heavy $14 million indebtedness to creditors and the rumored 26,000 unsold cars scattered from coast to coast. When the figures were totted up, Willys owed $18 million to various bankers who wanted their money.

Chase was willing to help but insisted on sending Walter Percy Chrysler into Willys territory. Della Chrysler, dismayed by the constant presence of her husband's cronies and their smelly stogies in her house, was happy to have her husband un-retire. Chrysler demanded $1 million per year for his services. Although taken aback, the bankers concluded the money would be well spent if Willys could be saved. John Willys was allowed to keep the title of president but with none of its authority. This would be Chrysler's show. Walt made this crystal clear when his first decision was to slash Willys' $150,000 salary in half. "I guess we've put our problems in the right man's hands," John laughed. He liked and admired Chrysler and had even tried to hire him away from Buick, but that power play had to rankle.

Next, Chrysler fired production manager Clarence Earl, who was no Knudsen and who soon proved he was no better as his own boss by taking over the Briscoe Motor Corporation and renaming its car the Earl. Ben Briscoe, who "found the call of patriotism too great to withstand," had spent the war years abroad directing the maintenance of Caproni seaplanes and Naval staff cars, and now sallied forth into the oil business in California and gold mining in Colorado. Earl moved quickly into receivership.

Department heads loyal to Earl rolled out of the company soon after he did; Chrysler cut to more sensible levels the workforce that John Willys had bragged was 100,000 men and made manufacturing economies to streamline operations. The lower-price field held no interest for Walt, nor was he enamored with sleeve-valve engines. The only car in the Willys lineup that intrigued him was the six under development in the New Jersey plant. When technical problems arose, Chrysler called in three former Studebaker engineers he regarded as "wizards": Carl Breer, Owen Skelton, and Fred Zeder. That one of John Willys' weak points was his naiveté about automobiles was revealed soon afterward, when Chrysler took him to the Elizabeth plant to check on the progress being made by the triumvirate that would forever after be known as the Three Musketeers. Getting off the freight elevator, Walt proudly pointed out the wooden mock-up and John asked, "Have you had it on the road yet?"

What had made Willys' company a success was John's skill as a salesman. That talent was really needed now. An upper berth on trains crisscrossing the continent was his accommodations for the next few months as he sought to shore up his dealership network. Even Chrysler admitted this was a turning point. "I've shown the boys I'm not dead," John said. He was forthright with his dealers: "I told them 'Wall Street didn't get me. I got myself; didn't play the game right'...The dealers decided I was a pretty good scout."

——

Wall Street got Billy Durant. Of course, it was his own fault. General Motors had seventy-five plants in forty cities and, in one month in early 1920, 6,150 cars was the total output of the entire corporation. As many as fifty GM executives reported directly to Durant, and their frantic efforts to reach him during this critical period were often unavailing because Billy was spending most of his time in the stock market, trying to support the price of GM stock.

The business collapse had been accompanied, as historically, by a break in stock market prices. Ever the optimist, Durant thought the GM tumble was merely a correction, and he could correct that all by himself. As GM stock prices slumped, Durant bought. He bought more as they slumped further, borrowing against his own holdings when his funds ran out. When friends told him they were facing ruin because of the plummeting GM price, he bought their stock, too. He neglected to tell GM directors about any of this.

Finally, Billy didn't know where he stood but was aware bankruptcy loomed. For a meeting about the situation with John Raskob and Alfred Sloan, he brought a sheaf of penciled notes and sheepishly admitted he had "no personal books or accounts and was wholly unable to give definitive statements as to total indebtedness" (Sloan's words). The entire corporation could be compromised if Durant went under.

The price demanded of Billy for bailing him out was GM. When news spread on Wall Street that Durant was gone and the corporation was now in the hands of du Pont and Morgan, brokers began buying GM stock again. Margery was proud that, rather than submitting a letter of resignation, her father called a board of directors meeting for November 30 to announce it. "You knew he was grief-stricken but no grief showed on his face," Alfred Sloan said. "He was smiling pleasantly, as if it were a routine matter, when he told us..." Then he went home. Margery remembered "all the tears running down his cheeks."

––––

Had Henry Ford not been so anxious to get rid of his stockholders, the business slump would have been a minor inconvenience. But to get unfettered control of his company, Ford had needed a $60 million loan, which he gritted his teeth and got from a bank. Thirty-five million had been paid back already. The remainder was due April 1921. His numbers people told him he wouldn't have it.

Ford confronted the situation with an attack on several fronts. First, against the advice of all of his executives, he lowered the price of the Model T. This had always worked well for the company in the past. The reduction this time of 25 to 30 percent, depending on body style, was the largest ever in the industry. "Now is the time to call a halt on war methods, war prices, war profiteering, and war greed," Henry said. His price reductions made the front page of probably every newspaper in the country. Editorials were heady in praise.

The industry recoiled in horror. The Dodge brothers and Hudson's Roy Chapin met with a few other automakers in Detroit and decided not to lower their prices. GM followed suit. Franklin, Studebaker, and Willys-Overland followed the Ford lead. Ned Jordan slashed $400 from his Playboy, Marmon reduced its prices by 20 percent. Ultimately, about half of the automakers lowered their prices.

The strategy worked, at least for Ford, but only for a month. When sales nosedived in November, Henry began cutting company costs. He slashed his office staff by almost half, sold off office equipment, and took out 60 percent of the company telephones. "Only comparatively few men in any organization need telephones," he said. Pocket knives would now be necessary to sharpen pencils because Henry curtailed ordering any new pencil sharpeners.

In December, Ford workers produced 78,000 cars, twice the number dealers could handle. On Christmas Eve, the plants were closed "for inventory," with the promise of being reopened the first week of January. Before year's end, the announcement came that "lack of orders" and the economic malaise meant operations would be suspended indefinitely. Detroit Bolsheviks distributed a circular, suggesting Ford workers ask the company to turn the factory over to them to make cars for their families. Ten thousand of them assembled to proffer the suggestion to management, but the demonstration was broken up. Fabulously wealthy as he was, Ford's financial predicament touched the hearts of many Americans, who still looked upon him as a folk hero. One Model T owner suggested that everybody with a Tin Lizzie lend Henry $100 until he could get back on his feet. Contributions that arrived at the company were returned.

Instead, Henry went on a diet, believing the less work his stomach had to do the clearer his thinking, and came up with an alternative plan. On January 26, 1921, Ford workers were called back to put together some more Model Ts. These cars, together with the backlog from December, were shipped out. At railway sidings all across America, dealers arrived to find far more cars than they had ordered, together with pricey packages of spare parts that cleaned out the factory's huge stockpiled inventory. Protest they might, but Ford intimated that not accepting the shipment would mean forfeiture of their franchises, which did not appeal to many. Because the Ford policy was payment on arrival, the dealers trotted to their local banks to borrow money to cover the shipments. Henry had the cash to pay off his loan in April.

By the spring of 1921, the Ford Motor Company was a very different place. In the ostensible interest of saving money, Henry had fired key personnel. The first round of departures came at the time of the stockholder buyout and began with Harold Wills, who, in a private arrangement, had been receiving a portion of Henry's own dividends for years. Ford didn't want to pay anybody dividends anymore, and he hadn't been happy with Wills since discovering and smashing the Wills-designed new Ford in the company garage upon his return from Europe several years earlier.

But Wills, an engineer with little to engineer now at Ford, wasn't unhappy about leaving either. He took the $1.6 million Ford buyout and, with close associate John Lee of the Sociological/Education Department, also recently fired, bought 4,250 acres on the banks of the St. Clair River and announced that a model industrial community called Marysville (after his wife) would be built there for the manufacture of a car of advanced concept to be called the Wills Sainte Claire. Wills, who had designed the distinctive Ford script, added the "e" to "Saint" and "Clair" for aesthetic effect.

Departing a month after Wills was Norval Hawkins, who had masterfully directed the marketing of the Model T for more than a decade and who had aroused his boss' ire by his independent thinking and his penchant for putting things down on paper. Once, after being asked to sign a requisition, Ford marched to the office where the forms were stored, asked the clerk for all of them and a can of gasoline, and ordered the pile to be taken out to the test yard and burned.

Frank Klingensmith's sin was his suggestion that borrowing money was a viable solution to the company's cash flow problems. His departure had been preceded a few days by the firing of advertising manager Charles Brownell, who lost his job when Henry eliminated the advertising department. A fifteen-year Ford veteran, Klingensmith had succeeded Jim Couzens as treasurer. Because Henry Ford didn't like to be seen as firing people, resignations were usually requested. "I have resigned," Klingensmith's January 3 formal statement read, "because I am not in full accord with some of the business policies contemplated by the company in the future." This probably referred to the dumping on dealers that followed later that month.

The departure that shook the industry the most was William Knudsen's. He had lost out in a power struggle with fellow Dane Charles Sorensen because Charlie was amenable to taking orders and Big Bill wasn't. The two men almost came to blows on occasion. Knudsen had laid the groundwork for his firing by questioning the wisdom of the perpetuity of the Model T and by the sheer force of his personality. Earlier, Henry had been similarly intimidated by Walter Flanders. "Mr. Knudsen was too strong for me to handle," Ford said. "You see, this is my business. I built it and, as long as I live, I propose to run it the way I want to run it." In what was both a compliment and an admission, Ford added, "I let him go, not because he was good, but because he was too good—for me."

Klingensmith invited Knudsen to join him in his new venture. Frank was now president of Gray Motor Corporation, the veteran Detroit engine builder now secretively at work on a Gray automobile to rival the Model T that was being developed by two engineers formerly of Packard and Cadillac. Knudsen asked how much money was backing the company and, when given the figure, said it wasn't enough. He accompanied Klingensmith to New York to talk to a banker, who offered sufficient backing but with stiff terms. "Kling," Big Bill said, "I don't want to go into the automobile business unless the company has enough money to see it through, and it can get enough money at a price it can afford to pay." Knudsen decided to wait for a better offer. Klingensmith raised $4 million but, like John Willys, found making a Model T competitor tough.

As for Willys, he wanted his company back. To get it, he played the game right, and cleverly, throwing his umbrella Willys Corporation of New York into receivership in order to come out on top at Willys-Overland of Toledo. John then packed up his family and moved back to Ohio. Around the same time, the bankers who had agreed to Chrysler's $1 million salary were meeting with him to discuss renewal. When the amount became a bone of contention—"Well, that's a great deal of money to pay anybody," one banker said—Chrysler stood up, graphically told all assembled where they could stick their job, and walked out.

Della Chrysler did not have to worry about smelly stogies in her house, however, because her husband was already involved in another resuscitation attempt: Maxwell-Chalmers. Following Walter Flanders' retirement at the end of 1918, his successors had borrowed madly to increase production and were caught flat-footed by the business slump. "On top of that," Chrysler said, "Maxwell...had contracted for many millions of dollars worth of parts to be manufactured into cars of a design that was no good." Sixteen thousand Maxwells languished on rail sidings because these dealers couldn't be browbeaten into taking them. For this rescue, Chrysler did not demand a huge immediate compensation but a comparatively modest salary of $100,000 and options on a large block of stock. "You will collect your reward in the future," Walt was told, "through ownership and its attendant satisfactions."

CHAPTER 35

Forever a Roller Coaster

WHILE IN NEW YORK for the National Automobile Show in January 1920, John Dodge caught a cold that developed into the flu, which then turned into pneumonia. He died on January 14. Since childhood, the brothers had been together, and this eternal separation devastated Horace. He died on December 10. Cirrhosis of the liver was the stated reason—and reasonable, given the Dodges' drinking habits—but a contributing factor was grief.

The brothers had precious little time to spend their Ford buyout money and made their wives, Matilda and Anna, the wealthiest widows in the world. They gave the Dodge Brothers' presidency to Frederick Haynes, who had resigned from Franklin in 1912 to throw his lot in with the Dodges as they developed their new automobile. His lot now was trying as Anna visited the plant often, Matilda "got after" him occasionally, and he had to answer to a board of directors no longer willing to serve as a rubber stamp.

But Haynes persevered. Emlen Hare didn't. In April 1921, little more than a year after the lavish launch at the Claridge, Mercer and Simplex pulled out of Hare's Motors, followed that summer by Locomobile, all three companies weakened by the experience. Meanwhile, Stutz was adrift in Indianapolis, largely because Harry Stutz was no longer there. To expand, Harry had taken his company public in 1916 and lost control to a Wall Street speculator named Allan A. Ryan. Ryan persuaded Stutz to stay for three years, whereon Harry left to manufacture the H.C.S. (his middle name was Clayton) elsewhere in Indianapolis, and Allan Ryan proceeded to engineer the infamous "Stutz corner" of 1920. His manipulating was flawless, but his plan backfired and Ryan was ruined. To help an acquaintance, Charles M. Schwab of Bethlehem Steel bought Ryan's stock, entrained for Indianapolis, and asked Albert Erskine to come down from South Bend to tour the Stutz facilities with him because he had never been in an automobile factory and now he owned one. Erskine was happy to take the day off from Studebaker to tour Stutz with his good friend.

———

"If ever there was a mess, that was it," Walter Chrysler said of Maxwell-Chalmers once he had a chance to look around. "Bankruptcy was forty-eight hours around the corner..." Phasing out Chalmers was the only sensible thing to do. Despite a dreadful car on the market now, Maxwell had earned a solid reputation when Jonathan Maxwell was in charge and Ben Briscoe wasn't absorbed in empire building. Chrysler used the good will and improved the product into the "Good Maxwell," that phrase candidly used in advertising. As he had at Buick and Willys, Walt streamlined production, got inventory under control, and reordered priorities. When he saw that three-quarters of the company creditors were old friends, he knew there was a good chance for success, and this was a good place on which to stake his future. "I could see possibilities," he said. "I went at it full steam."

There was one disappointment. Among the retrenching decisions during the Willys receivership was the sale of the Elizabeth property and everything on it, which included the six-cylinder car being developed by the Three Musketeers. At their request, Chrysler visited the plant to see the further progress and, after an hours-long inspection of the engine and the model, said to Zeder, "Fred, I'm with you." The two men shook hands, then threw their left arms around each other and cried. Walt really wanted that car.

The Maxwell bankers gave the okay for Chrysler to purchase the plant at auction on June 9, 1922. Early bidding showed three principals, the bidding for each done by a representative. Chrysler's was Senator James Smith, Jr., of New Jersey. Clarence Davies was rumored to represent either Studebaker or General Motors. The third bidder was a New York realty expert named Joseph P. Day. Davies stopped bidding at $4,465,000; Smith made a quick raise to $5.5 million; Day raised him $25,000; and Smith, without the authorization to go further, bowed out.

The Elizabeth plant now belonged to Billy Durant. Walt was furious. Everyone thought Durant would be "cleaned out" by $5.5 million. "I would have been willing, if the bankers had agreed, to bid up to $7.5 million," Chrysler said.

Yes, Billy was back. Returning from a six-week holiday after being booted out of General Motors, Durant had written sixty-seven of his friends to announce that he was organizing a new company. Within forty-eight hours, he had $7 million in checks and pledges, $2 million of which he returned because he needed only $5 million to start. The company was to be called Durant Motors. This was out of character for Billy; he had disliked his name being on the GM headquarters building (which now, of course, it would not be) and undoubtedly was persuaded in this case by his associates. On January 12, 1921, the new company was incorporated with no car to build and no place to build one.

Forty-seven days later, the former deficiency was taken care of with introduction of the Durant Four in Washington, D.C. The curious choice of the nation's capital for the launch was perhaps because of the concentration of government workers to throng the showroom at the close of their day's work. A crowded showroom signified success. So, apparently, did the Durant name. Thirty thousand Durant Fours were ordered before production began, and 146,000 stockholders rushed to invest in Durant Motors. Ultimately, the latter figure would be 250,000, second only to AT&T.

The Elizabeth plant auction that summer provided Billy a place to build the Durant Four and the bonus of the six-cylinder car the Three Musketeers had been developing for Chrysler. Billy liked the engineers' efforts, but for his top-of-the-line, Durant was thinking "a little bigger, a little more horsepower...a little more expensive." So Zeder, Skelton, and Breer were free to pay a visit to Walter Chrysler, who installed them in a disused area of the Chalmers plant and told them to carry on.

Durant's new company shook John Raskob to his wingtips. Was the Durant Billy's new Chevrolet? Billy assured Pierre du Pont, who had succeeded him as GM president, that he had no designs on the corporation, that he was now sixty, and only wanted "to make a real good car." This satisfied du Pont, but Raskob heard footsteps for years.

Du Pont was more concerned about taking the reins of a corporation that Billy had carried around largely in his head and making order of an aggregate of companies that competed rather than cooperated with each other. The plan to realign management that Alfred Sloan had earlier proposed to Durant was dusted off and presented to du Pont. Following its acceptance, Sloan was appointed vice president of operations, soon to ascend to the GM presidency when du Pont kicked himself up to the board chairmanship.

Sloan's plan had been adapted from the staff-line principle developed by the German army in the late nineteenth century and was a compromise between the du Pont ramrod rigidity and Durant's *laissez-faire*. That his plan would become the model for American corporations for generations to come was something Sloan could not have envisioned as he surveyed the GM scene in the midst of the business decline. Oakland was neatly summed up: "Some days they produced ten cars and some days they produced fifty cars. The situation is this—they turn out a lot of cars that are not what they should be and then they have to fix them up."

Oldsmobile went into the doldrums when its president since 1916, Edward Ver Linden, defected to Durant Motors. More desperate was Cadillac. The Lelands had taken key people with them to Lincoln in 1917, and chief engineer D. McCall White grabbed a number of his colleagues when he left in 1918 to produce the Lafayette for Charlie Nash. Cadillac's ranks were further depleted as president Richard H. "Trainload" Collins (the nickname derived from his years as Buick's super salesman) took three department heads with him to promote the Collins Six and subsequently acquire controlling interest in Peerless of Cleveland.

"You can imagine things looked dark...," Cadillac engineer Ernest Seaholm said. "All the leaders from the top down were gone and those of us left were confused and anxious." Seaholm took over as top engineer "due to my seniority possibly, and knowing my way around in this area." But things looked darkest at Chevrolet, which lost $1 million one month in 1921 and $5 million for the year. Only Buick was solid. When the suggestion was made to move some of its principals, including president Harry Bassett, the large congenial man who looked rather like the hound and who had ably followed Walter Chrysler, Sloan immediately wrote to du Pont that "It is far better that the rest of General Motors be scrapped than any chances taken with Buick's earning power."

Business conditions improved late in 1921. "It was a steady climb from 1922 on," John Willys said. "In the tail end of March we made a little, in May $750,000, and in June $1,000,000. The next year—1923—we made twelve or thirteen millions. We paid the banks their $18,000,000 in fifteen months—three months short of the time allowed—and had $300,000 velvet."

Hupmobile enjoyed an early recovery, bouncing from 13,626 cars in 1921 to 34,168 in 1922. Hudson production rose from 27,143 to 64,464 in the same period, many of the company sales being registered for its Essex coach offered at only $300 above the open touring car's $1,195 price tag, a differential that Roy Chapin would close year by year until, by the mid-1920s, the coach was selling for less than the tourer.

This move by Chapin was as important to the industry as his championing of motor trucks for delivery of matériel during the war. "A packing crate" was the derisive phrase the competition used to describe the new Essex, and it smacked of sour grapes. The "All Year Car" had been promoted by Kissel since 1913, but Hudson's carrying of the concept into the popular-priced field was momentous.

So long as cars remained fair-weather conveyances to all but those who could afford limousines, the government's classification of the automobile as a luxury had some merit. The Essex coach nullified that.

Most automakers took advantage of the business upswing. Four Auburn executives were encouraged to strike out on their own for Elkhart, sixty Hoosier miles to the northwest, to buy out the company of George and William Pratt, builders of carriages since 1873 and cars since 1908. The Auburn veterans called their new automobile the Elcar, made plans to double the Pratt plant capacity to 6,000 cars annually, and set out to grab a piece of the lucrative taxi business. Joining them were more than fifty Auburn workers, who moved their families to Elkhart either because they liked the promise of this new enterprise or didn't like what they saw at Auburn. Chicago capital, including two financial institutions and William Wrigley, now controlled the Auburn Automobile Company. Long-distance ownership and local management was not the optimal way to run an automobile factory. This heavy exodus left the Auburn company in desperate straits.

Desperate, too, were the Lelands. Production of 3,407 cars up to February 1922 was about half the projected figure, and Washington was telling them again that they owed back taxes on wartime income. The Treasury Department's previous claim for $5.7 million had been disproved and withdrawn; this one for $4.5 million arrived in the midst of Wilfred's negotiations for a $10 million bank loan and scared the bankers off. The Lincoln Motor Company was thrown into receivership just as Henry Leland was making arrangements with the coachbuilding houses of Brunn and Judkins to redesign the banal bodies his son-in-law had crafted. Aware that their company would be sold, the Lelands sought a buyer they could trust. Henry Ford, they decided, was their man. Although he hadn't forgotten who had sculpted Cadillac out of his own failed company, Ford had come to like the elder Leland and had long respected his mastery at engineering. The addition of a luxury car to the company product line appealed to Henry and especially to Edsel, whose sense of the aesthetic could never be appeased by a Model T.

The headline of the *Detroit News* on January 11, 1922, read "Ford Saves Lelands." This followed an extensive interview with Henry, during which he suggested that he neither wanted nor needed Lincoln but was willing to buy the company for reasons of sentiment and altruism. "It would be a stain against the motor-car industry and against Detroit," Henry said loftily, "to permit outsiders to secure control of the Lincoln plant merely because the Lelands have been caught in a financial pinch."

Lincoln became the property of the Ford Motor Company for the $8 million determined by the court. The *Detroit News* called the transaction "a marriage of volume and precision manufacturing." On February 16, at a party to celebrate his seventy-ninth birthday, the Fords presented Henry Leland a check for $363,000, the par value of his Lincoln stock. Henry Ford implied that all Lincoln stockholders would be reimbursed as well.

Ford had also pledged that the Lelands could continue to manage Lincoln as they always had, but within twenty-four hours, Charlie Sorensen was at the door with a delegation of Ford executives to look around. The Lelands, who had raised imperiousness to an art form, bristled at the presence of the interlopers. Sorensen had the subtlety of an avalanche and promptly bruised their egos with pointed remarks about Lincoln's old-fashioned and inefficient production methods. A horde of Ford workmen soon arrived to reorganize the plant. Included in the demolition was one wall of Henry Leland's private office. Ford machines and tools were brought in, and Lincoln's were yanked out. Lincoln men were fired, and Ford employees were installed in their places. When Sorensen told a Ford worker to use the cylinders that had been rejected by a Lincoln inspector, Henry Leland took a sledge hammer and smashed the cylinders to bits.

This was a marriage that could not be saved. In late May, Wilfred Leland, assured he could find financing, wrote to Ford, asking to buy back the company for what Henry had paid for it "plus a reasonable interest rate." The letter went unanswered, so did a second and then a third, pleading that Ford "turn the Lincoln plant back to us...to go on in our one-horse way producing and improving the Lincoln car." Finally, Wilfred drove to Fairlane, grandly swept past the guard, surprised Ford in his study, and begged to buy Lincoln back. "Not for $500 million," said Henry.

On June 10, a Ford emissary arrived at Wilfred's office to request his resignation. The father resigned, too. That same day, the Lelands took their belongings, as was also requested, and left. Ford paid the $4 million Lincoln had owed creditors but balked at reimbursing all Lincoln stockholders, which infuriated and embarrassed the Lelands. They took their case to the press and ultimately to court, where they lost and after which they remained bitter toward Ford to their deaths.

Edsel Ford made a beauty, and a success, of the Lelands' Lincoln. Henry didn't visit the factory much and didn't seem much interested. His focus was on the Rouge. By now, the foundry and the power plant, each the largest of its kind in the world, were in operation. Soon iron ore from Lake Superior ports and coal from ports along Lake Erie would be brought by Ford ships to the company's half-mile-long mill to be made into steel in a continuous process and in myriad varieties for the many parts of a Ford car. From iron ore to finished motor on the final assembly line would take only thirty-three hours. By the mid-1920s, the Rouge employed 42,000 workers in 93 separate buildings sprawled over 1,115 acres and was the greatest industrial colossus in the world.

Self-sufficiency had been the Ford plan, and at the Rouge, he had achieved it. Having rid his company of its strongest leaders, Ford was Henry's to run the way he wished. His stubbornness deepened and his prejudices—particularly a virulent anti-Semitism—hardened. The libel suit he brought against the *Chicago Tribune* brought him one more group to detest: the press. Nobody could hate better than Henry Ford.

———

"Durant to Build Car at Ford Price," *Automotive Industries* heralded in February 1922. Actually, Billy hoped to do even better than that. The price of a Model T without self-starter and demountable rims was now $348. The new Durant car, as yet unnamed, was to be offered fully equipped for the same price.

The car arrived, amid carefully frenzied hoopla, on March 9, again in Washington, D.C. Star was its name, a selection, some said, to attract the same Jewish customers that Ford was alienating.* The choice allowed headline writers of limited imagination to write about "Durant's Star Seen in the Ascendant." And it certainly did seem so. The Washington showroom was mobbed by visitors of every stripe, including dealers from the south and west who were fed up with the heavy-handedness of Ford, and Senator Newberry, who arrived to compare the Star, as *Automobile Topics* said, "with the product of the late aspirant for his own toga."

Try as he might, Billy wasn't able to provide the Star with starter and demountable rims for $348 but offered these features optionally for $95, $10 less than the Model T Ford price for the same package. The Star had a standard gearbox as opposed to the Model T's planetary, and

---

* Billy named another car in his new empire the Flint, after the city where he could always raise cash fast. Princeton was his new Cadillac; Eagle was in the price range between the Flint and the Star. The Princeton was a stillborn, and the Eagle (the thirteenth use of that name for a new car) died in infancy. Probably Billy selected Star less for ethnic reasons than his expectation that the car would be one.

the fine array of body styles included the industry's first production station wagon. By September, however, Henry lowered the price of the Model T by $50, a figure Billy could not hope to meet. He had played this scene with Ford in the past. Now, he huddled with Ver Linden and two dozen other executives who had followed him from GM, to decide what to do next.

Replacing the people who followed Durant was one of the more pressing tasks Alfred Sloan faced in his reorganization of General Motors. Determining whose loyalty remained with the man who was now a rival made the job more difficult. After several discussions, Sloan concluded that A.B.C. Hardy's allegiance was to GM and installed him in the Olds presidential chair formerly occupied by Ver Linden. To take "Trainload" Collins' place, he picked Herbert H. Rice, who had begun selling Cadillacs in Providence, Rhode Island, in 1903.

From the Ford castoffs, Sloan latched onto Norval Hawkins as general consultant to the General Motors Executive Committee, which had been created to prevent the impulsive decision-making of the Durant years. What Hawkins had done in marketing the Model T, he now adapted to GM products, and he championed the concept of covering the entire market while avoiding overlap among corporate member firms. Sloan was in complete agreement; he wanted GM everywhere except "the fancy-price field with small production."

After weeding out the weak Sheridan and Scripps-Booth, the focus turned to Chevrolet. An independent appraisal had recommended the company be eliminated. Sloan was adamantly opposed. Forget the report, Pierre du Pont said. The next order of business was a president for Chevrolet to replace Durant. Chosen was Karl W. Zimmerschied, a metallurgist who had joined GM during Durant's first reign. Because he had not been involved with Chevrolet when Billy organized it, Zimmerschied was deemed a GM man, and his implacable nature was seen as well attuned to this period when everyone seemed to have a different suggestion about what to do with Chevrolet.

Charles Kettering's idea was a copper-cooled motor that promised to have fewer parts, less weight, and higher performance than a water-cooled engine, as well as the novelty of air cooling. Franklin had been producing air-cooled cars in Upstate New York since shortly after the turn of the century, and Fox of Philadelphia was a new air-cooled car in the marketplace, but both were in the "fancy-price field with small production" and thus of no concern. The only problem with the copper-cooled engine was that it was a fiasco. "Throw it in the ashcan," Walt Chrysler had advised Durant when asked for his advice. From his laboratory in Dayton, Kettering, who had come up with the self-starter, proclaimed his latest invention "the greatest thing that has ever been produced in the automobile world" and, with the encouragement of Pierre du Pont, pressed onward.

Meanwhile, something had to be done about the Chevrolet that was on the market. During the first two years of the new decade, Model T production had doubled (to the million-unit range), while Chevrolet's had been halved (to sixty-odd thousand). November 1921 saw the appointment of Ormond E. Hunt, late of Hare's Motors, as Chevrolet chief engineer. Karl Zimmerschied told him he hated the copper-cooled engine. Finally, so did everyone else. Of the 759 cars completed, 239 were scrapped in production, another 20 were lost somewhere, and the rest were ultimately recalled. Kettering recovered from the "staggering blow" of the abandonment of his copper-cooled invention and went on to experiment in high-octane gasolines and high-compression engines.

What to do with Chevrolet remained the issue. Sloan and Hawkins concluded that it would be suicidal to compete with Ford head-on. "No conceivable amount of capital short of the United States Treasury could have sustained the losses required to take volume away from him at his own game," Sloan said. Instead, the strategy was to chip at Ford from the top, to create a price class just above the Model T's that would attract those with a few more dollars to spend and the desire for more than the basic transportation of the Tin Lizzie. An earlier Curtis Publishing survey had indicated such a strategy could work. "The World's Lowest Priced *Quality* Automobile," the ads said. "Unequalled in Style, Value and Economy...Nothing Compares with Chevrolet." The new model's designation was changed from Durant's Four-Ninety to Superior, and none but the irrevocably dense wondered what the Chevrolet was superior to.

There was one casualty at Chevrolet during this clamorous period: Karl Zimmerschied. He had a nervous breakdown and retired. Heading Chevrolet now was none other than William Knudsen, whom Sloan had earlier hired for GM's Executive Committee. Knudsen relished the assignment of taking on Henry Ford. For Big Bill, this was war.

And victory would be his within a few years. "I vant vun for vun," was Knudsen's one-sentence speech at a dealer meeting. The dealers scratched their heads, then caught on. As Chevrolet increasingly encroached into Ford territory, even Henry's yes men began saying no to the Model T, and he had to reluctantly agree to a new model.

———

Alexander Winton was weary. He hated where the industry was headed. Reluctant to change unless the idea was his, he had waited until World War I to adopt left-hand steering, the same time he changed his company's name from Winton Motor Carriage to Winton Motor Car. In the early 1920s, he was selling about 1,000 cars per year, most of them to repeat customers. The new Winton that a San Francisco man bought in December 1923 was the fourteenth since his first in 1901; two years later, an L.A. man bought his eighteenth new Winton.

Such owner loyalty was admirable, but these first-generation automobile owners were dying off by now. And Alexander Winton didn't care to make adjustments to entice new car buyers. Only once, in 1916, did Winton sales pass the 2,000 mark. Low production of a high-priced car was the Winton way, and when he realized the future meant competition with the likes of Ford and General Motors, he turned his back on the automobile business to pursue manufacture of the engine invented by Rudolf Diesel.

In April 1920, while watching the races at the Los Angeles Speedway, Elmer Apperson suffered a massive heart attack and died. Thereafter, his brother Edgar banked his war revenues, once they arrived, and took to his leisure. His name remained on the door, but he was seldom in the factory. The year 1921 was the last year Apperson sales passed the 1,000 mark. The company's liquidation followed five years later.

———

Elwood Haynes fought to the end. In 1922, a granite monument was erected on Pumpkinvine Pike to "the inventor, designer, and builder of America's first mechanically successful automobile." Two years earlier, before Elmer Apperson died, the two Kokomo companies had waged an advertising war disputing which of them deserved "first automobile" honors. That the monument remained standing was evidence that Edgar Apperson really didn't care anymore.

Haynes mustered sales of 5,600 cars and a profit in 1922, and a $1 million bond drive was successfully undertaken in Kokomo the following year. But the tide had turned against the company. A merger try in 1923 among Dorris, Winton, and Haynes fell through, and there was a rumor that Haynes may have talked consolidation with Apperson in 1924, which indicates how grievous the situation was. The Haynes Automobile Company went to the auction block in February 1925. Walter Chrysler bought the factory. Elwood Haynes was dead of pneumonia that April.

Charlie King gave up the automobile business in 1921, selling out to a Buffalo entrepreneur who ran the company into the ground within a few years. It was Charlie behind whom an envious Henry Ford had bicycled when King tested the first automobile built in Detroit in 1896. Now King spent the remainder of his career giving engineering advice when asked and serving on corporate boards such as the Fletcher Paper Company of Detroit.

Dallas Dort, Billy Durant's carriage-building partner, gave up after producing some 107,000 cars in a decade, paying his debts, and closing the doors of the Dort Motor Car Company in 1924. He died of a heart attack while playing golf at the Flint Country Club the following year. Joseph Cole died in 1925, too, less than ten months after he chose to liquidate his Indianapolis company.

Of all the post-World War I entries into the marketplace, perhaps the most intriguing was the Rickenbacker. It bore the name of the war's most celebrated hero, Captain Eddie, ace of aces. Behind the company were three of the industry's celebrated pioneers: the E-M-F trio...Barney Everitt, who had started with Ransom Olds; Bill Metzger, who had made Cadillac a success; and Walter Flanders, who had moved Henry Ford toward mass production. The first car in the medium-price field to feature four-wheel brakes, the Rickenbacker wasn't on the market long before a merger with Gray and Peerless was attempted. It failed. Frank Klingensmith left Gray in 1925 for an extended vacation in Australia. "Trainload" Collins had already been ousted from Peerless following two class suits brought against him by a rancorous stockholder.

The Gray was no more by 1926, and the Peerless followed five years later. Rickenbacker became history by 1927, the same year Harold Wills admitted defeat in Marysville. Partly the victim of his own pursuit for perfection, Wills was widely known in the industry for shutting down the assembly line whenever he thought an improvement could be made to the Wills Sainte Claire.

The Auburn Automobile Company was given a reprieve when its Chicago owners sent the local hotshot Moon salesman to Indiana to take charge. Errett Lobban Cord dressed up those parking-lot Auburns, which by now had instruments, and owned the company within a few years. Subsequently, he dazzled with the Model J Duesenberg and went stylishly front drive with the Cord. His specialty merchandise approach—Sloan's "fancy price field"—worked well until the Great Depression.

Likewise, Billy Durant's second empire (or third, depending on how you count them) failed because Billy became miffed that he couldn't compete with Ford and the corporation he had created. He turned his energies to the stock market, where he became the "bull of bulls" and was wiped out in the crash of 1929. With Durant Motors went Locomobile, which Billy had bought to be the jewel in his lineup. Mercer and Simplex had long since become a memory. Stutz was gone, too.

In the late 1920s, Fred Chandler sold out to Hupp, and Harry Jewett to the Graham brothers. Neither the Hupp nor the Graham survived World War II. In desperate straits, Stewart McDonald of Moon in St. Louis and the Kissel brothers of Hartford, Wisconsin, allowed themselves to be finagled by Archie Andrews, the wheeler-dealer behind the front-drive Ruxton, a short-time rival to the Cord. The Gardners didn't survive their encounter with Andrews either.

Rolls-Royce called it quits in Springfield in the early 1930s, and Pierce-Arrow became history in Buffalo before the decade ended. Packard endured longer because Alvan Macauley had become aware even before the Great Depression that survival was impossible solely in the luxury field. Finally, Packard thought survival was possible only with Studebaker. Willys placed its hopes on the Jeep. The companies long nurtured by Charlie Nash and Roy Chapin combined into American Motors, dropping the Nash and Hudson nameplates to focus on a car called the Rambler, which was the name Tom Jeffery had chosen for his first automobile at the turn of the century.

In the years since Oliver Evans first had the lunatic idea of horseless travel, minions had followed with a big dream and varying talent. It had been a raucous and rollicking epoch. Now Darwinian predictably took over. As year passed year, more automakers failed, and entries into the field became fewer. Those who had no interest in being big found they couldn't make it by staying small. In 1923, a total of 164 companies were producing automobiles in 23 states. By 1930, that figure had dwindled to 42 companies in 9 states.

The last new automaker to survive today strode into the marketplace at the Commodore Hotel during the New York Automobile Show in January 1924. The trade press marveled at the "skillfully prepared advertisement" that introduced the prominent figure in the industry who was unknown to the public at large.

Walter Chrysler's name was spelled phonetically.

Epilogue

IN MAY 1946, under the leadership of George Romney, the Automobile Manufacturers Association, descendant of the A.L.A.M.-*cum*-N.A.C.C., sponsored a golden jubilee to mark the beginning of the industry, the date representing the first series manufacture of an automobile by the Duryeas in Massachusetts. In 1896, too, Charlie King and Henry Ford drove their first cars on the streets of Detroit, which played to local pride, and it was the city's sesquicentennial. Automakers were anxious to celebrate. The long war was over; the "arsenal of democracy" had returned again to the business of building cars. Nearly 90 million vehicles had been produced thus far in America. From "miscellaneous" status shortly before World War I, the industry had grown—leapt, actually—to number one in the nation.

A mile of Woodward Avenue was painted gold for the occasion, as were the hooves of participating horses. The week-long festival included expositions and fireworks and a four-mile-long parade with a Jubilee Queen, scads of elaborate flower-bedecked floats, marching bands, and more than a thousand "ancient" automobiles. Living industry pioneers were named to an Automotive Hall of Fame. Only a handful of the people we have met in this book remained. Fortuitously, one of them was a Duryea: J. Frank.

Charles Duryea's obituary in 1938 had declared the 1895 car his solo undertaking, suggesting Charles was "the father of the automobile" and mentioning Frank only in passing. Charles' son, who had provided the obituary writer the biographical material, continued to work on behalf of his father's legacy. His uncle quietly demurred that the proper pronoun was "we."

Henry Leland had died at ninety in 1932. The following year, Albert Erskine died by his own hand as he and his beloved Studebaker Corporation careened toward bankruptcy. In 1936, pneumonia took Roy Chapin, who had taken time away from Hudson to serve as Secretary of Commerce in the Hoover administration. He was fifty-five. A decade earlier, Jim Storrow, who continued a vigorous business life despite illness, had succumbed to cancer at age sixty-two. In 1941, Harold Wills was the same age when he died in Detroit in the hospital named for his boss in Dearborn. The previous year, at his lavish estate on Long Island, Walter Chrysler had been taken at age sixty-five by a cerebral hemorrhage and years of overwork. Edsel Ford was only forty-nine when he died of stomach cancer in 1943 and, many thought, a heart broken by his father's predilection for a bully named Harry Bennett over his own son. Henry was devastated.

Automakers who survived to join Frank Duryea in the Automotive Hall of Fame were Edgar Apperson, William C. Durant, Henry Ford, Charles B. King, Charles W. Nash, Ransom Eli Olds, and Alfred P. Sloan, Jr. Big Bill Knudsen was given a special "Oscar" for his contributions to the industry. Charlie King recreated his drive of Detroit's first automobile.

Bygones by now were long begone. The automakers smiled broadly at each other and reveled in more attention than most of them, Henry Ford excepted, had been paid in a long time. Photos of the Charles (King and Nash), Ranse and Henry, and Ed and Frank in rapt conversation gladdened the heart. Billy Durant was too weak to attend; in ill health for more than four years, he was being quietly provided financial assistance by Alfred Sloan. The Golden Jubilee was the pioneering automakers' last hurrah.

Ironically, the only race car driver honored, the hell-raising Barney Oldfield, who had survived in Ford's 999 and the Blitzen Benz, was the first Golden Jubilee celebrant to die, less than four months later, of a cerebral hemorrhage at age sixty-nine. When the same malady claimed Bill Knudsen at the same age in 1948, he was acclaimed by the Detroit Common Council as "a war casualty entitled to the acclaim of every citizen of the United States."

Within a month of each other in 1947, Henry Ford and Billy Durant were gone. Billy was first, at eighty-five on March 18 in his apartment in New York City's Gramercy Park. Even the Durant-friendly *New York Times* obituary subtly suggested he was a has-been. "Once Motor Car Giant" was the headline of the irreverent *New York Post*. Although lower-echelon industry members with whom Billy had worked were at his funeral at Gramercy Park's Calvary Church, none of his fellow hall of famers attended.

Henry's death on April 7 was an event. His body lay in state in Greenfield Village as mourners waited in a mile-long queue to see him. *Life* magazine carried on its cover a photograph of a factory worker in overalls gazing mournfully into Ford's casket. On the day of the funeral, more than 30,000 people clustered outside St. Paul's Episcopal Cathedral. Twenty thousand were at the family cemetery in pouring rain. Henry's death was page-one news throughout the nation.

Ransom Olds died much more quietly in Lansing, at age eighty-six, in 1950. He and his wife Metta, who had cheerfully followed behind him with a block of wood on his test drives in the 1890s, had been married more than sixty years. He was a happy man but did not die truly content because of a lingering resentment that his contribution to the industry had been forgotten in the lionizing of Henry Ford.

The two Charles died nine years apart, Nash first in 1948 at age eighty-one. In retirement, Charlie had seldom ventured far from his mountainside home in Beverly Hills. The transplanted Californian's estate was valued in excess of $40 million. Saying "the spadework was over" in Detroit, Charlie King spent his final years in New York's Westchester County, still experimenting, now as an artist and architect. His will, opened in 1957, revealed that Charlie had donated his $500,000 collection of antique and classic automobiles to the Henry Ford Museum.

In 1957, at age eighty-six, Ed Apperson had returned to Kokomo to cut the ribbon marking Apperson Way, which began, ironically, across the street from the old Haynes plant. He commented to a reporter that "the highway slaughter today makes me doubtful of my contribution," and he died in a rest home in Phoenix, Arizona, in 1959. Alfred Sloan had a fatal heart attack in 1966 and spent his final hours in the research hospital he and a GM colleague had co-founded:

Memorial Sloan-Kettering in New York City. Obituaries proclaimed him a captain of industry. He was ninety.

Last of the Golden Jubilee hall of fame automakers to leave this world was Frank Duryea, at age ninety-seven in 1967. Obviously, early retirement had agreed with him. By now, it was acknowledged that he was responsible for the first Duryea. In 1959, when he was eighty-nine, Frank had been on hand for a parade of antique autos up Manhattan's Fifth Avenue from Washington Square to Central Park. Among the cars was one of the 1896 Duryeas. Peering into its engine, Frank said, "It's like a dream to look at the old fellow."

Research Sources

FOLLOWING ARE REFERENCES and further reading for this volume. Because, as noted in the Introduction, this book has been literally forty years in the making, much of the research was derived from articles and books written by the author during that period. Individual references to those works are cited, save for one: the *Standard Catalog of American Cars 1805–1942.* If an automobile company's lifetime production ranged from one to several hundred cars, the reader may assume the reference is from that volume.

Chapter 1

Bathe, Greville and Dorothy. *Oliver Evans: A Chronicle of Early American Engineering.* Historical Society of Pennsylvania, 1935.

Doerflinger, Thomas M. *A Vigorous Spirit of Enterprise: Merchants and Economic Development in Revolutionary Philadelphia.* University of North Carolina, 1986.

"An Eighteenth-Century Henry Ford," *The Mentor*, February 1922.

Evans, Oliver. "On the Origin of Steam Boats and Steam Waggons," *Delaware History,* Vol. 7, No. 2, September 1956.

_____. *Patent Right Oppression Opposed.* R. Folwell, 1813.

_____. *The Young Steam and Engineer's Guide.* H.C. Carey, 1805.

Klein, Philip S. and Ari Hoogenboom. *A History of Pennsylvania.* McGraw-Hill, 1973.

"Oliver Evans, Engineer," *Pennsylvania Arts and Sciences*, Vol. 1, 1936.

Olton, Charles S. *Artisans for Independence: Philadelphia Mechanics and the American Revolution*. Syracuse University, 1975.

Quimby, Ian M.G. *Apprenticeship in Colonial Philadelphia*. Garland, 1985.

Sellers, Coleman, Jr. "Oliver Evans and His Inventions," *Journal of Franklin Institute*, July 1886.

Teilhut, Darwin L. *Trouble Is My Master*. Little, Brown, 1942.

Chapter 2

Bailey, L. Scott. "The Other Revolution: The Birth and Development of the American Automobile," *The American Car Since 1775*. Automobile Quarterly, 1971.

Bathe, Greville. *Three Essays: A Dissertation on the Genesis of Mechanical Transport in America Before 1800*. St. Augustine, 1960.

Beecroft, David. "The History of the American Automobile Industry, Chapter 1," *The Automobile*, October 28, 1915.

Chevalier, Michael. *Society, Manners and Politics in the United States*. Weeks, Jordan, 1839.

Downs, Robert B. *Images of America: Travelers from Abroad in the New World*. University of Illinois, 1987.

Dunbar, Seymour. *A History of Travel in America*. Tudor, 1937.

Fitch, John. *The Autobiography of John Fitch*. American Philosophical Society, 1976.

Read, David. *Nathan Reid*. Hurd and Houghton, 1870.

Sarmiento, Domingo Faustino. *Travels in the United States in 1847*. Princeton University, 1970.

Shaler, N.S. "The Common Roads," *Scribner's Magazine*, October 1889.

Sutton, Horace. *Travelers: The American Tourist from Stagecoach to Space Shuttle*. William Morrow, 1980.

Turnbull, Archibald Douglas. *John Stevens, An American Record*. Century, 1928.

Chapter 3

Dudgeon, Richard. Various writings and monographs. New York Public Library.

Fletcher, William. *English and American Steam Carriages and Traction Engines*. Newton & Abbott, 1904.

_____. *The History and Development of Steam Locomotives on Common Roads*. Newton & Abbott, 1891.

The New York Times, October 6, 7, and 8, 1858 (burning of the Crystal Palace).

Roper, untitled and unsigned article, *The Hub*, July 1897.

Roper, Stephen. *The Engineer's Handy-book*. E. Claxton, 1881.

Scott, Robert F. "Richard Dudgeon, Machinist," *Automobile Quarterly,* Vol. VI, No. 3.

"A Very Early American Automobile," *Light Steam Power*, May–June 1966.

Wile, Frederic William. *A Century of Industrial Progress*. Doubleday, Doran, 1928.

Williams, Archibald. *The Romance of Modern Invention*. C. Arthur Pearson, 1903.

Chapter 4

Bailey, Sturges, Mrs. *Index to Hisory of the Fox River Valley, Lake Winnebago, and the Green Bay Region*. Wisconsin State Genealogical Society, 1981.

Current, Richard Nelson. *Wisconsin: A Bicentennial History*. Norton, 1977.

Harden, Horst O. *Samuel Morey and His Atmospheric Engine*. Society of Automotive Engineers, 1992.

Ingram, J.S. *The Centennial Exposition*. Hubbard, 1876.

Maas, John. *The Glorious Enterprise: The Centennial Exhibition*. American Life Foundation, 1973.

"Magee's Illustrated Guide of Philadelphia and the Centennial Exhibition," 1876.

McCabe, James D. *The Illustrated History of the Centennial Exhibition*. National Publishing, 1975.

Nesbit, Robert C. *The History of Wisconsin, Vol. III, 1873–1893*. State Historical Society of Wisconsin, 1985.

Newspaper articles in the *Weekly Northwestern* (Oshkosh), *Greenbay Advocate*, and *Milwaukee Sentinel*, and transcripts of the Laws of Wisconsin of the period, made available through the Milwaukee County Historical Society, Milwaukee Public Library, Milwaukee Public Museum, State Historical Society of Wisconsin, and the Oshkosh Public Museum.

"Official Catalogue of the [Centennial] Exhibition," 1876.

Scott, Robert F. "I Invented the Automobile," *Automobile Quarterly,* Vol. IV, No. 3.

Thompson, William Fletcher. *The History of Wisconsin*. State Historical Society of Wisconsin, 1973.

Walsh, Margaret. *The Manufacturing Frontier. Pioneer Industry in Antebellum Wisconsin*. State Historical Society of Wisconsin, 1977.

Chapter 5

Badger, Reid. *The Great American Fair: The World's Columbian Exposition & American Culture*. N. Hall, 1979.

Burg, David F. *Chicago's White City of 1893*. University of Kentucky, 1976.

"The Chicago Tribune Art Supplement—World's Columbian Exposition," 1893.

Electrical World and Electrical Engineer, January 21, 1899 (A.L. Riker electric).

Kimes, Beverly Rae. *The Star and the Laurel: The Centennial History of Daimler, Mercedes and Benz*. Mercedes-Benz of North America, 1986.

"Official Catalogue of the [World's Columbian] Exposition," 1893.

"Pictorial History of the Chicago Fair," *Harper's Weekly*, May 13, 1893.

"Preliminary Glimpses of the Fair," *Century Magazine*, February 1893.

Scientific American, May 6, June 3, August 19, and November 4, 1893 (exposition, various articles).

Smith, F. Hopkinson. "The Picturesque Side," *Scribner's Magazine*, November 1893.

Truman, Benjamin Cummings. *History of the World's Fair*. Arno, 1976.

Yarnell, Duane. *Auto Pioneering: A Remarkable Story of Ransom E. Olds.* DeKline, 1949.

Chapter 6

Anderson, Russell. "The First Automobile Race in America," Museum of Science and Industry, 1945.

Carriage Monthly, December 1895; *Harper's Weekly,* October 31, 1896; and Chicago newspapers (Chicago Times-Herald race report).

The Horseless Age, February 1896 (power and duty tests).

"An Industrial Achievement," Pope Mfg. Co., 1907.

King, Charles Brady. *Personal Side Lights of America's First Automobile Race.* Super-power, 1945.

May, George W. *Charles E. Duryea, Automaker.* Edwards Brothers, 1973.

Morris & Salom entry: *The Horseless Age,* November 1895, and December 1895.

Mueller Record, November 1945. Beverly Rae Kimes Archives.

New York Recorder, August 31, September 7, and November 6, 1895 (Macy Benz entry).

The New York Times, August 11, 1909 (obituary of Albert Pope).

Pope, Colonel Albert A. "Automobiles and Good Roads," *Munsey's Magazine*, May 1903.

Scharchburg, Richard P. *Carriages Without Horses: J. Frank Duryea and the Birth of the American Automobile Industry.* Society of Automotive Engineers, 1993.

Scientific American, November 16, 1895 (consolation race report).

"Thos. A. Edison's Views on Motor Carriages," *The Horseless Age*, November 1895.

Chapter 7

Cosmopolitan Magazine, January through May issues, 1896 (Cosmopolitan Race).

"The Future of the Motor Car," *Scientific American*, July 17, 1897.

Gill, Brendan. "Charles Brady King: To Spare the Obedient Beast," *The New Yorker,* May 18, 1946.

The Horseless Age, January, April, and May 1896 (Morris & Salom Electrobat).

"The Horseless Carriage in France and America," *Harper's Weekly,* March 1896.

Kimes, Beverly Rae. "Young Henry Ford," *Automobile Quarterly,* Vol. X, No. 2.

King, Charles Brady. *Charles Brady King, Engineer and Inventor.* Larchmont, 1932.

May, George S. "Duryea Motor Wagon Company," *The Automobile Industry, 1896–1920.* Facts on File, 1990.

Scott, Robert F. "The Elusive Mr. Pennington: A Study of Inventive Genius and Gyp Artistry," *Automobile Quarterly,* Vol. V, No. 4.

_____. "Haynes-Apperson," *Automobile Quarterly,* Vol. II, No. 3.

"Spreading Automobile," *Harper's Weekly,* July 1, 1899.

"The Status of the Horse at the Turn of the Century," *Harper's Weekly,* November 18, 1899.

Thomas, L.M. "Following the Mystery Tide: The Life and Cars of Charles B. King," *Automobile Quarterly,* Vol. 30, No. 3.

Chapter 8

Goddard, Stephen B. *Colonel Albert Pope and His American Dream Machine.* McFarland, 2000.

Kimes, Beverly Rae, and Richard M. Langworth. *Oldsmobile: The First Seventy-Five Years.* Automobile Quarterly, 1984.

Maxim, Hiram Percy. *Horseless Carriage Days.* Harper, 1936.

The New York Times, February 21 and 22 and July 11 and 13, 1899; *Scientific American,* February 18, 1899; and *The Hub,* May 1899 (Electric Vehicle Company).

_____. February 16, 1967 (obituary of J. Frank Duryea).

Pinkerton, Robert E. "Ed Apperson and the Horseless Carriage," *True's Automobile Yearbook,* No. 1, 1952.

"The Place of the Automobile," *Outing,* October 1900.

"The Promise of the Automobile," *Outing*, April 1900.

Winton, Alexander. "Get a Horse," *The Saturday Evening Post*, February 8, 1930.

"The Winton Motor Carriage," *Scientific American*, July 24, 1897.

Chapter 9

"Alexander Winton: A Sketch of His Career and the Development of the Winton Vehicles," *Motor Review*, May 15, 1902.

"Amzi Lorenzo Barber and the Barber Asphalt Paving Co.," *Stanley Museum Quarterly*, June 1999.

Doolittle, James Rood, ed. *The Romance of the Automobile Industry*. Klebold, 1916.

Gray, Ralph D. *Alloys and Automobiles: The Life and Times of Elwood Haynes*. Indiana Historical Society, 1976.

Harper's Weekly, July 22, 1899 (Winton New York trip).

_____. July 22, 1899, and *Scientific American*, July 27, 1901 (Winton automobile).

Martin, Terry. "The First of the Marque," *Packard: A History of the Motor Car and the Company*. Automobile Quarterly, 1978.

The New York Times, January 19 and December 7, 1900 (Electric Vehicle Company).

_____, October 3, 1940 (obituary of Freelan O. Stanley).

Nevins, Allan and Frank Ernest Hill. *Ford: The Times, The Man, The Company*. Charles Scribner's, 1954.

Niemeyer, Glenn A. *The Automotive Career of Ransom E. Olds*. Michigan State University, 1963.

Chapter 10

"Automobile Club's Run," *The New York Times*, November 13, 1899.

"Automobile Races at Newport," *The Automobile*, September 1901.

"The Automobile in Society," *The Automobile Magazine*, October 1899.

Baldwin, William Earle. "Society Women as Motorists," *The Automobile Magazine*, June 1900.

Bentley, John. *Great American Automobiles: A Dramatic Account of Their Achievements in Competition.* Prentice-Hall, 1957.

"Contradicts Itself," *Cycle and Automobile Trade Journal*, January 1900.

Gosden, Walter. "Alexander Winton, The Man and His Motorcars," *Automobile Quarterly*, Vol. 22, No. 3.

Hewitt, Edward Ringwood. *Those Were the Days: Tales of a Long Life.* World Book, 1943.

Kimes, Beverly Rae. "Nothing to Watch But the Road," *Automobile Quarterly*, Vol. II, No. 4.

_____. "Willie K: The Saga of a Racing Vanderbilt," *Automobile Quarterly*, Vol. XV, No. 3.

"Labeling of Motor Carriages," *The Automobile Magazine*, June 1901.

"The Modern Chariot," *Cosmopolitan Magazine*, June 1900.

"Names for Horseless Vehicles," *The Horseless Age*, March 1896.

The New York Times, January 3, July 3, 10, and 24, and October 31, 1899, and January 28, 1900 (various articles).

_____, December 7, 1899, and September 12, 1900 (automobile licensing).

_____, April 15, July 8 and 26, and September 7 and 9, 1900 (New York Automobile Show, pre-event races).

_____, July 23, 1900 (editorial) and November 4, 6, 7, 8, 10, and 11, 1900 (New York Automobile Show).

"Newport's Automobile Parade," *Harper's Weekly*, September 18, 1899.

"What's in a Name," *Harper's Weekly*, July 29, 1899.

Chapter 11

"The Automobile in America," *Munsey's Magazine*, 1906.

"The Automobile in America," *The Strand Magazine*, February 1900.

"The Automobile—A Miracle of the Twentieth Century," *Munsey's Magazine*, 1910.

Automobile Topics, February 24, 1936 (obituary of Roy Chapin).

"Automobile-Making in America," *The Review of Reviews,* September 1901, pp. 297–300.

"Automobilism in the States," *The Autocar*, March 15, 1902, pp. 263–265.

Collins, Michael J. "Raymond and Ralph Owen," *Pioneers of the U.S. Automobile Industry: The Design Innovators.* Society of Automotive Engineers, 2002.

Donovan, Neal. *Andrew L. Riker and the Electric Car.* McFerson College, 2003.

Kimes, Beverly Rae. "Ransom Eli Olds: The Man Behind the Marque," *Automobile Quarterly*, Vol. 41, No. 3.

MacFarlane, Peter Clark. "The Beginnings of the Automobile," *Collier's Magazine*, in three issues, January 1915.

Chapter 12

"Automobile Topics of Interest," *The New York Times*, July 20 and December 7, 1902.

Dunham, Terry B. and Lawrence R. Gustin. *The Buick: A Complete History.* Automobile Quarterly, 1980.

Hendry, Maurice D. *Cadillac, Standard of the World: The Complete History.* Automobile Quarterly, 1973.

Kimes, Beverly Rae. "The Benjamin Briscoe Story" *Automobile Quarterly*, Vol. XVII, No. 2.

Levine, Leo. *Ford: The Dust and the Glory.* Society of Automotive Engineers, 2000.

Nolan, William F. *Barney Oldfield.* G.P. Putnam's, 1961.

Rae, John B. "Henry Martyn Leland," *The Automobile Industry, 1896–1920.* Facts on File, 1990.

Chapter 13

Hill, Ralph N. *The Mad Doctor's Drive.* Stephen Greene, 1964.

Latham, George E. "The Automobile and Automobiling," *Munsey's Magazine*, May 1903.

McConnell, Curt. *Coast to Coast by Automobile*. Stanford University Press, 2000.

Munsey, Frank A. "Impressions by the Way," *Munsey's Magazine*, May 1903.

The New York Times, March 21, 1928 (obituary of James Ward Packard).

Norman, Henry. "The Coming of the Automobile," *The World's Work*, April 1903.

Saal, Thomas F. "Pope-Hartford: Too Good to Fail," *Automobile Quarterly*, Vol. 36, No. 1.

_____, Bernard J. Golias, and Joseph S. Freeman. *Famous But Forgotten: The Story of Alexander Winton*. Golias, 1997.

Sheridan, Martin. "The First Automobile Coast to Coast," *True Automobile Yearbook*, No. 1, 1952.

Chapter 14

A.L.A.M. advertisement, "Notice! To Manufacturers, Dealers, Importers, Agents and Users of Gasolene Automobiles," *The Automobile Review*, August 15, 1903.

Beebe, Lucius. *The Big Spenders*. Doubleday, 1966.

Early, Helen Jones and James R. Walkinshaw. *Setting the Pace: Oldsmobile's First 100 Years*. Oldsmobile Division of General Motors, 1996.

"The Future of the Automobile," *Munsey's Magazine*, May 1903.

Greenleaf, William. *Monopoly on Wheels: Henry Ford and the Selden Patent Suit*. Wayne State University, 1961.

Hyde, Charles K. "Horace Elgin Dodge" and "John Francis Dodge," *The Automobile Industry, 1896–1920*. Facts on File, 1990.

Kimes, Beverly Rae. "A Family in Kenosha: The Story of the Rambler and the Jeffery," *Automobile Quarterly*, Vol. XVI, No. 2.

Nolan, William F. "You Knew Him...Barney Oldfield," *Automobile Quarterly*, Vol. I, No. 1.

Chapter 15

A.L.A.M. "What Is the Selden Patent on Gasoline Automobiles?" Beverly Rae Kimes Archives.

Cameron, William T. *The Cameron Story.* International Society for Vehicle Preservation, 1990.

Flink, James J. *The Automobile Age.* The MIT Press, 1990.

Hiscox, Gardner D. *Horseless Vehicles, Automobiles, Motor Cycles.* Norman W. Henley, 1900.

Kennedy, E.D. *The Automobile Industry: The Coming of Age of Capitalism's Favorite Child.* Reynal & Hitchcock, 1941.

Rae, John B. *The American Automobile Industry.* Twayne, 1984.

Sloan, Alfred P., Jr. *Adventures of a White-Collar Man.* Doubleday, Doran, 1941.

Chapter 16

"The Advantages of the Electric Runabout for City Work," *The Horseless Age,* November 18, 1908.

"Army Tests an Automobile," *The New York Times,* October 11, 1901.

"The Automobile in Use To-Day," *Review of Reviews,* August 1899.

"Automobile Vehicles in Warfare," *Scientific American,* September 18, 1897.

"The Automobile in War," *Outing,* December 1903.

"Automobiles for City Street Cleaning Departments Are Desired," *The Automobile and Motor Review,* November 15, 1902.

"Automobiles for the Postal Service," *The Automobile Magazine,* February 1900.

Babcock, F.A. "The Electric Motor of Yesterday and To-Day," *Harper's Weekly,* March 16, 1907.

Budlong, M.J. "The Development of the Electric Automobile," *Harper's Weekly,* March 16, 1907.

Clark, Ronald W. *Edison: The Man Who Made the Future.* G.P. Putnam's, 1977.

Conot, Robert. *A Streak of Luck: The Life and Legend of Thomas Alva Edison.* Seaview, 1979.

Goss, M.L. "Yesterday and To-Day of the Electric," *Harper's Weekly,* November 16, 1907.

Holland, James P. "The Future of the Automobile," *Munsey's Magazine*, n.d.

"The Horseless Carriage as a War Machine," *Review of Reviews*, July 1896.

Jaderquist, Eugene. "Electrics: The Favorite of Doctors and Dowagers," *True Automobile Yearbook*, No. 4, 1955.

Josephson, Matthew. *Edison*. McGraw-Hill, 1959.

Moffett, Cleveland. "Automobiles for the Average Man," *Review of Reviews*, June 1900.

Morrell, Parker. *Diamond Jim: The Life and Times of James Buchanan Brady*. Simon & Schuster, 1934.

Munsey, Frank A. "Impressions by the Way," *Munsey's Magazine*, n.d.

"New Types of Automobile Carriages," *Harper's Weekly*, August 19, 1899.

"Not Roosevelt's First Ride," *The Motor World*, May 18, 1905.

Sutphen, Henry R. "Touring in Automobiles," *Outing*, May 1901.

Wachhorst, Wyn. *Thomas Alva Edison*. The MIT Press, 1981.

"White Autos in Military Service," *White Company Bulletin*, August 1905.

Wren, Genevieve. "Edward Joel Pennington," *The Automobile Industry, 1896–1901*. Facts on File, 1990.

Chapter 17

Durant, Margery. *My Father*. G.P. Putnam's, 1929.

Finney, E.J. *Walter Flanders: His Role in the Mass Production of Automobiles*. Privately printed, 1992.

Folsom, Richard B. "Henry Ford," *The Automobile Industry, 1896–1920*. Facts on File, 1990.

The Horseless Age, July 10, August 7, and September 18 and 25, 1907, and April 29 and June 17, 1908; and *The Automobile*, September 17, 1908 (Selden patent litigation).

Kimes, Beverly Rae. "Wouldn't You Really Rather Be a Buick?" *Automobile Quarterly*, Vol. VII, No.1.

Sorensen, Charles E. *My Forty Years with Ford*. W.W. Norton, 1956.

Young, Charles H. and William A. Quinn. *Foundation for Living: The Story of Charles Stewart Mott and Flint*. McGraw-Hill, 1963.

Chapter 18

Berger, Michael L. *The Devil Wagon in God's Country: The Automobile and Social Change in Rural America, 1893–1929.* Archon, 1979.

Brough, James. *Princess Alice: A Biography of Alice Roosevelt Longworth.* Little, Brown, 1975.

Felsenthal, Carol. *Alice Roosevelt Longworth.* G.P. Putnam's, 1988.

"How Fool Driving Affects the Popularity of the Automobile," *Outing*, February 1906.

"Motorists Sent to Jail Without Option of Paying Fine," *The Automobile and Motor Review*, November 8, 1902.

The New York Times, May 15 and 27, 1902 (editorials).

Swanberg, W.A. *Citizen Hearst: A Biography of William Randolph Hearst.* Macmillan, 1961.

Teichmann, Howard. *Alice: The Life and Times of Alice Roosevelt Longworth.* Prentice-Hall, 1979.

Wik, Reynold. "The Early Automobile and the American Farmer," *The Automobile and American Culture* (David L. Lewis and Laurence Goldstein, eds.). University of Michigan, 1980.

Chapter 19

Anderson, Rudolph E. *The Story of the American Automobile.* Public Affairs Press, 1950.

"Automobile Troubles That May Be Avoided," *Country Life in America*, May 1908.

Dayton, Helena Smith. "Leaves from the Diary of a Motorist," *Harper's Weekly*, June 20, 1908.

Flower, Raymond and Michael Wynn Jones. *100 Years on the Road: A Social History of the Car.* McGraw-Hill, 1981.

The Horseless Age, entire issue of January 7, 1903, and substantial portions of issues of February 11 and March 4, 1903, and November 1, 1905 (doctors and automobiles).

Jones, Forrest R. *Automobile Catechism.* Class Journal, 1906.

Paris, Burt J. *Care of Automobiles: A Non-Technical Treatise for the Business and Professional Man.* Doubleday, Page, 1908.

Partridge, Bellamy. *Excuse My Dust*. McGraw-Hill, 1943.

"The Passing of the Horse," *Carriage Monthly*, October 1895.

"The Passing of the Scared Horse Nuisance," *The Horseless Age*, August 1907.

"The Romance of Motoring," *Atlantic Monthly*, August 1908.

Scarritt, Winthrop E. "The Horse of the Future and The Future of the Horse," *Harper's Weekly*, March 16, 1907.

Chapter 20

"Automobile Number," *The Journal of the American Medical Association*, April 21, 1906.

Duryea, Charles E. "It Doesn't Pay to Pioneer," *The Saturday Evening Post*, May 16, 1931.

Haines, Harry B. "The Automobile and the Average Man," *Review of Reviews*, June 1907.

The Horseless Age, December 4, 1907, and January 22, 1908 (Panic of '07).

Kimes, Beverly Rae. "Behold the Highwheeler—The Sears, For Instance," *Automobile Quarterly*, Vol. IX, No. 1.

_____. "High Times, High Rollers—The Highwheeler in America," *Automobile Quarterly*, Vol. XV, No. 1.

_____. "John North Willys: His Magnetism, His Millions, His Motorcars," *Automobile Quarterly*, Vol. XVII, No. 3.

The New York Times, August 11, 1907 (obituary of Albert Pope).

_____, December 11, 1907; and *The Horseless Age,* December 11 and 18, 1907, and March 18 and September 26, 1908 (Electric Vehicle Company receivership).

Norman, Henry. "Can I Afford an Automobile," *The World's Work*, June 1903.

Ransley, Francis. "No Ordinary Brush," *The Automobile*, October 1988.

Sangree, Allen. "The 'Poor Man' and the Motor-Car," *Harper's Weekly*, January 13, 1906.

Scarritt, Winthrop E. "The Low-Priced Automobile," *Munsey's Magazine*, May 1903.

Snodgrass, Rhey T. "A Poor Man's Auto," *Collier's,* January 16, 1909.

Strouse, Jean. "The Brilliant Bailout," *The New Yorker*, November 22, 1998.

Towle, Herbert Ladd. "The Automobile of To-Morrow," *Scribner's Magazine*, May 1908.

Tucker, Franklin B. *Holsman History: 1901–1910.* Privately printed, 1993.

Willey, Dan Allen. "Who Can Automobile?" *Good Housekeeping*, May 1909.

Chapter 21

Briscoe, Benjamin. "The Inside Story of General Motors," *Detroit Saturday Night*, 1921.

Cohn, David L. *Combustion on Wheels: An Informal History of the Automobile Age.* Houghton Mifflin, 1944.

Crotty, Tom. "The Foresight of Henry Ford," *Automotive History Review*, Summer 1988.

Flink, James J. *America Adopts the Automobile: 1895–1910.* The MIT Press, 1970.

"Ford Light Touring Car for 1909," *The Automobile*, September 24, 1908.

"The Ford Model T," *The Horseless Age*, September 30, 1908.

Garrett, Garet. *The Wild Wheel.* Pantheon, 1952.

John, W.A.P. "That Man Durant," *MoToR*, January 1921.

Kimes, Beverly Rae. "Henry's Model T," *Automobile Quarterly*, Vol. X, No. 4.

Lewis, David L. *The Public Image of Henry Ford.* Wayne State University, 1976.

Lewis, Eugene W. *Motor Memories: A Saga of Whirling Gears.* Alved, 1947.

"The New Model T Ford Touring Car," *Cycle and Automobile Trade Journal*, October 1908.

Pound, Arthur. *The Turning Wheel: The Story of General Motors Through Twenty-Five Years.* Doubleday, Doran, 1934.

Chapter 22

Kimes, Beverly Rae. "Billy Durant: Hurrah for the Big Little Man," *Automobile Quarterly*, Vol. 40, No. 2.

_____. "A Few 'Whys' Worth Considering: Being a Narrative on the Cartercar," *Automobile Quarterly*, Vol. XII, No. 2.

McKenna, Ken. "Forgotten Men of Business: David Buick," *New York Herald Tribune*, March 6, 1961.

Niemeyer, Glenn A. *The Automotive Career of Ransom E. Olds*. Michigan State University, 1963.

Scharchburg, Richard. "Albert Champion," *The Automobile Industry, 1896–1920*. Facts on File, 1991.

Smith, Frederick L. "Motoring Down a Half Century," *Detroit Saturday Night*, 1928.

Weisberger, Bernard A. *The Dream Maker: William C. Durant, Founder of General Motors*. Little, Brown, 1989.

Chapter 23

Flink, James J. *The Automobile Age*. The MIT Press, 1990.

The Horseless Age, February 24, June 9, and September 15 and 22, 1909; and *The Motor World*, September 16 and 23, 1909 (Selden patent case).

_____, January 12 and 19, and February 16, 1910 (A.L.A.M./A.M.C.M.A).

Katz, John F. "Mister Fisher's Stoddard-Dayton," *Automobile Quarterly*, Vol. 23, No. 3.

Leland, Mrs. Wilfred C. and Minnie Dubbs Milbrook. *Master of Precision: Henry M. Leland*. Wayne State University, 1966.

MacManus, Theodore F. and Norman Beasley. *Men, Money and Motors: The Drama of the Automobile*. Harper, 1929.

The New York Times, July 29 and September 10, 1910 (Durant and GM).

"Says Durant Could Have Bought Ford for $8,000,000," *Automotive Industries*, April 16, 1927.

Seltzer, Lawrence H. *A Financial History of the American Automobile Industry*. Houghton Mifflin, 1928.

Chapter 24

"A.L.A.M. Banquet an Enjoyable Affair—Henry Ford a Guest," *The Horseless Age*, January 18, 1911.

Ellis, William Donohue. "The Man Who Said He Invented the Automobile," *True's Automobile Yearbook*, No. 3, 1954.

Gustin, Lawrence R. *Billy Durant: Creator of General Motors*. William B. Eerdmans, 1973.

The Horseless Age, January 11 and 18, 1911; and *The Automobile*, January 12, 1911 (Selden decision).

Kimes, Beverly Rae. "Reo Remembered," *Automobile Quarterly*, Vol. XIV, No. 1.

Chapter 25

Betts, Charles L., Jr. *Auto Racing Winners, 1895–1947*. Betts Brothers, 1948.

Bloemker, Al. *500 Miles to Go: The Story of the Indianapolis Motor Speedway*. Coward-McCann, 1961.

Catlin, Russ. "Speed King in a Silk Shirt—The Career of Bob Burman," *Automobile Quarterly*, Vol. XIX, No. 4.

"Christie in the Grand Prix: His Car and His Chances," *The New York Times*, May 19, 1907.

Cole, Dermot. *Hard Driving: The 1908 Auto Race from New York to Paris*. Paragon, 1991.

"German Auto First in Paris," *The New York Times*, July 27, 1908.

Helck, Peter. "Twenty-Four Hours to Go: A Saga of the Dirt Track Grinds in America," *Automobile Quarterly*, Vol. V, No. 1.

Kimes, Beverly Rae. "The Dawn of Speed," *American Heritage*, Vol. 38, No. 7, November 1987.

_____. "Gentlemen and Hellions," *The Star*, May–June 1988.

_____. "Lozier: The Big One That Got Away," *Automobile Quarterly*, Vol. VII, No. 4.

_____. "The Mighty Alco," *Automobile Quarterly*, Vol. XI, No. 2.

_____. "Packard Gray Wolf," *Automobile Quarterly*, Vol. XIX, No. 3.

_____. "The Rise and Fall of the Empire Empire," *Automobile Quarterly*, Vol. XII, No. 1.

_____. "The Vanderbilt Cup Races, 1904–1910," *Automobile Quarterly*, Vol. VI, No. 2.

Mahoney, Tom. *The Great Auto Race.* Scholastic, 1965.

Mulford, Ralph. "Racing with Lozier: A Memoir," *Automobile Quarterly*, Vol. XI, No. 2.

Pardington, A.R. "The Modern Appian Way for the Motorist," *Harper's Weekly*, March 16, 1907.

Street, Julian. "The Modern Mercuries," *Collier's*, January 16, 1909.

Chapter 26

"Chevrolet Plan to Manufacture...," *The New York Times*, October 25, 1914.

Chrysler, Walter P. *Life of an American Workman.* Dodd, Mead, 1937.

"500-Mile Sweepstakes Run Off at the Indianapolis Speedway," *The Automobile*, June 1, 1911.

Fox, Jack C. *The Indianapolis 500.* World, 1967.

Freeman, Joseph S. "Birth of the Bowtie: The Car That Ate General Motors," *Automobile Quarterly*, Vol. 34, No. 4.

Grayson, Stan. "The Little Cars That Couldn't," *Automobile Quarterly*, Vol. XII, No. 4.

Katzell, Raymond A., ed. *The Splendid Stutz.* Stutz Club, 1996.

Kimes, Beverly Rae. "Blueprints and Balance Sheets—The Company that Charlie Built," *Automobile Quarterly*, Vol. VI, No. 2.

MoToR, September 1912; *The Horseless Age*, October 23, November 13, 20, and 27, and December 18 and 25, 1912, January 8, August 7 and 21, September 18 and 25, and October 9, 16, and 23, 1912 (U.S. Motor receivership).

"Walter E. Flanders—Industrial Colossus," *Munsey's Magazine*, advertising section, n.d.

Yanik, Anthony J. "U.S. Motor: Benjamin Briscoe's Shattered Dream." *Automobile Quarterly*, Vol. 36, No. 2.

Chapter 27

Arnold, Horace L. and Fay I. Fasurote. *Ford Methods and the Ford Shops.* Engineering Magazine Co., 1915.

Borth, Christy. *Masters of Mass Production.* Bobbs-Merrill, 1945.

Bryan, Ford R. *Henry's Lieutenants.* Wayne State University, 1993.

Ford, Henry and Samuel Crowther. *My Life and Work.* Doubleday, 1922.

Greenleaf, William. *From These Beginnings: The Early Philanthropies of Henry and Edsel Ford.* Wayne State University, 1964.

Meyer, Stephen. *The Five-Dollar Day: Labor, Management and Social Control in the Ford Motor Company.* State University of New York, 1981.

Rae, John B. *The American Automobile.* University of Chicago, 1965.

White, Lee Strout. *Farewell to Model T.* G.P. Putnam's, 1936.

Wik, Reynold M. *Henry Ford and Grass-Roots America.* University of Michigan, 1972.

Womack, James P., Daniel T. Jones, and Daniel Roos. *The Machine That Changed the World.* Maxwell Macmillan, 1990.

Chapter 28

Butler, Don. *The History of Hudson.* Crestline, 1982.

Conde, John A. *The Cars That Hudson Built.* Arnold-Porter, 1980.

Davis, Donald Finlay. *Conspicuous Production: Automobiles and Elites in Detroit, 1899–1933.* Temple, 1998.

"Detroit to Produce...," *The Automobile*, December 19, 1912.

Godshall, Jeffrey I. "Hupmobile: Always a Good Car," *Automobile Quarterly*, Vol. 16, No. 1.

Grayson, Stan. "Artist's Conception: The Novel Cars of James Scripps Booth," *Automobile Quarterly*, Vol. XIII, No. 3.

_____. "The Brothers Dodge," *Automobile Quarterly*, Vol. XVII, No. 1.

Hendry, Maurice D. "Hudson: The Car Named for Jackson's Wife's Uncle," *Automobile Quarterly*, Vol. IX, No. 4.

Kimes, Beverly Rae. "E & M & F ... & LeRoy," *Automobile Quarterly*, Vol. XVII, No. 4.

Longstreet, Stephen. *A Century on Wheels: The Story of Studebaker*. Holt, Rinehart & Winston, 1952.

Marcosson, Isaac F. "The Automobile—A Miracle of the Twentieth Century," *Munsey's Magazine*, 1910.

Maxim, Hiram Percy. "Why the Industry Flocks Westward," *The Automobile*, July 16, 1914.

May, George S. "Hugh Chalmers," *The Automobile Industry, 1896–2000*. Facts on File, 1990.

Pound, Arthur. *Detroit: Dynamic City*. Appleton-Century, 1940.

Szudarek, Robert G. *How Detroit Became the Automotive Capital*. Privately printed, 1996.

Yanik, Anthony J. *The E-M-F Company*. Society of Automotive Engineers, 2001.

Chapter 29

"The Auto Otis Built," *The Otis Bulletin*, June–July 1950.

Clark, Henry Austin, Jr. "The Three Lives of the Simplex," *Automobile Quarterly*, Vol. II, No. 4.

"Distribution of Automobile Factories," *Cycle and Automobile Trade Journal*, June 1911.

Emmanuel, Dave. "Cole: The Pride of Indianapolis," *Automobile Quarterly*, Vol. 22, No. 2.

Hanley, George Philip and Stacey Pankiw. *The Marmon Heritage*. Doyle Hyk, 1985.

Hendry, Maurice D. "Pierce-Arrow: An American Aristocrat," *Automobile Quarterly*, Vol. XVIII, No. 3.

Homan, Arthur Lee. "Sic Transit Gloria Mundi," *Automobilist of Upper Hudson Valley*, Summer 1990.

Husting, Gene. "The Kissel Kaper," *Automobile Quarterly*, Vol. IX, No. 3.

Katz, John F. "Chandler: Built to Master a Mountain...and More," *Automobile Quarterly*, Vol. 24, No. 4.

_____. "The Pathfinder: Indiana's Aspiring Aristocrat," *Automobile Quarterly*, Vol. 25, No. 3.

Kimes, Beverly Rae. "The Artists Who Painted for Pierce-Arrow: Automobile Advertising's Grandest Era," *Automobile Quarterly*, Vol. XIV, No. 3.

_____. "Chadwick—Remember the Name," *Automobile Quarterly*, Vol. IX, No. 2.

_____. "A Little on the Biddle," *Automobile Quarterly*, Vol. XI, No. 3.

_____. "Lozier: The Big One That Got Away," *Automobile Quarterly*, Vol. VII, No. 4.

_____. "The Speedwell from Dayton: A Motorcar Worth Remembering," *Automobile Quarterly*, Vol. XIII, No. 1.

_____. "The Velies of Moline: Father, Son and Motorcar," *Automobile Quarterly*, Vol. XV, No. 4.

Knoble, Cliff. *Automobile Selling Sense*. Prentice Hall, 1923.

LaMarre, Thomas S. "White Steam: Sewing Up the Steam Car Market," *Automobile Quarterly*, Vol. 31, No. 4.

LaMarre, Thomas S. and Jonathan A. Stein, "Quest for Perfection: The Motorcars of Frank Stearns," *Automobile Quarterly*, Vol. 30, No. 3.

Powell, Sinclair. *The Franklin Automobile Company: The History of the Innovative Firm, Its Founder, The Vehicles It Produced, and The People Who Built Them*. Society of Automotive Engineers, 1999.

Quant, Val V. *The Classic Kissel Automobile*. Kissel Graph, 1990.

Scull, Penrose, with Preston C. Fuller. *From Peddlers to Merchant Princes: A History of Selling in America*. Follett, 1967.

Spinell, Art and Beverly Edwards, Mo Mehlsak, and Larry Tuck. *America's Auto Dealer: The Master Merchandisers*. Freed-Crown, 1978.

Chapter 30

Abbott, T.O. "The Lawmaker and the Automobile," *Outing*, August 1907.

Babbitt, Charles J. *The Law Applied to Motor Vehicles*. John Byrne, 1911.

Barber, H.L. *The Story of the Automobile: Its History and Development from 1760–1917*. A.J. Munson, 1917.

Boyd, T.A. *Professional Amateur: The Biography of Charles Franklin Kettering*. Dutton, 1959.

Bromley, Michael L. *William Howard Taft and the First Motoring Presidency*. McFarland, 2003.

Burchell, H.P. "Our Chaotic Automobile Laws," *Harper's Weekly*, May 16, 1908.

Cleveland, Reginald M. *The Road Is Yours: The Story of the Automobile and the Men Behind It*. Greystone, 1951.

Coit, David G. "Laws of the Road," *The Lever*, July 1910.

Collins, Herbert Ridgeway. *Presidents on Wheels*. Bonanza, 1971.

"Excuses for Speeding," *The Horseless Age*, July 8, 1908.

"Federal Registration," *Automobile Journal*, July 1911.

Huddy, Xenophon P. "Remarkable Provisions of Our Automobile Laws," *The Horseless Age*, September 25, 1907.

Humphrey, Seth K. "Automobile Selfishness," *Atlantic Monthly*, November 1908.

Kimes, Beverly Rae. "Adams-Farwell: You See It and You Still Don't Believe It," *Automobile Quarterly*, Vol. VIII, No. 2.

_____. "Cadwallader Washburn Kelsey: The Spirited Career of an Automotive Pioneer," *Automobile Quarterly*, Vol. XIII, No. 2.

LaMarre, Tom. "Detroit Electric," *Automobile Quarterly*, Vol. 27, No. 2.

McLaughlin, Charles C. "The Stanley Steamer: A Study in Unsuccessful Innovation," *Explorations in Entrepreneurial History*, October 1954.

Metcalf, Mark. "Presidents on Wheels," *Steelways*, January–February 1969.

Morris, Dave H. "The Legislative Needs of the Motorist," *Harper's Weekly*, March 16, 1907.

Powilson, W.L. "Brief History of the Glidden Tour," *The Bulb Horn*, October 1956.

"President Taft Gets a Garage," *The Motor World*, March 11, 1909.

Preston, Howard L. *Automobile Age Atlanta: The Making of a Southern Metropolis*. University of Georgia, 1979.

Scharff, Virginia. *Taking the Wheel: Women and the Coming of the Motor Age*. Macmillan, 1992.

Sinsabaugh, Chris. *Who, Me? Forty Years of Automobile History*. Arnold-Powers, 1940.

Smallzried, Kathleen Ann and Dorothy James Roberts. *More Than You Promise: A Business at Work in Society*. Harper, 1942.

"The White at the White House," *White Company Bulletin*, January 1910.

Chapter 31

Barnard, Harry. *Independent Man: The Life of Senator James Couzens*. Charles Scribner's, 1958.

Bonsall, Thomas E. "Edsel: The Forgotten Ford," *Automobile Quarterly*, Vol. 29, No. 3.

Fisher, Jane. *Fabulous Hoosier: A Story of American Achievement*. Robert M. McBride, 1947.

Gelderman, Carol. *Henry Ford: The Wayward Capitalist*. St. Martin's, 1981.

Heilig, John. "The Men Behind the Highway," *Automobile Quarterly*, Vol. 29, No. 3.

Hokanson, Drake. *The Lincoln Highway: Main Street Across America*. University of Iowa, 1988.

Joy, Henry B. "Seeing America and the Lincoln Highway," *Scientific American*, January 1, 1916.

Kraft, Barbara. *The Peace Ship: Henry Ford's Pacifist Adventure in the First World War*. Macmillan, 1978.

LaMarre, Thomas S. "One Piece at a Time: The Cars of C.H. Metz," *Automobile Quarterly*, Vol. 32, No. 4.

The New York Times, June 30 and December 22 and 24, 1915 (various articles on the Durant/GM coup).

Post, Emily. *By Motor to the Golden Gate*. Appleton, 1916.

Riggs, L. Spencer. "Carl G. Fisher: Indiana's Best-Kept Secret," *Automobile Quarterly*, Vol. 35, No. 2.

Rishel, Virginia. *Wheels to Adventure: Bill Rishel's Western Routes*. Howe Brothers, 1983.

Tuttle, Peter Guertin. *The Ford Peace Ship: Volunteer Diplomacy in the Twentieth Century*. New Haven, 1958.

Chapter 32

Bradley, W.F. *Motor Racing Memories: 1903–1921*. Motor Racing Publications, 1960.

Bullard, Arthur. *Mobilising America*. Macmillan, 1917.

Crowell, Benedict and Robert Forrest Wilson. *The Giant Hand: Our Mobilization and Control of Industry and Natural Resources, 1917–1918*. Yale University, 1921.

Cuff, Robert D. *The War Industrial Board: Business–Government Relations During World War I*. Johns Hopkins University, 1973.

Godshall, Jeffrey I. "Locomobile: Bridgeport's Beautiful Beast," *Automobile Quarterly*, Vol. 22, No. 4.

Grayson, Stan. "The Brothers Dodge," *Automobile Quarterly*, Vol. XVI, No. 1.

Powell, Major E. Alexander. *The Army Behind the Army*. Charles Scribner's, 1919.

Sibley, Hi. *Merry Old Mobiles on Parade*. Garden City, 1951.

"Stevens-Duryea Company Stops Manufacturing Cars," *The Horseless Age*, January 6, 1915.

Von Keler, T.M.R. "Europe's Fighting Motor Cars," *Scientific American*, October 3, 1914.

Chapter 33

Beamish, Richard Joseph and Francis Andrew March. *America's Part in the World War*. John C. Winston, 1919.

Cannon, William A. and Fred K. Fox. *Studebaker: The Complete Story*. Tab, 1981.

Grayson, Stan. "In the Cause of Liberty," *Packard: A History of the Motor Car and the Company*, Automobile Quarterly, 1978.

Hobhouse, Janet. *Everybody Who Was Anybody*. G.P. Putnam's, 1975.

Kollins, Michael J. "Hugh Chalmers," *Pioneers of the U.S. Automobile Industry: The Financial Wizards*. Society of Automotive Engineers, 2002.

Mellow, James R. *Charmed Circle: Gertrude Stein & Company*. Praeger, 1974.

Moulton, Harold Glenn. *The War and Industrial Readjustment.* University of Chicago, 1928.

The New York Times, May 26, 1943 (obituary of Edsel Ford).

The New York Times and *The New York Post*, March 19, 1947; and *Automotive News,* March 24, 1947 (obituary of William C. Durant).

Rogers, W.G. *Gertrude Stein Is Gertrude Stein Is Gertrude Stein.* Thomas Y. Crowell, 1973.

Sprigge, Elizabeth. *Gertrude Stein: Her Life and Work.* Harper, 1957.

Stevenson, William Yorke. *At the Front in a Flivver.* Houghton Mifflin, 1917.

Chapter 34

Beasley, Norman. *Knudsen: A Biography.* Whittlesey House, 1947.

Breer, Carl. *The Birth of Chrysler Corporation and Its Engineering Legacy.* Society of Automotive Engineers, 1995.

Burlingame, Roger. *Henry Ford.* Alfred A. Knopf, 1966.

Burst, Carl W., III and Andrew D. Young. "The Moon in All Its Phases," *Automobile Quarterly*, Vol. 25, No. 4.

Crow, Carl. *The City of Flint Grows Up.* Harper, 1945.

Curcio, Vincent. *Chrysler: The Life and Times of an Automotive Genius.* Oxford University, 2000.

"Describes Durant's Gen. Motors Sale," *The New York Times*, March 13, 1921.

Erskine, Albert. *History of Studebaker Corporation.* Studebaker Corporation, 1924.

Filippelli, Ronald L., ed. *Labor Conflict in the United States.* Garland, 1990.

Haimson, Leopold H. and Charles Tilly, eds. *Strikes, Wars, and Revolutions in an International Perspective.* Cambridge University, 1989.

Hendry, Maurice D. "Childe Harold Wills: A Career in Cars," *Automobile Quarterly*, Vol. 5, No. 2.

Kimes, Beverly Rae, ed. *The Classic Tradition of the Lincoln Motorcar.* Automobile Quarterly, 1971.

Kimes, Beverly Rae. "Kenworthy: An Automotive Odyssey," *Automobile Quarterly*, Vol. 42, No. 4.

Langworth, Richard M. "Ned Jordan: The Cars He Built," *Automobile Quarterly*, Vol. XIII, No. 2.

Lens, Sidney. *The Labor Wars: From the Molly Maguires to the Sitdowns.* Doubleday, 1973.

"Men in Wall Street's Eye: Albert Russel Erskine," *Barron's Magazine*, June 19, 1922.

Muldoon, Tony. "Hare's Today, Gone Tomorrow: Emlen Hare's Failed Empire," *Automobile Quarterly,* Vol. 35, No. 3.

Nevins, Allan and Frank Ernest Hill. *Ford: Expansion and Challenge, 1915–1933.* Charles Scribner's, 1957.

The New York Times, June 11 and 14, 1921 (Ford/Newberry fracas).

"Reo's Condition Is Best in its History," *Automobile Topics*, December 1, 1923.

"Rolls-Royce Making Substantial Progress," *Automobile Topics*, November 10, 1923.

Rosenbusch, Karla. "Assembling Quality: Gardner's Spring, Summer and Fall," *Automobile Quarterly*, Vol. 37, No. 1.

Scharchburg, Richard P. *W.C. Durant, "The Boss."* General Motors Institute, 1973.

Sinclair, Upton. *The Flivver King.* United Auto Workers of America, 1937.

Sloan, Alfred P., Jr. *My Years with General Motors.* Doubleday, 1964.

Willys receivership. *Automotive Industries*, February 16, 1920.

Chapter 35

Automobile Topics, June 11, 1932 (obituary of Hugh Chalmers).

_____, June 25, 1932 (obituary of Alexander Winton).

Automotive Industries, May 21, 1925, and *Automobile Trade Journal*, June 1925 (obituary of J. Dallas Dort).

_____, April 1, 1929 (obituary of Elmer Apperson).

_____, April 2, 1932 (obituary of Henry Martyn Leland).

Baldwin, Neil. *Henry Ford and the Jews.* Perseus, 2001.

Borgeson, Griff. "The Little-Known Battle of Two Henrys," *Motor Trend,* February 1967.

"Chrysler Puts Out a Six in Own Name," *Automobile Topics*, December 29, 1923.

"Collins Resigns as Peerless President," *Automobile Topics*, December 29, 1932.

"Durant to Build Car at Ford Price," *Automotive Industries*, February 16, 1922.

"Durant's Star Seen in the Ascendant," *Automobile Topics*, March 11, 1922.

Emanuel, Dave. "Drift, Salvation, Malaise: The Stutz Motor Car Company of America, 1916–1937," *Automobile Quarterly*, Vol. XX, No. 3.

"General Motors Is Mirror to Industry," *Automobile Topics*, March 11, 1922.

Godshall, Jeffrey I. "Ruxton: A Superb Automobile That Never Had a Chance," *Automobile Quarterly*, Vol. VIII.

Hendry, Maurice D. "Childe Harold Wills: A Career in Cars," *Automobile Quarterly*, Vol. V, No. 2.

Kimes, Beverly Rae. "Auburn from Runabout to Speedster," *Automobile Quarterly*, Vol. V, No. 4.

_____. "Hat in the Ring: The Rickenbacker," *Automobile Quarterly*, Vol. XIII, No. 4.

Latham, Caroline and David Agresta. *Dodge Dynasty: The Car and the Family That Rocked Detroit.* Harcourt Brace Jovanovich, 1989.

Madden, W.C. *Haynes-Apperson and America's First Practical Automobile.* McFarland, 2003.

The New York Times, March 27, May 26, July 14, 23, and 31, and November 8, 1921, and July 23, 1922 (Durant Motors).

Rosenbusch, Karla. "Rising to the Top: Chevrolet Between the Wars," *Automobile Quarterly*, Vol. 34, No. 4.

"Walter P. Chrysler Presented to Public," *Automobile Topics*, December 15, 1923.

Young, Rosamond McPherson. *Boss Kett: A Life of Charles Kettering.* Longmans, Green, 1961.

Index

About the Author

BEVERLY RAE KIMES has been writing about automobile history for more than four decades. Her first subject was Ransom Olds' curved dash Oldsmobile, for *Automobile Quarterly*, the magazine she joined after earning her M.A. from Penn State University, which had followed a baccalaureate from the University of Illinois. Both degrees were in journalism, with accompanying minors in history and literature.

Since 1963, Kimes has written hundreds of articles and authored or edited more than a dozen books. In the process, she has become the most honored automobile historian in America. Her books have won the Cugnot Award of the Society of Automotive Historians for "best book of the year" five times, and the society's Benz Award for "best article of the year" four times. Kimes has been cited by the Antique Automobile Club of America for most significant original research four times. Her articles have won the Moto of the National Association of Automotive Journalism three times, and "best of magazines" as well as "best of 2002" from the National Automotive Media Foundation.

A past president of the Society of Automotive Historians, Kimes is a recipient of its Friend of Automotive History Award. She is an Honorary Member of the Antique Automobile Club of America, has received the Certificate of Distinguished Service Award of the Classic Car Club of America (for whom she has served as executive editor since leaving *Automobile Quarterly* in 1981), and was the first historian to receive the Distinguished Service Citation of the Automotive Hall of Fame. Kimes' current board memberships include the National Automotive History Collection of the Detroit Public Library, the Saratoga Automobile Museum, and the Rolls-Royce Foundation.

Kimes lives with her husband, Jim Cox, in New York City and Matamoras, Pennsylvania, where they have an antique shop. They share their lives with Oscar, Maggie, Henry, and Ralph: to wit, two cats, one dog, and a 1930 Auburn 8-125 Sport Sedan, in which they have motored more than 45,000 miles.